Evidence-Based Reading Practices for Response to Intervention

Evidence-Based Reading Practices for Response to Intervention

edited by

Diane Haager, Ph.D.
California State University, Los Angeles

Janette Klingner, Ph.D.
University of Colorado at Boulder

and

Sharon Vaughn, Ph.D.
University of Texas at Austin

·P A U L·H·
BROOKES
PUBLISHING C?.®

Baltimore • London • Sydney

Paul H. Brookes Publishing Co.
Post Office Box 10624
Baltimore, Maryland 21285-0624

www.brookespublishing.com

Typeset by Barton, Matheson, Willse & Worthington, Baltimore, Maryland.
Manufactured in the United States of America by
Versa Press, Inc., East Peoria, Illinois.

The case studies appearing in this book are composites based on the authors' experiences;
these case studies do not represent the lives or experiences of specific individuals, and no
implications should be inferred.

Second printing, October 2007.

Library of Congress Cataloging-in-Publication Data

Evidence-based reading practices for response to intervention / edited by Diane Haager,
Janette Klingner, and Sharon Vaughn.
    p.   cm.
Includes bibliographical references and index.
ISBN-13: 978-1-55766-828-8 (pbk.)
ISBN-10: 1-55766-828-0 (pbk.)
    1. Developmental reading.   2. Reading disability.   I. Haager, Diane.
II. Klingner, Janette K.   III. Vaughn, Sharon, 1952–   IV. Title.

LB1050.53.E85 2007
371.91'44–dc22   2006035041

British Library Cataloguing in Publication data are available from the British Library.

Contents

About the Editors

Diane Haager, Ph.D., Professor, Charter College of Education, California State University, Los Angeles, 5151 State University Drive, Los Angeles, California 90032

Dr. Haager is a researcher and teacher educator in reading and learning disabilities. A professor at California State University, Los Angeles, she instructs teachers in methods for teaching students with high-incidence disabilities. She has worked in the public schools as a reading specialist and special educator and is the author of numerous books, chapters, and articles. Her research interests include issues related to effective reading instruction for English language learners, students with learning disabilities, and students at risk for reading failure.

Janette Klingner, Ph.D., Associate Professor, School of Education, University of Colorado at Boulder, 249 UCB, Boulder, Colorado 80309

Dr. Klingner is Associate Professor in Bilingual/English as a Second Language Special Education at the University of Colorado at Boulder in the Division for Educational Equity and Cultural Diversity. She was a bilingual special education teacher for 10 years before earning her doctoral degree in reading and learning disabilities from the University of Miami, Florida. She is a co-principal investigator for The National Center for Culturally Responsive Educational Systems, a technical assistance center founded to address the disproportionate representation of culturally and linguistically diverse students in special education. Her research interests include reading comprehension strategy instruction for diverse populations, the disproportionate representation of culturally and linguistically diverse students in special education, and professional development that leads to the sustained implementation of validated practices. In 2004, she was honored with the American Educational Research Association's Early Career Award.

Sharon Vaughn, Ph.D., Director, The Texas Center for Reading and Language Arts, Professor, College of Education, Department of Learning and Reading Disabilities, University of Texas at Austin, 228 Sanchez Building, Austin, Texas 78712

Dr. Vaughn is the H.E. Hartfelder Southland Corporation Regents Chair and Professor at the University of Texas at Austin. She is the recipient of the American Educational Research Association's Special Education State Improvement Grant Award for contribution to research. She has served as Editor-in-Chief of the *Journal of Learning Disabilities* and Co-editor of *Learning Disabilities Research and Practice,* and she is the author of numerous books and research articles.

About the Contributors

Jason L. Anthony, Ph.D., Ed.S., Assistant Professor, Division of Developmental Pediatrics, University of Texas Health Science Center, 2000 Fannin Street, Suite 2377, Houston, Texas 77030. Dr. Anthony's research focuses on the assessment of children, early intervention, literacy acquisition, and program evaluation.

Manuel T. Barrera, Ph.D., Dean, College of Education, Walden University, 155 5th Avenue South, Suite 100, Minneapolis, Minnesota 55401. In addition to his role as Dean at Walden University, Dr. Barrera is a researcher in the National Center on Educational Outcomes at the University of Minnesota where he conducts research on assessment and instruction of English language learners with learning-related disabilities. He maintains active research and scholarly interests in literacy, educational technology, and diverse learners with and without disabilities.

Andrea Canter, Ph.D., N.C.S.P., 4438 Pillsbury Avenue, Minneapolis, Minnesota 55419. Dr. Canter is an independent consultant and editor in Minneapolis and the former Lead Psychologist for the Minneapolis Public Schools. Prior to retirement from the schools in 2004, she was one of the lead investigators and trainers for the Minneapolis Schools Problem-Solving Model. She is currently the Editor of *Communiqué*, the newspaper of the National Association of School Psychologists.

Coleen D. Carlson, Ph.D., Associate Researcher Professor, University of Houston, Associate Director, Texas Institute for Measurement, Evaluation, and Statistics, University of Houston, 100 TLCC Annex, Houston, Texas 77204. Dr. Carlson's research interests include measurement development and psychometric evaluation, advances statistical methods, program evaluation, and early literacy and language development in English- and Spanish-speaking students.

Carolyn A. Denton, Ph.D., Assistant Professor, Department of Special Education, University of Texas at Austin, 1 University Station, Suite D5300, Austin, Texas 78712. Dr. Denton serves as a member of the board of directors of the Vaughn Gross Center for Reading and Language Arts. Her research is focused on reading intervention, response to intervention, the role of the reading coach, and the process of bringing research-validated educational practices to wide scale implementation.

Diane P. Fanuele, M.S., Assistant Research Coordinator, Child Research and Study Center, University at Albany, State University of New York, 1535 Western Avenue, Albany, New York 12203. Ms. Fanuele's primary responsibilities are data management and assisting with statistical analysis of data. She also assists with data collection administration and is responsible for the training and implementation of the classroom observation program at the Child Research and Study Center.

Jack M. Fletcher, Ph.D., Distinguished University Professor of Psychology, University of Houston, Medical Center Annex, 2151 West Holcombe Boulevard, Suite 222, Houston, Texas 77204. Dr. Fletcher, a child neuropsychologist, has completed research on many issues related to learning disabilities and dyslexia, including definition and classification, neurobiological correlates, and intervention. He was the 2003 recipient of the Samuel T. Orton award from the International Dyslexia Association.

Barbara R. Foorman, Ph.D., M.A.T., B.A., Francis Eppes Professor of Education and Associate Director, Florida Center for Reading Research, Florida State University, 227 North Bronough Street, Suite 7250, Tallahassee, Florida 32301. Dr. Foorman has more than 100 publications and many research grants in the area of reading development and instruction. She is Co-editor of the *Journal of Research on Educational Effectiveness* and serves on several editorial boards and advisory committees.

Douglas Fuchs, Ph.D., Nicholas Hobbs Professor of Special Education and Human Development, Vanderbilt University, Box 328 Peabody, Nashville, Tennessee 37203. Dr. Fuchs's research interests are reading disability, math disability, learning disability classifications issues, including responsiveness to intervention and reading instruction.

Lynn S. Fuchs, Ph.D., Nicholas Hobbs Professor of Special Education and Human Development, Vanderbilt University, Box 328 Peabody, Nashville, Tennessee 37203. Dr. Fuchs's research interests are math disability, reading disability, responsiveness to intervention, classroom-based assessment, and instructional methods.

Charles R. Greenwood, Ph.D., Director, Juniper Gardens Children's Project, Professor and Senior Scientist, Applied Behavioral Science, University of Kansas, 650 Minnesota Avenue, Kansas City, Kansas 66101. Dr. Greenwood's research interests are in the application of applied behavior analysis to the problems of young children, early care, and education broadly defined within a high-risk community.

Beth A. Harn, Ph.D., Assistant Professor, Center on Teaching and Learning, University of Oregon, 5292 University of Oregon, Eugene, Oregon 97403. Dr. Harn is a co-principle investigator and coordinator for Project CIRCUTS (Center to Improve Reading Competence Using Intensive Treatments Schoolwide) at the University of Oregon, which implements systemic prevention models to accelerate the early reading achievement of students with reading difficulties in kindergarten through third grade. She teaches classes in special education, including educational assessment and systems level academic interventions, and has expertise in early literacy assessment, instruction, and intervention.

Edward J. Kame'enui, Ph.D., Commissioner, National Center for Special Education Research, 555 New Jersey Avenue NW, Suite 510F, Washington, District of Columbia 20208. Dr. Kame'enui is the founding Commissioner for the National Center for Special Education Research in the Institute of Education Sciences, U.S. Department of Education. He is a faculty member at the University of Oregon, Eugene, where he holds the Dean Knight Professorship of Education in the College of Education. His areas of research interest include early literacy, vocabulary development, learning disabilities, schoolwide models of reading improvement, and the design of high-quality educational materials.

Debra Kamps, Ph.D., Senior Scientist and Director, Center for Early Intervention in Reading and Behavior, Juniper Gardens Children's Project, University of Kansas, 650 Minnesota Avenue, Kansas City, Kansas 66101. Dr. Kamps's background includes teaching students with behavior disorders, learning disabilities, and autism spectrum disorders, and her current activities are focused on research and teacher training. She has received 10 federally funded grants from the U.S. Department of Education, Office of Special Education Programs.

Matthew Y. Lau, Ph.D., N.C.S.P., School Psychologist and Program Facilitator, Special Education Services, Minneapolis Public Schools, Field Placement Coordinator, School Psychology Program, University of Minnesota, 323 Elliott Hall, 75 East River Road, Minneapolis, Minnesota 55455. As a practitioner and a trainer, Dr. Lau's professional interests are in the areas of the Problem-Solving Model, the Response-to-Intervention Model, and assessment issues related to students who are culturally and linguistically diverse.

Sylvia Linan-Thompson, Ph.D., Associate Professor of Special Education, University of Texas in Austin, 1 University Station, Suite D3500, Austin, Texas 78744. Dr. Linan-Thompson is a Fellow in the Mollie V. Davis Professorship in Learning Disabilities and the Director of the Vaughn Gross Center for Reading and Language Arts. She has investigated reading interventions for struggling monolingual English readers in primary grades, literacy acquisition of English language learners, and Spanish literacy development.

Deborah L. Linebarger, Ph.D., Assistant Professor, Annenberg School for Communication, University of Pennsylvania, 3451 Walnut Street, Philadelphia, Pennsylvania 19104. Dr. Linebarger's research focuses on the relationships among children's developmental status, their use of media, and their larger social worlds. Her research combines microlevel experimental work to detect the features used in media that elicit attention and contribute to comprehension of content and macrolevel program evaluation and intervention work that combines the knowledge gained through both descriptive and basic research and its application in various real-world contexts.

Jennifer Mahdavi, Ph.D., Assistant Professor, Sonoma State University, 1801 East Cotati Avenue, Rohnert Park, California 94928. Dr. Mahdavi uses her experience as a special education teacher to inform her research and her teaching of credential candidates.

Douglas Marston, Ph.D., Administrator, Research and Evaluation in Special Education, Minneapolis Public Schools, Adjunct Professor, Department of Educational Psychology, University of Minnesota, Room 107 Burton Hall, 178 Pillsbury Drive SE, Minneapolis, Minnesota 55455. Dr. Marston's research interests include Curriculum-Based Measurement, the Problem-Solving Model, and the Response-to-Intervention Model.

Paul Muyskens, Ph.D., School Psychologist in the Minneapolis Public Schools Department of Special Education, 807 Northeast Broadway, Minneapolis, Minnesota 55413. Dr. Muyskens' interests include the Problem-Solving Model, Curriculum-Based Measurement, and Alternate Assessment.

Rollanda E. O'Connor, Ph.D., Professor of Special Education and Reading, Graduate School of Education, University of California at Riverside, 1207 Sproul Hall, Riverside, California 92521. Dr. O'Connor's research interests include longitudinal early intervention research with students in grades kindergarten through third and reading interventions for older students with learning disabilities. She authored *Ladders to Literacy: A Kindergarten Activity Book, Second Edition* (Paul H. Brookes Publishing Co., 2005), and *Ladders to Literacy: A Preschool Activity Book* (Paul H. Brookes Publishing Co., 1998), both with Angela Notari-Syverson and Patricia F. Vadasy.

Andrew C. Papanicolaou, Ph.D., Director, Division of Clinical Neurosciences, Professor, Department of Neurosurgery, University of Texas Medical School, 1333 Moursund Street, Suite H114, Houston, Texas 77030. Dr. Papanicolaou, a Fulbright Scholar, founded the Summer Institute of Advanced Studies of the International Neuropsychological Society in 2002 and continues to act as the director for the program. He is the author of numerous scientific articles and of six books ranging from methodological and technical manuals for electrophysiological and functional brain imaging research, to clinical textbooks and theoretical monographs.

Amy L. Reschly, Ph.D., Assistant Professor, Department of Educational Psychology and Instructional Technology, University of Georgia, 329 Aderhold, Athens,

Georgia 30602. Dr. Reschly is an assistant professor in the School Psychology Program at the University of Georgia. Her research interests include the Problem-Solving Model and Curriculum-Based Measurement, dropout prevention, and student engagement at school and with learning.

Kristi L. Santi, Ph.D., The Santi Group, Post Office Box 20766, Houston, Texas 77225. Dr. Santi is a former teacher and the author of various early reading assessments and related products. She is active in research on early reading instruction and the effect of mentoring on student success.

Donna M. Scanlon, Ph.D., Associate Professor, University at Albany, State University of New York, 1535 Western Avenue, Albany, New York 12203. Dr. Scanlon is on the faculty in the Reading Department and is also the Associate Director of the Child Research and Study Center. Her research focuses on literacy development and instructional approaches to preventing reading difficulties.

Deborah C. Simmons, Ph.D., Professor of Special Education, Department of Educational Psychology, College of Education and Human Development, Texas A&M University, 4225 College Station, Texas 77843. Dr. Simmons' research and scholarship focuses on early intervention and the prevention of reading difficulties in the early grades.

Panagiotis G. Simos, Ph.D., Associate Professor, Department of Psychology, University of Crete, Gallos Campus, Rethymno, Greece 74100. Dr. Simos has developed and validated special applications of magnetoencephalography for functional brain mapping. He is involved in neuropsychological and brain imaging studies of language, reading, and memory and has published several articles on the neurophysiological profiles associated with specific reading disability (dyslexia), math disability, and attention-deficit/hyperactivity disorder.

Sheila G. Small, M.S., Research Coordinator, Child Research and Study Center, University at Albany, State University of New York, 1535 Western Avenue, Albany, New York 12203. Ms. Small is the Research Coordinator of the Child Research and Study Center (CRSC) and has been responsible for training assessment specialists, facilitating the collection of data, and serving as liaison with the schools involved in CRSC studies into literacy development.

Audrey McCray Sorrells, Ph.D., Associate Professor, Department of Special Education, College of Education, University of Texas at Austin, 1 University Station, D5300, Austin, Texas 78712. Dr. Sorrells' interests include teacher education and multicultural special education. Along with Dr. Janette Klingner, she has developed the six-part *Making Corrections* professional model to improve middle and secondary teachers' instruction in diverse classrooms with struggling readers.

Deborah L. Speece, Ph.D., Professor, Department of Special Education, University of Maryland, 1308 Benjamin Building, College Park, Maryland 20742. Dr. Speece directs the doctoral leadership training program in learning disabilities and is the former Editor of *Learning Disabilities Research & Practice.* Her research interests include classification issues in learning disabilities, including responsiveness to intervention, children at risk for school failure, and contextual features that influence school performance.

Joan M. Sweeney, M.S., Research Associate, Child Research and Study Center, University at Albany, State University of New York, 1535 Western Avenue, Albany, New York 12203. Ms. Sweeney's work has focused on providing professional development and coaching to both classroom and intervention teachers as they design programs to address their students' literacy needs. She has worked in the past as a special educator and reading teacher.

Barbara J. Terry, Ph.D., Assistant Research Professor, Juniper Gardens Children's Project, University of Kansas, 650 Minnesota Avenue, Kansas City, Kansas 66101. Dr. Terry is a former elementary teacher who has always liked the area of teacher training and staff development as it relates to implementing techniques and programs that have been researched and shown to be effective. At Juniper Gardens Children's Project (JGCP), she has worked on many of the educational research grants in researching, developing, and evaluating programs that enhance the educational achievement of children and students at risk, and she currently coordinates the postdoctoral leadership grant at JGCP.

Frank R. Vellutino, Ph.D., Professor and Director, Child Research and Study Center, University at Albany, State University of New York, 1535 Western Avenue, Albany, New York 12203. Dr. Vellutino holds a joint appointment in the Department of Psychology and the Department of Educational and Counseling Psychology. He has done considerable research in the study of literacy development and factors leading to difficulties in acquiring literacy skills.

Caroline Y. Walker, M.S., M.A., Doctoral Candidate, Department of Special Education, University of Maryland, 1308 Benjamin Building, College Park, Maryland 20742. Ms. Walker is the Title I Coordinator for the Howard County Public School System. Her research interests include reading disability subtyping, responsiveness to intervention, and effective reading interventions for upper elementary students.

Jeanne Wanzek, Ph.D., M.S.Ed., Research Assistant, Vaughn Gross Center for Reading and Language Arts, University of Texas at Austin, 1 University Station, Suite D5300, Austin, Texas 78744. Dr. Wanzek's research interests include effective instructional design and beginning reading instruction.

Althea L. Woodruff, Ph.D., Project Director and Lecturer, Vaughn Gross Center for Reading and Language Arts, University of Texas at Austin, 1 University Station, Suite D5300, Austin, Texas 78712. Dr. Woodruff has worked in several research areas, including analysis of different types of professional development for upper elementary and middle school teachers in teaching reading comprehension and the implementation of a Three-Tier framework for teaching reading in kindergarten through third grade classrooms.

Dedicated to Candace S. Bos:
scholar, author, researcher, teacher, and friend

Background and Overview of the Three-Tier Model

Overview of the Three-Tier Model of Reading Intervention

Sharon Vaughn and Janette Klingner

Since the mid-1970s, the identification of students with learning disabilities has been an ongoing topic of contention. Though perhaps not quite as heated as the math or reading "wars," issues about how best to identify students with learning disabilities have changed surprisingly little over the years. These issues include 1) subjectivity in student referral for services with teacher's perceptions weighing too heavily in the process, 2) inaccurate procedures for determining learning disabilities through emphasis on flawed methods such as IQ score–achievement discrepance as a primary practice, 3) students being identified using a "wait-to-fail" model rather than a prevention–early intervention model, 4) opportunity to learn and environment providing too little influence on who is identified as having a learning disability, 5) considerable variation among prevalence rates for learning disabilities from state to state, and 6) disproportionate numbers of minorities being identified and served inappropriately in special education.

These frequently discussed problems have nagged the field of learning disabilities. In fact, many advocates for individuals with learning disabilities worried that the category of learning disabilities might be disallowed under special education unless a more defensible identification process could be implemented. Because of this concern, several independent initiatives related to special education were undertaken. Fortunately, these initiatives, discussed in the following section, yielded convergent findings that set the stage for changes in the identification and intervention practices for students with learning disabilities.

The primary change was the recommended use of Response to Intervention (RTI) in which increasingly more intensive layers of intervention are used as a means to determine students with reading and learning difficulties. These layers of instruction are often thought of as tiers of instructions. While the number of tiers may vary, typically schools use three tiers: Tier 1, or primary instruction refers to one reading instruction provided by the classroom teacher to all students; Tier 2, or secondary intervention, refers to reading instruction provided to those students identified through universal screening and requiring supplementary reading interventions; and Tier 3, or tertiary intervention, refers to reading instruction proved to those students who continue to struggle as they learn and whose response to secondary intervention was inadequate.

SETTING THE STAGE FOR RESPONSE TO INTERVENTION

Since 2001, three major initiatives have set the stage for change in the identification process for students with learning disabilities. These three initiatives include the President's Commission on Excellence in Special Education (2002), the Learning Disabilities Summit sponsored by the Office of Special Education Programs (OSEP) of the U.S. Department of Education (Bradley, Danielson, & Hallahan, 2002), and the National Research Council report on minority students in special education (Donovan & Cross, 2002). Recommendations from each of these initiatives are briefly summarized in the following paragraphs.

The President's Commission on Excellence in Special Education held 13 public hearings throughout the United States of America and invited and received hundreds of written comments. The commission's findings (2002) revealed that the current special education system places too much emphasis on paperwork and placement and not enough emphasis on instruction and takes a "wait-to-fail" approach rather than focusing on prevention and intervention. The commission also recognized that the general education and special education systems operate separately rather than as a unified system serving students with disabilities. As a result of its findings, the President's Commission recommended that the education system shift its focus from monitoring to results, with special consideration given to implementing a prevention model that takes into account the fact that students with disabilities are also part of general education. "In short, the system must be judged by the opportunities it provides and the outcomes achieved by each child" (p. 9, 2002).

In August 2001, the OSEP-sponsored Learning Disabilities Summit assembled researchers in the field of learning disabilities. The goal of the summit was to determine the most current research and practice findings related to the identification of learning disabilities and identify alternative practices for resolving previously identified issues such as inaccurate procedures for determining learning disabilities, subjectivity of student referral for learning disabilities, and measurement problems related to identifying processing problems. The findings from this summit are reported in a book that is more than 800 pages in length (Bradley, Danielson, & Hallahan, 2002).

Although a complete summary of the findings reported in the book (Bradley, Danielson, & Hallahan, 2002) are beyond the scope of this introduction, the advisory team achieved consensus on eight key principles related to the identification of learning disabilities and the eventual use of RTI as a means of facilitating more appropriate identification of students with learning disabilities. The eight key principles are as follows:

- The concept of learning disabilities is a valid construct.

- Students with learning disabilities require special education.

- Individuals with learning disabilities have a disorder that is experienced across the life span.

- The exact prevalence of learning disabilities is unknown, though the rates may be as high as 6%.

- IQ-score–achievement discrepance is not an adequate practice for identifying students with learning disabilities.

- The link between processing disabilities and learning disabilities is difficult to measure and determine the correct treatment for most processing disabilities.

- RTI is the most promising method for identifying individuals with learning disabilities.

- A great deal is known about effective interventions for students with learning disabilities, yet ineffective interventions continue to be used.

A consistent finding has been that identifying and treating students with learning disabilities using traditional assessment practices may not accurately identify students with learning disabilities. Because students with learning disabilities exhibit unexpected underachievement, their poor response to typically effective practices may serve as a guide for identifying those students who require special education.

Donovan and Cross's (2002) report on minority students in special education provided similar recommendations to those of the advisory groups in the Learning Disabilities Summit (Bradley, Danielson, & Hallahan, 2002) and the recommendations of the President's Commission on Excellence in Special Education. Findings revealed that the dominant reason for referral to special education is reading and behavior problems. The council's recommendations were that early screening and intervention practices be instituted so that early identification and treatment can be provided. Because of the growing knowledge base about effective interventions for students with reading and behavior problems, educational systems can institute schoolwide behavior and reading programs aimed at reducing difficulties in students. Students who still exhibit problems after participating in these programs are likely to need special education rather than having been placed in special education because appropriate programs were not available. The committee recommended that

> Federal guidelines for special education eligibility be changed in order to encourage better integrated general and special education services. We propose that eligibility ensue when a student exhibits large differences from typical levels of performance in one or more domain(s) and with evidence of insufficient response to high-quality interventions in the relevant domain(s) of functioning in school settings (p. 362, Donovan & Cross, 2002).

RESPONSE TO INTERVENTION:
A NEW ERA IN IDENTIFICATION AND INSTRUCTION
FOR STUDENTS WITH LEARNING DISABILITIES

New directions for identifying students with learning disabilities resulted from these three initiatives. The Individuals with Disabilities Education Improvement Act (IDEA) of 2004 (PL 108-446) recommended RTI as a practice for identifying students with learning disabilities. Citing the consensus reports reviewed earlier, IDEA of 2004 made the following recommendations:

- Discontinuation of the use of the IQ-score–achievement discrepance criterion because it delays intervention until a student's performance is sufficiently low to meet the criterion rather than providing services early when they are likely to be most beneficial

- Early screening and intervention so the gap between a child's performance and the performance of his or her peers can be closed early

- Use of a multitiered intervention strategy

- District review of practices to accelerate learning so that students make adequate progress in special education

- Systematic, ongoing progress monitoring of a student's response to high-quality, research-based interventions

- Better integration of general and special education services

- Consideration of the role of context when referring, identifying, and serving students in special education

Although these recommendations seem very sensible and well-directed, the implementation seems somewhat overwhelming to many state and local education agencies; therefore, in response to IDEA of 2004, the National Association of State Directors of Special Education (2005) produced a document designed to assist educators in understanding the policy considerations and implementation practices needed for applying RTI. This document provides an excellent overview of both problem solving and standard protocol approaches to RTI. Perhaps of most value to individuals trying to obtain a better understanding of RTI is the question and answer format provided at the end of the document.

OVERVIEW

This book reflects some of the best research and thinking associated with RTI approaches that are being conducted nationally. Our intent is to provide a summary of what is known about RTI models and also raise questions for the reader to consider. We have divided the book into five sections. The first section provides background and an overview of the Three-Tier Model, the second section describes primary interventions, the third section discusses secondary interventions, the fourth section discusses tertiary interventions, and the fifth and final section addresses various issues associated with RTI implementation and research. We also included a list of web sites and resources we found helpful in the Appendix of General References at the end of this book.

Background and Overview of the Three-Tier Model

In Chapter 2, Vaughn, Wanzek, Woodruff, and Linan-Thompson discuss the potential of RTI to provide effective instruction, identify struggling readers early, provide appropriate interventions, prevent reading difficulties, and identify students with reading disabilities. They review 42 studies that address RTI for young struggling readers and raise important questions related to determining which students should be considered nonresponders and what secondary interventions should look like. They describe a possible Three-Tier Model and note how RTI can help educators make sound instructional decisions.

In Chapter 3, Fuchs and Fuchs describe the role of assessment within the three-tier approach to reading intervention, with a focus on three essential purposes. The authors also explain what curriculum-based measurement is and how it can be applied to satisfy those three assessment purposes. To illustrate the role of curriculum-based measurement within an RTI model, they present a case study of first-grade classrooms in a fictitious school and also outline a comprehensive framework spanning kindergarten through grade 6.

Primary Intervention

In Chapter 4, Foorman, Carlson, and Santi present the lessons they have learned from observing classroom reading instruction in the primary grades. They emphasize that the formal reading instruction provided in general education classrooms is of crucial importance as part of an RTI model. They suggest that more assessments are needed so that teachers can be better equipped to make data-based decisions for instructional purposes.

Chapter 5, by Greenwood, Kamps, Terry, and Linebarger, describes primary intervention as a means of preventing special education, particularly in urban schools. They summarize the research Greenwood and colleagues have conducted over a span of 20 years on classwide peer tutoring and other peer-assisted learning strategies and note that the prevalence of struggling and failing readers can be reduced through effective early instruction. They also discuss how to achieve wide-scale, systematic use of these instructional strategies.

Secondary Intervention

In Chapter 6, Denton, Fletcher, Simos, Papanicolaou, and Anthony describe their implementation of Three-Tier Model of Reading Intervention in two different studies. They provide detailed descriptions of students who participated in one of the studies, including contrasts between students who responded adequately and those who responded inadequately to an intensive intervention. They also discuss changes in brain function for participants who became adequate readers and for those who did not respond well to instruction.

In Chapter 7, O'Connor discusses layers of intervention that affect students' outcomes in reading, with a particular focus on secondary intervention. O'Connor shows that increasing the intensity of instruction in the second tier of an RTI model, while maintaining a focus on the alphabetic code, produces improvements—but not cures—for students. She notes that we still have much to learn about the type and intensity of instruction that can minimize reading disability and raises important questions about the decisions that must be made when using RTI.

Tertiary Intervention

Chapter 8, by Harn, Kame'enui, and Simmons, discusses essential features of interventions for kindergarten students most in need of support, particularly those students participating in the third tier of an RTI model. The authors provide data from a research study on kindergartners identified as being at risk for reading difficulties and conclude that effective third-tier interventions should be empirically based, carefully designed, purposefully implemented, and given high priority. In addition, student progress should be monitored closely.

In Chapter 9, Vellutino, Scanlon, Small, Fanuele, and Sweeney describe their model for preventing early reading difficulties through kindergarten and first-grade interventions. They summarize selected findings from their research. Their model deviates somewhat from the Three-Tier Model in that they provided support for kindergarten students identified as at risk for early reading difficulties before the students had received classroom instruction. Their intervention supplemented first-tier classroom literacy instruction without any attempt to modify the instruction.

Implementation Issues

Chapter 10, by Klingner, Sorrells, and Barrera, discusses considerations when implementing RTI models with culturally and linguistically diverse students. They note that RTI models show great promise for reducing the disproportionate placement of minority students in special education but caution that unless evidence-based interventions take into account what is known about appropriate assessments and interventions for culturally and linguistically diverse students, students' opportunities to learn may be compromised and they may still be placed inappropriately in special education.

Chapter 11, by Haagar and Mahdavi, discusses what can reasonably be expected of teachers in a Three-Tier Model. Teachers have increasing responsibilities with a three-tiered model. Providing research-based practices in the classroom, conducting universal screening and progress monitoring, and participating in professional development are but a few of the many activities for which teachers are responsible. This chapter provides guidance to educational leaders about how teachers might be reasonably engaged in this process.

In Chapter 12, Marston, Reschly, Lau, Muyskens, and Canter describe their years of work with a problem-solving model in Minneapolis Public Schools. They provide a historical perspective on multitiered models, discuss lessons learned, and offer recommendations. The foundation of the Minneapolis model is a sequential approach to problem solving that starts with the classroom teacher in general education and moves through increasingly intensive stages of intervention and evaluation, involving increasing levels of team collaboration.

Finally, Chapter 13, by Speece and Walker, raises important issues concerning RTI implementation and research. The authors discuss four elements of RTI models that they believe require further investigation: screening procedures, intensity and content of instruction, definition of responsiveness, and implications for "postprimary" children. They offer a broad perspective that situates validated instructional practices within the larger context of RTI and learning disabilities identification.

It is recognized that the implementation of RTI models will require validated practices in assessment and instruction. The information provided by the chapter authors can assist teachers and administrators in determining how this implementation might be initiated.

REFERENCES

Bradley, R., Danielson, L., & Hallahan, D.P. (2002). *Identification of learning disabilities: Research to practice.* Mahwah, NJ: Lawrence Erlbaum Associates.

Donovan, M.S., & Cross, C.T. (2002). *Minority students in special and gifted education.* National Research Council. Committee on Minority Representation in Special Education. Division of Behavioral and Social Sciences and Education. Washington, DC: National Academies Press.

President's Commission on Excellence in Special Education. (2002). *A new era: Revitalizing special education for children and their families.* Washington, DC: U.S. Department of Education.

2

Prevention and Early Identification of Students with Reading Disabilities

Sharon Vaughn, Jeanne Wanzek,
Althea L. Woodruff, and Sylvia Linan-Thompson

The importance of ensuring that children acquire adequate literacy skills in the primary grades has been well-documented; students who do not learn to read in the first and second grades are likely to continue to struggle with reading (Juel, 1988; Morris, Shaw, & Perney, 1990) and are at higher risk for academic failure and school dropout than children who develop proficient reading skills in the first years of formal schooling. That we are falling short of all students reading at or above grade level is also well-documented: The National Assessment of Educational Progress, our national report card, indicates that more than two thirds of fourth and eighth graders in the United States cannot handle challenging texts at proficient levels (National Center for Education Statistics [NCES], 2003). Even more alarming, the percentage of students reading at these low levels has remained relatively stable over the past 10 years. More specifically, fully 37% of fourth graders nationally cannot read at a basic level—that is, they cannot read and understand a short paragraph of the type found in simple children's books (NCES, 2003). Reading failure is especially prevalent among children living in poverty. Seventy percent of students from low-income families in the fourth grade cannot read at this basic level (Lyon, 2001). In an effort to improve the reading achievement of students, the No Child Left Behind Act of 2001 (PL 107-110) has incorporated systems for the early identification and intervention of students at risk for reading difficulties.

Further evidence of the need for early identification of children at risk for reading failure comes from data on the progress of children who are identified—typically after 1–2 years of reading failure—as having a reading-related disability and are provided with special education services. According to a report published by the Office of Special Education and Rehabilitative Services (2001), approximately 60% of students are identified too late to derive full benefit from special education services. The long-term consequences of late identification cannot be underestimated. For example, only 2% of students receiving special or compensatory education for difficulties learning to read will complete a 4-year college program (Lyon, 2001).

A large percentage of elementary students with reading difficulties qualify for special education services based on a marked discrepancy between their expected performance level in reading and their actual reading levels. Thus, the issue of reading difficulties also serves as an early warning signal for risk that if not heeded may lead to further problems and referral and placement in special education.

Two of the most significant factors associated with improved outcomes for students at risk for reading problems are early identification through screening and early intervention. Screening measures that permit the early and relatively accurate identification of students at risk for reading failure are now available. In addition, a large body of research exists on the types of interventions that are most effective for students who encounter difficulty in mastering the basic components of reading. Thus, at least for monolingual English-speaking students and increasingly for bilingual students (Vaughn, Linan-Thompson, Mathes et al., 2006; Vaughn et al., 2006), there is a growing database of validated early intervention practices.

What is now needed are models of schoolwide programs that incorporate best practices in all the critical areas mentioned above—effective reading instruction for all students; early identification of students at risk for reading problems; effective interventions for students at risk; professional development; the efficient and effective deployment of school resources to sustain the program; and, integrated into each aspect of the program, the involvement of parents and families.

RESPONSE TO INTERVENTION:
EARLY IDENTIFICATION OF LEARNING DISABILITIES

One of the issues in prevention and early identification of reading problems is the timing of referral for special education services. Under identification procedures in most states, students typically do not qualify for services within the category of learning disabilities (LD) until their academic failure is severe. This is due in large part to the use of the IQ-score–achievement discrepance method for identifying students with LD. This method inherently requires that students fall behind to a significant degree in areas such as reading before they can be considered eligible for special services. Although this model has been questioned for years on many grounds, including whether it accurately discriminates poor readers from typical readers or between subgroups of low-performing readers (Fletcher, Coulter, Reschly, & Vaughn, 2004; Fletcher, Francis, Rourke, Shaywitz, & Shaywitz, 1992; Siegel, 1992; Stuebing et al., 2002; Vellutino, Scanlon, & Lyon, 2000), it remains the primary procedure for identifying students with LD in the majority of states.

Alternatives to the IQ-score–achievement discrepance model have been proposed that focus on how a student responds to an initial intervention as a means for determining whether he or she needs special education (Fuchs & Fuchs, 1998; Gresham, 2002). A Response to Intervention (RTI) approach is based on monitoring students' progress, by means of curriculum-based measures, over the course of their participation in appropriate interventions. Students who make minimal or no gains can be provided a more intensive and specific intervention to determine their response over time. Students who fail to profit adequately from this more intensive intervention are those who may be considered by the school district and parents as having a learning disability. Essential to the effective implementation of an RTI model are 1) reliable and valid measures that are sensitive to intervention and can be administered multiple times, 2) validated intervention protocols for targeted outcomes such as reading decoding and comprehension (Vaughn, 2002), and 3) school-level models delineating a coordinated system of screening, intervention, and placement. The primary thrust for using identification models that incorporate RTI is to provide early intervention and/or prereferral services early to students who exhibit academic difficulties. The goal is to reduce inappropriate referral and identification and to establish a prevention model for students, thus eliminating the "wait-to-fail" model in place in many schools (Fletcher et al., 2004).

Research on Response to Intervention

Studies examining interventions for students with reading disabilities or difficulties reveal that even when the intervention group as a whole makes significant gains, some students do not respond as well to the intervention. These students may be considered *nonresponders* to the intervention. In recent years, it has become increasingly common for authors to report the number or percentage of nonresponders to the reported interventions. It is important to note that in almost all cases, students who are referred to as nonresponders are actually either low responders (meaning the slope for their response rate is not steep enough to accelerate their progress so that they would eventually be on-level readers) or their start point for the intervention was so low that even though they are responding they are not making sufficient progress to meet grade-level benchmarks.

To provide a review of the research that addresses RTI for young students with reading difficulties, we identified the corresponding literature in three stages. First, the 23 intervention studies included in the synthesis of literature by Al Otaiba and Fuchs (2002) encompassing the years 1966–2000 were obtained. Second, a three-step process was used to identify studies that took place from June 2000–August 2004, including 1) computer searches of PsycInfo and ERIC for the years 1999–2004, 2) hand searches of 10 major journals related to the topic for the years 2001–2004, and 3) examination of the reference section of a relevant meta-analysis to identify additional studies not captured through the computer and hand searches (Nelson, Benner, & Gonzalez, 2003). Third, a search of Dissertation Abstracts for the years 1996–2003 was conducted.

The criteria for inclusion of a study corresponded to the criteria set by Al Otaiba and Fuchs (2002):

1. Dissertations or studies were published in peer-reviewed journals.

2. Participants ranged from preschool to third grade.

3. Participants included students at risk for reading difficulties (e.g., students with low ability, low phonological awareness, low income, language disorders, LD).

4. Interventions targeted early literacy and were conducted in English.

5. Study outcomes addressed reading outcomes.

6. Studies reported descriptions of students who were unresponsive to intervention. Studies reporting a percentage of nonresponders without providing descriptive information on these nonresponders separately from the participants as a whole were not included.

A total of 42 studies met criteria for inclusion in the synthesis. Twelve studies described nonresponders without statistical analyses. Twenty-five studies examined factors that predicted nonresponse to reading intervention. Five studies examined the characteristics of nonresponders after multiple interventions. Unique characteristics of nonresponders in one study were reported in two different publications, yielding a total of 43 publications or dissertations. It is beyond the scope of this chapter to review and analyze all of these studies; however, Wanzek (2005) provides a summary of all of the studies. A consistent definition of nonresponse to intervention has not been applied in the field. Thus, nonresponse to intervention was defined in a variety of ways in the studies we located, including lack of grade-level outcomes, empirically derived criteria on specific measures (e.g., students below the 30th percentile on a word reading measure), and no progress or slow progress in intervention compared with other students. Often, even the criteria to determine "grade level" or "slow progress" were not specified. It is clear that before RTI can be used effectively as an identification approach, agreement on what constitutes response and nonresponse to intervention is needed. One suggestion for defining nonresponse has been to use both the slope of progress and the performance level for students (Fuchs, Fuchs, McMaster, & Al Otaiba, 2003). Using this definition, a student who is below average in achievement level and who makes minimal progress in an intervention is identified as not responding to the intervention. In contrast, a student who begins at a low performance level in an intervention and does not meet criterion by the end of the intervention may still show evidence of responding to the intervention if he or she displays a sufficient slope of progress. If the student's slope of progress continues to demonstrate response, then the student is responding and is not in need of more intensive interventions or special education. Although this approach of examining student performance level as well as student growth may be leading the field toward a more consistent definition of nonresponse, no such consistent process is yet in place. Thus, a consistent level of RTI is not available across studies.

In addition to inconsistencies in definitions of nonresponse, the fidelity of interventions was only reported in 17 of the studies synthesized. The lack of measuring the validity of the independent variable has been an ongoing problem in the field of education (e.g., Gresham, MacMillan, Beebe-Frankenberger, & Bocian, 2000). It is difficult to determine the general effectiveness of interventions employed if the fidelity of the implementation is unknown or unreported. Four of the five studies, however, reported in this chapter reported on the fidelity of implementation (Al Otaiba, 2000; Berninger et al., 2002; Vadasy, Sanders, Peyton, & Jenkins, 2002; Vaughn, Linan-Thompson, & Hickman, 2003), increasing the validity of the reported results.

Studies Providing Multiple Interventions

Five of the identified studies addressed the provision of multiple interventions (Al Otaiba, 2000; Berninger et al., 2002; Vadasy et al., 2002; Vaughn, Linan-Thompson et al., 2003; Vellutino et al., 1996). One study reported additional information on nonresponders in a second article (Vellutino et al., 2000). We selected these studies for review in this chapter because they relate closest to the Three-Tier Model we are proposing, which specifies the provision of multiple interventions for students whose RTI does not indicate the boost needed for them no longer to be considered at risk. Each of these studies identified nonresponders after one round of intervention and provided additional intervention(s) to students demonstrating insufficient response.

Four of the studies provided intervention to students at risk for reading difficulties for approximately one semester either in the spring of kindergarten (Al Otaiba, 2000) or in first grade (Berninger et al., 2002; Vadasy et al., 2002; Vellutino et al., 1996). The kindergarten intervention (Al Otaiba, 2000) focused on phonological awareness, letter sounds, and blending sounds into words. First-grade interventions involved instruction in letter sounds, word reading, story reading, and spelling. Students who had made insufficient progress after the semester of intervention were identified and received additional intervention during the following grade (i.e., first or second grade). In general, the second semester of intervention in each of these studies built on the first semester by reviewing concepts and increasing the difficulty of word reading as well as by incorporating comprehension instruction. In two studies, predictors of continued nonresponse were identified. Berninger and colleagues (2002) found that growth in word reading predicted response on word-reading measures after multiple interventions. Al Otaiba (2000) reported phonemic awareness, rapid automatic naming, grammatical closure, vocabulary, sentence imitation, word discrimination, and behavior as significant predictors of nonresponse to interventions. While Vadasy and colleagues (2002) did not identify predictors of continued nonresponse, the authors reported the additional intervention did not significantly improve outcomes for students.

Vellutino and colleagues (1996) also examined response to word reading and identified students making "low" growth or "very low" growth with students making "good" growth or "very good" growth after the first intervention. Both the first and second intervention included one-to-one instruction in fluency, phonological awareness, letter names and sounds, sight word reading, vocabulary, and writing. Predictors of group assignment included attention, phonemic awareness, rapid automatic naming, visual–verbal association, and verbal memory. Though predictors of continued nonresponse were not identified, the identified growth groups remained distinct on outcome measures after the second intervention. In a follow-up study, Vellutino and colleagues (2000) reported IQ score as unrelated to predicting response to intervention (Vellutino et al., 1996).

In another study, three intervention opportunities were provided within 10-week timeframes to second-grade students at risk for reading problems (Vaughn, Linan-Thompson, & Hickman, 2003). Students received instruction in fluency, phonological awareness, word analysis, spelling, and instructional passage reading on a daily basis. After each 10-week period, students who reached criteria on reading fluency were exited from the intervention. Therefore, the duration of the intervention was 10, 20, or 30 weeks depending on the progress made by each student. Some students demonstrated insufficient response throughout the 30 weeks and therefore never exited from intervention. The areas of reading fluency, comprehension, and rapid automatic naming were related to continued insufficient response over the entire 30 weeks. For the second-grade students participating in this study, phonemic awareness and decoding ability did not predict students who would not exit from the intervention. In contrast to Vadasy and colleagues (2002), however, the additional intervention allowed several more students to progress and meet exit criteria at both the 20-week and 30-week periods.

These studies, as well as our own work implementing a Three-Tier Model in reading, raise very interesting and provocative questions about RTI. Most of these questions have to do with implementing RTI in school settings. For example, should students who do not respond adequately to a validated intervention automatically be referred to special education? At what point in the lack of response to validated interventions should students be considered eligible for referral to special education? Who is the appropriate person to provide the validated intervention (e.g., classroom teacher, trained personnel, reading specialist)? How much confidence do we have that validated reading interventions are available for teachers to use, and how should teachers obtain the appropriate materials to implement them? These and many other questions are necessary to address so that general and special education teachers as well as educational leaders have the information they need to implement RTI appropriately.

Interventions for Students Demonstrating Insufficient Response

Torgesen (2000) suggested that students not responding to effective instruction may need more intensive intervention. In an effort to examine this hypothesis, a few researchers have investigated reading outcomes for students with reading difficulties when various levels of instructional intensity are provided. In these studies, intensity has been defined as decreasing group size for instruction and/or increasing the amount of time the student spends receiving instruction.

Although it is not surprising that whole-class instruction is less effective for students with disabilities than small-group or student-paired instruction (Elbaum, Vaughn, Hughes, & Moody, 1999; Schumm, Moody, & Vaughn, 2000), this finding does not provide evidence for what group size offers sufficient intensity for students to make adequate progress. To address this question of group size, an intervention was implemented in varying group sizes with second-grade students at risk for reading problems (Vaughn, Linan-Thompson, Kouzekanani et al., 2003). Students were randomly assigned to receive the intervention in either a group of 10 students with one teacher or a group of 3 students with one teacher or through one-to-one instruction. The same reading intervention was provided to students in all three group sizes. Results indicated students who received instruction in groups of 3 or one-to-one made considerably more gains on comprehension measures than students taught in groups of 10. Students receiving one-to-one instruction demonstrated significantly higher gains in fluency and phonological awareness than students in groups of 10. There were no significant differences between the students taught in groups of 3 and the students who received one-to-one instruction, indicating that the increased intensity of providing one-to-one instruction may not be necessary to improve student outcomes. A meta-analysis of one-to-one tutoring interventions found similar results in that one-to-one instruction yielded no different outcomes than small-group interventions (Elbaum, Vaughn, Hughes, & Moody, 2000).

Another way to conceptualize intensity is to consider the duration of interventions. In a meta-analysis of one-to-one instruction (Elbaum et al., 2000), the study samples were split into interventions lasting 20 weeks or less and interventions lasting longer than 20 weeks. Higher effects were yielded for interventions lasting 20 weeks or less, suggesting that students may make the largest gains early in an intervention. Though student progress is still evident in longer interventions, the sizeable gains made in the shorter time period also may suggest that the intensity level of intervention is not increased substantially by providing longer interventions.

A more specific examination of the effect of duration on intervention can be found in a study of second-grade students with reading difficulties who participated in a reading intervention that lasted either 10, 20, or 30 weeks (Vaughn, Linan-Thompson, & Hickman, 2003). The duration of the intervention was determined by each student's progress. Students who achieved a passing score—more than 55 correct words per minute—on a reading fluency measure and a passing score—50 or more correct words per minute—on progress-monitoring measures of fluency for at least 3 consecutive weeks were exited from the intervention, though their progress was still followed. Students who did not meet exit criteria after each 10-week intervention continued in the intervention for an additional 10 weeks. All 10 of the students who exited after 10 weeks of instruction as well as 10 of 12 students who exited after 20 weeks of instruction continued to make gains in reading fluency with classroom reading instruction only. This finding indicates a longer intervention assisted even more students in reaching a reading level that allowed them to benefit from core reading instruction. An additional 10 students met exit criteria after 30 weeks of instruction, but their progress was not followed after exiting. This study combined with Elbaum and colleagues' (2000) meta-analysis provide evidence that interventions up to at least 20 weeks can allow many students to make substantial gains in their reading outcomes.

Both of the studies that examined duration of intervention considered the effects of an increased number of days in intervention on students' outcomes. Another way to increase intervention time or intensity is to increase the number of sessions or hours of instruction a student spends in intervention over the same number of days (e.g., 2 hours per day for 10 weeks versus 1 hour per day for 10 weeks). Although the effects of this type of intervention intensity have not been studied specifically in the literature, interventions in the reading literature have typically been conducted for 20–50 minutes per day. A notable exception is a study conducted by Torgesen and colleagues (2001), who provided a reading intervention for two 50-minute sessions per day for 8–9 weeks to 8- to 10-year-old students with reading disabilities. The 67.5 hours of instruction yielded substantial improvements in word reading and comprehension that were maintained over the next 2 years of follow-up. This study suggests more instruction in a short period of time may benefit students with severe reading disabilities; however, the study was not designed specifically to investigate whether the increased time in intervention significantly improved outcomes over interventions of less time per day.

The research available on intensity of instruction (group size and duration of intervention) provides preliminary evidence that small-group instruction and increased duration of intervention may allow more students to succeed in reading. Further research is still needed to determine what levels of intensity of intervention can improve outcomes for students who do not make sufficient progress in generally effective reading interventions. Particularly for students at risk for reading disabilities, this research may assist schools in determining student need for intervention or referral and placement in special education, thus providing the most effective intervention in the most efficient manner and reducing the allocation of extensive resources over time.

THE THREE-TIER MODEL

We have organized a Three-Tier Model as a decision-making framework to support school districts in using resources to meet the instructional needs of all young readers, particularly those who struggle in the early elementary grades and those who do not make adequate progress after interventions are provided. The model focuses on prevention of reading problems and is aimed at identifying students as early as kindergarten and first grade, before they fall behind, and providing the academic interventions they need throughout the first 4 years of schooling. The model may be conceptualized as a safety net for struggling readers and as an alternative to a "wait-to-fail" model. The model consists of three tiers or levels of instruction: Tier 1 (core reading instruction with screening three times a year for all students and progress monitoring more frequently for students at risk for reading problems), Tier 2 (intervention and progress monitoring for students who are struggling), and Tier 3 (intensive interventions for students for whom the Tier 2 intervention was insufficient).

Tier 1

Tier 1 is comprised of three elements: 1) a core reading program or curriculum based on scientific reading research, 2) screening and benchmark testing of students at least three times each year (i.e., fall, winter, and spring) to determine instructional needs, and 3) ongoing professional development to provide teachers with the necessary tools to ensure every student receives quality reading instruction. Tier 1 reading instruction is designed to address the needs of the majority of a school's students. During core classroom reading instruction, students are at various levels of development in critical early reading skills. Some students are able to acquire the necessary skills with the standard instruction given by the teacher, whereas others require more intensive instruction in specific skill areas. When teachers implement an effective reading program that includes flexible grouping and targeting specific skills, they often are able to meet the needs of most students. Thus, in Tier 1, the instruction provided by the classroom teacher is sufficient to meet many students' needs.

Tiers 2 & 3

Focused classroom reading instruction is not sufficient to meet the needs of some children. To accelerate their progress and ensure that they do not slip further behind, these students require more strategic intervention in addition to the time allotted for their core reading instruction. Tier 2 is designed to meet the needs of these students by providing them with an additional 30 minutes of intensive, small-group reading instruction daily. The aim is to support and reinforce the skills being taught within the core reading program. In Tier 2, the interventionist may be the classroom teacher, a specialized reading teacher, or another support person specifically trained for Tier 2 intervention.

A small percentage of students who receive Tier 2 intervention continue to show marked difficulty in acquiring necessary reading skills. These students require instruction that is more explicit, more intensive, and specifically designed

Table 2.1.　The Three-Tier Model: Tiers of instruction

	Tier 1	Tier 2	Tier 3
Definition	"Core" curricular and instructional reading programs and strategies, including ongoing professional development and benchmark assessments three times per year	Programs, strategies, and procedures that take place in small groups designed and employed to supplement, enhance, and support Tier 1	Specifically designed and customized reading instruction that is extended beyond the time allocated for Tier 1 and Tier 2 and takes place in groups of 1–3 students
Focus	For all students in kindergarten through 3rd grade	For students with marked reading difficulties who have not responded to Tier 1 efforts	For students with marked difficulties in reading or with reading disabilities who have not responded adequately to Tier 1 and Tier 2 efforts
Program	Scientific-based reading instruction and curriculum emphasizing the five critical elements of beginning reading	Specialized, scientifically-based reading program(s) emphasizing the five critical elements of beginning reading	Sustained, intensive, scientifically based reading program(s) emphasizing the five critical elements of beginning reading
Instruction	Many opportunities to practice embedded throughout the school day	Additional attention, focus, support Additional opportunities to practice embedded throughout the day Preteach, review skills; frequent opportunities to practice skills	Carefully designed and implemented, explicit, systematic instruction Fidelity of implementation carefully maintained
Interventionist	General education teacher	Personnel determined by the school to provide intervention	Personnel determined by the school to provide intensive intervention
Setting	General education classroom	Appropriate setting designated by the school	Appropriate setting designated by the school
Grouping	Flexible grouping	Homogeneous small-group instruction (e.g., 1:4 or 1:5 teacher-to-student ratio)	Homogeneous small-group instruction (e.g., 1:3 teacher-to-student ratio)
Time	Minimum of 90 minutes per day	Minimum of 20 minutes per day	45–60 minutes per day
Assessment	Benchmark assessments at beginning, middle, and end of academic year	Progress monitoring twice a month on target skill to ensure adequate progress and learning	Progress monitoring weekly on target skill to ensure adequate progress and learning

to meet their individual needs. For these students, a 45- to 60-minute session of specialized, small-group reading instruction can be provided in Tier 3 in addition to Tier 1 instruction. The Tier 3 interventionist may be a specialized reading teacher, a special education teacher, or an external interventionist specifically trained for the intervention. For a more complete explanation of the components of the three tiers and the differences among them, refer to Table 2.1.

Relating the Tiers

Tiers 2 and 3 provide intensive, focused instruction for students identified by benchmark assessments as having low early literacy skills and as being at risk for reading difficulty. Generally, Tier 1 instruction (core classroom reading instruction) should meet the needs of 70–80% (or more) of learners. The lowest 20–30% may need additional support with Tier 2 intervention, and it is anticipated that 5–10% will require Tier 3 instruction for intensive intervention. The aim of the Three-Tier Model is to reduce the number of students with reading difficulties and put all students on track to becoming successful readers. Furthermore, the model holds promise as an integrated approach for all levels of instruction.

As illustrated in Figure 2.1, movement through the three tiers is a dynamic process, with students entering and exiting as needed. Once a student's needs are met and he or she is able to achieve grade-level benchmarks on the assessments,

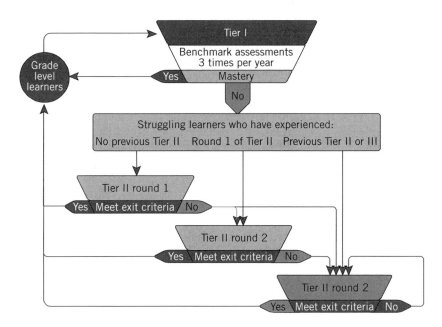

Figure 2.1.   An example of movement through Tiers 1, 2, and 3.

the intervention may no longer be required for that student. Screening and benchmark testing of all kindergarten through third-grade students three times per year (i.e., fall, winter, and spring) ensures that students who require additional help are 1) identified early, or 2) re-identified if they have previously received support and show that they need intervention again. In contrast to previous interventions for reading, the Three-Tier Model provides a system that is responsive to students' changing needs.

Assessment and Progress Monitoring within the Model

Assessment plays a central role in the Three-Tier Model. Two types of assessments are used to inform instruction: 1) screening and benchmark assessment to determine the need for intervention, and 2) progress-monitoring assessment to track student progress (Good, Simmons, & Smith, 1998; Simmons & Kame'enui, 1998). Benchmark assessments aid in early identification of students at risk for reading problems—a critical aspect of the Three-Tier Model. Testing of all students, kindergarten through third grade, is conducted in early fall, early winter, and late spring. For those who are not making adequate progress, teachers combine core classroom instruction (Tier 1) with an intervention (Tier 2 or Tier 3) matched to students' needs and use ongoing progress-monitoring data to adjust instruction and ensure students' academic growth.

Benchmark data can be entered into a database so that reading performance can be analyzed at the individual, classroom, grade, and school levels. Reports can then be issued to teachers and administrators to 1) identify students who will benefit from reading intervention, 2) customize reading instruction based on students' needs, and 3) help school personnel determine the effectiveness of Tier 1 (the core reading program) and decide the professional development needs of the teachers.

Students receiving Tier 2 or Tier 3 instruction receive frequent and ongoing progress monitoring (Kame'enui & Carnine, 1998; Pressley, Rankin, & Yokoi, 1996). Teachers' instruction improves when they use progress monitoring to 1) track student learning, 2) plan instruction, and 3) provide feedback to students (Fuchs, 1986). The use of these assessments, combined with timely intervention, yields fewer students with reading difficulties and ultimately reduces the number of students referred for special education services.

RESEARCH STUDY ON THE THREE-TIER MODEL

We initiated a 5-year project to examine the effectiveness of a school-based model for improving student outcomes (Vaughn, Linan-Thompson, Elbaum et al., 2004). The participants in this longitudinal study are kindergarten through third-grade students and their teachers at six schools. Before we began implementation of the model, the kindergarten and first-grade students and teachers in these

Table 2.2. Research study: Grade levels within each cohort and year

Cohorts	Year 1	Year 2	Year 3	Year 4	Year 5
Historical control	Kindergarten First grade	First grade Second grade	Second grade Third grade	Third grade	
Cohort 1		Kindergarten	First grade	Second grade	Third grade
Cohort 2			Kindergarten	First grade	Second grade

schools were identified as a historical control group (HC), with whom we could compare the students and teachers who would participate in the Three-Tier Model implementation. During the first year of the project, the kindergarten and first-grade students were assessed but none of their teachers received professional development (Tier 1) from the research team and none of the students were provided with intervention (Tier 2) by us. During the second year of the study, implementation of the Three-Tier Model began with professional development for all kindergarten teachers at the participating schools and delivery of Tier 1 instruction to all kindergarten students at the schools. As the students move from one grade to the next, teachers at each successive grade level participate in the ongoing professional development program and students continue to be provided with Tier 1 intervention (for a summary of the grade levels participating in each cohort during each year of the project, see Table 2.2). The project documents changes over time in the skills and perceptions of both students and teachers. With regard to students, the focus is on growth in reading skills. With regard to teachers, the focus is on improved teaching skills and perceptions concerning barriers and facilitators related to schoolwide implementation of the model.

In addition to supporting the Tier 1 instruction, students who meet risk criteria on the benchmark assessments for Tier 2 intervention are randomly assigned to receive either Tier 1 plus Tier 2 (Tier 1+2) or Tier 1 with typical school services (Tier 1+SS). Thus, a treatment group and a control group of at-risk readers are used for examining the Tier 2 instruction. Each classroom teacher has students in the Tier 1+2 group and the Tier 1+SS group to companion for Tier 1 teacher effects. Students who enter second grade and have not adequately responded to Tier 2 interventions are engaged in Tier 1 core instruction plus a Tier 3 intervention that is even more extensive (45–60 minutes per day) and more intensive (ongoing progress monitoring, smaller groups size) to address the more extensive reading needs of these students.

To better understand the extent to which a Three-Tier Model of Reading Intervention prevents reading difficulties and assists in the appropriate early identification of students with reading disabilities, we intend to use our sample and data set to address several critical research questions. We plan to address the relative influence of each tier of instruction by comparing the progress of the students who received the tiers of instruction with the progress of those who did not. We are interested in the patterns of response to these tiers and the characteristics of the students and teachers that differentiate the response to the various tiers of instruction. We also are interested in studying students who demonstrated reading difficulties in early grades (kindergarten and first grade) but no longer exhibited those difficulties in later grades (second and third grade) as well as students whose early skills indicated that they were on level but who demonstrated low performance in reading in later grades. In addition, we are interested in students who are identified for special education and require intervention in reading. The extent to which the number of students identified for special education changes over time and is influenced by the Three-Tier Model will be documented.

Preliminary Findings

To examine the effectiveness of both Tiers 1 and 2, we are comparing three groups of students who are struggling with basic literacy skills: 1) a historical control group, 2) a Tier 1 plus Tier 2 group, and 3) a Tier 1 with typical school services group (Tier 1 plus the school services group). During the first 2 years of our study, students in each of these groups were assessed at the middle and end of kindergarten and at the beginning of first grade. Across these time periods, we used three measures within the Dynamic Indicators of Basic Early Literacy Skills (DIBELS; Good & Kaminski, 2002) and two measures within the Woodcock Reading Mastery Tests–Revised (WRMT–R; Woodcock, 1987). Preliminary findings relate to several literacy skills: 1) naming upper- and lowercase letters fluently and accurately; 2) segmenting words into phonemes fluently; 3) decoding nonsense words; 4) decoding both simple and complex nonsense words accurately; and 5) reading words accurately.

In each of these areas, a pattern emerges across the three time periods when comparing the scores for the three groups of struggling readers. In the middle of kindergarten, all three groups looked very similar across the measures; however, at the end of kindergarten and beginning of first grade, differences emerged among the three groups. Specifically, at these two later time periods, the Tier 1+SS group demonstrated higher scores across the five assessed areas when compared with the historical control group. Such improvement in students' scores illustrates the effect that our Tier 1 intervention alone had on students' literacy skills. Further, the Tier 1+2 group's scores across the five skill areas exceeded both the historical control group's and the Tier 1+SS group's scores, a finding that validates the importance of combining a targeted, strategic intervention (i.e., Tier 2) with improved general classroom reading instruction (i.e., Tier 1).

SUMMARY

Appropriate identification and placement of students with LD into special education programs has been problematic since its inception. In no small part, the challenges of identifying individuals with LD are rooted in the inappropriate use of discrepancy between intelligence and achievement that has prevented many districts from providing early intervention. Although a great deal is known about validated interventions for struggling readers, there is a need for schoolwide programs to address student needs. The Three-Tier Model is a decision-making framework to assist schools and school districts in meeting the instructional needs of all young readers. The Three-Tier Model includes the implementation of a core reading program or curriculum based on scientific reading research, ongoing assessments to identify struggling readers and make appropriate instructional decisions, professional development for teachers to meet the needs of students, and interventions that increase in intensity as needed for individual students. The use of the Three-Tier Model can provide a framework for assisting educators in providing effective instruction, identifying struggling readers early, providing appropriate interventions, and making instructional decisions throughout the school year. Although there are many unanswered questions about RTI and its effective implementation in schools (Vaughn & Fuchs, 2003), we are optimistic that current and future research will assist in addressing these questions.

REFERENCES

Al Otaiba, S.D. (2000). Children who do not respond to early literacy intervention: A longitudinal study across kindergarten and first grade. *Dissertation Abstracts International, 61*(4), 1354A. (UMI No. 9970028)

Al Otaiba, S., & Fuchs, D. (2002). Characteristics of children who are unresponsive to early literacy intervention: A review of the literature. *Remedial and Special Education, 23,* 300–316.

Berninger, V.W., Abbott, R.D., Vermeulen, K., Ogier, S., Brooksher, R., Zook, D., et al. (2002). Comparison of faster and slower responders to early intervention in reading: Differentiating features of their language profiles. *Learning Disability Quarterly, 25,* 59–76.

Elbaum, B., Vaughn, S., Hughes, M., & Moody, S.W. (1999). Grouping practices and reading outcomes for students with disabilities. *Exceptional Children, 65,* 399–415.

Elbaum, B., Vaughn, S., Hughes, M.T., & Moody, S.W. (2000). How effective are one-to-one tutoring programs in reading for elementary students at risk for reading failure? A meta-analysis of the intervention research. *Journal of Educational Psychology, 92,* 605–619.

Fletcher, J.M., Coulter, W.A., Reschly, D.J., & Vaughn, S. (2004). Alternative approaches to the definition and identification of learning disabilities: Some questions and answers. *Annals of Dyslexia, 54*(2), 304–331.

Fletcher, J.M., Francis, D.J., Rourke, B.P., Shaywitz, B., & Shaywitz, S.E. (1992). The validity of the discrepancy-based definitions of learning disabilities. *Journal of Learning Disabilities, 25,* 555–561, 573.

Fuchs, L.S. (1986). Monitoring progress among mildly handicapped pupils: Review of current practice and research. *Remedial and Special Education, 7*(5), 5–12.

Fuchs, L.S., & Fuchs, D. (1998). Treatment validity: A unifying concept for reconceptualizing the identification of learning disabilities. *Learning Disabilities Research and Practice, 13,* 204–219.

Fuchs, D., Fuchs, L.S., McMaster, K.N., & Al Otaiba, S. (2003). Identifying children at risk for reading failure: Curriculum-based measurement and the dual-discrepancy approach. In H.L. Swanson, K.R. Harris, & S. Graham (Eds.), *Handbook of learning disabilities* (pp. 431–449). New York: The Guilford Press.

Good, R.H., & Kaminski, R. (2002). *Dynamic indicators of basic early literacy skills.* (6th ed.). Eugene, OR: Institute for the Development of Educational Achievement.

Good, R.H., Simmons, D.C., & Smith, S.B. (1998). Effective academic interventions in the United States: Evaluating and enhancing the acquisition of early reading skills. *School Psychology Review, 27,* 45–56.

Gresham, F.M. (2002). Responsiveness to intervention: An alternative approach to the identification of learning disabilities. In R. Bradley, L. Danielson, & D.P. Hallahan (Eds.), *Identification of learning disabilities: Research to practice* (pp. 467–547). Mahwah, NJ: Lawrence Erlbaum Associates.

Gresham, F.M., MacMillan, D.L., Beebe-Frankenberger, M.E., & Bocian, K.M. (2000). Treatment integrity in learning disabilities intervention research: Do we really know how treatments are implemented? *Learning Disabilities Research and Practice, 15,* 198–205.

Juel, C. (1988). Learning to read and write: A longitudinal study of 54 children from first through fourth grade. *Journal of Educational Psychology, 80,* 437–447.

Kame'enui E.J., & Carnine D.W. (1998). *Effective teaching strategies that accommodate diverse learners.* Upper Saddle River, NJ: Prentice Hall.

Lyon, G.R. (2001). *Measuring success: Using assessments and accountability to raise student achievement.* Address to U.S. House of Representatives Subcommittee on Education Reform, Committee on Education and the Workforce. Statement retrieved on September 30, 2004, from http://www.nrrf.org/lyon_statement3-01.htm

Morris, D., Shaw, B., & Perney J. (1990). Helping low readers in grades 2 and 3: An after-school volunteer tutoring program. *Elementary School Journal, 91,* 133–150.

National Center for Education Statistics. (2003). *National assessment of educational progress.* Retrieved December 23, 2003, from http://nces.ed.gov/nationsreportcard/reading/results2003

Nelson, J.R., Benner, G.J., & Gonzalez, J. (2003). Learner characteristics that influence the treatment effectiveness of early literacy interventions: A meta-analytic review. *Learning Disabilities Research and Practice, 18,* 255–267.

No Child Left Behind Act of 2001, PL 107-110, 115 Stat. 1425, 20 U.S.C. §§ 6301 *et seq.*

Pressley, M., Rankin, J., & Yokoi, L. (1996). A survey of instructional practices of primary teachers nominated as effective in promoting literacy. *Scientific Studies of Reading, 1,* 145–160.

Schumm, J.S., Moody, S.W., & Vaughn, S. (2000). Grouping for reading instruction: Does one size fit all? *Journal of Learning Disabilities, 33,* 477–488.

Siegel, L.S. (1992). An evaluation of the discrepancy definition of dyslexia. *Journal of Learning Disabilities, 25,* 618–629.

Simmons, D.C., & Kame'enui, E.J. (Eds.). (1998). *What reading research tells us about children with diverse learning needs: Bases and basics.* Mahwah, NJ: Lawrence Erlbaum Associates.

Stuebing, K.K., Fletcher, J.M., LeDoux, J.M., Lyon, G.R., Shaywitz, S.E., & Shaywitz, B.A. (2002). Validity of IQ-discrepancy classifications of reading difficulties: A meta-analysis. *American Educational Research Journal, 39,* 469–518.

Torgesen, J.K. (2000). Individual differences in response to early interventions in reading: The lingering problem of treatment resisters. *Learning Disabilities Research and Practice, 15,* 55–64.

Torgesen, J.K., Alexander, A.W., Wagner, R.K., Rashotte, C.A., Voeller, K.K.S., & Conway, T. (2001). Intensive remedial instruction for children with severe reading disabilities: Immediate and long-term outcomes from two instructional approaches. *Journal of Learning Disabilities, 34,* 33–58.

Vadasy, P.F., Sanders, E.A., Peyton, J.A., & Jenkins, J.R. (2002). Timing and intensity of tutoring: A closer look at the conditions for effective early literacy tutoring. *Learning Disabilities Research and Practice, 17,* 227–241.

Vaughn, S. (2002). Using response to treatment for identifying students with learning disabilities. In R. Bradley, L. Danielson, & D.P. Hallahan (Eds.), *Identification of learning disabilities: Research to practice* (pp. 549–554). Mahwah, NJ: Lawrence Erlbaum Associates.

Vaughn, S., & Fuchs, L.S. (2003). Redefining learning disabilities as inadequate response to treatment: The promise and potential problems. *Learning Disabilities Research and Practice, 18*(3), 137–146.

Vaughn, S., Linan-Thompson, S., Elbaum, B., Wanzek, J., Rodriguez, K.T., Cavanaugh, C.L., et al. (2004). *Centers for implementing K-3 behavior and reading intervention models preventing reading difficulties: A three-tiered intervention model.* Unpublished report, University of Texas Center for Reading and Language Arts.

Vaughn, S., Linan-Thompson, S., & Hickman, P. (2003). Response to instruction as a means of identifying students with reading/learning disabilities. *Exceptional Children, 69,* 391–409.

Vaughn, S., Linan-Thompson, S., Kouzekanani, K., Bryant, D.P., Dickson, S., & Blozis, S.A. (2003). Reading instruction grouping for students with reading difficulties. *Remedial and Special Education, 24,* 301–315.

Vaughn, S., Linan-Thompson, S. Mathes, P.G., Cirino, P.T., Carlson, C.D., Francis, D.J., et al. (2006). Effectiveness of Spanish intervention for first-grade English language learners at risk for reading difficulties. *Journal of Learning Disabilities, 39*(1), 56–73.

Vaughn, S., Mathes, P.G., Linan-Thompson, S., Cirino, P., Carlson, C., Francis, D.H., et al. (2006). First-grade English language learners at-risk for reading problems: Effectiveness of an English intervention. *Elementary School Journal, 107*(2), 153–180.

Vellutino, F.R., Scanlon, D.M., & Lyon, G.R. (2000). Differentiating between difficult-to-remediate and readily remediated poor readers. *Journal of Learning Disabilities, 33,* 223–238.

Vellutino, F.R., Scanlon, D.M., Sipay, E.R., Small, S.G., Pratt, A., Chen, R., et al. (1996). Cognitive profiles of difficult-to-remediate and readily remediated poor readers: Early intervention as a vehicle for distinguishing between cognitive and experiential deficits as basic causes of specific reading disability. *Journal of Educational Psychology, 88,* 601–638.

Wanzek, J. (2005). *The effects of varying amounts of time in reading intervention for students demonstrating insufficient response to intervention.* Unpublished doctoral dissertation, University of Texas at Austin.

Woodcock, R.W. (1987). *Woodcock reading mastery test-revised.* Circle Pines, MN: AGS Publications.

3

The Role of Assessment in the Three-Tier Approach to Reading Instruction

Lynn S. Fuchs and Douglas Fuchs

Research has established the efficacy of interventions to enhance the reading performance of students. In these research studies, students or classrooms are assigned randomly to contrasting interventions; reading growth across time is measured for participants in the various interventions; and the methods that promote superior outcomes for the great majority of students are identified.

Of course, no instructional method, even those validated as effective with randomized controlled research, works for all students. For this reason, as schools implement validated interventions within general education, the effects of those interventions on children's reading performance must be monitored so that children who do not respond adequately can be identified promptly. For these students, more intensive programs can then be implemented. For students who fail to respond to this second level of programming, a third level of instruction, with greater individualization, can be implemented while student response continues to be assessed. This iterative process, during which interventions of increasing intensity and individualization are conducted while responsiveness is gauged, describes a three-tier approach to intervention.

A key component of a three-tiered approach to intervention is assessment—for the purpose of identifying who should be the target of continued monitoring and attention, for quantifying responsiveness to intervention among those targeted for monitoring, and for tailoring individualized instructional programs for

Inquiries should be sent to Lynn S. Fuchs, Box 328 Peabody, Vanderbilt University, Nashville, TN 37203.

Some of the research described in this article was supported in part by Grants #324U010004, #H324DE000033, and #H324C000022 from the U.S. Department of Education, Office of Special Education Programs, and Grant HD 15052 from the National Institute of Child Health and Human Development to Vanderbilt University. Statements do not reflect the position or policy of these agencies, and no official endorsement by them should be inferred.

the most unresponsive subset of children. At the present time, state-of-the-art practice in assessing responsiveness to instruction and for tailoring individual programs centers on a form of progress monitoring known as Curriculum-Based Measurement (CBM).

In this chapter, we explain the role of assessment within a three-tier approach to reading intervention, with a focus on three essential assessment functions. Then, we describe what CBM is and how CBM can satisfy those three assessment functions. Next, to illustrate the role of assessment generally and CBM specifically within a three-tiered approach, we then present a case study conducted with first-grade students. Before closing, we describe a comprehensive CBM framework, which spans kindergarten through Grade 6, so that readers can apply the principles illustrated in the first-grade case study across the elementary grades.

THREE ASSESSMENT FUNCTIONS
ESSENTIAL TO THREE-TIERED READING INTERVENTIONS

Conducting a three-tier reading intervention requires the use of assessment to satisfy three functions. The first function is screening, in which a subset of the school population is targeted for subsequent attention. The second function is progress monitoring, in which responsiveness to instruction is quantified so that decisions can be formulated about which students should move in and out of the second and third tiers of instruction. The third function of assessment within a three-tiered reading intervention is informing instructional planning in ways that help teachers individualize instruction within the third instructional tier.

For screening, every student in the school is assessed during the first month of the school year, using a brief screening tool that demonstrates diagnostic utility for predicting future performance on important criterion measures (e.g., the reading state assessment). A cut score, which designates which children are likely to succeed or fail on the important criterion measures, is then applied. Children who fall below the criterion are targeted for subsequent attention.

This attention comes in the form of progress monitoring. As the Tier 1 general education program is implemented, the student's reading performance is measured frequently, at least once per week, and a rate of improvement is computed from the scores. Then a criterion is applied to determine whether that rate of improvement constitutes "responsiveness" to instruction, and that decision is used to move students into Tier 2. In a similar way, responsiveness is assessed and quantified at each instructional tier so that decisions about how to move students in and out of Tiers 2 and 3 can be formulated.

The third function of assessment within a three-tiered reading intervention centers on instructional planning. Tier 2 typically relies on small-group tutoring, which offers greater intensity than is possible in Tier 1 general education but which represents a standardized intervention protocol. Individualization typically is not emphasized in Tier 2. Once unresponsiveness has been demonstrated to the intensive but standardized intervention protocol in Tier 2, a student moves to the third tier, in which the signature feature is individualization. To individualize a student's program in ways that are responsive to a student's needs, assessment of the student's needs is required. This can be accomplished with a deductive or inductive approach. With a deductive approach, the child's cognitive abilities (e.g., rapid naming speed, concept formation, working memory) are assessed, and the results are used to design a program that capitalizes on the child's strengths while remediating cognitive deficiencies. With an inductive approach, alternative instructional components are systematically introduced; the child's reading progress is monitored and quantified with each component; and components that maximize growth are incorporated into the child's program while the components that have little effect on the child's improvement are abandoned. With an inductive approach, an instructional program is built cumulatively, as instructional features are empirically demonstrated to meet the child's needs. At the present time, research favors an inductive approach to assessing an individual's instructional needs.

CURRICULUM-BASED MEASUREMENT: SCIENTIFICALLY VALIDATED TO SATISFY THE THREE ASSESSMENT FUNCTIONS

CBM is a set of assessment methods that can be used to satisfy the three types of assessment decisions required for implementing a three-tiered reading intervention. CBM provides teachers with reliable, valid, and efficient indicators of academic competence with which to gauge individual student standing at one point in time for screening decision or to index student progress across time for gauging responsiveness to instruction (Deno, 1985). In addition, research demonstrates that teachers can use CBM to design more individualized instructional programs that enhance reading outcomes. In these ways, CBM satisfies the three assessment functions.

CBM differs from most forms of classroom assessment in several ways (Fuchs & Deno, 1991), including these three features. First, CBM is standardized so that the behaviors to be measured and the procedures for measuring those behaviors are prescribed, with documented reliability and validity. Second, CBM's focus is long-term so that testing methods and content remain constant, with equivalent weekly tests spanning much, if not all, of the school year; the primary reason for long-term consistency is so that progress can be monitored systematically over time. Third, CBM is fluency based so that students have a fixed amount of time to respond to the test stimuli. Therefore, improvement reflects an individual's capacity to perform critical behaviors not only with accuracy but also with ease.

To illustrate how CBM is used, imagine that a teacher establishes a reading goal for year-end performance as competent second-grade performance. Then, relying on established methods, the teacher identifies 30 reading passages of equivalent, second-grade difficulty. Each week, the teacher administers one test by having the student read aloud from a different passage for 1 minute; the score is the number of words read correctly. Each simple, brief assessment produces an indicator of reading competence because it requires a multifaceted performance. This performance entails, for example, a reader's skill at automatically translating letters into coherent sound representations, unitizing those sound components into recognizable wholes and automatically accessing lexical representations, processing meaningful connections within and between sentences, relating text meaning to prior information, and making inferences to supply missing information. As competent readers translate text into spoken language, they coordinate these skills in an obligatory, seemingly effortless manner (Fuchs, Fuchs, Hosp, & Jenkins, 2001).

Because this CBM passage reading fluency task reflects this complex performance, it can be used to characterize reading expertise and to track its development in the primary grades (e.g., Biemiller, 1977–1978; Fuchs & Deno, 1991). Within a normative framework, performance levels at a given point in time are compared between individuals to designate risk status for screening decisions. Using an intra-individual framework, the student's scores are graphed, and the slope is calculated on the series of scores to quantify reading improvement. These strategies for characterizing reading competence and growth have been shown to be more sensitive to inter- and intra-individual differences than those offered by other classroom reading assessments (e.g., Marston, Fuchs, & Deno, 1986). In addition, CBM is sensitive to growth made under a variety of interventions (Fuchs, Fuchs, & Hamlett, 1989b; Hintze & Shapiro, 1997; Hintze, Shapiro, & Lutz, 1994; Marston et al., 1986). In a related way, teachers' instructional plans, developed in response to CBM, incorporate a wide range of reading methods including, for example, decoding instruction, repeated readings, vocabulary instruction, story grammar exercises, and semantic mapping activities (Fuchs, Fuchs, Hamlett, & Ferguson, 1992). So, CBM is not tied to any particular reading instructional method. In a similar way, other CBM tasks (discussed later in this chapter) also serve as key indicators of overall reading performance, making them useful for screening and progress-monitoring decisions and other points in reading development.

Perhaps most importantly, however, studies indicate that CBM progress monitoring enhances teachers' capacity to plan programs for and effect achievement among students with serious reading problems. The methods by which CBM informs reading instruction rely on the graphed performance indicator. That is, decisions are tied to the rate of growth on the number of words read correctly in 1 minute: If a student's growth trajectory is judged to be adequate, the teacher increases the student's goal for year-end performance; if not, the teacher revises the instructional program. Research shows that these decision rules produce more varied instructional programs that are more responsive to individual needs (Fuchs et al., 1989b), with more ambitious student goals (Fuchs, Fuchs, & Hamlett, 1989a) and stronger end-of-year scores on commercial, standardized reading tests (e.g., Fuchs, Deno, & Mirkin, 1984). So, CBM can enhance the quality of instructional programming, even as practitioners use CBM to judge a student's responsiveness to instruction.

APPLYING CURRICULUM-BASED MEASUREMENT TO SATISFY THREE ASSESSMENT FUNCTIONS: A FIRST-GRADE CASE STUDY

To illustrate how CBM satisfies the three assessment functions within a three-tier approach to reading intervention, we present a case study of a fictitious school, which we call Carlton School. We focus on first grade. Before presenting the case study, we briefly describe the CBM measure used at first grade, the Tier 1 instructional context, and the nature of Tiers 2 and 3 instruction used in Carlton School's three-tiered reading intervention.

Curriculum-Based Measurement Measure

For screening, for gauging responsiveness at Tiers 1, 2, and 3, and for informing instructional planning, Carlton School uses CBM word identification fluency (CBM-WIF) at first grade. With CBM-WIF, students read a list of words for 1 minute. Performance scores are number of words read correctly, and each alternate form randomly samples 50 words from a pool of 100 high-frequency preprimer, primer, and first-grade words. If a student completes reading before 1 minute, the score is prorated to reflect words read per minute.

Alternate-form reliability/stability for CBM-WIF is .97. Validity for CBM-WIF performance level is also strong. For concurrent validity, correlations with the Woodcock Reading Mastery Test's Word Identification (Woodcock, 1998) subtest are .77 in the fall and .82 in the spring; the correlation with CBM passage reading fluency is .93 in the spring; and the correlation with the Comprehension Reading Assessment Battery—Comprehension score is .73 in the spring. For predictive validity, correlations from fall to spring on the same criterion measures range between .63 and .80.

CBM-WIF slope (i.e., weekly improvement based on a least-squares regression between calendar days and scores) has also been shown to be valid. The correlation between CBM-WIF slope and end-of-year first-grade Woodcock Reading Mastery Test's Word Identification (Woodcock, 1998) subtest is .70; with end-of-year CBM passage reading fluency, .85; and with end-of-year Comprehension Reading Assessment Battery—Comprehension, .66.

For screening, Carlton School assesses all students in September of first grade on two alternate forms of CBM-WIF, averaging performance across the two forms. At the beginning of first grade, Carlton School uses a CBM-WIF cut score of 15 for designating risk for reading failure by the end of first grade (i.e., any student scoring lower than 15 on CBM-WIF is deemed at risk of experiencing reading difficulty unless the student receives intervention). These students are targeted for subsequent progress monitoring as they participate in Tier 1 general education, and they are candidates for Tier 2 or Tier 3 instruction, in which progress monitoring also occurs.

For monitoring response to instruction and moving students in and out of instructional tiers, Carlton School measures at-risk students each week on a different form of CBM-WIF. At both Tiers 2 and 3, scores are graphed and slopes are calculated at decision points. Research indicates that typically developing first graders improve approximately 1.75 words per week on CBM-WIF. Based on a normative framework for at-risk students who respond positively to instruction, Carlton School uses a CBM-WIF slope of 1 word increase per week to designate positive response to intervention.

Tier 1 General Education

Tier 1 instruction at Carlton School can be described as "generally effective" for three reasons. First, every first-grade teacher uses a validated reading curriculum—Open Court. Second, Carlton's lead reading teacher observes each first-grade teacher's implementation of Open Court quarterly and has documented that the program is implemented with strong fidelity. The third form of evidence for the efficacy of Carlton School's first-grade Tier 1 reading program instruction is derived from the teachers' track records. That is, the previous year's first-grade cohort, on average, demonstrated a strong slope on CBM-WIF, improving an average of 1.8 words per week. This figure is commensurate with the weekly rate of improvement for typically developing students in first grade (1.75 words per week increase). Moreover, during the previous year, only 3 of 60 (i.e., 5%) first graders failed to achieve the end-of-year CBM-WIF benchmark of 60 words read correctly in 1 minute.

Tier 2 Instruction

Carlton School's Tier 2 instruction is modeled after a validated tutoring reading protocol at first grade. Students receive 45 minutes of instruction four times each week in groups of one to three students. The tutors are paraprofessionals who have completed training and are observed once each week by the lead reading teacher, who provides corrective feedback. Also, once each week, the lead reading teacher meets with all tutors for 1 hour to review students' CBM-WIF graphs and to ensure fidelity to the validated tutoring protocol. The tutoring sessions focus on phonological awareness, letter-sound recognition, decoding, sight word recognition, and short-story reading, with highly explicit instruction. Self-regulated learning strategies are also incorporated to increase motivation and goal-directed learning.

Tier 3 Instruction

Carlton School's third instructional tier represents individualized instruction. Students are tutored on a one-to-one basis by a certified special education teacher. The Tier-2–validated tutoring protocol is the starting-off point for inductively designing an effective reading program; that is, instructional components are added to the validated tutoring protocol as the effectiveness of those components for the individual learner as documented with CBM-WIF. For the purpose of inductively designing a more effective reading program that is responsive to the child's needs, the teacher increases the frequency of CBM data collection to twice weekly and uses the resulting database in two complementary ways.

The first strategy for using CBM to individualize instruction is "goal-based CBM decision making." With goal-based CBM decision making, the teacher relies on CBM norms that specify weekly rates of improvement for typically developing children to help establish a desired weekly rate of improvement for a particular child. She uses this to set a year-end goal, which is marked on the student's CBM graph. A line connecting this goal with the CBM baseline score (with which the student enters Tier 3) is called the "goal line." The teacher uses this goal to determine when to modify the instructional program because progress is insufficient to result in goal attainment (i.e., four consecutive CBM scores fall below the goal line or the student's CBM slope, based on at least 6 points, is lower than the goal line) or to increase the goal because progress is better than expected (i.e., four consecutive CBM scores fall above the goal line or the student's CBM slope, based on at least 6 points, is higher than the goal line).

The second strategy is called "CBM relative analysis," in which the teacher compares the student's CBM slope under contrasting instructional conditions. The teacher uses her understanding of the student's previous pattern of performance, her knowledge of the research literature, and her clinical judgment to formulate a hypothesis about which instructional feature may prove beneficial. She introduces this instructional component as she collects CBM data twice weekly. After 6–8 weeks of implementing this instructional component, the teacher inspects the graphed data points and quantifies the student's rate of improvement under this new instructional component. She compares this improvement rate to the student's weekly CBM slope without the new instructional component. If the component has produced a viable effect, the component is incorporated into the student's program; if not, the instructional feature is abandoned. In either case, the teacher then identifies the next instructional component to introduce so that its effects on the student's reading development can be assessed empirically.

Four Carlton Students

To illustrate how Carlton School's three-tiered reading intervention works for different students, we describe four first-grade children representing four scenarios under a three-tier approach to reading intervention.

The first student, Mariel, screened as not at risk. On the September CBM-WIF screening, Mariel's average score across the two alternate forms was 22.5. This score exceeded the cut point for designating reading-failure risk. Therefore, Mariel was deemed not at risk and was not a candidate for ongoing progress monitoring or for placement in Tier 2 or 3 instruction.

The next student, Terry, screened as at risk but deemed responsive to Tier 1. On the September CBM-WIF screening, Terry's average score across the two alternate forms was 10.5. This score fell below the cut point for designating reading-failure risk. Consequently, Terry was deemed at risk, and Terry's performance was monitored for 8 weeks under Tier 1 general education, with one CBM-WIF assessment conducted each week. At the end of 8 weeks, Terry's CBM-WIF slope (i.e., weekly increase) was 1.8, which exceeded the 1.0 criterion for positive response. Therefore, Terry was deemed responsive to Tier 1 instruction.

Another student, Liam, screened as at risk and was deemed unresponsive to Tier 1 but responsive to Tier 2. On the September CBM-WIF screening, Liam's average score across the two alternate forms was 5.5. This score fell below the cut point for designating reading-failure risk. Therefore, Liam was deemed at risk, and Liam's performance was monitored for 8 weeks under Tier 1 instruction, with one CBM-WIF assessment conducted each week. At the end of 8 weeks, Liam's CBM-WIF slope (i.e., weekly increase) was 0.4, which fell below the 1.0 criterion for positive response. Consequently, Liam was deemed unresponsive to Tier 1 instruction and entered Tier 2 instruction, again with weekly CBM-WIF monitoring. Under Tier 2, Liam's slope increased to 1.7, which exceeded the 1.0 criterion for positive response. Therefore, Liam was deemed responsive to Tier 2 instruction and returned to Tier 1 for continued progress monitoring with CBM.

The last student, Michael, screened as at risk and was deemed unresponsive to Tier 1 and Tier 2. On the September CBM-WIF screening, Michael's average score across the two alternate forms was 5.5, which fell below the cut point for designating reading-failure risk. Therefore, Michael was deemed at risk, and Michael's performance was monitored for 8 weeks under Tier 1 instruction, with one CBM-WIF assessment conducted each week. At the end of 8 weeks, Michael's CBM-WIF slope (i.e., weekly increase) was 0.2, which fell below the 1.0 criterion for positive response. Consequently, Michael was deemed unresponsive to Tier 1 instruction and entered Tier 2 instruction, again with weekly CBM-WIF monitoring. Under Tier 2, Michael's slope was 0.5, well below the 1.0 criterion for positive response. Therefore, Michael was deemed unresponsive to Tier 2 instruction. Consequently, Michael entered Tier 3, in which individualized instruction using CBM was implemented.

To initiate the Tier 3 program, the special education teacher considered the following pieces of information. First, given that 1) Michael's CBM slope under the Tier 2 validated tutoring protocol was a very low 0.5 and 2) typically developing students demonstrate a CBM-WIF slope of approximately 1.75, she decided that a realistic end-of-year goal for Michael might be a rate of improvement of 1.0 words per week on the CBM-WIF measure. The teacher calculated that 29 weeks remained in the school year. Michael's most recent 2 CBM-WIF scores averaged 16; so, the teacher drew the end-of-year goal at 45 (29 + 16). The teacher considered this to be a "working" goal: If the teacher succeeded in dramatically improving Michael's reading trajectory, CBM decision rules would guide her to make her end-of-year goal more ambitious.

The special educator's next challenge was to determine what instructional component to add to the Tier 2 validated tutoring protocol for Tier 3 analysis. The teacher considered the Tier 2 tutor's report that Michael experienced serious difficulty attending to instruction, even with a self-regulation intervention in place. She also considered her knowledge of the research literature to strengthen self-regulation with a strong reinforcement program. Thus, she began Tier 3 instruction, while assessing Michael's CBM-WIF performance twice weekly. At the end of 6 weeks, Michael's slope had increased to 0.83—a good improvement over Tier 2 instruction, indicating that the reinforcement component should be maintained in Michael's program. Of course, his weekly rate of improvement of 0.83 still fell short of the teacher's goal of 1.0 increase per week. So, the teacher reviewed Michael's performance, using her clinical judgment gleaned during the student's CBM-WIF performances to incorporate a computer program designed to strengthen word recognition of high-frequency words, as she continued to monitor the effects of that computer practice on Michael's CBM-WIF performance. In this manner, the teacher formatively evaluated the effectiveness of instructional components on Michael's reading development to inductively and empirically build a strong program for Michael.

A COMPREHENSIVE CURRICULUM-BASED MEASUREMENT FRAMEWORK

The Carlton School case study illustrates the three functions of assessment within a three-tiered reading intervention. It also shows how CBM can fulfill these three functions. Of course, the CBM-WIF task, although appropriate and useful at the first-grade level, does not address the developmental span across the elementary school years. For kindergarten students, for example, the CBM-WIF task produces a floor effect, with many students scoring 0. These students may make progress toward becoming a reader (e.g., connecting letters with sounds, blending sounds) even though performance on the CBM-WIF task, which remains at 0, indicates a lack of growth. For this reason, alternative tasks that are sensitive to beginning reading development are required. At the other end of first grade, once students have achieved a criterion CBM-WIF performance, the CBM-WIF task may fail to reveal continued development in the areas of passage reading or comprehension. For this reason, additional CBM tasks are required to implement a three-tiered reading intervention across the elementary grades.

Table 3.1. Sample technical data on the Comprehensive Curriculum-Based Measurement Framework

	Measure			
Technical feature	LSF	WIF	PRF	MF
Alternate-passage stability (3 weeks)	.92–.94	.97	.92–.97	.90
Criterion validity with WRMT	.58–.71	.77–.82	.71–.92	N/A
Criterion validity with CBM Passage reading fluency	.93	.86	N/A	.78–.86
Criterion validity with Gates MacGinitie, Stanford, Metropolitan Reading Test	N/A	N/A	N/A	.77–.89
Predictive validity with CBM Passage reading fluency*	.66–.68	.63–.80	.72–.86	N/A
Predictive validity with CBM (fall K to spring 1)	.54	N/A	N/A	N/A
Predictive validity with TerraNova*	.53	N/A	.65–.72	.67–.74
Predictive validity with TerraNova (fall K to spring 1)	.43	N/A	N/A	N/A

Key: LSF = letter-sound fluency; WIF = word identification fluency; PRF = passage reading fluency; MF = maze fluency; WRMT = Woodcock Reading Mastery Test; TerraNova = McGraw-Hill State Achievement test; N/A = not available; K = kindergarten; 1 = grade 1.

*For LSF, fall 1 to spring 1; for word identification fluency, 22 weeks; for passage reading fluency and for maze fluency, 22–30 weeks.

The Comprehensive CBM Framework addresses this developmental span. The framework grew out of a longstanding research program on CBM, which began in the mid-1970s under the direction of Stan Deno at the University of Minnesota. The framework comprises four reading behaviors that span reading development from kindergarten through sixth grade: letter-sound fluency, word identification fluency, passage reading fluency, and maze fluency. Table 3.1 displays sample technical data on traditional reliability and validity for these measures. In Table 3.2, we provide benchmarks associated with future reading success. End-of-year benchmarks indicate the CBM score students should achieve by year's end; slope benchmarks indicate the weekly CBM increase students should demonstrate.

Letter-Sound Fluency

The CBM letter-sound fluency task (Fuchs & Fuchs, 2001; Speece & Case, 2001) is employed to assess early reading development in kindergarten. Letter-sound fluency enjoys content validity for the following reasons. First, letter sounds are a standard feature of the kindergarten curriculum. Second, fluency with

Table 3.2. Benchmarks for the Comprehensive Curriculum-Based Measurement Framework

Measure	Grade	End-of-year benchmark	Slope benchmark
LSF	Kindergarten	40 letter sounds per minute	1 letter sound increase per week
WIF	Grade 1	50 words per minute	1.8 word increase per week
PRF	Grade 2	75 words per minute	1.5 word increase per week
	Grade 3	100 words per minute	1 word increase per week
	Grade 4	120 words per minute	0.6 word increase per week
MF	Grade 5	25 replacements per 2.5 minute	0.4 word increase per week
	Grade 6	40 replacements per 2.5 minute	0.4 word increase per week

Key: LSF = letter-sound fluency, WIF = word identification fluency, PRF = passage reading fluency, MF = maze fluency.

letter–sound correspondences constitutes a major achievement in learning to read because letter–sound correspondences are central to phonological decoding. Letter–sound correspondences, therefore, represent an important instructional target in kindergarten, providing teachers with useful information for guiding their instructional efforts. With letter-sound fluency, the teacher presents the child with a single page of 25 (different) lowercase letters, arranged in a 5-letter by 5-letter matrix (alternate forms vary the order of the letters and which 25 letters are represented). The student has 1 minute to say sounds. The teacher plots the number of correctly spoken sounds on the student's CBM graph. As shown in Table 3.1, letter-sound fluency is highly reliable and demonstrates strong criterion validity. It is also easy for teachers, aides, or volunteers to learn to administer.

Letter-sound fluency can be used to identify students at risk. Letter-sound fluency can also be used in a progress-monitoring framework to track the development of beginning reading competence across kindergarten. With CBM letter-sound fluency, teachers monitor progress toward a goal of 40 letter sounds correct in 1 minute by the end of kindergarten. This benchmark is associated with strong reading performance by the end of first grade. In fact, as soon as a child achieves this criterion during the kindergarten year, the teacher should transition the student to CBM word identification fluency for the purpose of monitoring continued reading progress.

Word Identification Fluency

After the student meets the 40 letter sounds per minute benchmark or at the beginning of Grade 1 (whichever occurs first), the CBM task becomes WIF (Fuchs, Fuchs, & Compton, 2004). With word identification fluency, the teacher presents the child with a single page of high-frequency words, configured in three columns, two with 17 words and one with 16 words. Alternate forms are generated by randomly sampling words, with replacement, from a high-frequency word list (e.g., Zeno, Ivens, Millard, & Duvvuri, 1995). The student has 1 minute to read words, and the teacher plots the number of correctly read words on the student's CBM graph.

As shown in Tables 3.1 and 3.2, and as illustrated in the Carlton School case study, WIF predicts future reading competence well, and a benchmark of 50 words read correctly by the end of first grade can be used to forecast future reading success. Students who do not achieve this benchmark should be assessed further to determine the need for more intensive instruction. Students who achieve this first-grade benchmark, however, are likely to experience reading success in second grade.

Passage Reading Fluency

From second through the end of fourth grade, CBM passage reading fluency performs well as an overall indicator of reading competence. It simultaneously reflects a student's progress in decoding, word identification, fluency, and comprehension. With CBM passage reading fluency, the teacher presents the child with a passage representing the difficulty expected at the end of the student's grade (a different passage representing the same difficulty is used at each testing). The teacher directs the student, using a standard set of directions, to read accurately, quickly, and with meaning. The student has 1 minute to read. If the student hesitates on a word for 3 seconds, the teacher provides the word. The teacher scores hesitations, substitutions, and deletions as errors and plots the number of words read correctly on the student's CBM graph.

As shown in Table 3.1 (and as documented widely in the literature; see, for example, Marston, 1989), CBM passage reading fluency is a strong measure of overall basic reading competence. In addition, a variety of studies illustrate how the passage reading fluency task can be used as a progress-monitoring tool (e.g., Fuchs et al., 1984; Fuchs et al., 1989b). When teachers monitor student progress, they adapt instructional programs in response to student progress more frequently and their students achieve better on standardized achievement tests. The benchmark for forecasting continued adequate reading success increases with grade (see Table 3.2). Beginning in fifth grade, the teacher transitions the student to the next task within the Comprehensive CBM Framework: CBM maze fluency.

Maze Fluency

At Grades 5 and 6, the CBM maze fluency task (Fuchs & Fuchs, 1992) is employed to monitor continued development of reading comprehension skill. With maze fluency, the student is presented with a passage from which every seventh word has been deleted and replaced with three choices. Only one choice represents a semantically correct replacement for the blank. The distracters are of similar length to the correct replacement but are not phonologically or visually confusing with the correct replacement (alternate passages of equivalent difficulty are used for each measurement; see Fuchs & Fuchs, 1992). The teacher reads the text while selecting replacements for the blanks (a variety of software programs are available to collect data automatically while the student works at the computer). The student has 2.5 minutes to work. The teacher plots the number of correct replacements on the student's CBM graph.

As shown in Table 3.1, maze fluency functions well as a CBM task. It demonstrates strong reliability and validity. Moreover, research documents that teachers can use the maze fluency CBM task as a progress-monitoring tool to enhance instructional planning and to boost student learning. Fuchs, Fuchs, Hamlett, and Ferguson (1992) conducted a study in which 33 special educators and 63 students with learning disabilities or behavior disorders were assigned randomly to three groups. Two groups relied on CBM maze fluency for 17 weeks to monitor student progress and develop instructional programs; one group functioned as the control. Both CBM groups achieved better than the control group on several key reading outcome measures assessing fluency and comprehension. As with passage reading fluency, the benchmark for forecasting future reading success increases with grade (Table 3.2).

SUMMARY

An essential feature of a three-tiered reading intervention is assessment. Within a three-tiered model, assessment is used for three purposes: to identify which students to target for careful monitoring, to quantify responsiveness to intervention among those targeted for monitoring, and to tailor individualized instructional programs for the most unresponsive subset of children. At the present time, state-of-the-art practice in assessing responsiveness to instruction and for tailoring individual programs centers on CBM, which can be used productively for all three assessment functions. In this chapter, we have illustrated how CBM can be applied in this manner and we have provided a framework of CBM tasks to address the developmental span within the elementary grades.

REFERENCES

Biemiller, A. (1977–1978). Relationship between oral reading rates for letters, words, and simple text in the development of reading achievement. *Reading Research Quarterly, 13,* 223–253.

Deno, S.L. (1985). Curriculum-based measurement: The emerging alternative. *Exceptional Children, 52,* 219–232.

Fuchs, L.S., & Deno, S.L. (1991). Paradigmatic distinctions between instructionally relevant measurement models. *Exceptional Children, 57,* 488–501.

Fuchs, L.S., Deno, S.L., & Mirkin, P.K. (1984). Effects of frequent curriculum-based measurement on pedagogy, student achievement, and student awareness of learning. *American Educational Research Journal, 21,* 449–460.

Fuchs, L.S., & Fuchs, D. (1992). Identifying a measure for monitoring student reading progress. *School Psychology Review, 21,* 45–58.

Fuchs, L.S., & Fuchs, D. (2001). *Letter-sound fluency task.* Available from L. Fuchs, 238 Peabody, Vanderbilt University, Nashville, TN 37203.

Fuchs, L.S., Fuchs, D., & Compton, D.L. (2004). Monitoring early reading development in first grade: Word identification fluency versus nonsense word fluency. *Exceptional Children, 71,* 7–21.

Fuchs, L.S., Fuchs, D., & Hamlett, C.L. (1989a). Effects of alternative goal structures within curriculum-based measurement. *Exceptional Children, 55,* 429–438.

Fuchs, L.S., Fuchs, D., & Hamlett, C.L. (1989b). Effects of instrumental use of curriculum-based measurement to enhance instructional programs. *Remedial and Special Education, 10*(2), 43–52.

Fuchs, L.S., Fuchs, D., Hamlett, C.L., & Ferguson, C. (1992). Effects of expert system consultation within curriculum-based measurement using a reading maze task. *Exceptional Children, 58,* 436–450.

Fuchs, L.S., Fuchs, D., Hosp, M., & Jenkins, J.R. (2001). Oral reading fluency as an indicator of reading competence: A theoretical, empirical, and historical analysis. *Scientific Studies of Reading, 5,* 239–256.

Hintze, J.M., & Shapiro, E.S. (1997). Curriculum-based measurement and literature-based reading: Is curriculum-based measurement meeting the needs of changing reading curricula? *Journal of School Psychology, 35,* 351–375.

Hintze, J.M., Shapiro, E.S., & Lutz, G. (1994). The effects of curriculum on the sensitivity of curriculum-based measurement in reading. *The Journal of Special Education, 28,* 188–202.

Marston, D. (1989). A curriculum-based measurement approach to assessing academic performance: What is it and why do it? In M.R. Shinn (Ed.), *Curriculum-based measurement: Assessing special children* (pp. 18–78). New York: The Guilford Press.

Marston, D., Fuchs, L.S., & Deno, S.L. (1986). Measuring pupil progress: A comparison of standardized achievement tests and curriculum-related measures. *Diagnostique, 11,* 71–90.

Speece, D.L., & Case, L.P. (2001). Classification in context: An alternative approach to identifying early reading disability. *Journal of Educational Psychology, 93,* 735–749.

Woodcock, R.W. (1998) *Woodcock Reading Mastery Test–Revised.* Circle Pines, MN: AGS Publishing.

Zeno, S.M., Ivens, S.H., Millard, R.T., & Duvvuri, R. (1995). *The educator's word frequency guide.* New York: Touchstone Applied Science Associates.

Primary Intervention

Classroom Reading Instruction and Teacher Knowledge in the Primary Grades

Barbara R. Foorman, Coleen D. Carlson, and Kristi L. Santi

In the Three-Tier Model of Reading Intervention, Tier 1—the classroom—is crucially important; it is here in the interaction between a teacher and his or her students that formal reading instruction in the primary grades initially occurs. The logic of making classroom reading instruction as effective as possible is self-evident: Children will become successful readers from the beginning and, with fewer children needing expensive pull-out interventions, those interventions can be delivered in small group sizes with sufficient intensity and duration to produce significant achievement gains (Foorman, Breier, & Fletcher, 2003; Torgesen, 2004). In short, prevention is the best intervention (Foorman, Francis, Shaywitz, Shaywitz, & Fletcher, 1997). In spite of the logic of improving classroom reading instruction in the primary grades, few empirical studies exist to show how instruction can be changed. In this chapter, we first briefly review the research on effective classroom reading. Second, we present lessons learned from observing first-through fourth-grade students in inner-city classrooms of primarily African American students and teachers. Third, we present lessons learned from observing primary-grade bilingual classrooms in Texas and southern California. Fourth and finally, we conclude with a strategy for capturing teacher change that we are implementing in a randomized study of mentoring primary-grade teachers to implement assessment-driven instruction.

This work was supported by grants from the National Institute of Child Health and Human Development, HD30995, "Early Interventions for Children with Reading Problems"; HD39521, "Oracy/Literacy Development in Spanish-Speaking Children"; and a grant from the Institute of Education Sciences (IES), R305W020001, "Scaling Up Assessment-Driven Intervention Using the Internet and Handheld Computers." The authors would like to thank Michele Hoffman, Lee Branum-Martin, and Paul Cirino for their help with preparation of graphs and data analysis.

RESEARCH ON EFFECTIVE CLASSROOM READING INSTRUCTION

What does it mean to be an effective primary-grade teacher? How is teacher quality measured? These are questions that need to be answered to successfully implement the No Child Left Behind Act of 2001 (PL 107-110). Unfortunately, the research base to provide a precise response to these questions is woefully thin. Shulman (1986) makes a distinction between content knowledge, pedagogical knowledge, and pedagogical content knowledge that is useful in addressing the questions of effectiveness and quality. *Content knowledge* is the disciplinary knowledge reflected in the curriculum, whereas *pedagogical knowledge* includes teachers' understanding of instructional strategies. *Pedagogical content knowledge,* then, includes "ways of representing and formulating the subject that makes it comprehensible to others" (Shulman, 1986, p. 9), as well as understanding how to address individual differences in the learning of content.

Teachers' Knowledge of Content, Pedagogy, and Pedagogical Content

What are the critical elements of reading instruction? Researchers describe the critical *content* of effective reading instruction as phonemic awareness, phonemic decoding, fluency in word recognition and text processing, construction of meaning, vocabulary, spelling, and writing (Foorman & Torgesen, 2001; Rayner, Foorman, Perfetti, Pesetsky, & Seidenberg, 2001; Snow, Burns, & Griffin, 1998). Research also shows

1. *Explicit* instruction in phonemic awareness and phonemic decoding is important for improving reading achievement in struggling readers and those at risk of reading difficulties (Ehri et al., 2001; Foorman, Francis, Fletcher, Schatschneider, & Mehta, 1998; Torgesen et al., 2001).

2. It is difficult to improve the fluency skills of older remedial readers, even after intensive intervention (Torgesen et al., 2001); and the vocabulary gap between readers and nonreaders increases exponentially over time (Anderson, Wilson, & Fielding; 1988; Cunningham & Stanovich, 1998).

3. Thirty-seven percent of fourth graders have "below basic" reading comprehension scores on the National Assessment of Educational Progress (NAEP; National Center for Education Statistics [NCES], 2003), a consequence of dysfluent reading and poor vocabulary.

4. Half of the questions on the NAEP require students to write a response to what they have read, yet writing and spelling instruction receive little attention in current reading initiatives.

To counter this inattention to spelling and writing and to address the validity of literacy as a unitary construct, we tested multilevel confirmatory factor analyses of reading and language outcomes using data from 1,342 students in 127 classrooms in Grades 1–4 in 17 high-poverty schools (Mehta, Foorman,

Branum-Martin, & Taylor, 2005). Results supported a unitary literacy factor for word reading, reading comprehension, and spelling, with the role of phonological awareness as an indicator of literacy declining over the grades. Writing was the least related to the literacy factor but the most influenced by teachers effects. In fact, sheer time spent teaching writing positively predicted writing outcomes. Language competence, as measured by receptive vocabulary and verbal IQ–score tasks, was distinct at the student level but perfectly correlated with literacy at the classroom level. Thus, at least in this sample, oral and written language skills appear to be so interrelated with reading skills that they form a single construct and, hence, deserve equal attention instructionally.

Measuring the Various Kinds of Teachers' Knowledge

Recent surveys of teachers' content knowledge of reading have moved beyond assessment solely of content (McCutchen et al., 2002; Moats, 1994; Wong-Fillmore & Snow, 2002) to assessment of pedagogy and pedagogical content knowledge (Foorman & Moats, 2004; Phelps & Schilling, 2004). Foorman and Moats's survey added to the section on linguistic knowledge a section with protocols of student's oral reading and writing. Phelps and Schilling (2004) factor-analyzed their survey and found two, rather than three, kinds of knowledge— knowledge of content and knowledge of teaching and content. In addition, they found that knowledge of comprehension used in teaching was distinct from more common knowledge of reading.

Two studies have shown that teacher knowledge gained through professional development workshops relates positively to student achievement (Foorman & Moats, 2004; McCutchen et al., 2002). Classroom observation in the McCutchen and colleagues (2002) study confirmed that kindergarten and first-grade teachers who participated in professional development workshops implemented more explicit instructional strategies, which, in turn, were associated with higher student achievement. A composite measure of teacher effectiveness was found to be related to variables from a Spanish and English version of the Foorman and Moats (2004) survey that was completed by kindergarten teachers participating in our bilingual classroom study, including positive (though modest) relations to student engagement and negative (though again modest) relations to time spent in noninstructional activities (Cirino, Pollard-Durodola, Foorman, Carlson, & Francis, in press). In addition, teacher effectiveness, oral language proficiency, and teacher knowledge were found to have significant effects (in conjunction with initial performance level) for end-of-year student outcomes in both Spanish (identification of letters and words) and English (a phonological awareness composite).

What these empirical studies of teacher knowledge show is that the movement from assessing teachers' content knowledge of reading to assessing pedagogical content knowledge has been a step in the right direction. The relationship between pedagogical content knowledge and student learning and achievement, however, is mediated by teaching effectiveness variables most commonly captured by classroom observations. The kinds of instructional variables that differentiate effective from less-effective teachers include instructional pacing and format, active student engagement, delivery of planned activities, motivational strategies and emphasis, and judgments of student learning (Phillips, Fuchs, Fuchs, & Hamlett, 1996).

AN EMPIRICAL APPROACH TO CLASSROOM OBSERVATIONS

Classroom researchers have been arguing since the 1970s about the validity and reliability of three types of measures of instruction: 1) direct classroom observations, 2) teacher reports, and 3) artifacts such as textbooks and student work. If observers had high interrater reliability, then direct observations of classrooms were considered valid (Shavelson, Webb, & Burstein, 1986). If teacher reports on a questionnaire or log were corroborated by artifacts, then their responses were considered valid (Burnstein et al., 1995). Camburn and Barnes (2004) recommend that these three types of measures of instruction be triangulated to improve validity. Their comparison of teacher log data with researcher observation data, however, led them to conclude that "some of our evidence cast reasonable doubt on whether observers of classroom instruction can provide judgments that are completely interchangeable with those of teachers" (Camburn & Barnes, p. 67). We take the view that these three sources of data—classroom observations by researchers, teacher reports, and artifacts—are all potentially valid sources of information about teaching effectiveness and can serve as predictors of student outcomes. The issue of validity is moot, however, if data sources are unreliable. Therefore, we have worked to develop a reliable system for observing classroom reading/language arts instruction that we have used to test the moderating effects of teacher variables in predicting gains in reading and spelling achievement. In our research, we also ask teachers to complete a survey regarding their knowledge of teaching reading/language arts and to report to us the frequency with which they engage in certain instructional activities. These procedures are described in detail elsewhere (Foorman, Goldenberg, Carlson, Saunders, & Pollard-Durodola, 2004; Foorman & Schatschneider, 2003), but we briefly describe the classroom observation system to provide a context for the results presented from two large-scale studies of classroom reading instruction.

Our classroom observation system captures within each minute the following categories: instructional format (whole class, small group with or without teacher monitoring), subject code (reading/language arts, English language development, social studies, science, math), transitions between subjects, 20 superordinate content codes, language of materials, presence of an instructional aide, teacher and student language, and student engagement (on task or off task). To make the precise judgments necessary for high interrater reliability, observers wear headsets with prerecorded directions about when to observe and when to code. In bilingual classrooms observers code in the following way on odd minutes:

- First 15 seconds: Record instructional format, content, subject, materials, aide

- Next 5 seconds: Record observation

- Next 10 seconds: Observe teacher language
- Next 5 seconds: Record teacher language
- Next 10 seconds: Observe student engagement
- Next 5 seconds: Record student engagement
- Next 5 seconds: Record instructional aide
- Next 5 seconds: Wait for next minute; no observation or recording

During even minutes, observers record both teacher and student language. Every 20 minutes observers take a 2-minute break. Observations continue throughout the reading/language arts block as well as during the English language development block when it exists. Each teacher is observed multiple times (4–6 times in the Houston, TX–Washington, DC study and 3 times in the bilingual study). Interrater reliability is computed on 10% of the observations and has proven to be adequate (>.80; Foorman et al., 2004; Foorman & Schatschneider, 2003).

Detailed descriptions of the content codes are provided in appendices of Foorman and colleagues (2004), Foorman and Schatschneider (2003), and Foorman, Schatschneider, Eakin, Fletcher, Moats, & Francis (2006). Therefore, we simply list the codes in Table 4.1. Less than 2% of the data were uncodable.

Table 4.1.   Content codes for observing reading and language arts instruction

1.	Oral language/discussion (with subcodes of listening comprehension, English language strategies, Spanish language strategies)
2.	Mechanics (grammar, capitalization, and punctuation)
3.	Vocabulary (instruction in knowledge of word meanings)
4.	Phonemic awareness (instruction in the sound structure of language)
5.	Book and print awareness (conventions of print, format of books)
6.	Letter recognition and reproduction
7.	Alphabetic instruction (instruction in letter–sound relations)
8.	Word work (instruction in how to recognize, blend, decode, or encode words in isolation or in connected text)
9.	Structural analysis (instruction in morphemic units)
10.	Previewing a text before reading
11.	Reading text (teacher reads aloud, students read aloud, students read silently)
12.	Reading comprehension (literal or inferential questions asked; written response)
13.	Writing composition (student composition; student dictation; teacher-led instruction)
14.	Students reading their own writing
15.	Formal spelling instruction
16.	Spelling in the context of reading
17.	Feedback (corrective praise, punitive)
18.	Giving directions/preparing for instruction
19.	Noninstructional behaviors (e.g., intercom announcements, lining-up, washing hands, teacher out of classroom, discipline, chaos)

Classroom Observations in Houston, TX, and in Washington, DC

From 1997 to 2002, we followed approximately 1,200 kindergarten- to fourth-grade students from 17 elementary schools in inner-city Houston, TX, and in Washington, DC who had chronically low achievement (i.e., below the 15th percentile in standardized achievement) and provided professional development to the teachers. The schools ranged in size from 125 to 726 students (with the median being 492 students) and varied in participation in the federal lunch program from 84% to 100% (with the median being 97%). More than 95% of the students and more than 90% of the teachers in these schools were African American.

Professional Development

We employed a cross-sequential design to examine the conditions under which students in adjacent grade-level cohorts became successful readers. Accordingly, our research staff and master teachers from the school district worked with approximately 107 teachers in kindergarten and Grade 1 in the first year, Grades 1–2 in the second year, Grades 2–3 in the third year, Grades 3–4 in the fourth year, and Grade 4 in the fifth year. This way we were able to see the benefits of working with the teachers in Grades 1–4 over 2 years. Professional development consisted of summer workshops lasting 2–4 days and follow-up meetings throughout the year. Because of a congressional supplement to the Washington, DC site, the DC project director, Dr. Louisa Moats, was able to offer two or three 3-credit courses each year focused on fundamental concepts of teaching reading (phonological awareness, decoding and spelling instruction, writing, vocabulary, and comprehension) and how these concepts could be implemented in the reading programs used in the schools. Four different reading programs were being used across the 17 schools: Houghton Mifflin (1996), Open Court (1995), Reading Mastery (Englemann & Bruner, 1995), and Success for All (Slavin, Madden, Dolan, & Wasik, 1996). Program consultants and master teachers familiar with these reading programs worked with the teachers in their classrooms to help them implement these programs with fidelity and in a manner that addressed individual differences. An early reading assessment tool, the Texas Primary Reading Inventory (TPRI; Texas Education Agency. 1998–2000), was used to identify students' learning needs (see Foorman & Moats, 2004, and Moats & Foorman, 2003, for more information).

Student Achievement

A sign of the effectiveness of our professional development was the growth in reading comprehension scores across the grades. In kindergarten, we saw growth in experimenter-designed measures of letter names and letter sounds and phonological awareness (Foorman, Chen, Carlson, Moats, Francis, & Fletcher, 2003). Performance in Grades 1–4 on the Passage Comprehension subtest of the Woodcock-Johnson Psycho-Educational Battery–Revised (WJ–R; Woodcock & Johnson,

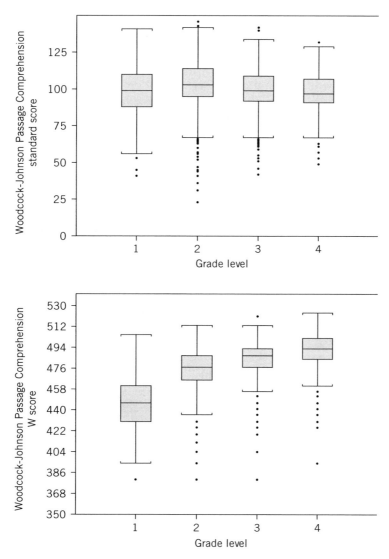

Figure 4.1. Woodcock-Johnson Passage Comprehension standard scores (top) and W scores (bottom) for students in Grades 1, 2, 3, and 4.

1989) is shown in the box plots presented in Figure 4.1. Standard scores are shown in the top of Figure 4.1 and W scores in the bottom. Standard scores have a mean of 100 (i.e., the 50th percentile) and a standard deviation of 15 points. They are useful for making comparisons with a representative sample of individuals similar in age or grade. W scores have a mean of 500, representing typical achievement in

Grade 5, and, being Rasch-based, reflect item-level difficulties at different points on the distribution. Box plots not only provide information about the mean, indicated by the line across the box, but, in addition, the height of the box represents the spread of scores from the 25th to the 75th percentile. A bar extends above or below the box to depict scores that fall up to plus or minus 1.5 interquartile range units from the 25th or 75th percentile. Additional dots represent outliers. Thus, what is immediately apparent in these box plots of standard scores and W scores is that students' scores in each grade were highly variable and that the metric matters (Seltzer, Frank, & Bryk, 1994). Standard score means were solidly at national averages in Grades 1, 2, and 3 but tended to fall off in Grade 4, illustrating what many refer to as "the fourth grade slump" (Chall, Jacobs, & Baldwin, 1990). W scores continued to rise across the grades but at a less accelerated rate and seemed to reach a plateau.

The two major factors attributed to the decline in reading comprehension scores in fourth grade are low vocabulary and lack of fluency (Rayner et al., 2001; Snow et al., 1998). Fluency can be seen as both a cause and a consequence of reading comprehension. Fluency as the quick and accurate recognition of words (LaBerge & Samuels, 1974) frees up cognitive resources to allow for attention and memory to what is read (Stanovich, 1986). Those who read easily read more and, hence, build more word knowledge and word meanings (Cunningham & Stanovich, 1997). Fluency is a consequence of comprehension in the sense that one reads with expression when the meaning is understood (Schwanenflugel, Hamilton, Kuhn, Wisenbaker, & Stahl, 2004). In our Houston, TX–Washington, DC dataset of more than 1,000 students, mean fluency scores, as measured by words correct per minute on passages from the Comprehensive Reading Assessment Battery (CRAB; Fuchs, Fuchs, & Hamlett, 1989) were 62.40 (SD = 33.33) in Grade 2, 83.72 (SD = 36.24) in Grade 3, and 101.35 (SD = 36.67) in Grade 4. This compares to Hasbrouck and Tindal's (1992) 50th percentile scores of 94 (SD = 39), 114 (SD = 39), and 118 (SD = 37) words correct per minute in Grades 2, 3, and 4, respectively, in a dataset of more than 7,000 students in schools in five midwestern and western states.

The relatively low fluency scores of the Houston, TX–Washington, DC students are indicative of more general difficulties in automatizing word recognition processes also evident in low standardized spelling scores at the 30th percentile, on average. Because spelling requires a complete orthographic representation of a word, it indexes consolidation of phonological and morphological processing as well as the spelling conventions of English. This consolidation of sublexical processes is essential to developing fluency (Wolf & Katzir-Cohen, 2001) and explains why spelling predicts significant unique variance in reading comprehension (Foorman & Ciancio, 2005).

Vocabulary is critical to comprehension as well (Rand Reading Study Group, 2002). If a reader cannot grasp the meanings of words read, then how is he or she to understand the meaning of the sentences and text as a whole? The vocabulary ability of the students in our study, as measured by the Peabody Picture Vocabulary Test–Revised, a standardized test of receptive vocabulary (Dunn & Dunn, 1981), remained, on average, at the seventh percentile from kindergarten through Grade 4. The vocabulary instruction from the basal reading program was not sufficient, given the low levels of vocabulary students brought to school in kindergarten (Foorman, Chen et al., 2003). We noticed from our classroom observations (see Figures 4.2 and 4.3) that instructional time allocated to teaching vocabulary increased from 3.5% in Grade 1 to 8% by Grade 4. The histograms represent the percent time in various reading/language arts activities across the total time observed during the year (i.e., 4 to 6 observations per teacher). From these histograms, we see the expected shift from time spent in alphabetic instruction and word work in Grades 1 and 2 (Figure 4.2) to more time in reading books and reading comprehension in Grades 3 and 4 (Figure 4.3). Time spent in writing instruction increased in Grade 4 in the Houston site because writing was tested by the state. Throughout the grades, the time wasted in giving directions/preparing to teach and in noninstructional behaviors (e.g., disciplining students, transitions, announcements, teacher out of the classroom, chaos) was notable. Surprisingly, instructional time was allocated to spelling and to vocabulary, yet standardized scores in these areas were low. When spelling was explicitly taught, observational ratings confirmed that the quality of instruction was poor. Teachers tended to use the spelling workbook for independent seat work without the teacher-led lesson on spelling patterns. In the case of vocabulary, the practice of introducing a few words before reading proved insufficient to build vocabulary size.

Vocabulary Enrichment Project

Realizing the dire consequences of chronically low vocabulary scores, we developed a 20-week, 5-day a week Vocabulary Enrichment Project (VEP) for Grade 3 (Foorman, Seals, Anthony, & Pollard-Durodola, 2003; Seals, Pollard-Durodola, Foorman, & Bradley, 2007a; Seals, Pollard-Durodola, Foorman, & Bradley, 2007b) that targeted 15 words per week or 300 words over 20 weeks. Because 95% of the participating 1,200 students from Houston and Washington, D.C. were African American, we designed the program around biographies and realistic and historical fiction depicting African American heroes and heroines. We had observed a high frequency of features of African American Vernacular English (AAVE) in the participating students. Therefore, one of our goals was to build knowledge of literate language by increasing students' sensitivity to differences between AAVE and standard American English. Targeted words were mature oral vocabulary words from Dale and O'Rourke's (1981) Living Word Vocabulary, which had high printed-word frequency for upper elementary grades (according to Zeno, Ivens, Millard, & Duvvuri, 1995) and were located in the selected literature.

An evaluation of the VEP was conducted with 27 third-grade teachers from 5 of the 17 schools participating in the research study. Schools were matched on demographics and then assigned to either an intervention or a control group. The 12 teachers in the control group taught vocabulary from the basal reading

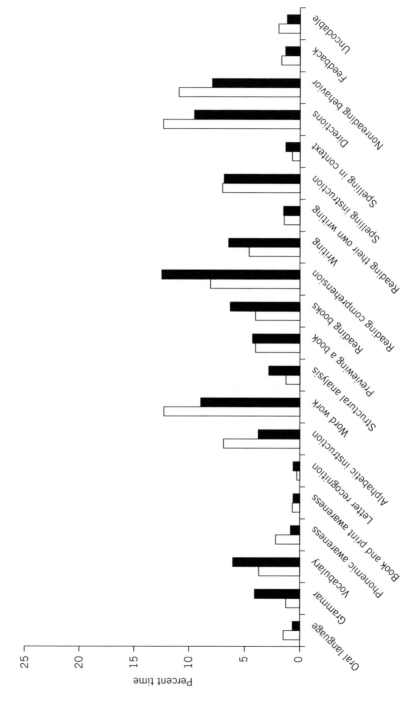

Figure 4.2. Percent time in reading activities and language arts activities for students in Grades 1 and 2. (*Key:* ☐ = Grade 1, ■ = Grade 2.)

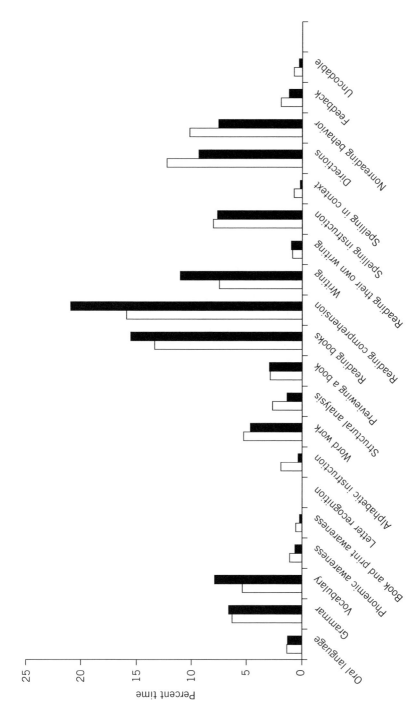

Figure 4.3. Percent time in reading activities and language arts activities for students in Grades 3 and 4. (*Key:* ☐ = Grade 3, ■ = Grade 4.)

program. The 15 VEP teachers received two days of after-school training and follow-up coaching in the classroom. Fidelity of implementation was monitored and percentage of expected components exceeded the criterion of .80. Students in the VEP and control classrooms completed at pretest and at posttest 1) a vocabulary test of 50 words selected at random from the 300 words taught during the year and analyzed according to Item Response Theory (IRT) and 2) the Word Identification subtest of the WJ-R (Woodcock & Johnson, 1989). Other language and literacy tests were administered only as posttests: Peabody Picture Vocabulary Test–Revised (PPVT-R; Dunn & Dunn, 1981); Word Attack and Passage Comprehension from the WJ-R (Woodcock & Johnson, 1989); the Similarities subtest from the Wechsler Intelligence Scale for Children (WISC-III; Wechsler, 1991), and reading comprehension from the Comprehension Reading Assessment Battery (CRAB) (Fuchs et al, 1989). We found significant growth in vocabulary on the IRT-based measure for the VEP students compared with the controls (eta-squared = 0.14). As others have found, however, these results did not generalize to improvements in verbal reasoning, reading comprehension, or decoding. We concluded that efforts to increase the size of vocabulary would need to start much earlier—in preschool and in kindergarten—if transfer to reading achievement were to be observed.

Modeling Teacher Effects

It is often assumed that teachers have a large impact on student achievement, yet most of these claims are based on descriptions of what effective teachers and schools look like (see Bohn, Roehrig, & Pressley, 2004, and Taylor, Pearson, Clark, & Walpole, 2000, for recent reviews). Multilevel growth models—often called "value-added" models—hold promise for addressing growth of individual students as well as growth of cohorts of students as required by the No Child Left Behind Act of 2001. These models can identify schools or teachers that appear more effective than others, but they cannot specify what those teachers do that make them more effective (Raudenbush, 2004). Two studies have attempted to model how teachers' instructional practices moderate student reading achievement in high-poverty schools. The first study was by Taylor, Pearson, Peterson, and Rodriguez (2003), and the second study was ours (Foorman et al., 2006).

The Taylor and colleagues (2003) study examined instructional practices and reading outcomes in 88 classrooms in nine schools with nine randomly selected students per classroom in Grades 1–5. Their classroom observational system was based on 1-hour-long observations three times a year during reading/language arts activities. Specifically, observers took 5 minutes of field notes, then recorded 1) proportion of students on task, 2) who was providing instruction, 3) grouping pattern, 4) the major literacy activity, 5) the two or three most salient literacy events, 6) materials used, 7) teacher interaction styles observed, and 8) expected student responses. Within the curricular codes for salient literacy events (#5), the nature of instruction was categorized (e.g., comprehension skill versus comprehension strategy, higher-level versus lower-level questioning, coaching versus telling, modeling, recitation, students actively versus passively responding). Interrater coding was adequate (i.e., >.81) and was improved on by substituting experts' ratings in cases of disagreement in the 10% of data used for reliability computation. Hierarchical Linear Models (HLM; Raudenbush & Bryk, 2002) analyses were conducted separately for Grade 1 versus Grades 2–5 and by each dependent variable (e.g., fluency, comprehension on a standardized reading test, comprehension on a basal reader test, writing).

This is clearly a high-inference coding system. In a more recent study using the same classroom observation system, Taylor, Pearson, Peterson, and Rodriguez (2005, p. 52) provided the following definitions for comprehension skill instruction and comprehension strategy instruction:

> *Comprehension skill instruction:* Students are engaged in a comprehension activity (other than a comprehension strategy) that is at a lower level of thinking (e.g., traditional skill work such as identifying main idea, cause-effect, fact-opinion).
>
> *Comprehension strategy instruction:* Students are using a comprehension strategy that will transfer to other reading and in which this notion of transfer is mentioned (e.g., reciprocal teaching, predicting; if predicting were done, but transfer was not mentioned, this would be coded as "c" [comprehension skill instruction]).

Taylor and colleagues' (2003) results showed that higher-level questioning contributed to growth in reading and writing in Grades 1–5, frequent phonics instruction was negatively related to fluency growth in Grades 2–5, comprehension skill instruction was negatively related to students' growth on standardized reading comprehension in Grades 2–5, and comprehension strategy instruction was positively related to students' writing growth in Grade 1. There were also significant results with regard to teacher stance and student response mode: Active responding was positively related and passive responding was negatively related to gains in standardized reading comprehension in Grades 2–5; coaching was positively related to gains in fluency in Grades 2–5; modeling was related to improvements in writing in Grades 2–5; and telling was negatively related to students' writing growth in Grade 1. Taylor and colleagues (2003) conclude that teachers who emphasize higher order thinking either through the questions asked or activities assigned stimulated greater growth in student outcomes. These potentially important findings are tempered by the lack of information about the HLM models run. For example, results were not presented for the unconditional models or the baseline conditional models that included covariates of fall reading and grade. We assume that effects of instructional predictors were judged relative to the baseline model that included the effects of the covariates, but we are not told how many of the 19 instructional predictors were entered into any one analysis, how they were centered, or how Type I error was controlled given the number of potentially significant interactions. This latter problem of Type I error was highlighted in three statisticians' criticisms of the 2005 expansion of the Taylor and colleagues study (Alvermann & Reinking, 2005).

Our (Foorman et al., 2006) study of the impact of instructional practices in Grades 1 and 2 on reading and spelling achievement in 17 high-poverty schools differed from the Taylor and colleagues (2003) study in several ways. First, our sample of 17 schools was at a higher poverty level (84%–100%, with a median of 97%) than the 9 schools in the Taylor and colleagues (70%–95%) study. Second, our schools used school reform curricula, which we entered as covariates in our design. Third, our classroom observation approach was lower inference and involved coding teacher behaviors at 5–10 second intervals rather than post hoc coding of 5-minute narratives. Fourth, our analytic approach incorporated several steps to reduce Type I error: 1) We factor analyzed our 20 superordinate time allocation variables to reduce them to seven components, which, along with grade (Grade 1 versus Grade 2), initial word reading, and overall ratings of teaching effectiveness were used as predictors in HLM analyses of outcomes in Letter-Word Identification, Word Attack, and Passage Comprehension from the WJ-R (Woodcock & Johnson, 1989) and spelling dictation from the Kaufman Test of Educational Achievement (Kaufman & Kaufman, 1985); 2) Because of the number of potentially significant interactions, we set the criterion for alpha at $p < .01$.

When the year-long results of the 107 first- and second-grade classrooms in 17 inner-city schools were examined, we (Foorman et al., 2006) found that effects of ratings of teaching effectiveness on reading and spelling outcomes ranged from 0.1%–4%, in contrast to effects of initial reading ability, which ranged from 31%–50%. Yet, it is important to remember that reading outcomes in first and second grade were solidly at national averages in this high-poverty sample. Good teaching made a small difference in improving achievement in reading comprehension above and beyond students' fall reading scores. In addition, there was a tendency for teachers rated high in effectiveness to allocate instructional time in ways that maximized word-reading outcomes. Specifically, highly rated first-grade teachers' positive impact on word attack outcomes was associated with more time in phonemic awareness and alphabetic activities compared with noninstructional activities such as disciplining students, interrupting instruction with long transitions, or being absent from the classroom. Moreover, effective teachers' positive impact on letter–word outcomes was associated with their lack of instruction in grammar, mechanics, and spelling. In contrast to reading, the picture for spelling outcomes was not as positive. Students in these classrooms ended the year with average spelling achievement at the 30th percentile. Although teachers rated highly effective tended to have students with higher spelling outcomes, this result was largely predicted by initial reading ability. Moreover, the more time that less effective teachers spent teaching grammar, mechanics, and spelling, the lower the spelling outcomes for high-ability students. Apparently, for students in these classrooms, it was not sufficient to relegate spelling instruction to workbook activities without teacher-led instruction on spelling patterns.

Thus, these results illustrate how difficult it is for teachers to change the rank order of abilities that students bring to the classrooms in the fall. It would be a mistake to assume that reading development is immutable—one interpretation of Juel's (1988) finding that 87%–88% of fourth-grade reading status was predicted by reading status in first grade. In our case, 31%–50% of first- and second-grade reading and spelling achievement was predicted by reading ability at the beginning of the year. Thus, reading status was not immutable; students were improving in reading and were performing solidly at the national average in reading (Figure 4.1). In this sample, however, a change in status was not associated with a change in rank, as was evident in the Phillips, Norris, Osmond, and Maynard's (2002) study of 187 Canadian children in Grades 1–6. In our sample, where students started the year was moderately associated with where they ended up, and teaching practices did little to alter this rank order. Our professional development, however, appeared to make a difference (Foorman, Chen et al., 2003; Foorman & Moats, 2004; Foorman et al., 2006). Perhaps additional professional development focused on differentiating instruction based on skill differences among students might be necessary to lessen the impact of initial reading ability on achievement and, potentially, to change the rank of students in classrooms.

Classroom Observations in Bilingual Classrooms in Texas and in Southern California

In addition to observing reading/language arts lessons in inner-city classrooms of primarily African American students and teachers, we have also observed primary-grade bilingual classrooms in schools in urban Texas (Houston and Austin), border Texas (Brownsville), and southern California. The 34 schools participating in this project were selected based on the following criteria: 40% or more Hispanic enrollment; 30% or more English language learners in kindergarten and Grade 1; average or above-average performance based on accountability ratings in Texas and comparable API ratings in California; and low to moderate income. In the kindergarten bilingual classrooms in these 34 schools, we found that ratings of teaching effectiveness related positively with percentage of on-task time for students and related negatively with percentage of noninstructional time (Cirino et al., in press). Similarly weak effects for ratings of teaching effectiveness on language and literacy outcomes, controlling for initial abilities, were apparent in these bilingual classrooms (Cirino et al., in press). These bilingual classrooms, however, engaged in more oral language instruction and varied, by definition, in the amount of English used for instruction relative to Spanish.

Time Allocation to Reading/Language Arts Activities

As we had seen in the Houston, TX–Washington, DC study (Foorman et al., 2006), ratings of teaching effectiveness did not predict percentage of time in small-group (Tier 2 in the Three-Tier Model of Reading Intervention) instruction in these bilingual classrooms (Cirino et al., in press). The percentage of instructional time in various content areas of reading/language arts in 89 bilingual kindergarten

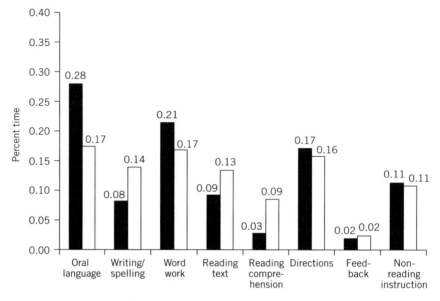

Figure 4.4. Percent time in instruction on specific content areas in Kindergarten and Grade 1 as averaged across three waves within the school year. (*Key:* ☐ = Kindergarten, ■ = Grade 1.)

instructional groups and in 124 bilingual Grade 1 instructional groups in the participating 34 schools is shown in Figure 4.3. We analyzed data within instructional group rather than within classroom teacher because approximately half the students had one teacher for both reading/language arts and English language development and half had a separate teacher for each of these subject areas. Furthermore, due to departmentalization, sometimes one teacher taught reading/language arts to all students at that grade. Our classroom observations covered both the reading/language arts block and, if it existed, the English language development block. The content areas shown in Figure 4.4 were obtained by collapsing the 16 instructional activity codes across the three waves of data collection during the school year:

- The oral language area consists of oral language, grammar, and vocabulary.

- The word work area consists of phonemic awareness, book and print awareness, letter recognition, alphabetic instruction, word work, and structural analysis.

- The reading comprehension area consists of previewing a book and reading comprehension activities.

- The writing/spelling area consists of writing compositions, students reading their own writing, formal spelling instruction, and spelling activities in the context of reading instruction.

It is interesting to note differential allocations of time in first-grade bilingual versus nonbilingual classrooms by comparing Figure 4.4 with Figure 4.2. The most notable difference was in the oral language area: 17% of instructional time was spent in oral language, grammar, and vocabulary activities in bilingual classrooms in contrast with about 10% in nonbilingual classrooms (and this 17% was reduced from 28% in kindergarten bilingual classrooms). Another notable difference was in time allocated to reading books: 13% of time in bilingual first-grade classrooms compared with 4% in nonbilingual first-grade classrooms. Time allocation in the other content areas and the noncontent areas were very similar.

As part of our time sampling system, we coded at precise intervals within odd-numbered minutes whether the teacher's instruction was in Spanish, English, or mixed, or whether coding was impossible because the teacher's voice was inaudible or the observer missed the code. Fortunately, the percentage of data that was inaudible or missed was very small (< 1%). During even minutes, the teacher's and the students' language was coded. Observers were trained to use the mixed code only when language during the 10-second time interval was 50% Spanish and 50% English. If any one language dominated the time interval, then that was the language coded. Language mixing was more evident in the Texas sites than in the Southern California site in our cross-sectional analyses of 105 classrooms in kindergarten through Grade 2 (Foorman et al., 2004).

Teachers' Language and Program as Predictors of Outcome

A major question of interest was the extent to which the type of bilingual program (transition, dual-language, immersion, or maintenance) or the teacher's language use better predicted student language and literacy outcomes. We addressed this question within the K–2 longitudinal arm of the study, and here we report on data from kindergarten and Grade 1. We investigated the impact of K–1 teachers' language use in 34 schools in the four sites (three in Texas and one in southern California). The vast majority of these schools had a single bilingual program, as described by the principal, but five schools had two models, giving a total of 39 instances of four types of bilingual programs: 1) 15 primary-language schools that transitioned students to English in first or second grade or later (transition); 2) 8 dual-language or two-way immersion schools that strove for a balance of native Spanish and native English speakers, with the goal of maintaining both languages (dual-language); 3) 14 schools in which instruction was in English (immersion); and 4) 2 schools representing the "developmental bilingual education" model that emphasizes "the importance of supporting the long-term linguistic, academic, and cognitive development of English language learners" (Ramirez, 1992, pp. 19–20). We refer to this fourth program model as "maintenance" and note its similar goals with dual-language. As mentioned above, there were 89 instructional groups in kindergarten and 124 in Grade 1 in these 34 schools. We randomly selected 10 students from bilingual classrooms (3 low, 3 high, and 4 moderate achievers according to their teachers) to administer language and literacy measures at the beginning and end of the school year. The total number of K–1 students in these analyses was 1,016.

The first step in our analyses was to create a variable we called English ratio. This variable represented the percentage of total reading/language arts (and English language development) time in English plus half of the "mixed" language category, which, by definition was half English and half Spanish. Second, we plotted the English ratio by school across the three waves of classroom observations in kindergarten and the three in Grade 1 for each of the four program models. We also plotted these data within school and observed large variability within instructional group; however, we present only the school-level data here for each of the three waves of observation during kindergarten and first grade for all four programs in Figure 4.5. Figure 4.5 also shows the plotted data for the 8 dual-language schools, the 14 immersion schools, and the 15 transition schools. Data for the 2 maintenance schools are not shown because they follow the same pattern as the dual-language schools. Two points are immediately apparent in these graphs: First, there is a lot of school-level variability in the ratio of teacher instructional language within programs; and, second, on average, the four-program distinction dissolves into two—immersion and nonimmersion. Third, we tested whether bilingual program predicted the observed language ratio and found that it did in both grades, with the immersion program having the highest ratio of English, the transition program having the least, and dual language and maintenance falling in between.

Kindergarten students were individually assessed at the beginning and end of the year on experimental measures of letter names and sounds and word reading, phonemic awareness (utilizing Wagner, Torgesen, & Rashotte's (1999) Comprehensive Test of Phonological Processing), and the oral language composite from the Woodcock Language Proficiency Battery–Revised (Woodcock, 1991; Woodcock & Munoz-Sandoval, 1995). The oral language composite consists of the average of Picture Vocabulary, Listening Comprehension, and Verbal Analogies. These same measures were administered at the beginning and end of Grade 1, except that the word reading list was replaced with the WJ-R Letter–Word Identification subtest (Woodcock & Johnson, 1989). All measures were administered in both English and in Spanish. Grade 1 language and literacy outcomes in English and Spanish were analyzed, controlling for beginning of kindergarten performance, with kindergarten and Grade 1 observed language and bilingual program as predictors. These results are described in detail elsewhere (Carlson & Foorman, 2004) and will be briefly summarized here. First, we summarize the English outcomes:

1. In general, program classification did not add uniquely to the prediction of Grade 1 outcomes above and beyond observed language of instruction.

2. For letter names and sounds and phonemic awareness, the relationship between instructional language and skills varied as a function of program. Specifically, students in an immersion program who received more English

instruction in kindergarten had higher skills in these two areas. In addition, students in a dual-language program who received more English instruction in kindergarten had higher skills in letter names and sounds.

3.   Students who received instruction predominantly in English in kindergarten or Grade 1 showed higher English oral language and word reading skills than students who received more instruction in Spanish in either year. Relationships were stronger in Grade 1 than in kindergarten.

Results of analyses of Spanish literacy and language outcomes in Grade 1, controlling for beginning of Kindergarten performance, were:

1.   Program classification did not add uniquely to the prediction of Grade 1 outcomes above and beyond observed language.

2.   Students who received instruction predominantly in English across both kindergarten and Grade 1 showed lower skills in Spanish letter naming and sound identification, phonemic awareness, and word reading skills than students who had some instruction in Spanish in either one or both years.

3.   Students who received more instruction in Spanish than in English in kindergarten had higher Spanish oral language skills. Interestingly, Grade 1 language alone did not contribute uniquely to Spanish oral language outcomes.

Lessons Learned from Observing Bilingual Classrooms

The first lesson learned from observing these kindergarten and Grade 1 bilingual classrooms is that there was a lot of variability in the language of instruction at the classroom level within school and at the school level within program. Because of this variability, the ratio of English to Spanish was conceptually and empirically an appropriate variable for capturing classroom instructional language because it captured unique variance in predicting language and literacy outcomes above and beyond the program name. The utility of specific program labels becomes questionable when the data seemed to fall into two camps: 1) virtually all English (English immersion), and 2) a mix of approximately 65% Spanish and 35% English. The fact that dual-language, maintenance, and transition programs looked similar, on average, in terms of the language of instruction, should serve to dissipate some of the passionate rhetoric around which of these approaches is better for Spanish-speaking children (see August & Hakuta, 1997; Ramirez, 1992; Thomas & Collier, 1997). The empirical results are clear in this dataset: The more English used in instruction, the higher the English language and literacy outcomes; the more Spanish used in instruction, the higher the Spanish outcomes. A sobering caveat, however, is that the oral language outcomes in Grade 1 for both Spanish and English were low (i.e., 13th percentile and 1st percentile, respectively), in spite of the relatively large percentage of time spent on oral language instruction in the classroom (28% in kindergarten and 17% in Grade 1). Examination of the subcodes within oral language showed that most of the time was devoted to informal discussions during calendar and sharing time. The subcodes relevant to

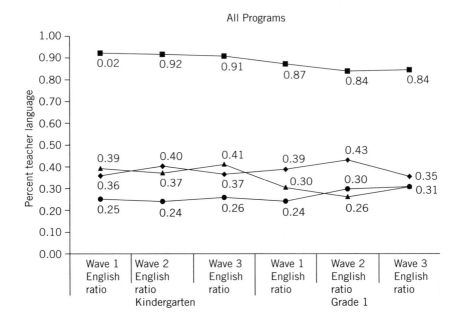

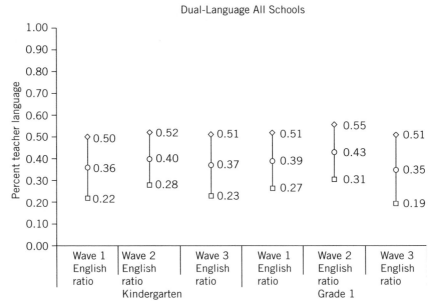

Figure 4.5. Percentage of the use of English observed in teachers' language during three observation waves in Kindergarten and in Grade 1 for all programs (top left), dual-language schools (bottom left), immersion schools (top right), and transition schools (bottom right). (*Key:* ◆ = dual language; ■ = immersion; ▲ = maintenance; ● = transition; □ = one standard deviation below; ○ = mean; ◇ = one standard deviation above.)

(continued)

Figure 4.5. *(continued)*

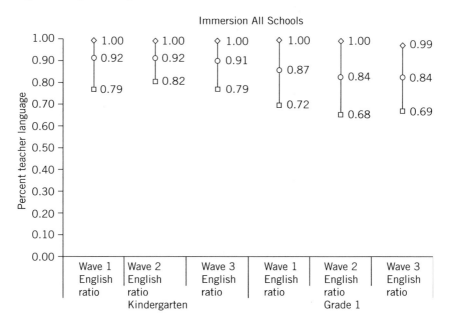

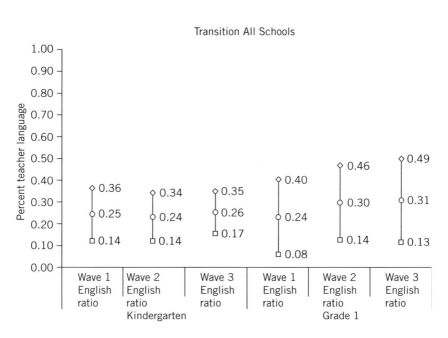

targeting the semantic and syntactic aspects of language and narrative structure (i.e., vocabulary, teaching the structure of English or Spanish, and listening comprehension) had minimal data (Saunders, Foorman, & Carlson, 2006).

CONCLUSION

Federal initiatives stemming from the No Child Left Behind Act of 2001 and the reauthorization of the Individuals with Disabilities Education Improvement Act (IDEA) in late 2004 (PL 108-446) emphasize early intervention in a multitiered approach. Making classroom instruction as effective as possible at Tier 1 minimizes "curriculum casualties" and reduces overidentification of risk that potentially overwhelms instructional resources at Tiers 2 and 3. Reform of Tier 1 has been validated in research studies (e.g., Borman, Hewes, Overman, & Brown, 2003; Foorman et al., 1998) and by the instructional practices exemplified in "beat-the-odds schools" (e.g., Denton, Foorman, & Mathes, 2003; Taylor et al., 2000). Many of the characteristics of effective schools are systemic, such as strong leadership, strong accountability, positive climate, and parental support. But many characteristics are instructional, such as increased reading time and use of data-based decisions.

Our system for conducting classroom observations has added to the literature on the reform of Tier 1 by reliably quantifying time allocated to the format and content of reading/language arts instruction. In addition to using these time allocation variables to describe instructional practice, we have used them, along with initial ability, as predictors of student outcomes and have discovered several important results. First, we corroborated McCutchen and colleagues' (2002) finding that teacher content knowledge was modestly related to gains in student outcomes (Foorman & Moats, 2004). The finding in our bilingual study that content knowledge interacts with other teacher variables (i.e., ratings of effectiveness and oral language proficiency), however, supports the pedagogical content knowledge construct validated by Phelps and Schilling (2004). Second, we found support for Taylor and colleagues' (2003; 2005) finding that effective teachers have more engaged students and less wasted instructional time (Cirino et al., in press). Third, we did not find that percentage of time in small-group instruction was related to ratings of teaching effectiveness or to student achievement (Cirino et al., in press). Fourth, we found that time spent on the critical elements of reading instruction mattered. For example, time spent teaching writing predicted writing outcomes (Mehta et al., 2005), and the addition of a vocabulary intervention resulted in students learning more words relative to controls (Foorman, Seals, et al., 2003). Moreover, effective teachers improved students' word reading skills by teaching phonemic awareness and alphabetic skills and not wasting instructional time. We learned, however, that it was the quality of instructional time that was crucial. For example, time spent on spelling instruction did not predict spelling outcomes because spelling instruction consisted of workbook activities without the teacher-led lesson on spelling patterns.

A content area noticeably missing from our classroom observations was that of assessment. Assessment was not totally absent from the classrooms observed in Houston, TX, Washington, DC, Austin, TX, Brownsville, NE, and southern California because an early reading assessment was administered in all Texas sites and in the K–1 classrooms in Washington, DC at least twice a year. What was not apparent was ongoing assessment to track student skill development and to make instructional decisions. Two of the school reform programs in place in Houston, TX, and in Washington, DC (i.e., Success for All and Reading Mastery) did have 8-week assessments or mastery tests built into the curriculum. It was not, however, apparent that results of these tests informed instruction for individual students or groups of students. In short, there was no evidence of data-driven instruction. Because of the importance of differentiating instruction at Tier 1 to minimize the numbers of students needing the second or third tiers, we have embarked on a randomized study in more than 200 schools of the technological aides and teacher supports needed to scale assessment-driven instruction in K–2 classrooms. One thing we are learning is the value of seasoned mentors who can make sure technology support is provided and work with teachers on translating results of early reading assessment to instruction. Web mentoring provided by tools on our project web site does not appear to substitute for the in-person, ongoing professional development afforded by these mentors. By empowering teachers to take ownership of assessment-driven instructional practices, the mentors seem to be slowly changing the core of schooling so fundamental to educational innovation in general (Elmore, 2004) and to the success of multitiered interventions in particular.

REFERENCES

Alvermann, D.E., & Reinking, D. (2005). Revealing an exchange between authors and reviewers about statistical significance. *Reading Research Quarterly, 40*(1), 6–10.

Anderson, R.C., Wilson, P.T., & Fielding, L.G. (1988). Growth in reading and how children spend their time outside of school. *Reading Research Quarterly, 23,* 285–303.

August, D., & Hakuta, K. (1997). *Improving schooling for language-minority children.* Washington, DC: National Academies Press.

Bohn, C.M., Roehrig, A.D., & Pressley, M. (2004). The first days of school in the classrooms of two more effective and four less effective primary-grade teachers. *The Elementary School Journal, 104,* 269–287.

Borman, G.D., Hewes, G.M., Overman, L.T., & Brown, S. (2003). Comprehensive school reform and achievement: A meta-analysis. *Review of Educational Research, 73,* 125–230.

Burnstein, L., McDonnell, L.M., VanWinkle, J., Ormseth, T., Mirocha, J., & Guiton, G. (1995). *Validating national curriculum indicators.* Santa Monica, CA: RAND.

Camburn, E., & Barnes, C. (2004). Assessing the validity of a language arts instruction log through triangulation. *Elementary School Journal, 105,* 49–73.

Carlson, C.D., & Foorman, B.R. (2004, October). *How language of instruction relates to literacy outcomes in kindergarten and grade 1.* Presented at the meeting of the NICHD Bilingual Grants, Washington, DC.

Chall, J.S., Jacobs, V.A., & Baldwin, L.E. (1990). *The reading crisis: Why poor children fall behind.* Cambridge, MA: Harvard University Press.

Cirino, P., Pollard-Durodola, S., Foorman, B.R., Carlson, C.D., & Francis, D.J. (in press). Teacher characteristics, classroom instruction, and student literacy and language outcomes in bilingual kindergarteners. *Elementary School Journal.*

Cunningham, A.E., & Stanovich, K.E. (1997). Early reading acquisition and its relation to reading experience and ability 10 years later. *Developmental Psychology, 33,* 934–945.

Cunningham, A.E., & Stanovich, K.E. (1998, Spring/Summer). What reading does for the mind. *American Educator, 22,* 8–15.

Dale, E., & O'Rourke, J. (1981). *Living word vocabulary.* Chicago: World Book/Childcraft International.

Denton, C., Foorman, B., & Mathes, P. (2003). Schools that 'beat the odds': Implications for reading instruction. *Remedial and Special Education, 24,* 258–261.

Dunn, L.M., & Dunn, L.M. (1981). *Peabody Picture Vocabulary Test–Revised.* Circle Pines, MN: AGS Publishing.

Ehri, L.C., Nunes, S.R., Willows, D.M., Schuster, B.V., Yaghoub-Zadeh, Z., & Shanahan, T. (2001). Phonemic awareness instruction helps children learn to read: Evidence from the National Reading Panel's meta-analysis. *Reading Research Quarterly, 36*(3), 250–287.

Elmore, R.F. (2004). *School reform from the inside out: Policy, practice, and performance.* Cambridge, MA: Harvard Education Press.

Englemann, S., & Bruner, E. (1995). *Reading Mastery I.* Chicago: SRA/McGraw-Hill.

Foorman, B.R., & Breier, J.I., & Fletcher, J.M. (2003). Interventions aimed at improving reading success: An evidence-based approach. *Developmental Neuropsychology, 24*(2&3), 613–639.

Foorman, B.R., Chen, D.T., Carlson, C., Moats, L., Francis, D.J., & Fletcher, J.M. (2003). The necessity of the alphabetic principle to phonemic awareness instruction. *Reading and Writing, 16,* 289–324.

Foorman, B.R., & Ciancio, D. (2005). Screening for secondary intervention: Concept and context. *Journal of Learning Disabilities, 38*(6), 494–499.

Foorman, B.R., Francis, D.J., Fletcher, J.M., Schatschneider, C., & Mehta, P. (1998). The role of instruction in learning to read: Preventing reading failure in at-risk children. *Journal of Educational Psychology, 90,* 37–55.

Foorman, B.R., Francis, D.J, Shaywitz, S.E., Shaywitz, B.A., & Fletcher, J.M. (1997). The case for early reading interventions. In B. Blachman (Ed.), *Foundations of reading acquisition and dyslexia: Implications for early intervention* (pp. 243–264). Mahwah, NJ: Lawrence Erlbaum Associates.

Foorman, B.R., Goldenberg, C., Carlson, C.D., Saunders, W.M., & Pollard-Durodola, S.D. (2004). How teachers allocate time during literacy instruction in primary-grade English language learner classrooms. In P. McCardle and V. Chhabra (Eds.), *The voice of evidence in reading research* (pp. 289–328). Baltimore: Paul H. Brookes Publishing Co.

Foorman, B.R., & Moats, L.C. (2004). Conditions for sustaining research-based practices in early reading instruction. *Remedial and Special Education, 25*(1), 51–60.

Foorman, B.R., & Schatschneider, C. (2003). Measurement of teaching practices during reading/language arts instruction and its relationship to student achievement. In S.

Vaughn & K.L. Briggs (Eds.), *Reading in the classroom: Systems for the observation of teaching and learning* (pp. 1–30). Baltimore: Paul H. Brookes Publishing Co.

Foorman, B.R., Schatschneider, C., Eakin, M., Fletcher, J.M., Moats, L.C, & Francis, D.J. (2006). The impact of instructional practices in grades 1 and 2 on reading and spelling achievement in high poverty schools. *Contemporary Educational Psychology, 31*(1), 1–29.

Foorman, B., Seals, L., Anthony, J., & Pollard-Durodola, S. (2003). Vocabulary enrichment program for third and fourth grade African American students: Description, implementation, and impact. In B. Foorman (Ed.), *Preventing and remediating reading difficulties: Bringing science to scale* (pp. 419–441). Timonium, MD: York Press.

Foorman, B.R., & Torgesen, J.K. (2001). Critical elements of classroom and small-group instruction promote reading success in all children. *Learning Disabilities Research and Practice, 16*(4), 202–211.

Fuchs, L.S., Fuchs, D., & Hamlett, C.L. (1989). Monitoring reading growth using student recalls: Effects of two teacher feedback systems. *Journal of Educational Research, 83,* 103–110.

Hasbrouck, J., & Tindal, G. (1992). Curriculum-based oral reading fluency norms for students in grades 2–5. *Teaching Exceptional Children, 24,* 41–44.

Houghton Mifflin Co. (1996). *Invitations to literacy.* Boston: Author.

Individuals with Disabilities Education Improvement Act of 2004, PL 108-446, 20 U.S.C. §§ 1400 *et seq.*

Juel, C. (1988). Learning to read and write: A longitudinal study of 54 children from first through fourth grades. *Journal of Educational Psychology, 80,* 437–447.

Kaufman, A.S., & Kaufman, N.L. (1985). *Kaufman Test of Educational Achievement.* Circle Pines, MN: AGS Publishing.

LaBerge, D., & Samuels, S.J. (1974). Toward a theory of automatic information processing in reading. *Cognitive Psychology, 6,* 293–323.

McCutchen, D., Abbott, R.D., Green, L.B., Beretvas, S.N., Cox, S., Quiroga, T., et al. (2002). Beginning literacy: Links among teacher knowledge, teacher practice, and student learning. *Journal of Learning Disabilities, 35,* 69–87.

Mehta, P., Foorman, B.R., Branum-Martin, L., & Taylor, W.P. (2005). Literacy as a unidimensional multilevel construct: Validation, sources of influence, and implications in a longitudinal study in grades 1–4. *Scientific Studies of Reading, 9*(2), 85–116.

Moats, L.C. (1994). The missing foundation in teacher education: Knowledge of the structure of spoken and written language. *Annals of Dyslexia, 44,* 81–102.

Moats, L.C., & Foorman, B.R. (2003). Measuring teachers' content knowledge of language and reading. *Annals of Dyslexia, 53,* 23–45.

National Center for Educational Statistics (2003). *The nation's report card: Reading highlights 2003.* Washington, DC: U.S. Department of Education.

No Child Left Behind Act of 2001, PL 107-110, 115 Stat. 1425, 20 U.S.C. §§ 6301 *et seq.*

Open Court Reading. (1995). *Collections for young scholars.* New York: McGraw-Hill.

Phelps, G., & Schilling, S. (2004). Developing measures of content knowledge for teaching reading. *Elementary School Journal, 105,* 31–48.

Phillips, L.M., Norris, S.P., Osmond, W.C., & Maynard, A.M. (2002). Relative reading achievement: A longitudinal study of 187 children from first through sixth grades. *Journal of Educational Psychology, 94,* 3–13.

Phillips, N.B., Fuchs, L.S., Fuchs, D., & Hamlett, C.L. (1996). Instructional variables affecting student achievement: Case studies of two contrasting teachers. *Learning Disabilities Research & Practice, 11,* 24–33.

Ramirez, J.D. (1992). Executive summary. *Bilingual Research Journal, 16,* 1–62.

Rand Reading Study Group. (2002). *Reading for understanding: Toward an R&D program in reading comprehension.* Santa Monica, CA: RAND.

Raudenbush, S.W. (2004). What are value-added models estimating and what does this imply for statistical practice? *Journal of Educational and Behavioral Statistics, 29*(1), 121–129.

Raudenbush, S.W., & Bryk, A.S. (2002). *Hierarchical linear models: Applications and data analysis methods* (2nd ed.). Thousand Oaks, CA: Sage Publications.

Rayner, K., Foorman, B., Perfetti, C.A., Pesetsky, D., & Seidenberg, M.S. (2001). How psychological science informs the teaching of reading. *Psychological Science in the Public Interest, 2,* 31–74.

Saunders, W., Foorman, B.R., & Carlson, C.D. (2006). Do we need a separate block of time for oral English language development in programs for English learners? *Elementary School Journal, 107*(2).

Schwanenflugel, P.J., Hamilton, A.M., Kuhn, M.R., Wisenbaker, J.M., & Stahl, S.A. (2004). Becoming a fluent reader: Reading skill and prosodic features in the oral reading of young readers. *Journal of Educational Psychology, 96,* 119–129.

Seals, L.M., Pollard-Durodola, S.D., Foorman, B.R., & Bradley, A. (2007a). *Vocabulary power: Lessons for students who use African American Vernacular English* (student workbook level 1). Baltimore: Paul H. Brookes Publishing Co.

Seals, L.M., Pollard-Durodola, S.D., Foorman, B.R., & Bradley, A. (2007b). *Vocabulary power: Lessons for students who use African American Vernacular English* (teacher's manual level 1). Baltimore: Paul H. Brookes Publishing Co.

Seltzer, M., Frank, K., & Bryk, A. (1994). The metric matters: The sensitivity of conclusions about growth in student achievement to the choice of metric. *Educational Evaluation and Policy Analysis, 16,* 41–49.

Shavelson, R.J., Webb, N.M., & Burstein, L. (1986) Measurement of teaching. In M.C. Wittrock (Ed.), *Handbook of research on teaching* (3rd ed., pp. 50–91). New York: Macmillan.

Shulman, L.S. (1986). Those who understand: Knowledge growth in teaching. *Educational Researcher, 15*(2), 4–14.

Slavin, R.E., Madden, N.A., Dolan, L.J., & Wasik, B.A. (1996). *Every child, every school: Success for all.* Thousand Oaks, CA: Corwin Press.

Snow, C.E., Burns, M.S., & Griffin, P. (1998). *Preventing reading difficulties in young children.* Washington, DC: National Academies Press.

Stanovich, K.E. (1986). Matthew effects in reading: Some consequences of individual differences in the acquisition of literacy. *Reading Research Quarterly, 21,* 360–407.

Taylor, B.M., Pearson, P.D., Clark, K., & Walpole, S. (2000). Effective schools and accomplished teachers: Lessons about primary-grade reading instruction in low-income schools. *The Elementary School Journal, 101,* 121–165.

Taylor, B.M., Pearson, P.D., Peterson, D., & Rodriguez, M.C. (2003). What matters most in promoting reading growth? Toward a model of reading instruction maximizing cognitive engagement in literacy learning. *The Elementary School Journal, 104*(1), 3–28.

Taylor, B.M., Pearson, P.D., Peterson, D., & Rodriguez, M.C. (2005). The CIERA school change framework: An evidence-based approach to professional development and school reading improvement. *Reading Research Quarterly, 40*(1), 40–69.

Texas Education Agency (1998–2000). *Texas Primary Reading Inventory (TPRI)*. Austin, TX: Author.

Thomas, W.P., & Collier, V. (1997). *School effectiveness for language minority students.* Washington, DC: National Clearinghouse for Bilingual Education.

Torgesen, J.K. (2004). Avoiding the devastating downward spiral: The evidence that early intervention prevents reading failure. *American Educator, 28*(3), 6–19.

Torgesen, J.K., Alexander, A.W., Wagner, R.K., Rashotte, C.A., Voeller, K., Conway, T., et al. (2001). Intensive remedial instruction for children with severe reading disabilities: Immediate and long-term outcomes from two instructional approaches. *Journal of Learning Disabilities, 34,* 33–58.

Wagner, R.K., Torgesen, J.K., & Rashotte, C.A. (1999). *Comprehensive Test of Phonological Processing.* Austin, TX: PRO-ED.

Wechsler, D. (1991). *The Wechsler Intelligence Scale for Children* (3rd ed.). San Antonio, TX: Psychological Corporation.

Wolf, M., & Katzir-Cohen, T. (2001). Reading fluency and its intervention. *Scientific Studies of Reading, 5,* 211–238.

Wong-Fillmore, L., & Snow, C.E. (2002). What teachers need to know about language. In C.T. Adger, C.E. Snow, & D. Christian (Eds.), *What teachers need to know about language* (pp. 7–54). McHenry, IL: Delta Systems Co.

Woodcock, R.W. (1991). *Woodcock Language Proficiency Battery–Revised* (English Form). Chicago: The Riverside Publishing Co.

Woodcock, R.W., & Johnson, M.B. (1989). *Woodcock-Johnson Psycho-Educational Battery–Revised.* Allen, TX: DLM Teaching Resources.

Woodcock, R.W., & Munoz-Sandoval, A.F. (1995). *Woodcock Language Proficiency Battery–Revised* (Spanish Form). Chicago: The Riverside Publishing Co.

Zeno, S.M., Ivens, S.H., Millard, R.T., & Duvvuri, R. (1995). *The educator's word frequency guide.* New York: Touchstone Applied Science Associates.

5

Primary Intervention

A Means of Preventing Special Education?

Charles R. Greenwood, Debra Kamps,
Barbara J. Terry, and Deborah L. Linebarger

The failure to learn to read is an impairment of ability. The prevalence of significant reading disability in children is 17%–20% (1 in 5) children, while more than 33% (1 in 3) struggle to learn to read. Statistics indicate that 25% of twelfth graders score below the basic level in reading and that no significant change has occurred in fourth-grade reading progress since 1992 (National Assessment of Educational Progress [NAEP], 2003; for additional information see review by NAEP, 2002). Estimates are that 74% of poor readers in the third grade remain poor readers in ninth grade (Fletcher & Lyon, 1998). Allington (2001) observed that remedial reading generally is not very effective in making children more literate. Because struggling readers are more likely to drop out of school and to engage in criminal behavior and substance abuse (Whitehurst & Lonigan, 2001), prevention of reading difficulties is a matter of survival.

Difficulties learning to read occur most often in central city, urban schools, where the majority of students of low socioeconomic status (SES) and minority/ethnic students are educated (NAEP, 2003; Snow, Burns, & Griffin, 1998). Students educated in central city schools perform lower in fourth-grade reading than do students attending urban-fringe, suburban, or rural schools. Students who are free-lunch eligible (indicating low SES) perform lower than those who are not free-lunch eligible (indicating average and above-average SES). African and Latino Americans perform lower in reading achievement than do white or Asian students (NAEP, 2003). They are overrepresented in special education primarily because of problems with reading achievement and behavior and underrepresented in programs for the gifted (Ferguson, Kozleski, & Smith, 2003). Teachers in urban

A number of colleagues deserve thanks for their substantial contributions to this work, including Drs. Mary Abbott and Jay Buzhardt. Preparation of this manuscript was partially supported by grants H327A000038, H324X010011, and H324T990014 from the Office of Special Education Programs (OSEP) of the U.S Department of Education.

schools are often the least qualified, lacking the necessary credentials and/or assigned to teach subjects that are out of their areas of expertise (Cohen, 2003). Because of the need for special education, the costs to educate children in urban schools are greater than they should be. Loss to the national economy due to this constraint on the intellectual capacity of the workforce is enormous (Brooks-Gunn, Currie, & Besharov, 2000; Karoly et al., 1998). Can the prevalence of struggling, failing readers be reduced by providing more potent instruction? Can the need for special education for reading disability be prevented (or reduced) with educational interventions? These fascinating questions are increasingly answered in the affirmative.

In this chapter, we discuss the use of schoolwide, primary intervention in the general education classroom, with and without the inclusion of students with identified disabilities. This prevention approach, the Three-Tier Model of Reading Intervention, considers monitoring individual student progress outcomes relative to three levels of risk: primary (Tier 1), secondary (Tier 2), and tertiary (Tier 3; Walker & Shinn, 2002). In Tier 1, proactive evidence-based practices are implemented with all children to prevent the onset of a delay or disability, thereby avoiding the emergence of reading problems—in this case, struggling and failing readers by the fourth and fifth grades. Children who have reading difficulties receive Tier 2 interventions—typically additional help provided in small groups. Children who do not respond to Tier 2 interventions receive special education—Tier 3—services. In Tier 3, intervention is focused on treating the actual disability. Although primary and secondary interventions may have failed students who end up receiving Tier 3 interventions, early detection and intervention at the secondary level may have minimized the overall influence of the disability over the student's lifetime.

The prevention approach presumes knowledge of risks, disability conditions, early identification, precursor skills, screening, progress monitoring, and application of effective intervention. Prevention models are increasingly common (e.g., schoolwide positive behavioral support [Marquis et al., 2000]), early intervention programs for pre-school age children (e.g., Fox & Little, 2001). Prevention requires that all children be screened early and frequently enough to evaluate status and response to intervention. Decision making within a prevention model seeks to move a child from Tier 1 to Tier 2 or Tier 3-level intervention based on data reflecting their individual Response to Intervention (RTI), as noted by other chapter authors in this volume. In this chapter, we limit discussion to issues that enhance the effectiveness of Tier 1 instruction.

EVIDENCE THAT READING PROBLEMS CAN BE REDUCED

ClassWide Peer Tutoring (CWPT), peer-assisted learning strategies (PALS), is one excellent example—for which rigorous evidence from a 12-year randomized trial is available—of teacher-implemented reading intervention in elementary school.

Follow-ups occurred in middle and high school (Greenwood, Maheady, & Delquadri, 2002). The design of the study contrasted 1) teacher-led instruction with 2) CWPT combined with teacher-led instruction in Title 1 (low SES) elementary schools in one school district. Title 1 schools were randomly assigned to use CWPT in daily reading, spelling, and math instruction for 30 minutes per session (90 minutes daily, four days per week). Also controlled in the design was school SES. A second comparison group of non-Title 1 (average to above-average SES) schools used the same curricula and conventional teacher-led instruction in the same school district. Studies that were statistically controlled in the 'intent to treat' multivariate repeated measures and analyses of all students' test scores at the end of fourth grade where initial differences in IQ–score and achievement (reading, language arts, and math) were compared against the scores from the fall of first grade.

Results indicated that CWPT used progressively throughout Grades 1–4 significantly improved low-SES students' classroom engagement during instruction and reduced socially inappropriate behavior; and 2) accelerated reading, language, and math performance on standardized achievement tests compared with both the low- and average- to above-average-SES control groups (Greenwood, 1991a, 1991b; Greenwood, Delquadri, & Hall, 1989). Greenwood also reported that low-SES CWPT students at fourth grade were not significantly different in achievement—adjusted for initial ability and achievement—from the average-to above-average-SES comparison group students. It appeared that the CWPT group had closed the achievement gap existing among groups at first grade.

These accelerated effects in elementary school for low-SES CWPT group students compared with average- to above-average-SES controls were associated with 1) higher achievement outcomes in reading, language, math, social studies, and science, and 2) lower use of special services in middle school (Greenwood, Terry, Utley, Montagna, & Walker, 1993). In high school, the low-SES CWPT group was significantly less likely to drop out of school compared with the low-SES control group (Greenwood, 1996; Greenwood & Delquadri, 1995).

Effect sizes between the low-SES CWPT and the low–SES control groups averaged .72, ranging from .37 (math) to .57 (reading) to −.83 (a reduction in inappropriate behavior) to 1.41 (academic engagement) in the original elementary school study. Effect size is an indicator of the magnitude of the intervention effect between an experimental and control group in terms of standard deviation units. According to Cohen (1988), effect sizes in rank order of .20, .50, and .80 represent small, moderate, and large effect sizes, respectively. This means that, on average, 72% of CWPT group students performed higher than control group students on these outcomes. At the middle school follow-up, the average effect size was .44, ranging from .35 (language) to .39 (reading) to .57 (math) on achievement test measures. The effect size for reduction in special education services between groups was .54; the proportion of students served in less restrictive services compared with controls was .73. The effect size for reduction in the number of students who were high school dropouts was .66.

Additional analyses of the elementary school data focused on fitting three alternative theoretical models to the achievement data. Results indicated that a model in which students' engagement in academic responding (e.g., reading aloud, silent reading) mediated the relationship between classroom instructional ecology (task-materials and teacher behavior) and achievement, compared with two models in which engagement had only direct effects on achievement, provided the best fit (Greenwood, Terry, Marquis, & Walker, 1994). These analyses supported the notion that CWPT affected gains in achievement through at least one major pathway—increasing engagement in academic responding—and therefore, the intensity of primary-level instruction. The vignette below shows an example of this.

> [Following high school graduation,] Marquis Roby, now a college freshman, remembers that he looked forward to working with a partner and competing for points when he used it [reading and spelling CWPT] in third grade at Chelsea Elementary School. "Back then, we thought it was more for fun [than for learning]," said Roby, who will be transferring from Kansas State University to the University of Kansas. "But you did learn a lot from it," he said. "You learned faster because you would sit there and you would spell the words and see what you spelled wrong. You were determined to get it right." Roby learned to spell and read well enough that he now aspires to be a journalist (Horsley, 1995, December 24).

Greenwood and colleagues (1989) reported that general education teachers were employing CWPT strategies relatively effectively. Given all available opportunities to use CWPT each day, however, as individual teachers they varied; and as a group, they only achieved partial implementation. Consequently, reported results likely underestimate maximum attainable effects with CWPT fully implemented. Yet, important benefits were observed by fourth grade and later in middle school in which achievement effects were maintained and generalized to science and social studies achievement and in which CWPT students were seen to be comparatively less frequent users of special education services. This experimental, longitudinal study provided strong evidence that it is possible to prevent reading problems by using effective prevention–intervention strategies systematically and at an early age to prevent later difficulties. The Greenwood and colleagues' study is the only study of which we are aware that reports later-life outcomes of PALS interventions.

To date, PALS interventions have been evaluated across a range of subject matters, including reading, with a variety of students and in different elementary classroom settings. In a recent synthesis (n = 90 group comparative studies in elementary school), Rohrbeck, Ginsberg-Block, Fantuzzo, & Miller (2003) reported the following:

- The average effect size for PALS was .59 (i.e., 59% of PALS group students exceeded the achievement of non-PALS group students), a moderate effect size overall.

- Students from urban, low-income, and minority backgrounds experienced larger gains than students from suburban, middle- to high-income backgrounds.

- Younger students experienced larger gains in achievement than older students.

- Greater academic effects were produced by programs in which students controlled more of the PALS procedures, including goal setting, guiding tutoring roles, monitoring of progress, evaluating performance, reward selection, and reward administration.

- PALS programs that included individual rather than group evaluation procedures were associated with better outcomes.

- PALS programs in which interdependent reward contingencies, rather than individualized or group contingencies, produced greater achievement.

Thus, evidence exists that it is possible to decrease the number of children who receive special education services for reading problems and that this can be true for students in urban schools where students are taught to play the roles of both teacher and learner, progress is monitored frequently, and contingencies of reinforcement for performance are used.

Qualities of a Science-Based Reading Intervention

Science-based reading interventions such as CWPT and PALS are those that teach scientifically validated skills (e.g., precursor, readiness, reading, comprehension) using scientifically validated practices. Because it is increasingly well-known which skills must be learned by when in one's schooling to be ready to learn future skills and which strategies for teaching these skills are measurably superior to others (National Reading Panel, 2000), this combination of the right skills and the right practices is critical (see Figure 5.1).

Skills Required for Reading

Adequate early reading instruction includes opportunities for children to acquire knowledge of two interdependent domains of information. First, children need sources of information that will directly support their understanding of the meaning of print (i.e., outside-in processes: vocabulary knowledge, conceptual knowledge, story schemas, comprehension). Second, children need to be able to translate print into sounds and sounds into print (i.e., inside-out processes: phonemic awareness, letter–sound correspondence). To acquire this knowledge, it is increasingly clear that children must be taught these critical skills in early experiences with parents and teachers (Whitehurst & Lonigan, 2001).

The core elements of a science-based reading program prior to third grade include phonemic awareness, phonemic decoding skills, an increasing lexicon of words (vocabulary) identifiable at a "single" glance (fluency), and comprehension (see upper-right panel in Figure 5.1). Students arriving in third grade with these skills will be able to read third-grade text accurately and fluently with variable levels of understanding (Moats, 1999; National Reading Panel, 2000). Reading skill components that differentiate reading achievement after third grade include

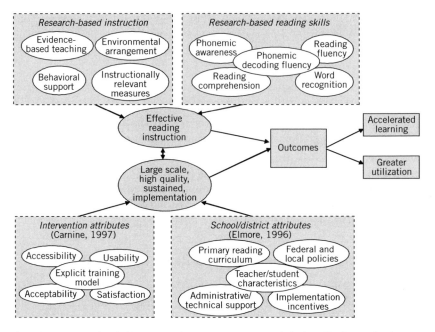

Figure 5.1.   Scalability of effective practice conceptual framework linking effective reading instruction and large-scale, high-quality, sustained implementation to accelerated learning and increased utilization outcomes.

continued growth in the lexicon of words, acquisition of the complex vocabulary that appears primarily in written text, acquisition of strategies for processing different types of text (e.g., narrative, expository), growth in conceptual and background knowledge, and growth in reasoning/inferential skills. The most important outcome of elementary reading instruction is comprehension of written material (Block, Gambrell, & Presley, 2002; Torgesen, 1998, 2002).

Science-Based Instructional Strategies

Science-based instructional strategies are practices validated through rigorous experimental research, including randomized trials (Embry, 2004). The recognized components of effective teaching strategies include teaching practices (student and materials interaction strategies), environmental arrangement, behavioral support, and instructionally relevant measurement for progress monitoring. PALS interventions are one example of a class of practices that, when aligned with teacher-led activities in the reading curriculum, is highly effective and relatively easy to replicate (see review by Rohrbeck et al., 2003). Example interventions included in this class are cooperative learning, peer teaching, and peer tutoring.

In CWPT, a PALS strategy, students engage in peer-assisted, collaborative instructional activities (teaching practice) in which they support each others' learning (Greenwood et al., 1989). In addition to learning materials, students are arranged into dyads during a portion of weekly reading instruction (environmental arrangement). Rules are used to teach and guide appropriate social and tutoring behavior (behavioral support), including peer teaching interactions consisting of task presentation, correction, awarding of points, and praise for correct responding (Greenwood, Delquadri, & Carta, 1997). Curriculum-based measurement strategies (instructionally relevant measurement) are used to monitor individual and class progress in the curriculum consisting of research-based reading skills (i.e., phonemic awareness, decoding, and comprehension among others) (Greenwood, Reynolds, Abbott, & Tapia, 2004).

CWPT enables general educators to meet the instructional needs of a wide range of students including those at risk who benefit most in the presence of intense and explicit instruction. As part of a primary curriculum, CWPT helps students become highly engaged with instructional materials and experience multiple opportunities to respond and practice compared with typical teacher-directed instruction (Greenwood, 1996).

When explicit reading curricula are combined with CWPT (as in Beginning Reading CWPT [BR-CWPT]) or kindergarten peer-assisted learning strategy (K-PALS), as described below), instruction becomes both intensive and explicit (i.e. all steps are taught directly) (Mathes, Torgesen, Allen, & Howard Allor, 2002). With implicit instruction, many students simply do not learn the necessary skills because teachers do not teach them.

CWPT, compared with teacher-led instruction, offers distinct advantages—at reasonable effort and cost—with respect to enhancing explicitness and intensity of instruction. These advantages are that: 1) groups of students can operate on different levels of the curriculum and use different procedures that meet their individual needs without overwhelming the students or the teacher, 2) students receive one-to-one mentoring with corrective feedback, 3) the volume of reading is dramatically increased, 4) mastery and fluency of new material is established rapidly, 5) academic, social, and behavior skills are learned at the same time, 6) students with disabilities can access the general education reading curriculum through cooperative learning groups (Atwater, Carta, Schwartz, & McConnell, 1993; Dugan, Leonard, Watkins, Rheinberger, & Stackhaus, 1995; Kamps, Leonard, Potucek, & Garrison-Harrell, 1995) and CWPT (Kamps, Barbetta, Leonard, & Delquadri, 1994), 7) teachers and students find CWPT a highly acceptable practice, and 8) cost and resources are reasonably low compared with traditional teacher-directed instruction. The existence of science-based reading practices such as PALS strategies alone cannot reduce the prevalence of reading problems; such practices must be systematically used over time to produce the desired benefit.

Are Science-Based Strategies Being Used?

What is known from research concerning the widespread use (i.e., scalability) of effective practice also is captured in Figure 5.1 (Carnine, 1997; Elmore, 1996; National Reading Panel, 2000). This framework posits that implementation of science-based reading instruction is a function of the attributes of the intervention itself (e.g., materials, media, technology, acceptability) and school entities (e.g., district, school, teachers, students) that interact to differentially affect the large-scale, high-quality, sustained implementation.

It is known that effective reading instruction and implementation quality interact to produce desired reading outcomes and widespread patterns of utilization across teachers, schools, and districts. Use of effective instruction leads to increased student learning and administrators and teachers who are excited to continue to use that particular method and to advocate for its use by others. Intervention attributes and schooling contexts interact to differentially promote usage that is further advanced by accelerated learning outcomes that when used help to sustain subsequent usage.

Although teachers around the nation report being exposed to PALS methods (Henke, Chen, & Goldman, 1999), they typically are not using its science-based components—those that have been linked to achievement outcomes (Rohrbeck et al., 2003). These components include using group reward contingencies, self-management of learning activities, fidelity of implementation, and individualized evaluation of progress in the curriculum. Nationwide, there is an estimate of 2–3 million U.S. public school teachers and 32–35 million students in Grades 1–8; how many of these teachers actually use PALS? No one really knows.

There is no national survey of instructional practices used by teachers from which the prevalence of PALS interventions usage can be reliably inferred. In addition, many science-based practices have not yet been translated from research to use in real schools with classroom teachers (and not researchers) as implementers. Most lack the necessary comfort-level features (e.g., acceptability, satisfaction) and tools (e.g., accessibility, usability, training models) that school building faculty require to bring them into their practice (Carnine, 1997). In addition, the fact that the most effective practices vary in scope and that few portend to be total solutions to the out-of-the-box comprehensive reading curriculum that most schools are hoping to find makes translation to practice difficult. For example, PALS procedures are not yet widely included in methods within elementary reading curricula or in professional development activities (Rohrbeck et al., 2003). Instead, most research-based practices are curricula components and/or strategies such as CWPT that, when integrated by teachers within existing curricula, help create more comprehensive solutions to the teaching of reading. Few research-based practices are complete solutions with convincing evidence that they work equally well across the wide diversity of real school settings and learners that define elementary schools in America (American Federation of Teachers, 1998; Moats, 1999).

Even in light of the national No Child Left Behind (NCLB) Act of 2001 (PL 107-110) policies mandating the use of science-based reading curricula, few schools offer the supports and incentives necessary to establish full implementation and sustained use over time and through staff transitions (Elmore, 1996). For example, determinants of large-scale, high-quality, and sustained implementation of effective practices include use or consideration of 1) the locally mandated reading curriculum and strategies, 2) teacher (e.g., knowledge of reading) and student characteristics (e.g., school readiness), 3) administrative and technical IT support, and 4) incentives to implementation.

SCIENCE-BASED PRACTICES RECOMMENDED FOR PRIMARY INTERVENTION?

Peer-Assisted Learning Strategy

CWPT and BR-CWPT contain the components associated with greater effectiveness reported by Rhorbeck and colleagues (2003).

ClassWide Peer Tutoring

CWPT tutoring pairs belong to either a competing or a cooperating team, based on the teacher's discretion, as a key motivational strategy founded on the social–psychological principles of cooperative learning and the behavior analysis principles of interdependent reinforcement (Greenwood & Hops, 1981; Stevenson & Newman, 1986).

CWPT was based on the observation that even students who failed to make progress in teacher-led instruction were able to make rapid and sustained progress when taught one-to-one by a highly qualified tutor outside of the classroom (Delquadri, 1978). The development of CWPT became a search for an effective, sustainable, acceptable approach to providing such instruction to all students as part of primary instruction (Greenwood, Maheady, & Delquadri, 2002). Consequently, the following key principles guided the design: 1) application of CWPT in the general education classroom with all students participating, 2) explicit strategies for including English language learners (ELLs) and students with disabilities, 3) maximum adaptability to local curricula to promote acceptability, and, therefore, scalability, by classroom teachers, and 4) use of computer software to support progress monitoring and teacher implementation.

The core reading process involves daily 35–45 minute sessions in which half the students in a classroom tutor and supervise the reading of the other half. After 15 minutes of tutoring, the teacher signals the tutor and tutee dyads (one triad if class has an unequal number of students) to stop and trade roles. In the next 15 minutes, the tutors become tutees, and vice versa, for a second tutoring round on the same material. Because the primary goal of CWPT is to accelerate intensity (i.e., engagement and volume of responding of all students in the material), its immediate effects on reading are in terms of accuracy, fluency, and comprehension of the material.

In Reading CWPT (R-CWPT), daily sessions typically occur three or more times per week in coordination with teacher-led instruction. During these sessions, background knowledge is activated, new material is introduced, and students read to the teacher as determined by the adopted curriculum, with formative evaluation of progress. Teacher planning and design decisions that shape the core process include flexible methods of peer pairing, choice of curriculum, and peer-teaching strategies.

In R-CWPT, tutor and tutee pairs change weekly or with every new unit of material to avoid the negative effects of boredom and the stigma of always being the tutee and never being the tutor. Partners are assigned by the teacher and typically are paired from among members of the same or adjacent reading groups. To include the lowest-performing students, teachers pair higher- with lower-functioning students. Some additional strategies include having the higher-functioning student read first as a model for the lower-functioning student. These and other decisions are all made privately by the teacher as part of his or her weekly planning.

Curriculum Integration Issues of ClassWide Peer Tutoring

CWPT is adaptable with respect to integration with local curricula, making it readily scalable. At the elementary level, CWPT is integrated to create a comprehensive reading program for Grades 1–5, focused on science-based beginning reading skills, fluency, and reading comprehension. Combined with teacher-led instruction and aligned peer-teaching materials, CWPT may be used to scaffold phonemic activities, word vocabulary, spelling, passage reading accuracy/fluency, and retell reading comprehension, as appropriate, before and after third grade. CWPT is also used for literature-based activities in which peer tutors are guided by teacher-developed study guides (Greenwood & Hou, 2001; Greenwood et al., 2004).

For example, when applied to phonemes or letter names, CWPT tutees say the sounds or letter names associated with the flashcard item presented by the tutor. The tutor provides correction and tallies the tutee's responses using points. At a later time, the teacher assesses the fluency of letter naming and phonemic segmentation using formative measures and the CWPT-LMS.

When applied to word and passage reading, tutees read brief passages from the curriculum to their tutor. The tutor provides points for correctly read sentences and error correction. Teachers assess the fluency of the students' reading using oral reading rate measures. When applied to comprehension, the tutee responds to who, what, when, where, and why questions (and/or other comprehension promoting tasks) concerning the passage asked by the tutor. They may also respond to prediction and other questions. The tutor corrects responses and provides feedback using materials and their own knowledge. When applied to advanced subject matter (e.g., literature, science), peer teaching is guided by study guides. These procedures are thoroughly described in the teacher's CWPT manual that delivers as part of the CWPT-LMS software.

Adaptations of the curricula can be made to include individual students with disabilities or ELLs, including variations in content, tasks and materials, and behavioral supports inclusion of paraprofessionals in the tutoring process as translators or for assistance. For example, in CWPT program in inclusive classrooms, students with autism and behavioral disabilities also earned points for appropriate social interactions such as offering help and sharing information (Kamps et al., 1995). For example, a child with a hearing impairment and his or her paraprofessional participate in CWPT with a peer tutor without disabilities, wherein the paraprofessional provides sign language translation. A somewhat similar translation strategy works for ELLs.

For example, the teacher of ELLs may use another student in the classroom to help introduce the spelling or vocabulary to the entire class in the second language, in addition to having the items presented in writing and/or in combination with pictures. For passage reading, a non-English or limited-English speaker can be paired with a more fluent bilingual speaker to assist with pronunciation and comprehension of text (Arreaga-Mayer, 1998).

Beginning Reading-ClassWide Peer Tutoring

Although CWPT was designed to be adapted to existing curricula, BR-CWPT (curricula and teacher support software) directly links science-based early-reading skills with CWPT activities adapted for preschoolers, kindergartners, and, where desired, early elementary students (Terry & Greenwood, 2004). The BR-CWPT curricula is comprised of 16 science-based skill modules that can be selected and flexibly used by teachers for initial instruction and reused for review and refresher sessions. Each of the modules is supported by computer software (see below) for creating the CWPT task materials (visual/picture flashcards) specific to each module for use in the peer-tutoring sessions.

The following is a list of BR-CWPT curriculum modules and, in parentheses following the module name, the skills taught within each module:

1. Word Discrimination (hear a sentence; identify beginning, middle, and end words; then hear a series of words, and repeat the words to make a sentence)

2. Letter–Sound Association (hear a sound, repeat it, say its letter name; hear a sound, write its letter)

3. Letter–Symbol Identification (see a letter, say its name; hear a letter, write it)

4. Beginning Sounds (hear a word, say the beginning sound)

5. Ending Sounds (hear a word, say the ending sound)

6. Two-Letter Sound Blends (hear a word; say the two-letter sound blend)

7. Sound Identification (hear a word, say all sounds in the word)

8. Sound Blending (hear a sequence of sounds, say the word)

9. Matching Sounds (hear a word and a sound, say if the sound is present in the word)

10. Common Sounds (hear two words, say the sound that is common in both words)

11. Subtracting Sounds (hear a word, take out a sound, say the word/sound(s) that are left)

12. Switching Sounds (hear a word, switch one sound for another, and say the new word)

13. Working with Syllables (hear a series of syllable sounds, say them fast to say the word; hear a word and say the syllable sounds)

14. Sight Word Vocabulary (using the Dolch sight words, see a word and say it; hear the word and write it)

15. CWPT Oral Reading (see grade-level sentences, paragraphs, passages; read orally at an 85% accuracy level)

16. CWPT Comprehension (read grade-level material; answer related comprehension questions orally and written, including vocabulary, factual, recall, sequential, and inferential information)

Each of the 16 individual modules is designed as a complete teaching unit that includes both teacher and PALS activities. Each module provides the teacher with the objective, the necessary prerequisite skills, student mastery criteria, curriculum materials, peer teaching tasks (flashcards for each module), and considerations pertaining to each particular skill of the module. In addition to the instructional/lesson format, each module includes suggested activities for applying the newly acquired knowledge in practical ways; provides ideas on how to sequence the content; and suggests options for dealing with both students who have and have not yet mastered the material.

When students have learned the rules and can perform the roles of tutor and tutee, BR-CWPT sessions officially begin. Reoccurring module activities are preassessments (7–10 minutes), mini-lessons (10–20 minutes), CWPT (6–10 minutes), suggested activities (8–10 minutes), and mastery postassessments (7–10 minutes). A preassessment is conducted prior to any teaching or tutoring. These assessments are created using the Assessment Generator software and are based on the content that is being tutored for the week and that will be reassessed for mastery at posttest.

Each pre- and posttutoring assessment is conducted weekly and takes approximately 6–10 minutes per assessment. Given prior to instruction, the pretest contains items that reflect the content that will be tutored for the week. The posttest is given following instruction of the same tutored material. An example of a preassessment session on word discrimination skills follows.

Once the assessment forms and writing instruments have been distributed, the teacher says, "Class, look at the three pictures in row 1. I will say the name of each picture, and I want you to repeat the name after me. As we say the names of the pictures, I will tell you to think of which picture is at the beginning of the row, the middle of the row, and the end of the row. You will do this quietly to yourself, and then I will tell you to circle the picture that is in the position I say, either beginning, middle, or end. Let's do the first row. The first picture is a bell. Everyone repeat the word 'bell.' Now think of where it is located in the row: beginning, middle, or end. The second picture is a house. Everyone repeat the word 'house,' and think of where it is located in the row: beginning, middle, or end. The third picture is a football. Everyone repeat the word 'football.' Now think of where it is located in the row: beginning, middle, or end. Now take your pencil [or crayon] and circle the picture that is in the middle of the first row. Now let's do the same steps in row 2."

The teacher continues the same procedures and instructions for each of the remaining rows until the entire assessment had been completed by each student. For the postassessment, the same preassessment form is used but the answers or targeted items are changed. Once the assessment is completed, the teacher collects all of the papers and grades and records the scores on a weekly test-scores chart. A master key for scoring the completed tests is used. Students scoring 70% or below on the pretest are considered within range for learning the content, and students scoring 85% or above on the posttest are considered to have mastery of the content.

Similar to CWPT, BR-CWPT is based on a game format with the entire classroom divided into two teams of equal ability competing to be the winning team by earning the most points during the tutoring process. BR-CWPT, however, differs from CWPT in several ways. For CWPT activities, students are paired up with a same-age peer to work together to learn the academic task (e.g., hear a word, say the two-letter sound blend). The tutor presents the flashcard to the tutee for a response. The tutee responds orally and in writing (when appropriate). The tutor then assesses the correctness of each response.

In BR-CWPT, students use a card placemat as an organizer for separating content flashcards that are answered correctly and incorrectly (see Figure 5.2). The teacher uses a large replica of the placemat to show the students where the flashcards go, where the help card is, and how it should be used by the tutor to stack flashcards that are responded to correctly (or incorrectly) by the tutee. Incorrectly answered flashcards are placed on the question mark. Correctly answered flashcards are placed on the smiley face. A help sign is also located on the tutoring placemat. The bottom portion of the teacher's placemat chart has example rows from the students' point sheet so that the teacher can demonstrate how tutors are to award points to the tutee for each correct answer.

During tutoring sessions in which oral responses are made, the two students are seated across from one another with the tutoring placemat in between them.

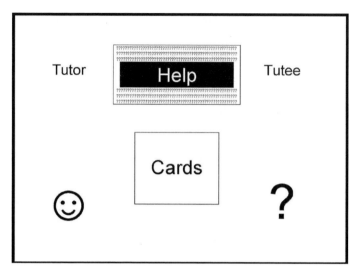

Figure 5.2.   Beginning Reading ClassWide Peer Tutoring placemat.

For the Common Sounds module, the tutor in each pair picks up the first flashcard with two pictures on it, shows it to the tutee, and says, "This is a picture of a box and a bus. Tell me the common sound in *box* and *bus*." The tutee responds with the common sound in the two words. If the response is correct, the tutor turns the cards to show the common letter; says, "Good job"; places the flashcard on the smiley face on the placemat; and tells the tutee to give him- or herself one point on his or her pointsheet. If incorrect, the tutor says, "Nice try. The sounds in *box* are *(b) (o) (x)* and the sounds in *bus* are *(b) (u) (s);* so the common sound in *box* and *bus* is *(b)*." "Again, what is the common sound in *box* and *bus?*" The tutee responds and the tutor gives positive feedback and places the cards on the question mark on the placemat. The tutor picks up the next card, then continues the procedure until all the cards have been dispersed to the smiley-face or the question mark piles. When all the cards have been shown, the tutor continues tutoring practice by redoing the question mark cards until they have been moved to the smiley-face card pile. If time remains, the process starts over with the smiley-face card pile and continues until the bell sounds the end of the first round. When the timer signals the end of the first round, the teacher praises the students for "good tutoring" and tells them to reverse tutor–tutee roles. When ready, the teacher resets the timer for the second round of tutoring for the same amount of time and says "Begin." The students carry out the same tutoring procedure until the end of the second round, signaled by the timer.

During tutoring sessions for which written responses are required, a writing worksheet is used. Each writing worksheet is divided into four columns. The column on the far left is used by the tutee to make his or her first written attempt, responding to the tutor's flashcard prompt. Here is an example using a spelling tutoring task that requires both oral and written responses. The tutor says, "Spell the word *cat*." The tutee says aloud (as she writes in the far left column of the first row), "Cat, c-a-t." The tutor says, "Correct. Give yourself one point on the tutoring point sheet. Now spell *will*." The tutee says and writes in the far left column of the second row, "Will, w-e." The tutor immediately says, "Stop. The correct spelling of *will* is w-i-l-l." "Practice it three times."

The tutee moves to the second column of the second row, says, and then writes, "w-i-l-l," (moving across to the third column) "w-i-l-l," (moving across to the final column of the second row), *"w-i-l-l"*. The tutor says, "Very nice job," and places the flashcard on the question mark side of the placemat because the tutee made an error on that word. No points are awarded for any assisted answer, and the tutee correctly practices missed words three times in both the oral and written form.

This tutoring exchange continues through as many flashcards as possible until the timer sounds the end of the tutoring session for the students. The teacher then resets the timer for the same amount of time, and the student who was the tutor in each dyad now becomes the tutee, and vice versa, so that the second student has a chance to practice the content and to earn points for the team. At the end of the second round of tutoring, the points earned by all members of the two separate class teams are tallied to determine the winning team for the day. Point scores are tallied and a winning team declared after every peer-tutoring session. The team who has the most points at the end of the entire week is that week's overall winner. Each team should have won several times during the tutoring week. The posttest assessment covering the tutored material is given at the end of each module to evaluate individual student's gains and determine whether more teaching is needed before proceeding to material contained in the next module. Once very young students begin to read text, teachers can conduct the CWPT sessions as outlined in *Together We Can!: ClassWide Peer Tutoring for Basic Academic Skills*.

In What Populations and Contexts Have ClassWide Peer-Tutoring Practices Been Validated?

The original CWPT intervention research took place in the 1980s primarily in urban elementary schools in Northeast Kansas City, Kansas. This community is a traditionally low-SES, high-risk area that became part of the Missouri/Kansas Bi-State Enterprise Zone during the first Clinton Administration. First reports of effectiveness appeared in *Education and Treatment of Children, Journal of Applied Behavior Analysis, Exceptional Children,* and *Journal of Educational Psychology*. With the advent of mainstreaming, the least restrictive environment principle, and inclusion, students with learning disabilities (LD), behavior disorders (BD), mental retardation, and autism were included in the context of instruction in the general education classroom. These early CWPT applications focused primarily on teaching reading, spelling, vocabulary, and math in the Title 1/Chapter 1 urban schools in the area with majorities of African American students. Independent replications occurred in other urban schools around the country (Greenwood et al., 2002). More recent research on CWPT conducted in urban schools and classrooms including students with disabilities and ELLs in the same school district as in the original studies have reported positive results in elementary school (Arreaga-Mayer, 1998; Greenwood, Arreaga-Mayer, Utley, Gavin, & Terry, 2001), middle school, and high school (Kamps, Arreaga-Mayer, Veerkamp, Utley, & Greenwood, 2004; Veerkamp, 2001).

Kindergarten Peer-Assisted Learning Strategy, First-Grade Peer-Assisted Learning Strategy, and Peer-Assisted Learning Strategy for Grades 2–6

Developed in the early 1990s (Mathes, Fuchs, Fuchs, Henley, & Sanders, 1994; Simmons, Fuchs, Fuchs, Hodge, & Mathes, 1994), PALS, which is similar to CWPT, was an effort to provide teachers with an effective, feasible, and acceptable intervention for the entire class in which students with LD could be meaningfully included in instruction. Built around the CWPT core process, PALS includes a number of effective peer-teaching strategies linked to reading curricula. In addition, it can be linked to computerized formative evaluation systems using curriculum-based measurement (CBM)-enabling teachers to gear instruction to the group as well as to the needs of specific students.

K-PALS focuses on teaching emergent reading skills (e.g., phonemic skills, pronunciation, alphabetic knowledge). PALS Grade 1 sessions are divided into classwide activities that include 1) phonemic segmentation skills, 2) partner reading of connected text, 3) story retell after partner reading, 4) paragraph shrinking, and 5) prediction relays. PALS Grades 2–6 includes partner reading, paragraph shrinking, and prediction activities.

Higher-performing students are paired with lower-performing students by rank ordering class members, splitting the list at the median, and then pairing the first student in the upper half with the first student in the lower half and so forth. This step may be performed by the teacher or by the computer program accompanying the materials. Classroom textbook resources are used, and teachers may individualize the difficulty of the reading materials for each pair, with a specific emphasis on the needs of the weaker reader. Similar to CWPT, both coaches (tutors) and players (tutees) read the assigned material.

During Partner Reading/Story Retell, the higher-performing student reads first, as a model, followed by the lower-performing student reading the very same material. The lower-performing student then sequences major events from the material read. During Paragraph Shrinking, the higher-performing student resumes reading new text and stops after each paragraph to summarize the material. The lower-performing student then continues reading with new material and summarizes each paragraph. During Prediction Relay, students continue reading new textbook material with the higher-performing student reading aloud and stopping after each page to summarize information and make a prediction about what will happen next. The lower-performing student repeats the same procedure. Coaches (tutors) present points to players (tutees) for reading each sentence correctly, as in CWPT, and for summarizing, making reasonable predictions, and working cooperatively. Additional work has extended PALS to middle- and high-school applications with reading and subject matter instruction (Fuchs et al., 2001).

Similar to CWPT, convincing evidence supports PALS' superiority in teaching reading compared with conventional general education instruction in reading (e.g., Mathes et al., 2003). Results indicated that, using PALS, all students with and without LD made measurably greater progress on test scores in the same amount of time. Both teachers and students reported high levels of satisfaction with PALS instruction (Mathes et al., 1994). In addition, these authors reported that students with LD were better liked, made friends, and were better known by peers during K-PALS and PALS Grade 1 instruction than in conventional teacher-led instruction. Similar to CWPT, these findings also have been extended to students with BD (Locke & Fuchs, 1995). PALS reading and math were approved by the Program Effectiveness Panel of the National Diffusion Network and are undergoing review in the What Works Clearinghouse of the U.S. Department of Education.

In What Populations and Contexts Have Peer-Assisted Learning Strategies Practices Been Validated?

The original PALS research took place in the early 1990s, with first reports of effectiveness appearing in *Learning Disabilities Research and Practice* and *Journal of Learning Disabilities*. A major piece of this work took place in general education classrooms in metropolitan Nashville, TN Title 1 (low-SES) schools. The primary goal of PALS was the development of reading instructional intervention capable of improving the reading achievement of students with LD compared with the gains made by low-achieving and typically achieving students in the same classrooms and schools (Al Otaiba & Fuchs, 2002; Fuchs, Fuchs, & Burish, 2000; Fuchs, Fuchs, Mathes, & Simmons, 1997; Fuchs et al., 2001). Disaggregating PALS results for these groups in randomized trials emerged as an increasingly important design for investigating students responsive to intervention (Fuchs et al., 2001). Other general education contexts in which PALS has been shown effective include math instruction in elementary school (Fuchs, Fuchs, Phillips, Hamlett, & Karns, 1995), instruction with students who have behavior disorders, and subject matter instruction in middle school (Fuchs et al., 2001).

Media-Assisted Teaching Strategies: Between the Lions

Building on their success in teaching preschoolers school readiness via television (i.e., Sesame Street), producers at PBS, in collaboration with leading reading experts, have created a new television program for young children. The program, *Between the Lions*, incorporates science-based early-literacy skills into its broadcasts (Strickland & Rath, 2000, August). The goal of the producers was to reach all segments of society—especially children who have little or no access to print resources and few informal literacy opportunities in their homes—with this program. Television offers a powerful way to serve the literacy needs of children who have "low redundancy of educational opportunity" because 99% of U.S. homes have a television set (Mielke, 1994; Statistical Abstracts, 2000, p. 126; online at http://www.pbs.org/readytolearn/research/btlkansassum.pdf).

This series was created with the intent of teaching young children important emergent literacy skills (Whitehurst & Lonigan, 1998). *Between the Lions* presents children with an environment and experiences designed to foster emergent literacy. These experiences focus on both holistic processes (e.g., understanding different reading/writing contexts, prior knowledge, motivation) as well as direct instruction comprised of visual and auditory stimuli (e.g., print on screen with changing initial/final consonants) that have been specifically designed to teach concepts of print, the alphabetic principle, phonemic awareness, and letter–sound correspondences.

In a test of the effectiveness of *Between the Lions* in a randomized trial, 17 one-half hour episodes from the first season of the new series were used (Linebarger, 2000; Linebarger, Kosanic, Greenwood, & Doku, 2003). Randomized experimental viewing groups of kindergarten and first-grade children watched one *Between the Lions* episode each day. The viewing group watched the program in their classrooms in the afternoon during their computer free time from the end of February through the beginning of April with days off for spring break and district-scheduled vacation days. Children in the control group continued their usual instruction and schedule during the viewing phase.

Analyses controlled for the effects of initial differences at pretest, family SES, and home literacy experiences. The most prominent finding was improvement in the emergent literacy skills for kindergarten children who watched *Between the Lions*. These improvements were moderated by the child's reading risk status. Significantly higher word recognition and Test of Early Reading Ability scores were achieved for *Between the Lions* viewers compared with nonviewers (Cohen's d effect sizes ranged from .46 to .91, averaging .70) (Hresko, Hammill, & Reid, 2001). In addition, higher means and accelerated slopes for *Between the Lions* viewers were noted for phonemic awareness and letter–sound tasks (accounting for 58% and 47% of the variance in the intercept and 36% and 0% of the variance in the slope, respectively). Children who were most at risk for reading failure improved on concepts of print tasks (first graders) and word recognition tasks (both kindergarten and first graders). Given that television represents universally available technology for reaching all children, having children view a program such as *Between the Lions* should help a significant portion of students by extending early literacy instruction and reinforcing and motivating children within the home and in the classroom.

With confirmation of the ability of the program by itself to support children's acquisition of early literacy skills, the creators of the program decided to develop instructional materials to accompany the program's curriculum and involve educators in the learning process. A demonstration project—the Mississippi Literacy Initiative—was funded to evaluate whether these instructional materials, in combination with viewing the program, could further support children's literacy skill development. The Mississippi Literacy Initiative was created and delivered in preschool, kindergarten, and first-grade classrooms in two different contexts: the Choctaw Indian Reservation and the Delta region of Mississippi. Teachers showed the students two half-hour *Between the Lions* episodes each week and received training in how to use a set of related children's books and resources along with the series to help teach reading. In a school-year–long evaluation, researchers found improvements in basic early literacy skills for both populations (Prince, Grace, Linebarger, Atkinson, & Huffman, 2002).

Reports of the effectiveness of *Between the Lions* have only recently appeared in the *Journal of Educational Psychology*. Participants in this first randomized trial were 164 kindergarten and first-grade students. These children were recruited from classrooms in three elementary schools in the greater Kansas City metropolitan area. Eighty-one percent of the children were European American, 7% were Hispanic, 6% were African American, and 6% were from other backgrounds. Thirty-six percent of the families reported incomes below $30,000; 28% reported incomes between $30,000 and $45,000; and 36% reported incomes above $45,000. Eight percent of the children had an identified disability. Additional *Between the Lions* trials are in progress (Annenberg School for Communication of the University of Pennsylvania, 2001), most notably one involving an American Indian Head Start Initiative involving 12 different tribes in the southwestern U.S. with both home and Head Start components.

RECOMMENDATIONS FOR IMPLEMENTATION, POLICY, AND RESEARCH

Clearly, schools must implement preventive reading approaches to meet the wide range of needs among students. Three-tier models help provide early screening and the flexibility to increase the intensity of instruction as needed by individual students. In three-tier models, primary-level instruction provides the base-level influence on students success in learning to read and on the number of students who will eventually experience reading problems, thus the need for secondary- and tertiary-level instruction. As a rule of policy and practice, schools must adopt science-based curriculum. To boost the intensity and effectiveness of Tier 1 instruction, schools and classroom teachers should include the value-added benefits of PALS reading activities. Related recommendations include preservice teacher preparation that includes PALS and systematic in-service training that also incorporates PALS. To boost the explicitness, intensity, and effectiveness of primary-level instruction, schools and classroom teachers should include the value-added benefits of science-based media such as *Between the Lions* in the early grades.

Although these recommendations derive logically from a review of research findings, the gap between what is known to work and its subsequent spread to classrooms outside the research setting is well-known (e.g., Carnine, 1997; Elmore, 1996; Greenwood & Abbott, 2001; Klingner, Ahwee, Pilonieta, & Menendez, 2003). Since 2002, NCLB has attempted to address this problem by mandating that schools use science-based curricula in their reading instruction. The U.S. Department of Education's *What Works Clearinghouse* is creating a resource of information concerning science-based intervention practices. Yet, questions of progress remain to be addressed. It is unclear what percentage of the population of elementary and middle-school teachers in the U.S.—estimated to be between 2 and 3 million teaching 32–35 million first- to eighth–grade students—is now using science-based reading practices such as direct instruction, PALS, or *Between the Lions.* The annual rate of uptake in teachers' use of science-based reading practices in the light of NCLB or the effects of other policies or practices designed to accelerate the use of these practices also is unknown.

Outside of the field of education, however, scalability (or "diffusion") of new practices is a topic of some sophistication. For example, the "S-shaped" diffusion curve is known to describe the manner in which most innovations scale up—the initial rate of adoption is slow, followed by acceleration in the rate of adoption, and concluding with a deceleration in rate (Rogers, 2003). One of the earliest studies investigated 259 farmers' reports of hybrid seed corn use in two Iowa communities (Ryan & Gross, 1943). Ten percent of farmers implemented hybrid seed corn during the first 5 years of the 13-year study, followed by a large increase to 40% in the next 3 years, and then a leveling off over the next 5 years until all but two of the farmers reported using the new corn. Similar s-curved uptakes have been reported for educational innovations such as kindergartens, modern mathematics, and driver's education courses. Similar data on annual progress adopting and implementing science-based reading practices is needed to understand progress and factors positively affecting progress (see Figure 5.1).

At least five scalability factors are hypothesized in the literature: 1) perceived relative advantage, 2) compatibility with existing needs, 3) perceived ease of use (complexity), 4) trialability, and 4) observability. Policies such as NCLB tend to create a context for assessing reading interventions based on both relative advantage and compatibility with existing needs because of their measurable superiority to other methods of teaching reading. Characteristics of the science-based intervention (e.g., usability, accessibility; see Figure 5.1) support the perception of ease of use among teachers. The interaction between intervention characteristics and local policies facilitate trialability and observability.

An initial effort to scale up CWPT across nine schools in five states distant from the developers of CWPT identified three factors that affected adoption, implementation, and sustainability. Full implementation occurred fastest in schools in which

1) CWPT had strong support from school administrators, 2) teachers and administrators communicated early and frequently (at least 10 times with each other and the researcher) with researchers during the implementation process, and 3) initial implementation began earlier rather than later in the school year.

Although many teachers report exposure to PALS, PALS are not part of the majority of reading curricula and they do not often play a role in either teacher preparation or in-service training, despite empirical findings indicating that they should (Rohrbeck et al., 2003). So why isn't this method used in every inner-city school in the country? Why is there such difficulty getting research-oriented teaching practices applied in the classroom? Simply put, not enough educators are aware of these methods, and too few truly believe that these interventions are capable of closing the achievement gap (Greenwood & Maheady, 2001). The good news, however, is that there appears to be an increasingly active national market for science-based practices. Local policies are driving professional development and support for implementation. And, in increasing numbers, science-based interventions are being translated for implementation by teachers in local schools.

Translation of Science-Based Practice for Implementation by Teachers

The spirit behind the translation from research to practice is caught in this quote from Mrs. Mayberry, an elementary school teacher, regarding her experience using the CWPT-LMS:

> "This is the first time in my teaching career (of 26 years) that I've ever had a university team train me and make sure I could do it and provide me with all the materials." She said, "I've read lots of studies in my career and, 'Yeah, that sounds good but how do you do it?' With this, I was pleased." (Horsley, 1995, December 24).

A necessary step in translation is the development of teacher-friendly models for learning and implementing science-based practice. Of course this refers to the how-to manuals for guiding implementation and also to materials and media that expand, explain, and show the necessary examples and lessons learned. Other examples include the fact that media such as *Between the Lions* can be viewed directly on national television or more systematically in school via DVDs or videos making it readily accessible and usable by teachers. Two additional examples include PALS software tools that increase usability and ease of implementation. These are the CWPT-LMS and the BR-CWPT teacher support software.

The ClassWide Peer Tutoring-Learning Management System

A learning management system is a software or web application used to plan, implement, and assess a complex learning process, such as CWPT. The CWPT-LMS provides the classroom teacher with a way to create and deliver content using PALS activities, monitor individual and group participation, assess student performance, and implement adaptations to increase performance (Greenwood et al., 2004).

Setting up a R-CWPT program using the CWPT-LMS software begins by entering a student roster and identifying the subject matter to be taught (e.g., reading, spelling). Given this information, a database is created that anticipates daily data entry reflecting points earned by individual children and weekly accuracy/fluency progress information (pre- and post-peer tutoring). These data are used by an expert system to diagnosis individual and group problems and to recommend solutions to try in the next week of tutoring. Planning for a new week of tutoring includes assigning partners (dyads and one triad given an odd number of students) and partners to teams. The software allows the teacher to select either a competing or cooperating team format and designate tutoring pairs in several ways, including 1) ability matching using data available in the CWPT-LMS, 2) teacher designation, or 3) at random. The program also provides tools for removing, backing up, or transmitting data online to researchers and for restoring previously deleted data. For example, data from a previous year or other teachers' programs can be restored from a diskette on which the data has been saved or backed up and then reanalyzed.

The software's charting tools let the teacher monitor individual student and class progress in the curriculum. Charts are automatically available for displaying trends in the class average, in individual students' progress, and in all students' pre- and post-CWPT progress within each week. A fourth chart is diagnostic with respect to student outcomes and implementation concerns. Further support is provided by an expert system that renders specific suggestions for altering the next week's program as well as explaining the reasons for doing so based on available student data. Provided in easy-to-read text, teachers can reflect on the strategies needed in the next week to improve class and individual progress. The CWPT-LMS advisor contains more than 150 separate messages referenced to specific outcome patterns (Greenwood, Finney et al., 1993; Greenwood, Terry, Arreaga-Mayer, & Finney, 1992). The CWPT-LMS Resource CD contains interactive video clips, photos, an online manual, interactive how-to lessons, and other CWPT materials providing teachers concrete examples of R-CWPT.

The Beginning Reading Peer-Tutoring Teacher Support Software

This software expedites teachers' planning and implementation through four programs: Flashcard Generator, Assessment Generator, Tutoring Templates Catalog Generator, and Cut-and-Paste Tool (see Figures 5.3, 5.4, and 5.5). The Flashcard Generator allows the teacher to create/generate both picture or word flashcards and/or a combination of the two. It generates three distinct types of flashcards:

1. A module-based flashcard with pictures and correct responses on the backside of the flashcard for each individual reading skill module

2. A standard basic learning flashcard that includes number words/numerals/ counting dots, color words/colors, shapes (geometric)/shape words,

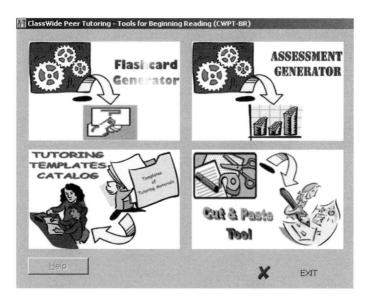

Figure 5.3. Beginning Reading ClassWide Peer Tutoring teacher support software user interface illustrating its four tool sets: Flashcard Generator, Assessment Generator, Tutoring Templates Catalog, and Cut-and-Paste Tool.

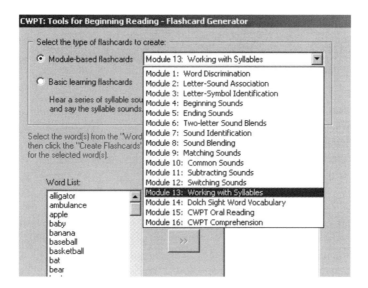

Figure 5.4. Beginning Reading ClassWide Peer Tutoring Flashcard Generator's tools for selecting module-based flashcard.

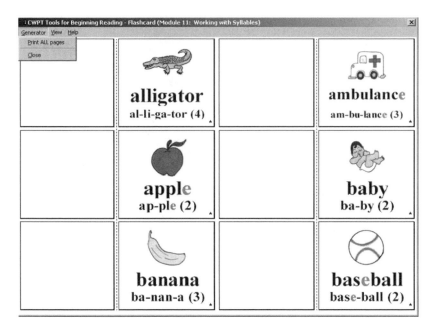

Figure 5.5. Beginning Reading ClassWide Peer Tutoring Flashcard Generator's print-ready peer-tutoring flashcard materials for Module 11: Working with Syllables.

punctuation marks/words, directional arrows/words, instructional words, the days of the week, the Dolch Sight Word list, and alphabet letters (upper case/lower case/and the combination of each)

3. Pictures and words for the most common kindergarten picture/word list

The Flashcard Generator also allows the teacher to customize by creating combinations of various module flashcards and author flashcards specific to the content/skills they wish to teach.

The Assessment Generator has two specific functions. The first is to provide two assessment forms that can only be printed off for use for individual student assessments at the beginning, middle (optional), and end of the year to document student acquisition and mastery progress. One of the two tests is the Student Global Assessment, and it provides measurement of all items in the Basic Learning Flashcard modules. The second test probes performance on the Dolch Sight Word list. These two assessments may be used multiple times with all students.

The Assessment Generator also allows a teacher to create CBM assessments specific to the content being taught. This assessment links back to any and all of the basic pictures and visuals in the Flashcard Generator, allowing teachers to create and utilize other specific content.

The Tutoring Templates Catalog Generator allows teachers access to all of the forms and materials needed to implement BR-CWPT, including the tutoring placemat, help card, comprehension prompt card, smiley-face point sheet, point sheets, tutoring worksheets, test scores chart, and oral reading/comprehension assessment form. These forms are available for printing only and cannot be modified. The Cut-and-Paste Tool allows the user to import words and word lists from other computer sources and use them in the program.

RESEARCH

The current state of knowledge regarding how to successfully teach reading has been informed to date by three distinct research foci: 1) The skills and precursors of reading and learning to read, 2) experimental studies that identify measurably superior instructional interventions when used by classroom teachers, and 3) implementation research regarding the use of effective instructional interventions by teachers in local schools. Clearly, continued research in each of these areas is needed and, based on new findings, instructional practices in local schools should change accordingly to account for our improving knowledge of effective practice. In particular, there is a need for research on reading comprehension including the skills, their measurement, and effective intervention components.

In our view, however, implementation research is in greatest need because the least is known regarding the extent to which effective intervention practices, such as reading PALS, are influenced, positively or negatively, by local innovations, drift in fidelity of implementation, and by natural differences in schooling contexts. For example, if local schools decide to implement PALS, what factors (e.g., training, administrative support, individual teacher differences) affect the time to reach full implementation in that year? What factors affect the ability to maintain full implementation for longer than just one school year? We have only scratched the surface of implementation questions such as these.

CONCLUSION

In this chapter, we considered three questions within the context of primary-level instruction and the Three-Tier Model of Reading Intervention: Can we reduce the prevalence of struggling and failing readers? What instructional strategies might be successfully used with all students to affect this problem? What factors might be successfully used to achieve widescale, systematic use of these instructional strategies? An increasing number of studies provide strong evidence that the number of struggling and failing readers can be reduced by making sure that preventive reading instruction (explicit and intensive) is implemented in all schools. In the case of CWPT, a PALS strategy, measurably superior prevention effects were extended from the first 4 years of elementary school to middle school to high

Table 5.1.   Methodologically rigorous evidence (randomized trials) supporting the effectiveness of ClassWide Peer Tutoring

Citation	Description	Indicator	Effect size
Greenwood, Delquadri, & Hall (1989)	Prospective, longitudinal randomized trial, nine schools, Grade 1 through Grade 4 (n = 416)	Reaching achievement Language achievement Arithmetic achievement Academic engagement	0.57 0.60 0.37 1.41
Greenwood (1991a; based on a randomly selected subsample of students in each classroom)	Multiyear behavior trajectories, Grade 1 though Grade 3 (n = 115)	Academic engagement Task manager Inappropriate behavior	0.63 0.61 0.83
Greenwood, Terry, Utley et al. (1993)	Follow-up at Grade 7 (n = 303)	Reading achievement Language achievement Arithmetic achievement Social studies achievement Science achievement Reduction in special education services Less restrictive services	0.39 0.35 0.57 0.39 0.48 0.54* 0.73*
Greenwood & Dalquadri (1995)	Follow-up at Grade 12 (n = 231)	Reduction in school dropouts	0.66*

Key: n = number of students.

Note: These four peer-reviewed publications report the longitudinal achievement, behavior, and lifestyle changes of a single ClassWide Peer Tutoring trial.

All effect sizes are Cohen's.

*Effect size calculated for Chi-square.

school (see Table 5.1). Thus, prevention is possible, and evidence shows that using a preventive reading approach in the design of primary-level reading instruction will reduce the prevalence of students with reading problems who are in need of secondary- and tertiary-level instruction.

Primary-level strategies reviewed in this chapter that qualify as preventive reading strategies include using a science-based reading curriculum for explicitness with PALS activities for intensity and educational media such as *Between the Lions* for both explicitness and intensity. In addition, both PALS and *Between the Lions* increase sources of social–emotional support for children at risk for learning to read. PALS provide a rich source of positive peer interaction including prompting, feedback, correction, and positive reinforcement. Programs such as *Between the Lions* provide interesting and attention-provoking listening and viewing experiences in which the material has been well scaffolded; such that skills build in small steps; with generalization to learning the next skills. These are effective strategies that can be used to prevent reading problems.

Research studies reporting effective reading instruction are an essential but insufficient solution to the problem of struggling and failing readers. Effective strategies must be translated for use by classroom teachers in the form of models, materials, media, and software that lead to classroom implementation (Greenwood, Delquadri, & Bulgren, 1993). Based on the ideas of Carnine (1997) and Elmore (1996), we reviewed attributes of interventions and local school organizations that tend to promote or detract from utilization (see Figure 5.1). These attributes included the primary reading curriculum, policies shaping the reading program, teacher and student body characteristics, incentives, and administrative and IT technical support. When correctly configured to support implementation, these qualities provide strong contexts in support of large-scale, high-quality, sustainable implementation. These factors are thought to influence adoption and use as well as the annual rate of uptake of effective practice. High-quality research demonstrating the effects of these components on scalability, however, still needs to be completed. This is very good news, however, because forms of effective preventive reading instruction and their widescale implementation are increasingly achievable by teachers in local schools. And, where students are not responsive to Tier 1 instruction, additional procedures in the form of Tier 2 and Tier 3 intervention are available, as noted in the other chapters in this volume.

REFERENCES

Al Otaiba, S., & Fuchs, D. (2002). Characteristics of children who are unresponsive to early literacy instruction. *Remedial and Special Education, 23,* 300–316.

Allington, R.L. (2001). *What really matters for struggling readers: Designing research-based programs.* New York: Addison-Wesley.

American Federation of Teachers. (1998). *Building on the best, learning from what works: Seven promising reading and language arts programs.* Washington, DC: Author.

Annenberg School for Communication of the University of Pennsylvania. (2001). *NEWS: Deborah Linebarger to assess effectiveness of American Indian Literacy Initiative in New Mexico.* Retrieved August 8, 2006, from http://www.asc.upenn.edu/news/newsDetail.asp?id=111&newstype=main

Arreaga-Mayer, C. (1998). Language sensitive peer-mediated instruction for culturally and linguistically diverse learners in the intermediate elementary grades. In R.M. Gersten & R.T. Jimenez (Eds.), *Promoting learning for culturally and linguistically diverse students* (pp. 73–90). Belmont, CA: Wadsworth Publishing.

Atwater, J.B., Carta, J.J., Schwartz, I.S., & McConnell, S.R. (1993). Blending developmentally appropriate practice and early childhood special education: Redefining best practice to meet the needs of all children. In B.L. Mallory & R.S. New (Eds.), *Diversity and developmentally appropriate practices: Challenges for early childhood education* (pp. 185–201). New York: Teachers College Press.

Block, C.C., Gambrell, L.B., & Presley, M. (2002). *Improving comprehension instruction: Rethinking research, theory, and classroom practice.* San Francisco: Jossey-Bass.

Brooks-Gunn, J., Currie, J., & Besharov, D.J. (2000). *Early childhood intervention programs: What are the costs and benefits?* (Congressional Research Briefing Summary). Washington, DC: Department of Health and Human Services.

Carnine, D. (1997). Bridging the research-to-practice gap. *Exceptional Children, 63*(4), 513–521.

Cohen, J. (1988). *Statistical power analysis for the behavioral sciences* (2nd ed.). Mahwah, NJ: Lawrence Erlbaum Associates.

Cohen, J.S. (2003, December 20, 2003). *Poor kids get least qualified teachers: Illinois' standards too lax, critics say.* Chicago Tribune, pp. 1, 22.

Delquadri, J.C. (1978). *An analysis of the generalization effects of four tutoring procedures on oral reading responses of eight learning disability children.* Unpublished doctoral dissertation, University of Kansas, Lawrence.

Dugan, E.D.K., Leonard, B., Watkins, N., Rheinberger, A., & Stackhaus, J. (1995). Effects of cooperative learning groups during social studies for students with autism and fourth-grade peers. *Journal of Applied Behavior Analysis, 28,* 175–188.

Elmore, R.F. (1996). Getting to scale with good educational practice. *Harvard Educational Review, 66*(1), 1–26.

Embry, D.D. (2004). Community-based prevention using simple, low-cost, evidence-based kernals and behavioral vaccines. *Journal of Community Psychology, 32*(5), 575–592.

Ferguson, D., Kozleski, E., & Smith, A. (2003). Transforming general and special education in urban schools. In F.E. Obiakor, C.A. Utley, & A.F. Rotatori (Eds.), *Effective education for learners with exceptionalities* (Vol. 15, pp. 43–74). New York: JAI Press.

Fletcher, J.M., & Lyon, G.R. (1998). Reading: A research-based approach. In W.M. Evers (Ed.), *What's gone wrong in America's classrooms.* (pp. 49–90). Palo Alto, CA: Board of Trustees of the Leland Stanford Junior University, Hoover Institution Press.

Fox, L., & Little, N. (2001). Starting early: School-wide behavior support in a community preschool. *Journal of Positive Behavioral Support, 3,* 251–254.

Fuchs, D., Fuchs, L., & Burish, P. (2000). Peer-assisted learning strategies: An evidence-based practice to promote reading achievement. *Learning Disabilities Research & Practice, 15*(2), 85–91.

Fuchs, D., Fuchs, L.S., Mathes, P.G., & Simmons, D.C. (1997). Peer-assisted learning strategies: Making classrooms more responsive to diversity. *American Educational Research Journal, 34,* 174–206.

Fuchs, D., Fuchs, L.S., Thompson, A., Svenson, E., Yen, L., Al Otaiba, S., et al. (2001). Peer-assisted learning strategies: Extensions downward into kindergarten/first grade and upward into high school. *Remedial and Special Education, 22*(1), 15–21.

Fuchs, L.S., Fuchs, D., Phillips, N.B., Hamlett, C.L., & Karns, K. (1995). Acquisition and transfer effects of classwide peer-assisted learning strategies in mathematics for students with varying learning histories. *School Psychology Review, 24*(4), 604–620.

Greenwood, C.R. (1991a). Longitudinal analysis of time engagement and academic achievement in at-risk and non-risk students. *Exceptional Children, 57,* 521–535.

Greenwood, C.R. (1991b). ClassWide Peer Tutoring: Longitudinal effects on the reading language and mathematics achievement of at-risk students. *Journal of Reading, Writing, and Learning Disabilities International, 7,* 105–124.

Greenwood, C.R. (1996). Research on the practices and behavior of effective teachers at the Juniper Gardens Children's Project: Implications for the education of diverse learners. In D. Speece & B.K. Keogh (Eds.), *Research on classroom ecologies: Implications for inclusion of children with learning disabilities* (pp. 39–67). Mahwah, NJ: Lawrence Erlbaum Associates.

Greenwood, C.R., & Abbott, M. (2001). The research to practice gap in special education. *Teacher Education and Special Education, 24*(4), 276–289.

Greenwood, C.R., Arreaga-Mayer, C., Utley, C.A., Gavin, K., & Terry, B.J. (2001). Class-Wide Peer Tutoring Learning Management System: Applications with elementary-level English language learners. *Remedial and Special Education, 22*(1), 34–47.

Greenwood, C.R., & Delquadri, J. (1995). ClassWide Peer Tutoring and the prevention of school failure. *Preventing School Failure, 39*(4), 21–25.

Greenwood, C.R., Delquadri, J., & Bulgren, J. (1993). Current challenges to behavioral technology in the reform of schooling: Large-scale high-quality implementation and sustained use of effective educational practices. *Education and Treatment of Children, 16,* 401–440.

Greenwood, C.R., Delquadri, J., & Carta, J.J. (1997). *Together we can!: ClassWide Peer Tutoring for basic academic skills.* Longmont, CO: Sopris West.

Greenwood, C.R., Delquadri, J., & Hall, R.V. (1989). Longitudinal effects of ClassWide Peer Tutoring. *Journal of Educational Psychology, 81,* 371–383.

Greenwood, C.R., Finney, R., Terry, B., Arreaga-Mayer, C., Carta, J.J., Delquadri, J., et al. (1993). Monitoring, improving, and maintaining quality implementation of the Class-Wide Peer Tutoring program using behavioral and computer technology. *Education and Treatment of Children, 16,* 19–47.

Greenwood, C.R., & Hops, H. (1981). Group contingencies and peer behavior change. In P. Strain (Ed.), *The utilization of classroom peers as behavior change agents* (pp. 189–259). New York: Plenum.

Greenwood, C.R., & Hou, S. (2001). *The ClassWide Peer Tutoring Learning Management System (CWPT-LMS): Manual for Teachers.* Kansas City: Juniper Gardens Children's Project, University of Kansas.

Greenwood, C.R., Reynolds, S., Abbott, M., & Tapia, Y. (2004). *Together we can: Class-Wide Peer Tutoring Learning Management System (CWPT-LMS).* Kansas City, KS: Juniper Gardens Children's Project, University of Kansas.

Greenwood, C.R., & Maheady, L. (2001). Are future teachers' aware of the gap between research and practice and what should they know? *Teacher Education and Special Education, 24*(4), 333–347.

Greenwood, C.R., Maheady, L., & Delquadri, J. (2002). ClassWide Peer Tutoring. In M.R. Shinn, H.M. Walker, & G. Stoner (Eds.), *Interventions for achievement and behavior problems* (2nd ed., pp. 611–649). Washington, DC: National Association for School Psychologists (NASP).

Greenwood, C.R., Terry, B., Arreaga-Mayer, C., & Finney, R. (1992). The ClassWide Peer Tutoring Program: Implementation factors moderating students' achievement. *Journal of Applied Behavior Analysis, 25,* 101–116.

Greenwood, C.R., Terry, B., Marquis, J., & Walker, D. (1994). Confirming a performance-based instructional model. *School Psychology Review, 23,* 625–668.

Greenwood, C.R., Terry, B., Utley, C.A., Montagna, D., & Walker, D. (1993). Achievement placement and services: Middle school benefits of ClassWide Peer Tutoring used at the elementary school. *School Psychology Review, 22*(3), 497–516.

Henke, R.R., Chen, X., & Goldman, G. (1999). What happens in classrooms? Instructional practices in elementary and secondary schools: 1994–95. *Education Statistics Quarterly, 1*(2). Retrieved August 8, 2006, from http://nces.ed.gov/programs/quarterly/vol_1/1_2/2-esq12-a.asp

Horsley, L. (1995, December 24). Two heads are better than one. *Kansas City Star*, pp. B1, B3.

Hresko, W.P., Hammill, D.P., Reid, D.K. (2001). *Test of Early Reading Ability–TERA3* (3rd ed.). Upper Saddle River, NJ: Pearson Education.

Kamps, D., Arreaga-Mayer, C., Veerkamp, M.B., Utley, C.A., & Greenwood, C.R. (2004). *Multi-content ClassWide Peer Tutoring and self-management interventions: Research improving teaching practice and literacy outcomes for middle school students with disabilities in urban poverty and suburban schools.* (Final Report to OSEP, H324D00052). Kansas City, KS: Juniper Gardens Children's Project, University of Kansas.

Kamps, D., Leonard, B., Potucek, J., & Garrison-Harrell. L. (1995). Cooperative learning groups in reading: An integration strategy for students with autism and general classroom peers. *Behavior Disorders, 21*(1), 89–109.

Kamps, D.M., Barbetta, P.M., Leonard, B.R., & Delquadri, J. (1994). Classwide peer tutoring: An integration strategy to improve and promote peer interactions among students with autism and general education peers. *Journal of Applied Behavior Analysis, 27*(1), 49–61.

Karoly, L.A., Greenwood, P.W., Everingham, S.S., Hoube, J., Kilburn, M.R., Peters, S., et al. (1998). *Investing in our children: What we know and don't know about costs and benefits of early childhood interventions.* Santa Monica, CA: RAND.

Klingner, J.K., Ahwee, S., Pilonieta, P., & Menendez, R. (2003). Barriers and facilitators in scaling up research-based practice. *Exceptional Children, 69*(4), 411–429.

Linebarger, D. (2000, June). *Summative evaluation of Between the Lions.* Kansas City: University of Kansas: Unpublished report prepared for the WGBH Educational Foundation.

Linebarger, D., Kosanic, A.Z., Greenwood, C.R., & Doku, N.S. (2003). Effects of viewing the television program "Between the Lions" on the emergent literacy skills of young children. *Journal of Educational Psychology, 96*(2), 297–308.

Locke, W.R., & Fuchs, L.S. (1995). Effects of peer-mediated reading instruction on the on-task and social interaction of children with behavior disorders. *Journal of Emotional and Behavioral Disorders, 3,* 92–99.

Marquis, J.G., Horner, R.H., Carr, E.G., Turnbull, A.P., Thompson, M., Beherns, G.A., et al. (2000). A meta-analysis of positive behavior support. In R. Gersten, E. Schiller, & S. Vaughn (Eds.), *Contemporary special education research: Syntheses of the knowledge base on critical instructional issues* (pp. 137–178). Mahwah, NJ: Lawrence Erlbaum Associates.

Mathes, P., Fuchs, D., Fuchs, L.S., Henley, A.M., & Sanders, A. (1994). Increasing strategic reading practice with Peabody ClassWide Peer Tutoring. *Learning Disabilities Research and Practice, 8*(4), 233–243.

Mathes, P.G., Torgesen, J.K., Allen, S.H., & Howard Allor, J.K. (2002). *First grade PALS (Peer-Assisted Literacy Strategies).* Longmont, CO: Sopris West.

Mathes, P.G., Torgesen, J.K., Menchetti, J.C., Santi, K., Nicholas, K., & Robinson, C.A. (2003). Comparison of teacher-directed versus peer-assisted instruction to struggling first-grade readers. *Elementary School Journal, 103,* 459–479.

Mielke, K. (1994). Sesame Street and children in poverty. *Media Studies Journal, 8,* 125–134.

Moats, L. (1999). *Teaching reading is rocket science: What expert teachers of reading should know and be able to do.* Washington, DC: American Federation of Teachers.

National Assessment of Educational Progress. (2002). *12th grade report card: Math and reading, 2003.* Retrieved August 1, 2006, from www.nces.ed.gov/nationsreportcard/reading/results

National Reading Panel. (2000). *Teaching children to read: An evidence-based assessment of the scientific research literature on reading and its implications for reading instruction.* Washington, DC: National Institute of Child Health and Human Development.

No Child Left Behind Act of 2001, PL 107-110, 115 Stat. 1425, 20 U.S.C. §§ 6301 *et seq.*

Prince, D.L., Grace, C., Linebarger, D.L., Atkinson, R., & Huffman, J.D. (2002). *Between the Lions Mississippi literary initiative: A final report to Mississippi Educational Television.* Report prepared for Mississippi Educational Television and WGBH Educational Foundation. Starkville, MS: The Early Childhood Institute, Mississippi State University.

Rogers, E. (2003). *Diffusion of innovations* (5th ed.). New York: The Free Press.

Rohrbeck, C.A., Ginsberg-Block, M.D., Fantuzzo, J.W., & Miller, T.R. (2003). Peer-assisted learning interventions with elementary school students: A meta-analytic review. *Journal of Educational Psychology, 95*(2), 240–257.

Ryan, B., & Gross, N. (1943). The diffusion of hybrid seed corn in two Iowa communities. *Rural Sociology, 8,* 15–24.

Simmons, D.C., Fuchs, D., Fuchs, L.S., Hodge, J.P., & Mathes, P.G. (1994). Importance of instructional complexity and role reciprocity to ClassWide Peer Tutoring. *Learning Disabilities Research and Practice, 4,* 203–212.

Snow, C.E., Burns, M.S., & Griffin, P. (1998). *Preventing reading difficulties in young children.* Washington, DC: National Academies Press.

Statistical Abstracts. (2000). Washington, DC: Government Publishing Office.

Stevenson, H.W., & Newman, R.S. (1986). Long-term prediction of achievement and attitudes in mathematics and reading. *Child Development, 57,* 646–659.

Strickland, D.S., & Rath, L.K. (2000, August). *Between the Lions: Public television promotes early literacy. Reading Online, 4.* Retrieved August 1, 2006, from http://www.reading online.org/articles/art_index.asp?HREF=/articles/strickland/index.html

Terry, B., & Greenwood, C.R. (2004). *ClassWide Peer Tutoring infused into the beginning reading curriculum of young children.* Kansas City: Juniper Gardens Children's Project, University of Kansas.

Torgesen, J. (1998). Catch them before they fall: Identification and assessment to prevent reading failure in young children. *American Educator, 22,* 32–39.

Torgesen, J.K. (2002). The prevention of reading difficulties. *Journal of School Psychology, 40,* 7–26.

Veerkamp, M.B. (2001). *The effects of ClassWide Peer Tutoring on the reading achievement of urban middle school students.* Unpublished doctoral dissertation, University of Kansas, Lawrence.

Walker, H.M., & Shinn, M.R. (2002). Structuring school-based interventions to achieve intregrated primary, secondary, and tertiary prevention goals for safe and effective schools. In S.R. Shinn, H.M. Walker, & G. Stoner (Eds.), *Academic and behavioral interventions II: Preventive and remedial approaches.* Washington, DC: National Association of School Psychologists.

Whitehurst, G.J., & Lonigan, C.J. (1998). Child development and emergent literacy. *Child Development, 69,* 848–872.

Whitehurst, G.J., & Lonigan, C.J. (2001). Emergent literacy: Development from prereaders to readers. In S.B. Neuman & D.K. Dickinson (Eds.), *Handbook of early literacy research* (pp. 11–29). New York: The Guilford Press.

Secondary Intervention

6

An Implementation of a Tiered Intervention Model

Reading Outcomes and Neural Correlates

Carolyn A. Denton, Jack M. Fletcher, Panagiotis G. Simos,
Andrew C. Papanicolaou, and Jason L. Anthony

T his chapter illustrates one implementation of a three-tier approach to reading intervention previously described in two research reports. Mathes and colleagues (2005) conducted a study of Tier 1 and Tier 2 intervention provided to struggling first-grade readers in six schools. During the following school year, Denton, Fletcher, Anthony, and Francis (2006) studied the effectiveness of a Tier 3 intervention for some of the students who had not responded adequately to instruction and intervention delivered in Tiers 1 and 2 of the Mathes and colleagues study. This program of research included an investigation of neural correlates to the reading progress of students participating in the three tiers of instruction (Simos, Fletcher, Foorman et al., 2002; Simos, Fletcher, Sarkani, Billingsley, Francis et al., in press; Simos, Fletcher, Sarkani, Billingsley, Denton et al., in press).

First, we will describe each of the intervention studies. Then we will provide detailed descriptions of students who participated in the Tier 3 intervention study, including contrasts between students who responded adequately and inadequately to the intensive intervention provided in this study. Finally, we will illustrate changes in brain function for participants who became adequate readers and those who did not respond well to the instruction in each tier.

The program of research described in this chapter was supported by a grant from the National Science Foundation, National Institute of Child Health and Human Development, and the U.S. Department of Education under the Interagency Educational Research Initiative, NSF 9979968.

DESCRIPTION OF THE INTERVENTION RESEARCH

Tiers 1 and 2

The study of Tier 1 and Tier 2 instruction took place in six schools in a large urban center (Mathes et al., 2005). The school district serves predominantly economically disadvantaged, minority students, but these schools did not meet Title 1 criteria. The schools were selected because of evidence of strong core reading programs. The researchers screened all students in the participating schools at the end of kindergarten or beginning of first grade to identify students who were at risk for reading difficulties because of severe difficulties in phonological awareness, letter–sound correspondence, and word reading—strong predictors of ease of reading acquisition (see Scarborough, 1998). Students who were identified as at risk were then randomly assigned to receive one of three conditions: 1) Tier 1 classroom instruction only (*number of students [n]* = 92), 2) Tier 1 plus Tier 2 intervention consisting of Proactive Beginning Reading Instruction (Mathes, Torgesen, Menchetti, Wahl, & Grek, 1999; *n* = 83), a highly prescriptive reading program based on a direct instruction model, or 3) Tier 1 plus Tier 2 intervention consisting of Responsive Reading Instruction (Denton & Hocker, 2006; *n* = 80), a model adapted from the guided reading model in which teachers plan lessons in response to student needs indicated through ongoing assessment. All three of these conditions were present in each of the six participating schools. The study was conducted with two cohorts of first graders over 2 school years (referred to as cohorts 1 and 2 in the following).

Tier 1 Intervention

Thirty first-grade teachers delivered the Tier 1 classroom reading instruction in the participating schools over the 2 years of the study. Sixteen of these teachers participated in both years of the study. All of the teachers were receiving ongoing professional development in reading through district and state reading initiatives that emphasized critical elements of reading instruction in the primary grades. To further support the quality of classroom reading instruction, the researchers provided the participating classroom teachers with student assessment data—both the comprehensive screening data and ongoing progress monitoring graphs of growth in oral reading fluency for all participating students. In addition, the researchers provided classroom teachers with 1 day of professional development during each year of the project that focused on the use of assessment data to differentiate instruction for struggling readers and on the use of peer-tutoring strategies (Mathes, Torgesen, Allen, & Allor, 2001).

Four of the participating schools had adopted the same basal reading program, whereas the other two schools had selected a different basal program; however, there was wide variation in the levels of teachers' implementations of the two programs. Some teachers followed the basal programs closely, some did not use the basal series at all, and many used parts of the adopted program along with other materials. Both of the adopted programs included instruction in the critical areas of phonemic awareness (PA), phonics, fluency, vocabulary, and comprehension. Observations conducted during classroom reading instruction indicated that teachers were highly likely to 1) encourage students to express their ideas verbally, 2) provide instruction in the meanings of vocabulary words, and 3) teach the strategy of identifying words by sounding them out. The overwhelming majority of teachers provided instruction in letter–sound correspondences. Teachers in schools that had adopted Basal 1 were somewhat more likely to provide direct instruction in sound–symbol patterns, word structure, or spelling rules and to directly teach comprehension strategies than teachers using Basal 2.

At-risk students who were assigned to the Tier 1-only condition also received whatever services their schools typically provided to struggling readers. Only two of the six schools, however, provided any supplemental small-group intervention to the first graders identified as at risk. This school-provided intervention was of relatively low intensity (delivered in groups of four to eight students) and did not typically include explicit, systematic instruction.

Tier 2 Intervention

At-risk students assigned to the Tier 2 intervention conditions received the Tier 1 instruction described above in addition to daily 40-minute small-group intervention for about 30 weeks in first grade. In both Tier 2 conditions, instruction was provided in groups of three students to one teacher by certified teachers who were trained and supervised by the researchers. Three teachers provided Proactive Beginning Reading Instruction and three provided Responsive Reading Instruction. The same six teachers participated during both years of the study. Before providing intervention in the study, the intervention teachers participated in about 42 hours of professional development delivered by the developers of their respective programs. At the beginning of the second year of the study, an additional 12 hours of professional development was provided. Across both years of the study, intervention teachers also participated in monthly half-day in-service meetings and received frequent onsite coaching from the intervention developers.

Proactive Beginning Reading Instruction incorporates a highly structured direct instruction approach based on a detailed scope and sequence, with students applying phonics skills in fully decodable text. In the Proactive Beginning Reading Instruction condition in this study, teachers delivered explicit instruction in PA, phonics, fluency, and comprehension following scripted lesson plans. The format of lesson delivery consisted of teacher modeling, followed by guided practice in which students responded in unison, and ending with independent practice as students took individual turns performing each skill.

In the Responsive Reading condition, teachers provided explicit instruction in PA, phonics, and word reading based on a recommended sequence of introduction of phonic elements and the need for instruction in these elements evidenced by student assessments. In this condition, students read text that was leveled for difficulty but not phonetically decodable. Students in the Responsive Reading Instruction group spent relatively less time practicing skills in isolation and more time reading and writing connected text than those in the Proactive Beginning Reading Instruction group. Responsive Reading teachers followed a lesson cycle consisting of 1) fluency building, 2) assessment, 3) explicit PA and phonics instruction, 4) supported reading of instructional-level text, and 5) supported writing of connected text. Teachers selected activities from a "menu" of options based on the observed needs of their students for each part of the lesson. Although students in the Responsive Reading group read text leveled for difficulty according to the Fountas and Pinnell (1999) system rather than reading decodable text, they were explicitly taught to use sound–symbol correspondences and a "sounding-out" strategy to read and spell unknown words. The use of context and pictures for word identification was discouraged, but the use of context to self-monitor and self-correct errors was explicitly taught. Intervention teachers focused on comprehension before reading by preteaching difficult vocabulary words, engaging students in prediction of text content, and encouraging students to link the book's subject matter to prior knowledge. As students read, teachers provided feedback, scaffolding, and modeling to assist students in applying the skills they had learned. During and after reading, teachers engaged students in discussion of the text meaning and asked students to retell or summarize portions of the text. To promote fluency, students engaged in partner reading and repeated reading of instructional-level text with modeling and feedback provided by the teacher.

Intervention teachers were observed every 8 weeks to verify their fidelity of implementation of each intervention program and their overall quality of instruction. Using a 3-point rating scale, observers rated each activity or lesson component for appropriate pacing, implementation of prescribed procedures, error correction with appropriate scaffolding, and student engagement and attentiveness. Teachers also received global ratings of readiness of instructional materials, appropriate student seating arrangement, and instructor warmth and enthusiasm. On average, both sets of intervention teachers conducted their respective interventions with high levels of fidelity.

Results of Tier 1 and Tier 2 Intervention

At the end of first grade, students in the Proactive Beginning Reading Instruction and Responsive Reading Instruction groups performed significantly better in phonological awareness, word reading, and oral reading fluency (Cohort 2) than those who received only Tier 1 intervention (Mathes et al., 2005). Results of the two small-group interventions differed significantly on only one outcome, the Word Attack subtest of the Woodcock-Johnson III Tests of Reading Achievement (WJ III: Woodcock, McGrew, & Mather, 2001). The Proactive Beginning Reading Instruction group performed significantly better on this measure of pseudo-word reading than the Responsive Reading Instruction group.

Mathes and colleagues (2005) reported rates of student response to Tier 1 and Tier 2 intervention using a cut point of performance below the 30th percentile on the WJ III Basic Reading Skills cluster (using grade-based norms) to denote inadequate response. Using these criteria, only 15 of the 92 students (16%) who received only Tier 1 instruction, 6 of the 83 students (7%) who received Tier 1 plus Tier 2 in the Responsive Reading Instruction intervention, and 1 of the 80 students (< 1%) who received Tier 1 plus Tier 2 in the Proactive Beginning Reading Instruction group were reading below the average range at the end of the intervention period. Another widely used benchmark for adequate response to instruction is an oral reading fluency rate of at least 40 words correct per minute (WCPM) at the end of Grade 1. Using this criterion, 43% of the Tier 1-only group, 33% of the students who received the Proactive Beginning Reading Instruction Tier 2 intervention, and 25% of the Responsive Reading Instruction Tier 2 group failed to meet the benchmark for adequate response.

Tier 3

Fourteen students who had demonstrated inadequate response to Tier 1 or Tier 1 plus Tier 2 intervention in the Mathes and colleagues (2005) study received a subsequent Tier 3 intervention in a study described in Denton and colleagues (2006). Students in the Tier 3 study received a 16-week intervention provided daily in groups of two students to one teacher. During the first 8-week period, students received a 2-hour intervention targeting PA and phonemic decoding based on the Phono-Graphix program (McGuiness, McGuiness, & McGuiness, 1996). This was followed by 8 weeks of a 1-hour intervention targeting reading fluency based on the Read Naturally program (Ihnot, Mastoff, Gavin, & Hendrickson, 2001).

The interventions were delivered by six trained teachers, four of whom had been Responsive Reading Instruction and Proactive Beginning Reading Instruction intervention teachers in the Mathes and colleagues (2005) study. Five of the six were certified teachers, and the sixth was a highly-qualified reading instructor who had extensive experience providing intervention in a clinical setting. All teachers received a full week of clinical training in Phono-Graphix from a certified trainer who was on the research team and a 2-day training in Read Naturally from the first author of this chapter, who was experienced in implementing Read Naturally in intervention settings and in training teachers in the intervention.

Of the students who had performed below the 30th percentile in WJ III Basic Reading Skills cluster at posttest in Mathes and colleagues (2005), only eight were available to participate in the Tier 3 study. Denton and colleagues (2006) added to the sample six students from the Tier 1 and 2 study on the basis of low oral reading fluency. All of these students had scores below the Basic Reading Skills cluster 30th percentile threshold at baseline of the Tier 3 study. Thirteen students with severe reading difficulties who had not received Tier 1 and 2 intervention in Mathes and colleagues (2005) also were included in the sample to increase the sample size and the power to detect program effects.

Tier 3 Intervention

During the first 8-week period of Tier 3, students received intervention for about 2 hours per day, 5 days per week, using the Phono-Graphix program (McGuiness et al., 1996). In this program, students are taught to read and spell using 140 letters and letter combinations that represent the sounds in English phonology. Early in the program, teachers focus on the alphabetic principle, basic letter–sound correspondences, and PA, and in the more advanced stages students learn to read and spell multisyllable words. The program includes extensive opportunities for practice using letter and word cards and application of skills in decodable text.

The 8-week Phono-Graphix intervention was followed with 8 weeks of the Read Naturally program (Ihnot et al., 2001), which students received for 1 hour each day of the week. Read Naturally, designed to promote oral reading fluency for students reading at grade levels 1–8, is based on a sequence of activities in which students engage in repeated reading of instructional-level expository passages with modeling and feedback and track their own fluency progress. Students follow a sequence of procedures with each passage until established criteria are met. These procedures include 1) timed readings, 2) graphing fluency rates, 3) practice with and without modeling provided by the teacher, an audio tape, compact disk, or computer application, and 4) brief comprehension activities. To "pass" a passage, the student must meet three criteria during a final oral reading: The student must meet his or her individualized fluency goal rate, have no more than three errors, and read with appropriate phrasing. Teachers in the Tier 3 study followed the standard Read Naturally procedures, but they also directly taught students to apply the decoding strategies they had learned in Phono-Graphix to read difficult words. This instruction was included in the Read Naturally intervention to encourage students to generalize the decoding skills they had applied in decodable text during the Phono-Graphix phase to nondecodable text at their instructional reading levels and to text they encountered in their regular classrooms.

Intervention Fidelity observations of teachers' implementations of the two Tier 3 interventions indicated uniformly high-level fidelity to the programs and high implementation quality. Observations indicated that teachers followed the programs closely, had their materials well-organized, had students seated appropriately, exhibited warmth and enthusiasm, monitored student performance, provided appropriate feedback, redirected off-task behavior, and communicated expectations to students clearly and explicitly.

Results of Tier 3 Intervention

As random assignment was not feasible, the Tier 3 study employed a multiple baseline design between groups and between interventions. The first group of students in the study (Group 1; n = 16) participated in the Phono-Graphix phase of the study for 8 weeks from October through December and the Read Naturally phase from January through March. The second group of students (Group 2; n = 11) began Phono-Graphix in January (with a no-treatment baseline phase from October through January) and received the Read Naturally intervention from March through May. The raw scores on all decoding, fluency, comprehension, and spelling outcomes at assessment Wave 1 (Phono-Graphix pretest for Group 1 and baseline for Group 2) were not significantly different between the two cohorts, and Group 1 and Group 2 did not differ significantly on preintervention assessments (i.e., Assessment Wave 1 for Group 1 and Wave 2 for Group 2). Thus, outcomes for the two groups were combined to evaluate the effects of the Phono-Graphix and Read Naturally phases of the intervention.

Participants demonstrated significant growth in decoding, fluency, and reading comprehension over the 8-week Phono-Graphix phase of intervention. Although the research design did not control for the effects of maturation, there is evidence that the improvement was the result of the intervention in that students in Group 2 had relatively small changes in scores for any measure during their no-intervention baseline phase, ranging from negligible for decoding to moderate for fluency skills. Effect sizes indicated that the Phono-Graphix intervention had large effects on decoding skills and moderate effects on reading comprehension. The effects of Phono-Graphix intervention on fluency and spelling were about the same as the baseline effects.

Following this intensive 8-week intervention with 8 weeks of reading fluency intervention using the Read Naturally program had significant effects, with moderate to large effect sizes, on the abilities of participants to fluently and accurately read words in lists and connected text. Effect sizes for decoding and comprehension associated with the Read Naturally phase were in the small to moderate range, consistent with the changes during the baseline phase for the Group 2 students. The combination of the Phono-Graphix and Read Naturally interventions was associated with a pattern of moderate to large effect sizes for the full 16-week intervention across all reading and spelling measures, consistently exceeding the changes in the no-intervention baseline phase for Group 2.

The response of individual students to Tier 3 intervention in this study was highly variable, with changes in WJ III Basic Reading Skills cluster scores across the 16-week intervention ranging from –6 to 26 standard score points. Denton and her colleagues examined the response of individual students from three subgroups: 1) those who had received Tier 1 intervention in Grade 1 but continued to have reading impairments (n = 9), 2) those who had received both Tier 1 and Tier 2 intervention in Grade 1 and continued to have impairments (n = 5), and 3) those who had not participated in the Mathes and colleagues' (2005) study but had been nominated by their current teachers as having serious reading difficulties (n = 13). Because of the very low pretest scores of many of the study participants, adequate response to Tier 3 intervention was defined as a gain of at least .5 standard deviations in WJ III Basic Reading Skills cluster scores over the 16-week intervention period rather than meeting the 30th percentile benchmark. Students in this study were more likely to respond well to Tier 3 intervention if they 1) had received both Tier 1 and Tier 2 intervention rather than Tier 1 only, 2) were in the first or second grade rather than third grade, and 3) were not currently served by special education.

INDIVIDUAL RESPONSE TO MULTIPLE TIERS OF INTERVENTION

As described above, fourteen students participated in both the Mathes and colleagues (2005) study of Tier 1 and Tier 2 intervention and the Denton and colleagues (2006) study of Tier 3 intervention. This section provides more detailed descriptions of these students and contrasts the characteristics of students who responded adequately with those who responded less adequately to Tier 3 intervention.

Participants

Table 6.1 contains demographic information for each participant along with the intervention tiers they received and their special education status. We did not in-

Table 6.1.   Intervention tiers received and student characteristics at Tier 3 pretest

Student	Tiers	Age	Gender	WASI Full-Scale IQ score	Special education
1	1, 3	9	M	86	Yes
2	1, 2, 3	8	M	80	No
3	1, 3	9	F	68	No
4	1, 3	9	F	79	No
5	1, 3	9	M	98	No
6	1, 3	8	F	78	No
7	1, 2, 3	8	F	76	No
8	1, 3	10	M	86	Yes
9	1, 3	10	M	88	Yes
10	1, 2, 3	8	M	102	No
11	1, 2, 3	10	F	95	Yes
12	1, 2, 3	10	M	64	Yes
13	1, 3	9	M	99	No
14	1, 3	9	F	87	Yes

Key: WASI = Wechsler Abbreviated Scales of Intelligence.

clude ethnicity in this table in order to protect the anonymity of the participants. The sample of 14 students had an average age of 9 years at the beginning of the Tier 3 study and was 36% white, 36% African American, 21% Hispanic, and 7% Asian. Eight participants were males and six were females. Parents of 13 of the 14 students reported the highest level of education of the participant's mothers. Of these 13 mothers, two had attended high school but not graduated, four were high school graduates but had no postsecondary education, and seven reported attending at least one course in a college or technical school after high school.

Full Scale IQ Scores

Table 6.1 also includes Full Scale IQ scores derived from the Vocabulary and Matrix Reasoning subtests of the Wechsler Abbreviated Scales of Intelligence (WASI; Wechsler, 1999). The WASI is designed so that the Full Scale IQ score can be derived from either two or four subtests. Both forms are linked to the WISC–III/WAIS–III normative sample. In this program of research, the two-subtest form, which yields only the Full Scale IQ score, was used to describe the sample. The reliabilities of the two-subtest form exceed .92 in the age range of the study, and the correlation of the two-subtest form composite IQ score with the WISC–III composite IQ score is .81. Table 6.1 indicates that participants in the Tier 3 study had Full Scale IQ scores that ranged from 64 to 102, with a mean of 85 (standard deviation [SD] 11.4).

Beginning of First Grade Phonemic Awareness and Rapid Naming Scores

At the beginning of Grade 1, students in the Mathes and colleagues (2005) study were administered multiple measures of PA, the results of which were combined into a single composite and reported on a scale derived from Item Response Models, that is, as a Theta score (Schatschneider, Francis, Foorman, Fletcher, & Mehta, 1999). The PA measures included the tasks of segmenting and blending phonemes and larger word parts as well as phoneme elision. The participants also completed an assessment of rapid automatized naming (RAN) of letters, in which students were required to rapidly identify a brief, repeated sequence of known letters in order to assess the speed with which they could access this information. As reflected in Table 6.2, PA Theta scores at the beginning of first grade for the students who ultimately received Tier 3 intervention ranged from –2.169 to 0.221. The mean PA Theta score for a group of typically developing first-grade readers in Mathes and colleagues (2005) was .017 (SD .567), with scores ranging from –2.48 to 1.4. Beginning of first-grade RAN scores for students in the Tier 3 study, reported in the number of letters correctly identified per minute, ranged from 13 to 66.67. The typically developing readers in Mathes and colleagues (2005) identified, on average, 68 letters per minute (SD 15; range 41–120).

Table 6.2.   Phonemic awareness Theta scores and rapid automatic naming of letters raw scores at Tier 1 or Tier 1+2 pretest

Student	PA Theta	RAN letters per minute
1	−0.845	49.00
2	−2.169	61.22
3	−1.327	50.36
4	−1.649	44.00
5	−0.162	66.67
6	−0.188	45.00
7	−1.856	38.00
8	−0.928	40.00
9	−0.783	31.00
10	−1.750	13.00
11	−1.237	55.56
12	−2.499	44.00
13	0.221	62.50
14	−1.299	40.91

Key: PA = phonemic awareness; RAN = rapid automatized naming of letters.

Measures

Students who received Tier 1 and/or Tier 2 intervention in the Mathes and colleagues (2005) study and Tier 3 intervention in the Denton and colleagues (in press) study received multiple assessments of reading and reading-related skills. In Tables 6.3 and 6.4, we report outcomes at the end of Tier 1 and Tier 2 intervention and at 1-year maintenance testing (for Cohort 1 only) for the WJ III Basic Skills cluster and Passage Comprehension subtests, as well as oral reading fluency scores and standard scores for the Sight Word Efficiency subtest of the Test of Word Reading Efficiency (TOWRE; Torgesen, Wagner, & Rashotte, 1999) at the end of Grade 1. For the Tier 3 study, we report outcomes for the same WJ III and TOWRE subtests and reading rate scores from the Gray Oral Reading Tests (GORT–4; Wiederholt & Bryant, 2001).

In the WJ III Word Attack subtest, students read nonwords; and in Letter–Word Identification, they name letters and read real words in lists. Passage Comprehension is measured through a cloze procedure, in which students read a sentence or brief passage in which certain words have been taken out and are required to produce the missing words or acceptable substitutions for them. The TOWRE Sight Word Efficiency subtest is an assessment of fluency in reading words presented in lists, and the GORT–4 is similar to an informal reading inventory, in that students' oral reading accuracy, fluency, and comprehension are measured on reading passages at varying levels of difficulty.

Table 6.3. Woodcock-Johnson Tests of Achievement-III standard scores at Tier 1 or Tier 1+2 posttest, at 1-year maintenance (for Cohort 1) and at three time points for Tier 3

| | Basic reading skills | | | | | Passage comprehension | | | | |
| | Tier 1 or Tier 1+2 | | Pretest | Tier 3 | | Tier 1 or Tier 1+2 | | Pretest | Tier 3 | |
Student	Posttest	Maintenance	Pretest	Posttest PG	Posttest RN	Posttest	Maintenance	Pretest	Posttest PG	Posttest RN
1	90	84	82	86	85	87	82	76	82	78
2	93c	a	89	99	98	87	a	79	91	92
3	95c	88	83	88	87	81	83	82	78	85
4	b	84	80	87	88	b	82	79	77	84
5	98c	92	84	93	90	94	89	88	84	90
6	89	a	88	100	99	84	a	83	91	99
7	88	a	82	94	96	86	a	80	85	87
8	69	78	73	83	85	71	76	77	84	79
9	66	69	68	73	74	60	61	62	68	65
10	95c	a	90	104	100	85	a	89	88	87
11	76	81	78	88	86	84	86	86	87	90
12	72	73	75	76	69	74	76	63	76	77
13	95c	91	93	98	97	92	92	91	95	97
14	87	82	85	87	87	86	88	88	83	83

Key: PG = Phono-Graphic phrase; RN = Read Naturally phrase.

[a]No 1-year maintenance data available because the student was repeating Grade 1 or beginning Grade 2.

[b]Tier 1 Woodcock-Johnson-III posttest data not available for the student.

[c]Level of response was determined using oral reading fluency and 1-year maintenance assessments.

117

Table 6.4. Oral reading fluency and word reading efficiency scores at Tier 1 or Tier 1+2 posttest and three time points for Tier 3

Student	ORF Tier 1 or Tier 1+2 Posttest	TOWRE Sight Word Efficiency Tier 1 or Tier 1+2 Posttest	TOWRE Pretest	TOWRE Tier 3 Posttest PG	TOWRE Tier 3 Posttest RN	GORT-4 Fluency Pretest	GORT-4 Fluency Tier 3 Posttest PG	GORT-4 Fluency Tier 3 Posttest RN
1	11	86	73	71	79	65	65	70
2	13	86	89	79	93	80	85	90
3	26	88	85	87	96	80	85	90
4	10	86	81	85	79	75	80	75
5	16	87	88	92	89	75	80	*
6	8	80	80	89	86	70	75	85
7	11	85	81	91	85	75	80	80
8	9	64	79	86	81	70	75	80
9	7	61	61	64	67	55	60	60
10	18	86	82	85	83	70	75	85
11	26	77	85	86	95	65	70	80
12	12	70	79	86	89	65	70	70
13	47	88	87	97	97	75	75	70
14	15	84	90	92	86	85	90	80

Key: ORF = oral reading fluency, reported in words correct per minute; TOWRE = Test of Word Reading Efficiency standard scores; GORT-4 = Gray Oral Reading Test-4 standard scores; PG = Phono-Graphic phrase; RN = Read Naturally phase.

*GORT-4 fluency data were not available for the student at posttest.

118

In addition, Tier 3 intervention teachers completed the Swanson, Nolan, and Pelham (SNAP–IV; see Swanson et al., 2004) rating scale for each of their students. The SNAP–IV scale is designed to assist in the assessment of attention–deficit/hyperactivity disorder (ADHD) and other behavior disorders, particularly oppositional defiant disorder, that are often present in students with ADHD. In order to meet criteria for identification of ADHD, at least six of nine established symptoms involving either Hyperactivity–Impulsivity or Inattention, or both, in the Diagnostic and Statistical Manual–IV (DSM–IV) must be endorsed. Although the results must be interpreted with caution because teacher ratings are not sufficient by themselves for clinical diagnoses of ADHD, they provide indications of the presence of attention and behavior difficulties in instructional situations. The results of this measure are provided in subsequent descriptions of students with adequate and inadequate response to intervention.

Response to Tier 1 or Tiers 1+2

As reflected in Table 6.1, Students 2, 7, 10, 11, and 12 received both Tiers 1 and 2 in the Mathes and colleagues (2005) study, whereas the other nine students received only Tier 1 classroom intervention. At the end of kindergarten or beginning of first grade, each of these students had been identified as having significant risk of reading difficulties, based on low performance on tests of phonological awareness, letter–sound correspondence, word reading, and text reading.

Tier 2 Intervention

All five of the Tier 2 students had received supplemental daily intervention using the Responsive Reading Instruction program (Denton & Hocker, 2006) described above. Students 11 and 12 were part of the first cohort of participants in the 2-year Tier 1+2 study, whereas Students 2, 7, and 10 were in the second cohort. Three intervention teachers provided the Responsive Reading intervention in the Mathes and colleagues (2005) study. All three of the Cohort 2 students had received the intervention from the same teacher, whereas Students 11 and 12 were each instructed by one of the other two participating Responsive Reading Intervention teachers.

Reading Outcomes

Table 6.3 includes age-based standard scores for the WJ III Basic Skills cluster and Passage Comprehension subtest at the end of the Tier 1+2 intervention year. For Cohort 1 students, we also have included scores for the administration of the WJ III 1 year later to illustrate level of maintenance of effects. Table 6.3 also contains outcomes on these measures at three points in the Tier 3 study, which will be discussed later in this chapter. We chose to include all WJ III outcomes in a single table to facilitate the examination of each student's progress over time. Similarly,

Table 6.4 provides oral reading fluency scores and TOWRE Sight Word Efficiency scores at the end of the Tier 1 and/or Tier 2 intervention year, along with scores for the same TOWRE subtest and for GORT–4 fluency at pretest, midpoint, and posttest for the Tier 3 study.

The WJ III Basic Skills cluster group mean for this group of poor responders at the end of the intervention year in Mathes and colleagues (2005) was 86 (SD 11). At the end of the intervention year, students in Cohort 1 of the Tier 1+2 study had a mean Basic Skills standard score of 83 (SD 12), and a mean score of 82 (SD 7) one year later, indicating that this group of students was making no progress in closing the gap with their typically performing peers. Similarly, the mean score for all 14 students in WJ III Passage Comprehension was low and remained stable for the Cohort 1 students at 1-year maintenance testing. Students who received one to two tiers of intervention demonstrated very low oral reading fluency at the end of first grade, with a mean score of 16 WCPM (SD 11). Only one student in the group was able to read more than 26 WCPM at the end of first grade. This lack of fluency was also reflected in standard scores for the TOWRE Sight Word Efficiency measure, which ranged from 61 to 88 with a mean of 81 (SD 9).

Mathes and colleagues (2005) used basic skills performance at or above the 30th percentile using grade-based standard scores as the criteria for adequate response to intervention. We are reporting age-based standard scores because several of the poor responders were retained in first grade during the year following intervention, a situation that would inflate the 1-year maintenance scores if grade-based norms were used. Five students had WJ III Basic Skills cluster age-based standard scores at or above the 30th percentile at the end of the intervention year, classifying them as "responders" to intervention using one common criteria for response. These students, however, had low fluency at the end of that year. Three of the five students were in Cohort 1 of the Mathes and colleagues study. One-year maintenance scores for these students indicated a substantial decline in WJ III Basic Skills, and none of the five students performed above the 30th percentile at baseline of the Tier 3 study.

Characteristics of Adequate and Inadequate Responders to Tier 3

As described above, Denton and colleagues (2006) established a benchmark for adequate response to Tier 3 intervention of a standard score gain in age-adjusted scores on the WJ III Basic Skills of at least .5 standard deviation, or 8 standard score points. Using this criterion, seven of the students described in this section had adequate response and seven did not. We will contrast scores and characteristics of students in each group. Then we will provide detailed information about the two individual students with the highest level of growth in basic reading skills and the two students who made the least gain on that outcome.

Demographic Characteristics

Four females and three males had adequate response to Tier 3 intervention. Three of these students were repeating first grade, two were in second grade, and three were in third grade. Parents of all except one of the students reported that English was the primary language spoken in the home. Of the seven students with inadequate response to Tier 3 intervention, two were females and 5 were males. Two were in Grade 2 and five were in Grade 3. All spoke English as the dominant home language.

Full Scale IQ Score

There was little difference between the mean WASI Full Scale IQ scores for the Tier 3 adequate responders (85; SD 10) and inadequate responders (84; SD 14). The scores for the inadequate response group, however, ranged from 64 to 99, and the group included two students with WASI IQ scores below 70. In contrast, the range of scores for the adequate response group was 76–102.

Behavior Characteristics

The SNAP–IV data indicated that two of the students with adequate Tier 3 response had characteristics associated with severe ADHD, combined type, along with significant behavior problems including oppositional defiant disorder. One other student in this group had indications of mild ADHD, inattentive type. The other four students had no indications of attention or behavioral conditions. In contrast, all but one of the students with inadequate response to Tier 3 had indications of attention or behavior disorders. Two students in this group had characteristics associated with ADHD, combined type, one of whom also had indications of oppositional defiant disorder. Four other students had indications of ADHD, inattentive type.

Phonemic Awareness
and Rapid Naming at the Beginning of First Grade

The mean beginning of first grade PA and RAN scores of students who would later respond well and less adequately to Tier 3 intervention did not differ greatly. Interestingly, the group means for both of these variables indicate somewhat greater impairment in the adequate responders than in the inadequate responders. The mean first-grade PA Theta score for the adequate responder group was –1.40 (SD .67; range –2.17 to –0.19) whereas the inadequate responder group mean was –0.96 (SD .88; range –2.50 to .221). At the beginning of first grade, the Tier 3 adequate response group was able to name, on average, 42.40 letters per minute (SD 15.42; range 13 to 55.56), whereas the inadequate response group mean was 49.20 letters per minute (SD 12.32; range 31.0 to 66.67). In contrast, typically developing first-grade readers in the same study had a mean PA Theta score of .017 and were able to name an average of 68 letters per minute, as reported above.

Progress in Intervention Programs

Table 6.5 contains means and standard deviations at pretest and posttest for strong and weak responders to Tier 3 intervention on the primary assessment associated with the Phono-Graphix program. This instrument measures three phonemic awareness skills along with knowledge of the alphabetic code. The tasks in the assessment are 1) blending phonemes (teacher pronounces a word phoneme-by-phoneme and student must produce the intact word; maximum score 15), 2) phoneme segmentation (teacher pronounces an intact word or nonword and student must pronounce the phonemes in the word or nonword separately; maximum score 63), 3) auditory processing (an elision task in which the student must pronounce words and nonwords with certain phonemes taken out, e.g., "Say nest without the /s/"; maximum score 10), and 4) code knowledge (identification of sounds associated with letters and letter combinations; 100% maximum score). The mean scores of strong and weak responders were similar on each of these tasks, although standard deviations were larger for the weak responder group, indicating more score variation. After 8 weeks of Phono-Graphix intervention, most of the students in each group reached the maximum scores for the phonemic awareness tasks, and mastery of the code knowledge task was above 90% for nearly all students, regardless of response group. For the adequate response group, scores on this measure ranged from 82% to 98%, whereas in the inadequate response group they ranged from 80% to 100% mastery.

Table 6.5. Read America diagnostic tests (Phono-Graphix) at pre and posttest for the Phono-Graphix phase of Tier 3 intervention

Student	Blending Pretest	Blending Posttest	Phoneme segmentation Pretest	Phoneme segmentation Posttest	Auditory processing Pretest	Auditory processing Posttest	Code knowledge Pretest	Code knowledge Posttest
1	13	15	49	63	3	10	66%	94%
2	9	15	46	62	3	10	62%	94%
3	8	13	49	63	1	10	54%	90%
4	12	15	49	63	2	8	56%	90%
5	10	15	62	63	7	10	64%	92%
6	14	15	51	63	5	10	56%	90%
7	9	15	49	62	4	9	54%	90%
8	13	15	41	61	3	10	52%	82%
9	8	14	44	62	5	7	50%	80%
10	12	15	58	63	3	10	64%	88%
11	13	15	53	63	5	10	58%	98%
12	8	12	46	63	2	9	64%	94%
13	12	15	45	63	6	10	60%	100%
14	10	15	50	63	5	10	46%	88%

Note: The maximum score for Blending is 15, for Phoneme Segmentation is 63, for Auditory Processing is 10, and for Code Knowledge is 100%.

During the 8-week Read Naturally phase, teachers collected weekly oral reading fluency data for each student on an unpracticed Read Naturally passage at the text level they were reading in the program. On average, both the adequate response and inadequate response groups began the program reading Grade 2.0 passages at a rate of 53 words correct per minute (SDs 8, 15). By the end of their programs, the average text level of both groups was Grade 3.0, and the poor response group read these passages slightly more fluently (61 WCPM, SD 22) than the adequate response group (57 WCPM, SD 6), although the rates of students in the latter group were more uniform (ranges 33–85 WCPM and 49–66 WCPM, respectively).

Outcome Measures

The Tier 3 adequate and inadequate responder groups differed most on outcomes for WJ III Basic Skills (see Table 6.3), the criterion on which the groups were identified, and on GORT–4 fluency (see Table 6.4). The mean standard score for the adequate response group on WJ III Basic Skills at pretest for the Tier 3 study was 83 (SD 6) and at posttest was 93 (SD 7), whereas the group of poor responders had a pretest mean of 81 (SD 8) and a posttest mean of 84 (SD 10). On the GORT–4 fluency measure, the mean standard score at pretest for the adequate responders was 72 (SD 4), and the posttest mean was 82 (SD 4); whereas the students who responded inadequately had a pretest mean of 71 (SD 10) and a posttest mean of 73 (SD 10). As a group, the weak responders had slightly lower standard scores on the TOWRE Sight Word Efficiency subtest at pretest ($M = 80$, $SD = 10$) than the strong responders ($M = 82$, $SD = 3$), but there was little difference between the groups on the TOWRE Sight Word Efficiency subtest at posttest ($M = 86$ for both strong and weak responders, $SD = 5$, 10, respectively) or on WJ III Passage Comprehension. The pretest Passage Comprehension mean for the adequate response group was 82 ($SD = 4$), whereas at posttest the group mean was 88 ($SD = 6$). The inadequate response group had a pretest mean on this measure of 79 ($SD = 12$) and an average posttest score of 82 ($SD = 10$).

Individuals with Strong Response to Tier 3

The two students who had the strongest response to intensive Tier 3 intervention in this study were Anita, who gained 14 standard score points in WJ III Basic Skills, and Joshua, who gained 10 standard score points over the intervention period.

Anita's Case Example

Anita gained 14 standard score points over the 16-week intervention period, more than any other student described in this chapter. Anita was repeating first grade, she was not served by special education, and her home language was English. The SNAP–IV data and anecdotal records indicated that she had severe ADHD (combined type) and significant oppositional defiant disorder. The two-subtest WASI indicated that she had a Full Scale IQ score of 76. At the beginning of first grade, her PA Theta score was –1.856, and Anita was able to name 38 known letters in one minute, indicating performance below the mean for the Tier 3 students in this study.

Anita had received both Tier 1 and Tier 2 intervention during the year prior to the Tier 3 study, ending that year with a WJ III Basic Skill standard score of 88, a Passage Comprehension standard score of 86, and an oral reading fluency score (on grade 1.7 materials) of 11 WCPM. Anecdotal records indicated that Anita was often out of her regular classroom during the Tier 1+2 intervention year and was difficult to engage in Tier 2 intervention because of her challenging behaviors.

At the beginning of the Tier 3 intervention, Anita was able to correctly blend the phonemes in 9 out of 15 words, segment 49 of 63 phonemes within words, complete 4 of 10 auditory processing (elision) tasks correctly, and identify correctly 54% of the items on the Phono-Graphix Code Knowledge task. At the same time, she had a WJ Basic Skills standard score of 82, a Passage Comprehension score of 80, and a GORT–4 fluency standard score of 75.

After 8 weeks of Phono-Graphix intervention, she had mastered the Phono-Graphix blending and segmenting tasks, and had 90% accuracy on auditory processing. Her posttest score on the code knowledge assessment was also 90%. Thus, she demonstrated a high level of mastery on the Phono-Graphix assessment. Anita had standard scores at this point of the intervention sequence of 94 in WJ III Basic Skills, 85 in WJ III Passage Comprehension, and 80 in GORT–4 fluency, reflecting substantial growth in her ability to decode words and nonwords, with lower (but educationally significant) gains in comprehension and fluency of 5 standard score points in 8 weeks. During the Read Naturally intervention phase, Anita progressed from reading Grade 1.0 passages at 52 WCPM with 98% accuracy to Grade 2.0 passages with 90% accuracy but only at a rate of 49 WCPM. Over the full 16-week intervention period, besides gaining 14 standard score points in WJ III Basic Skills, this student gained a total of 7 standard score points in WJ III Passage Comprehension and 5 in GORT–4 fluency.

Joshua's Case Example

Joshua had the second highest gains in WJ III Basic Skills standard score points. Joshua was a Grade 3 student who was served by special education because of an identified learning disability. His home language was English, and he did not exhibit significant behavior or attention difficulties. His WASI two-subtest IQ score was 86. At the beginning of first grade, Joshua's PA Theta score was –0.928, reflecting somewhat milder impairment than most other Tier 3 students described in this chapter, and he was able to name 40 known letters in one minute. During the year of the Tier 3 intervention, he received his reading instruction in the resource room, although the intervention replaced that instruction for the 16-week period in which he participated in it.

Joshua received Tier 1 and Tier 3 intervention but did not participate in supplemental Tier 2 intervention in Grade 1. At the end of first grade, his WJ III Basic Skills standard score was 69; whereas at the end of Grade 2 (1-year maintenance testing), it was 78. He performed slightly better in Passage Comprehension, with an end-of-first-grade standard score of 71, but at the end of second grade, his comprehension score was 76, somewhat lower than his score in Basic Skills at that time point. Joshua had very low oral reading fluency at the end of first grade, able to read Grade 1.7 passages at only 9 WCPM.

By January of Grade 3 (prior to Tier 3 intervention) Joshua's scores in basic reading skills had declined to 73, and his comprehension score had remained essentially unchanged. His GORT–4 fluency standard score of 70 indicated that he still had serious difficulties with fluent reading. His Phono-Graphix pretest reflected severe difficulties with segmenting phonemes (65% correct) and auditory processing (30% correct), as well as limited code knowledge (52% accuracy), but relative strength in blending phonemes (87% accuracy).

After 8 weeks of the Phono-Graphix program, Joshua had perfect or near-perfect scores on all of the phonemic awareness tasks and a score of 82% on the code knowledge measure. He had gained 10 standard score points on WJ III Basic Skills, 7 on Passage Comprehension, and 5 in GORT–4 fluency. In the 8-week Read Naturally intervention phase, Joshua progressed from 43 to 63 WCPM on Grade 3.0 passages. During this time, he gained an additional 2 standard score points in WJ III Basic Skills, lost 5 points in Passage Comprehension, and gained an additional 5 points in GORT–4 fluency.

Individuals with Weak Response to Tier 3

The two students who had the weakest response to intensive Tier 3 intervention in this study were Shandrell, who lost 6 standard score points in WJ III Basic Skills, and Marilee, who gained only 2 points over the intervention period.

Shandrell's Case Example

Shandrell was in Grade 3. He was served by special education under the Other Health Impaired category. His home language was English. SNAP data indicated characteristics of ADHD (inattention type), and the WASI two-subtest measure indicated a Full Scale IQ score of 64. At the beginning of first grade, Shandrell's PA Theta score of –2.499 indicated severe impairment and was the lowest of any Tier 3 student described in this chapter. His RAN score of 44 letters per minute was near the average for this group of Tier 3 students. Shandrell received both Tier 1 and 2 intervention in Grade 1. After a year of intervention, he was able to read grade 1.7 passages at a rate of only 12 WCPM, his WJ III Basic Skills standard score was 72, and his Passage Comprehension score was 74. These scores were basically unchanged at the end of Grade 2.

At the beginning of Tier 3 intervention in Grade 3, Shandrell's Basic Reading score was 75, and it remained approximately the same after 8 weeks of Phono-Graphix intervention. Shandrell made standard score gains in Passage Comprehension during the Phono-Graphix phase, going from 63 to 76, and he gained 5 standard score points in GORT–4 fluency. His progress on the Phono-Graphix assessment was good, going from 53% to 80% mastery in phoneme blending, 73% to 100% mastery in phoneme segmenting, 20% to 90% mastery in the elision task, and 64% to 94% mastery of code knowledge.

In the Read Naturally program, Shandrell progressed from first- to second-grade text, and was able to read Grade 2.0 text at a rate of 78 WCPM by the end of the program (with 90% accuracy). During this period, his comprehension and fluency scores remained stable, but his WJ Basic Skills score declined 7 points to a 69. The Basic Reading Skills cluster is a composite of Letter–Word Identification and Word Attack. Closer inspection revealed that Shandrell had a standard score of 77 in the word-reading task, but only 61 in the nonword task. This pattern was supported in TOWRE scores collected during the same time period, which indicated a score in Sight Word Reading Efficiency of 86 but a score on Phonemic Decoding Efficiency (nonword reading) of only 73.

Marilee's Case Example

Marilee was in the third grade and spoke English as her home language. Data indicated that she had a WASI Full Scale IQ score of 87 and had characteristics of ADHD (combined type). She was served by special education because of an identified learning disability. She received only Tier 1 intervention in the first grade. Both Marilee's PA Theta score (–1.299) and RAN score (40.91) at the beginning of Grade 1 were near the group mean for Tier 3 students in this study but well below the means for the typically developing first-grade readers. At the end of first grade, her WJ III Basic Skills standard score was 87, and 1 year later it had fallen to 82. At the end of first grade, her Passage Comprehension standard score was 86 and her oral reading fluency rate on grade-level passages was 15 WCPM. At the end of Grade 2 her comprehension score was relatively stable at 88.

In her third-grade year pretest for Tier 3 (administered in September), Marilee's Basic Reading score was nearly the same as at the end of first grade, and this increased only slightly after 8 weeks of Phono-Graphix, even though she reached 100% mastery on all of the intervention assessment phonemic awareness tasks and reached 88% mastery of code knowledge. Her Basic Skills score remained unchanged after 8 weeks of Read Naturally. Marilee lost ground in Passage Comprehension, declining from 88 to 83 during the first 8 weeks of intervention and remaining unchanged after the next 8 weeks of intervention. Her GORT–4 fluency score rose 5 points during Phono-Graphix phase but fell 10 points during the Read Naturally phase, although she progressed from a grade 2.5 passage at 58 WCPM to grade 3.5 text at 62 WCPM on the intervention materials.

Neural Correlates of Reading Intervention

In the past few years, research has utilized functional neuroimaging methods to evaluate the neural correlates of reading. Summaries of this research, including descriptions of the procedures, can be found in several sources (see Fletcher, Simos, Papanicolaou, & Denton, 2004; Shaywitz & Shaywitz, 2004). Figure 6.1 outlines the major regions of the brain involved in word recognition. Briefly, in proficient readers, reading a word initially activates the visual cortex (as with any activity involving vision) and then an area of the brain on the undersurface of the posterior temporal and occipital lobes, which we defined roughly as the occipital-temporal in Figure 6.1. This area of the brain mediates analysis of the visual features of the word. Then there is almost simultaneous activation of different areas of the frontal and posterior temporal–parietal areas of the brain, with the area roughly representative of Wernicke's area much more predominant in the left (language) hemisphere. The frontal area, roughly corresponding to Broca's area in Figure 6.1, would be especially activated if the response required speaking the word, whereas the areas in Figure 6.1 representing the middle and superior temporal gyrus have much to do with phonological and semantic processing. These findings are apparent across different imaging modalities as well as in studies of individuals with acquired lesions (see Fletcher et al., 2004).

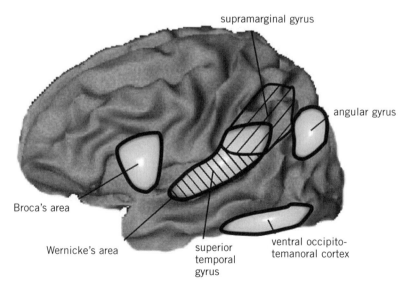

Figure 6.1. Model of a neural network for reading, showing four major participating areas. Broca's area is responsible for phonological processing involving articulation mapping, as in the pronunciation of words. Wernicke's area (which includes portions of the superior temporal and supramarginal gyri) is responsible for phonological processing involving letter–sound correspondence. The angular gyrus is a relay station that links information across modalities. The visual association cortex in the occipito-temporal region is responsible for graphemic analysis. (From Fletcher, J.M., Simos, P.G., Papanicolaou, A.C., & Denton, C. [2004]. Neuroimaging in reading research. In N. Duke & M. Mallette [Eds.], *Literacy research methodologies.* [p. 265]. New York: The Guilford Press; reprinted by permission.)

Magnetic Source Imaging

To investigate the neural processes of young children with and without risk for reading difficulties and changes in brain functioning associated with levels of response to tiered early reading intervention, functional neuroimaging data were collected at different phases of the interventions in Mathes and colleagues (2005) and Denton and colleagues (2006) (Simos, Fletcher, Foorman et al., 2002). The neuroimaging was conducted using magnetoencephalography (MEG), also known as magnetic source imaging (MSI). In contrast to better-known functional imaging methods such as functional magnetic resonance imaging (fMRI), which localizes brain activation through assessments of metabolism (blood flow), MSI is a neurophysiological method that localizes brain function by detecting changes in the biomagnetic energy generated when neurons fire and produce electrical discharges (Papanicolaou, 1998). Brain electrical activity has been measured for many years through methods such as electroencephalography (EEG) and evoked potentials, often in response to a cognitive task. Such methods, however, lack precision for localizing specific areas of brain activation because of surface interference from the scalp and skull. In MSI, brain electrical activity is not directly assessed; rather, the magnetic fields that emanate in and out of the brain when signals travel across neurons are detected and used to identify the sources of the magnetic energy. Unlike metabolic methods such as fMRI, MSI provides information not only about which areas of the brain are active as a person performs different tasks, but when and how quickly this activity occurs. It is also easier to use with young children because it is quieter than fMRI, the head is not enclosed in a tube, and an adult can stand next to the child throughout the procedure.

Our research group has used MSI extensively in children and adults at various levels of reading proficiency (Papanicolaou et al., 2003). Reliable neural correlates of different reading processes have been mapped, which permitted us to link the neuroimaging procedures to intervention. In the three MSI studies tied to Mathes and colleagues (2005) and Denton and colleagues (2006), students performed tasks such as providing letter sounds, reading pseudowords, and reading sight words as fast as possible as their brain activity was monitored. Note that this intervention sample is younger, more diverse, and defined by risk characteristics in comparison with our intervention study of students with identified reading disabilities, which used imaging tasks for real words and pseudowords that did not require oral responses (Simos, Fletcher, Bergman et al., 2002). Thus, the results of the imaging studies of young students reported in this chapter should not be reviewed as replication of Simos, Fletcher, Bergman, and colleagues (2002).

Neuroimaging of At-Risk and Not-At-Risk Readers at the End of Kindergarten

In Simos, Fletcher, Foorman, and colleagues (2002), the focus was on 45 students from the first cohort, (30 at-risk, 15 not-at-risk) from Mathes and colleagues

(2005). These students were about 6.5 years of age and had just completed kindergarten. Students were designated as at risk or not at risk for reading difficulties using the screening procedures previously described in this chapter. A letter sound naming task was analyzed because most children in this age range could read few sight words and virtually no pseudowords. Those at risk for reading difficulties showed brain activation profiles that were quite different from the not-at-risk students. In particular, there was lack of engagement of the superior temporal region of the left hemisphere, an area associated with the conversion of print to sound (see Figure 6.1). There was also more engagement of the same area in the right hemisphere, which was also found in studies of children with identified reading problems. The temporal course (timing and sequence) of activation was consistent with these findings. These results were quite similar to those in our studies of older children and adults with severe decoding difficulties (Papanicolaou et al., 2003) and consistent with other imaging studies indicating that individuals with severe reading impairments typically have reduced activation in the regions of the brain associated with phonological processing (Shaywitz & Shaywitz, 2004).

Neuroimaging After First-Grade Tier 1+2 Instruction

In Simos and colleagues (in press), 33 (17 at risk, 16 not at risk) of the 45 participants in Simos, Fletcher, Foorman, and colleagues (2002) participated in a follow-up MSI session at the end of first grade, along with a few additional participants who provided data from the second cohort of students in Mathes and colleagues (2005). The purpose of this study was to examine changes in brain activation associated with Tier 1+2 intervention and to compare processing patterns of at-risk students who received intervention to those of typically developing first-grade readers. The sample would have been larger for the second cohort, but a major flood closed the MSI lab for several months in the summer and fall of 2002. The at-risk group included 14 students who had responded adequately to Tier 1 or Tiers 1 and 2 intervention and three who were inadequate responders. Simos and colleagues (in press) found that, after a year of intervention, activation profiles for at-risk first-grade readers who responded adequately to Tier 1+2 instruction were more similar (but not identical) to those of typically developing readers on both tasks, especially in the temporal course of activation.

Neuroimaging of Adequate
and Inadequate Responders to Tier 3 Instruction

The final study (Simos et al., in press) involved 15 of the students who participated in the Denton and colleagues (2006) study. These students were imaged before the intervention began and after each 8-week intervention phase. Overall changes associated with intervention represented a shift toward patterns seen in proficient readers, including 1) increased activation in an area of the temporal lobe that is typically involved in lexical–semantic processing and 2) a shift in the rela-

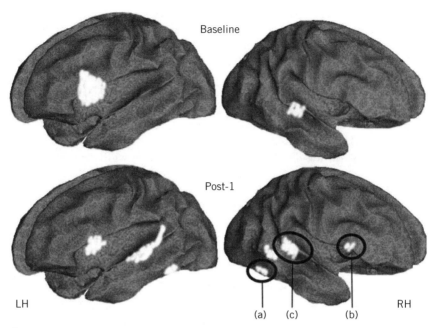

Figure 6.2.   Changes in neuromagnetic activity in response to consonant–vowel–consonant (e.g., "kak") and vowel–consonant–vowel pseudowords (e.g., "ama") following the first 8 weeks (Phono-Graphix phase) of successful Tier 3 remediation. At baseline (upper set of images) the brain activity was restricted to right hemisphere superior-temporal regions (c) and the left inferior frontal area (b). When retested 8 weeks later, dramatic increases in the degree of activity were noted in the left hemisphere (superior temporal lobe—area marked (c) on the right hemisphere but in the left hemisphere). There was also a smaller increase in activation in visual association areas (a) and a reduction in activity in frontal regions (b). A notable change in the activation profiles after intervention featured early activation in (a) followed by activity in (c), which was in turn followed by activity in (b). This temporal pattern of regional activation is characteristic of children and adults who never experienced difficulties in learning to read. LH and RH represent the left and right hemispheres, respectively. (Adapted from Simos, P.G., Gletcher, H.M., Sarkari, S., Bilingsley, R.K., Francis, D.J., Castillo, E.M., et al. [2005]. Early development of neurophysiological processes involved in normal reading and reading disability. *Neuropsychology, 19,* 794; adapted with permission.)

tive timing of regional activity in the temporal and frontal cortices to a pattern such as that observed in nonimpaired readers. Most of these changes were apparent after the first 8 weeks of intervention—after the Phono-Graphix phase. Specifically, an analysis of activity for all participants during the fluency task, which required naming of sight words as fast as possible, revealed changes in brain activity following intervention in the posterior part of the middle temporal gyrus involving increased degree of activity and reduced onset latency; the lateral occipital–temporal region involving decreased onset latency of activation; and inferior frontal gyrus involving increased onset latency.

Representative examples of the findings can be seen in Figure 6.2, which presents an example of a responder to the Phono-Graphix phase of the intervention in Denton and colleagues (2006). The tendency for the right hemisphere to be more involved in at-risk than in not-at-risk readers is clearly apparent in both figures. Neither, however, shows the marked hypoactivation of the middle and superior temporal region in the left hemisphere that characterizes older identified poor readers (Papanicolaou et al., 2003) and nonresponders in Mathes and colleagues (2005).

Discussion

This chapter illustrates the possibilities and challenges inherent in a three-tier reading intervention model. Because of the small number of students who participated in both the Tier 1+2 study and the Tier 3 study, the conclusions of this chapter should be considered tentative. For each of the following observations, many additional questions emerge. Clearly, response to tiered reading intervention is an area ripe for research.

Levels of Response to Three Tiers of Intervention

The first rather obvious observation is that the percentage of students who respond adequately to intervention is dependent on the criteria and benchmarks established to denote adequate response. In the Mathes and colleagues (2005) Tier 1 and 2 study described in this chapter, response was notably higher using the criteria of WJ III Basic Skills cluster standard scores at or above the 30th percentile than the criteria of oral reading fluency at or above 40 WCPM. Studies of reading intervention have employed various methods of determining response to intervention (see, for example, O'Connor, 2000; Speece & Case, 2001; Torgesen, 2000; Vellutino et al., 1996). The question of determination of adequate response to Tier 2 intervention is critical, given the amendments of 2004 to the Individuals with Disabilities Education Improvement Act (IDEA; PL 108-446), which support the use of response to quality instruction and intervention as one criteria for the identification of a learning disability.

Even less is known about what constitutes adequate response to Tier 3 intervention. Denton and her colleagues (2006) set the criteria of a gain of .5 standard deviations on the WJ III Basic Skills cluster over their 16-week intervention. This goal was selected because of the limited duration of the study and the very low pretest standard scores of several participants. Arguably, it could be said that some students identified by Denton and colleagues as inadequate responders to Tier 3 were showing signs of response but required a more extended intervention. For example, one student, Patrick, gained 6 WJ III Basic Skills cluster standard score points over the 16-week intervention, going from a score of 68 to 74. Although Patrick's decoding skills clearly remained severely impaired, it is noteworthy that his age-adjusted standard score had remained relatively unchanged from the end of first grade to the beginning of Grade 3, when he began Tier 3 intervention, despite receiving special education services, but rose 6 points after 16 weeks of concentrated, systematic, explicit small-group intervention. Patrick's comprehension and fluency scores remained uniformly low, reinforcing the need for extended intervention.

Ultimately, the goal must be performance in the average range on key reading skills, including decoding, fluency, and comprehension. Tier 3 is defined, in part, by extended duration of intervention (see Denton & Mathes, 2003). Nevertheless, it is critical that research inform practice in the application of benchmarks to denote when students no longer require intensive Tier 3 intervention. In the current service model, it is rare that students with reading disabilities make substantial progress toward the goal of average performance for their age and grade, an accomplishment that would indicate that they no longer require intensive intervention (see Hanushek, Kain, & Rivkin, 1998). If the goal of a three-tier intervention model is that all students become competent readers, thought must be given to the determination of levels of performance at which a student has a good chance of success without further intensive intervention.

Characteristics of Adequate and Inadequate Responders to Tier 3 Intervention

This chapter provided a detailed description of students who responded well and less adequately to an intensive Tier 3 intervention. Three overriding observations can be made based on these descriptions.

First, the Tier 3 intervention described in this chapter was offered for a 16-week period, with the first 8 weeks consisting of explicit, systematic code-based instruction provided for 2 hours per day and the second 8 weeks targeting fluency and the application of decoding skills in nondecodable text. All instruction was provided by highly qualified teachers in groups of two students with one teacher. In our current educational system, this level of intensity of instruction is seldom provided, even in special education settings. The fact that there was a great deal of variance in levels of response, even to this intensive intervention, illustrates the challenges inherent in teaching all students to read.

The second major observation based on the description of response to Tier 3 intervention in this chapter is that the characteristics and pretest scores of students with high and low response to Tier 3 were strikingly similar in most domains. The exceptions are that students who responded poorly to Tier 3 in this sample were more likely to be male, in Grade 3, and served by special education. In addition, students who received only Tier 1 intervention prior to Tier 3 were less likely to respond well to Tier 3 than those who received all three tiers of intervention. The group of inadequate responders also included a higher percentage of students with indications of ADHD and challenging behavior, such as oppositional defiant disorder; however, the student with the highest level of response to intervention had strong indications of both of these conditions. There was little difference in beginning of first grade PA or RAN mean scores of high and low responders to Tier 3, although the student with the weakest response to Tier 3 started first grade with the most impaired PA Theta score. Further research is needed to identify student characteristics that may predict adequate and inadequate response to Tier 3 instruction.

Finally, the descriptions of strong and weak responders to Tier 3 in this chapter provide support for providing Tier 2 intervention to severely impaired readers in Grade 1 and for beginning Tier 3 intervention in Grade 2. Students who had received both Tiers 1 and 2 as first graders tended to respond better to Tier 3, and students who were repeating first grade or starting second grade responded more readily to Tier 3 than third-grade students. Moreover, there is a need for improved methods of identifying students who require Tier 2 intervention. A large percentage of students determined to be at risk for reading difficulties in the Mathes and colleagues (2005) study attained benchmarks for adequate response at the end of first grade after receiving only Tier 1 classroom instruction. Research should systematically investigate the effectiveness of identifying students for Tier 2 and beginning Tier 2 supplemental intervention in January of Grade 1 rather than at the beginning of the school year as a way to improve the determination of need for Tier 2.

Insights from Brain Imaging Research

The neuroimaging research shows important links between patterns of neurological processing and gains in reading scores in students at different levels of proficiency. The parallels in the brain activity profiles in students at risk for reading difficulties, those who do not respond adequately to instruction, and older identified poor readers is striking. After intervention, a variety of results are apparent that appear to vary with the age and intensity of the intervention and seem to represent both normalizing and compensatory processes. The most important conclusion arising from this body of research is one that offers tremendous promise— that instruction changes the way the brain functions. Severe reading disabilities are not finite conditions that condemn a student to a lifetime of illiteracy. Even though there are marked differences in the ways that the brains of individuals with and without reading disabilities function when attempting reading or reading-related activities, these patterns can be changed through instruction. The research described in this chapter illustrates that this is true for young students who are at risk for serious reading difficulties and for older students with persistent reading difficulties. Further research is needed to further define neural markers related to adequate and inadequate response to intervention and to the development of fluent reading as well as longitudinal research investigating the degree of stability of these changes in brain function over time.

Implications for Practice

There is a disagreement among educators, researchers, and police makers about whether Tier 3 intervention should be offered in special education or general education. Some cite the low feasibility of the provision of high-intensity intervention within general education and question whether the purpose of intervention delivered within a three-tier model is to remediate academic difficulties or to demonstrate the presence of a reading disability based on the need for instruction beyond what is normally offered in general education (i.e., Fuchs, 2003; Fuchs, Mock, Morgan, & Young, 2003). A competing question is whether a student can be determined to have a disability based on the inability to thrive with general education instruction alone or whether inadequate response to carefully designed instruction delivered in small groups is a better indication of learning disabilities. Further, there is evidence that even severe and persistent phonological processing impairments can be remediated through instruction delivered in small-group formats (i.e., Denton et al., 2006; Torgesen et al., 2001), which may enable students to continue to make adequate progress in reading without extensive long-term support. Whether Tier 3 is conceived as being offered within general or special education, it is critical that researchers systematically examine student response to such highly intensive interventions within a three-tier model.

The Need for Individualization at Tier 3

The diverse characteristics of Tier 3 students described in this chapter, along with the wide variation in response to Tier 3, indicate that Tier 3 instruction may need to be designed specifically in response to student strengths and needs. This instruction may need to be highly individualized as to content, instructional delivery, level of intensity, and duration of instruction. The traditional emphasis of special education on individualized educational programming may be particularly well-suited for the kind of instruction required by students who respond inadequately to quality Tier 2 supplemental intervention.

A Fundamental Shift in Services

It is clear that the level of intensity of Tier 3 intervention described in this chapter is not possible in most special education programs, much less in general education. It is also clear that some students who received the Tier 3 intervention in Denton and colleagues (2006) needed even more extended—or different—intervention in order to become competent readers. This presents a formidable challenge to educators. The possibilities inherent in a three-tier reading intervention model include the reduction of students who are misidentified as having learning disabilities that require special education. Many resource rooms serve too many students to make the delivery of truly individualized, intensive instruction possible. If schools provide quality Tier 1 and 2 interventions to all young students in the school who need it, there is a possibility that Tier 3, offered by special education, could serve only the students with the greatest level of impairment. This would enable special educators to offer instruction designed to close the gap between individuals with reading impairments and their more able peers rather than to move students with severe reading difficulties from grade to grade with the most positive outcomes consisting of maintaining their relative standing below those of their typically functioning peers rather than falling farther behind.

In light of research that indicates the potential to fundamentally restructure the way the brain functions when a person attempts to read, there is evidence that much more is possible than current typical practice. The educational community must ask whether it is important and reasonable to expect that even students with severe reading difficulties can be taught to read competently, closing the gap with their peers. If this is a goal worth pursuing, a three-tier reading model would appear to offer a structure in which it is a possibility.

REFERENCES

Denton, C.A., Fletcher, J.M., Anthony, J.L., & Francis, D.J. (2006). An evaluation of intensive intervention for students with persistent reading difficulties. *Journal of Learning Disabilities, 39,* 447–466.

Denton, C.A., & Hocker, J.K. (2006). *Responsive reading instruction: Flexible intervention for struggling readers in the early grades.* Longmont, CO: Sopris West.

Denton, C.A., & Mathes, P.G. (2003). Intervention for struggling readers: Possibilities and challenges. In B.R. Foorman (Ed.), *Preventing and remediating reading difficulties: Bringing science to scale* (pp. 229–251). Timonium, MD: York Press.

Fletcher, J.M., Simos, P.G., Papanicolaou, A.C., & Denton, C. (2004). Neuroimaging in reading research. In N. Duke & M. Mallette (Eds.), *Literacy research methodologies* (pp. 252–286). New York: The Guilford Press.

Fountas, I.C., & Pinnell, G.S. (1999). *Matching books to readers.* Portsmouth, NH: Heinemann.

Fuchs, D., Mock, D., Morgan, P.L., & Young, C.L. (2003). Responsiveness-to-intervention: Definitions, evidence, and implications for the learning disabilities construct. *Learning Disabilities Research & Practice, 18,* 157–171.

Fuchs, L.S. (2003). Assessing intervention responsiveness: Conceptual and technical issues. *Learning Disabilities Research & Practice, 18*(3), 172–186.

Hanushek, E.A., Kain, J.F., & Rivkin, S.G. (1998). *Does special education raise academic achievement for students with disabilities?* National Bureau of Economic Research, Working Paper No. 6690, Cambridge, MA. Accessed on September 6, 2002, from http://www.nber.org/papers/w6690

Ihnot, C., Mastoff, J., Gavin, J., & Hendrickson, L. (2001). *Read naturally.* St. Paul, MN: Read Naturally.

Individuals with Disabilities Education Improvement Act of 2004, PL 108-446, 20 U.S.C. §§ 1400 *et seq.*

Mathes, P.G., Denton, C.A., Fletcher, J.M., Anthony, J.L., Francis, D.J., & Schatschneider, C. (2005). The effects of theoretically different instruction and student characteristics on the skills of struggling readers. *Reading Research Quarterly, 40,* 148–182.

Mathes, P., Torgesen, J.K., Allen, S.H., & Allor, J.H. (2001). *First grade PALS (Peer-Assisted Literacy Strategies).* Longmont, CO: Sopris West.

Mathes, P.G., Torgesen, J.K, Menchetti, J.C., Wahl, M., & Grek, M.K. (1999). *Proactive beginning reading.* Available from P.G. Mathes, Institute for Reading Research, Southern Methodist University, Post Office Box 750381, Dallas, TX 75275.

McGuiness, C., McGuiness, D., & McGuiness, G. (1996). Phono-Graphix: A new method for remediating reading difficulties. *Annals of Dyslexia, 46,* 73–96.

O'Connor, R. (2000). Increasing the intensity of intervention in kindergarten and first grade. *Learning Disabilities Research & Practice, 15,* 43–54.

Papanicolaou, A.C. (1998). Fundamentals of functional brain imaging. Lisse, The Netherlands: Swets & Zetilinger.

Papanicolaou, A.C., Simos, P.G., Breier, J.I., Fletcher, J.M., Foorman, B.R., Francis, D.J., et al. (2003). Brain mechanisms for reading in children with and without dyslexia: A review of studies of normal development and plasticity. *Developmental Neuropsychology, 24,* 593–612.

Scarborough, H.S. (1998). Early identification of children at risk for reading disabilities: Phonological awareness and some other promising predictors. In P. Accardo, A. Capute, & B. Shapiro (Eds.), *Specific reading disability: A view of the spectrum.* Timonium, MD: York Press.

Schatschneider, C., Francis, D.J., Foorman, B.R., Fletcher, J.M., & Mehta, P. (1999). The dimensionality of phonological awareness: An application of item response theory. *Journal of Educational Psychology, 91,* 439–449.

Shaywitz, S.E., & Shaywitz, B.A. (2004). Neurobiologic basis for reading and reading disability. In P. McCardle & V. Chhabra (Eds.), *The voice of evidence in reading research* (pp. 417–442). Baltimore: Paul H. Brookes Publishing Co.

Simos, P.G., Fletcher, J.M., Bergman, E., Breier, J.I., Foorman, B.R., Castillo, E.M., et al. (2002). Dyslexia-specific brain activation profile becomes normal following successful remedial training. *Neurology, 58,* 1203–13.

Simos, P.G., Fletcher, J.M., Foorman, B.R., Francis, D.J., Castillo, E.M., Davis, R.N., et al. (2002). Brain activation profiles during the early stages of reading acquisition. *Journal of Child Neurology, 17,* 159–163.

Simos, P.G., Fletcher, J.M., Sarkari, S., Billingsley, R.L., Francis, D.J., Castillo, E.M., et al. (2005). Early development of neurophysiological processes involved in normal reading and reading disability. *Neuropsychology, 19,* 787–798.

Simos, P.G., Fletcher, J.M., Sarkari, S., Billingsley, R.L., Denton, C.A., & Papanicolaou, A.C. (in press). Intensive instruction affects brain magnetic activity associated with reading fluency in children with persistent reading disabilities. *Journal of Learning Disabilities.*

Speece, D.L., & Case, L. (2001). Classification in context: An alterative to identifying early reading disability. *Journal of Educational Psychology, 93,* 735–749.

Swanson, J., Schuck, S., Mann, M., Carlson, C., Hartman, K, Sergeant, J., et al. (2004). *Categorical and dimensional definitions and evaluations of symptoms of ADHD: The SNAP and the SWAN ratings scales.* Retrieved December 20, 2004, from http://www.adhd.net

Torgesen, J.K. (2000). Individual differences in response to early interventions in reading: The lingering problem of treatment resisters. *Learning Disabilities Research & Practice, 15,* 55–64.

Torgesen, J.K., Alexander, A.W., Wagner, R.K., Rashotte, C.A., Voeller, K., Conway, T. et al. (2001). Intensive remedial instruction for students with severe reading disabilities: Immediate and long-term outcomes from two instructional approaches. *Journal of Learning Disabilities, 34,* 33–58.

Torgesen, J.K., Wagner, R., & Rashotte, C.A. (1999). *Test of Word Reading Efficiency.* Austin, TX: PRO-ED.

Vellutino, F.R., Scanlon, D.M., Sipay, E.R., Small, S.G., Pratt, A., Chen, R., et al. (1996). Cognitive profiles of difficult-to-remediate and readily remediated poor readers: Early intervention as a vehicle for distinguishing between cognitive and experiential deficits as basic causes of specific reading disability. *Journal of Educational Psychology, 88,* 601–638.

Wechsler, D. (1999). *Wechsler Abbreviated Scales of Intelligence.* New York: The Psychological Corporation.

Wiederholt, J.L., & Bryant, B.R. (2001). Gray Oral Reading Tests (GORT-4) (4th ed.). Austin, TX: PRO-ED.

Woodcock, R.W., McGrew, K.S., & Mather, N. (2001). *Woodcock-Johnson III Tests of Achievement.* Itasca, IL: The Riverside Publishing Co.

Layers of Intervention that Affect Outcomes in Reading

Rollanda E. O'Connor

C hildren can experience reading difficulties for various reasons, but among the most frustrating, painful, and preventable is poor instruction during the primary years. The layered approach to easing children's reading difficulties, what is now called the Three-Tier Model of Reading Intervention, begins with improved instructional routines in general education that are meant to ensure that all students have adequate opportunity to learn to read. From the studies in the 1980s that focused on early identification of reading disabilities (Juel, 1988; Share, Jorm, MacLean, & Matthews, 1984) and the kindergarten–first-grade intervention studies of the 1990s (Ball & Blachman, 1991; Cunningham, 1990; O'Connor, Jenkins, & Slocum, 1995; Torgesen, Wagner, & Rashotte, 1997; Vellutino et al., 1996), researchers began to identify the elements of instructional packages that are described in earlier chapters in this book (e.g., Chapter 4). The components that were deemed essential in these studies of effective early intervention are mirrored in current recommendations for general class reading instruction for students in the primary grades, an approach that begins with systematic instruction in the alphabetic code and phonemic awareness and extends to development of vocabulary, fluent reading, and comprehension.

LAYERED INTERVENTIONS IN READING

Although the essential components necessary for reading acquisition were identified by researchers through experimental studies, teachers are the ones who most need this knowledge. Teachers can and do change their instruction in response to professional development (Darling-Hammond, 2000; Garet, Porter, Desimone, Birman, & Yoon, 2001; McCutchen et al., 2002), and so researchers began to ask whether teachers could incorporate the activities used in experimental interven-

This chapter was supported in part by Grant #H324M980187-00 from the U.S. Office of Education, Office of Special Education Programs.

tions into their everyday instruction. The professional development that was provided to teachers in the first attempts at Layer 1 intervention was substantial (Blachman, Ball, Black, & Tangel, 1994; Greenwood, Tapia, Abbott, & Walton, 2003; O'Connor, 2000; Simmons, Kame'enui, Stoolmiller, Coyne, & Harn, 2003; Vaughn, 2003), as were the changes teachers made as they went about their work of teaching students to read.

Findings from the studies on changing teachers' practices suggest that professional development alone (with the accompanying improvement in teachers' instructional practices) can improve the reading outcomes for many students initially identified as struggling readers (Greenwood et al., 2003; O'Connor, 2000; O'Connor, Fulmer, Harty, & Bell, 2005; Simmons et al., 2003; Vaughn, 2003). This first layer of intervention—also called primary, or Tier 1, intervention—has helped to reduce false positives in research reports, in which students who received inadequate instruction were falsely diagnosed with reading disabilities and then viewed as cured of those disabilities as a result of a particular intervention. Primary intervention also has helped researchers make more accurate estimates of real risk and—because fewer students are falsely diagnosed with reading disabilities—has made secondary, or Tier 2, interventions more cost-effective.

The Three-Tier Model of Reading Intervention begins with changes in general education instruction. Evidence suggests that classroom instruction in phonemic awareness, letter–sound relations, and the alphabetic principle is effective for many students across a range of characteristics (Blachman, Ball, Black, & Tangel, 1994; 2000; Foorman, Francis, Fletcher, Schatschneider, & Mehta, 1998; O'Connor, 2000; O'Connor, Notari-Syverson, & Vadasy, 1996). Nevertheless, not all students respond to whole-class or large-group instruction, even when it is focused on effective instructional practices and activities. It is for these students that Tier 2 intervention is designed. As of 2006, many examples of the combination of Tier 1 and Tier 2 interventions have been implemented nationally.

Studies of Tier 2 interventions (also called Layer 2) deviate from the intervention studies common throughout the 1990s in which students in experiments were taught skills quite different from those presented in general class instruction. Rather, Tier 2 intervention builds on the reading instruction in the general education classroom, which—as a result of improvements drawn from the research and taught to teachers through professional development—is assumed to be well-designed and effective for most students in the class. Therefore, it is less likely that students who lag behind their peers in these classes are lagging as a result of a poor instructional environment.

Tier 2 is based on the notion that several possibilities could affect how well students benefit from good instruction in the primary grades; therefore, the additional instruction in Layer 2 is designed to address one or more of these possibilities. For example, students may be unprepared for the starting point of Tier 1 instruction (in which case Tier 2 instruction might begin by shoring up literacy preskills); students might need more instructional time to learn what their peers learn (in which case Tier 2 might provide more of the same instruction as Tier 1, but with additional repetition and review); students may need more explicit instruction than is provided in general class instruction (in which case Tier 2 teachers might task-analyze the concepts taught by the general education teacher to make the steps more transparent or the linkages between sound, print, and words clearer); or students might need another approach to reading instruction altogether (in which case instruction might encompass teaching methods distinctly different in content and/or method from Tier 1 instruction). This last possibility has received less attention in the research community than secondary intervention, but as the focus shifts to students who continue to struggle with reading acquisition despite the combined efforts of researchers and teachers, it can be expected that Tier 3 intervention will focus on more divergent and intensive approaches to teaching reading. This chapter focuses on secondary intervention, which is the next resort in a three-tier model of reading intervention when progress data show insufficient growth for particular learners in Tier 1 instruction.

EXPERIMENTS IN TIER 2

One of the earliest trials of general education class teachers providing Tier 1 instruction in phonemic awareness and letter knowledge was conducted by Blachman and colleagues (1994). Teachers and their teaching assistants learned to conduct the activities (later published as *Road to the Code,* Blachman et al., 2000) with their own students in small groups of four or five students. This approach combines the professional development aspects of primary intervention with the small-group feature of secondary intervention. The teachers' small-group instruction included auditory segmenting, Say-It-and-Move-It activities (i.e., for each isolated speech sound, students learned to move a disk into a designated space), and letter names and sounds. Following the 11-week intervention, students were able to read significantly more phonetically regular words and nonwords than students in a comparison group.

When the general class instruction includes an emphasis on the alphabetic code and small reading groups, as in Blachman and colleagues (1994), one may wonder whether there is need to add a second layer of intervention. In one small Tier 2 study involving kindergartners (O'Connor & Jenkins, 1995), the participants had been diagnosed with developmental delay and received 30 minutes of reading instruction in small groups 4 days per week by their teacher. The teacher implemented a code-based beginning reading program, Reading Mastery I (RMI; Engelmann & Bruner, 1995), with high fidelity. When the study began, these students had received 60 hours of instruction in RMI and had completed between 60 and 120 lessons in the program. To test the additive effect of Tier 2 intervention, students were matched within reading group on gender, reading ability, and lesson coverage and were assigned randomly to 1) secondary intervention that increased the explicitness of sound-to-letter coding by focusing on manipulating letter tiles to represent the sounds in words or 2) a control group in which students read the same words an equivalent number of times.

In the secondary intervention, the instructor used Segment-to-Spell (O'Connor, Notari-Syverson, & Vadasy, 2005) to encourage the student to form words from RMI with magnetic letters for 10 minutes. The student segmented each word, represented each speech segment with a letter, and then read back the word that was spelled. This activity is similar to Blachman and collegues' (1994) Say-It-and-Move-It, except that all sound in each word were represented by letters (rather than with disks or markers), and children read the word after they spelled it. When a student misspelled a word, the instructor used oral segmenting—which was part of RMI instruction for all the participants—as a prompt. Despite both groups receiving the same code-based instruction (Tier 1) and the same number of exposures to the same core of words, the students who received secondary intervention (i.e., segmenting each word and representing each phoneme with a letter) improved over the control group in reading real and nonsense words and in spelling. Although this study showed that instruction that focused intensely on demonstrating the alphabetic principle was useful for students with disabilities whose classroom instruction was code-based, it did not attempt to isolate the relative effects of Tier 1 and Tier 2 intervention. In addition, experiments beyond kindergarten that included more elaborate reading instruction were needed.

The work of Blachman, Tangel, Ball, Black, and McGraw (1999) became much more like the three-tier model of early reading intervention as they followed their kindergarten participants into first grade. In addition to the reading instruction provided by first-grade teachers who had been taught principles of reading acquisition (i.e., Tier 1 intervention), students who had made inadequate progress received an additional half hour of instruction for 12 weeks (i.e., Tier 2 intervention). This instruction built on the kindergarten skills and added more decoding and blending with letters (similar to Segment-to-Spell [O'Connor, Notari-Syverson et al., 2005], described previously) and reading stories constructed from decodable words, along with a few minutes of writing practice. Again, students scored significantly higher than those in the comparison classrooms that received neither Tier 1 nor Tier 2 intervention, and they were also were less likely to be retained in first grade or referred for remedial reading.

Because the previous studies combined aspects of both primary and secondary intervention, our research team piloted a three-tier model to intervention from 1997 to 1999 to test the effect of each tier of intervention over time (O'Connor, 2000). We worked in three high-poverty schools in which more than 70% of students received free or reduced-price lunches. Among the 189 kindergartners, 67% were African American and fewer than 10% spoke English as their second language. Historically, nearly half of the student population received remedial or special education by third grade. In these schools, professional development alone (Tier 1) reduced the percentage of students at risk in kindergarten from 40% to 30%. Adding direct, small-group intervention (Tier 2) further reduced the percentage at risk to 18% by October of first grade. To generate further reduction in this proportion of students at risk, ongoing intervention was provided in successive 14-week blocks through first grade. The percentage of poor readers steadily declined; however, 7% made poor progress despite nearly 2 years of intervention, and the percentage of the treated sample later referred for special education did not change. The study did not explore whether more intensive intervention in kindergarten and first grade could have reduced the number of students who continued to experience reading difficulties. Moreover, approximately 20% of parents of eligible students declined permission for their children to participate in Tier 2, so it was not possible to obtain an unbiased estimate of risk reduction.

Coyne, Kame'enui, Simmons, and Harn (2004) described a similar three-tier model of intervention, with a particular focus on the students who had responded well to Tier 2 intervention in kindergarten. They randomly assigned strong kindergarten responders to well-implemented, code-based general class reading instruction in first grade (Tier 1) or continued Tier 2 intervention in addition to the code-based general class instruction. They found no advantage for continued intervention in first grade for the students who had responded well in kindergarten and suggested that the early boost in kindergarten acted as inoculation against future reading problems. The strong word-reading skill levels of these students, measured with subtests of the Woodcock Reading Mastery Tests, support this suggestion. The reading fluency—measured in February—of the students initially at risk, however, was not as strong as that of the average readers in this district (26 words per minute compared with 34 words for average readers), leaving open the possibility that more support could be needed as rate begins to overstep accuracy as a predictor of reading competence (Jenkins, Fuchs, van den Broek, Espin, & Deno, 2003). In addition, not all kindergarteners in the original sample were strong responders to Tier 2 intervention. Across Tier 2 conditions in kindergarten, 9%–18% of students remained in the risk category and so failed to be inoculated. The authors conclude with the importance of conceiving of prevention and intervention as broad, schoolwide efforts.

Vaughn (2003) took this approach and added important information on "dosage" of successive layers of intervention. For students deemed unresponsive to scientifically based reading instruction, Tier 2 intervention consisted of 10–12 weeks of supplemental instruction in groups of three to five students. This instruction followed the content of the general class instruction; however, pacing was matched to the learning in the group, and students received many more opportunities to respond and more corrective feedback than they could receive in the whole-class grouping. After the first round of Tier 2 intervention, students who made good progress returned to general education class instruction alone, and those who had not made progress were assigned to another round of Tier 2—a much more intensive condition with even smaller groups, more instructional time, and frequent adjustment of instruction based on results from ongoing measurement of student progress (see Chapter 3 for examples of progress monitoring).

As in Greenwood and colleagues (2003) and O'Connor (1999; 2000), Vaughn (2003) found positive effects for professional development of teachers, with stronger gains for at-risk students who also received Tier 2 as needed. This study has not yet concluded, and the participants will continue in the interventions as needed until third grade. Some will also participate in tertiary (Tier 3) intervention; however, these proportions and results are not yet available. In the meantime, Vaughn conducted a study with second graders to determine how long Tier 2 intervention should continue with students at risk. In her sample, 31% of students receiving Tier 2 intervention caught up to average reading performance in 10 weeks of supplemental instruction, 53% in 20 weeks, and 76% in 30 weeks; 24% remained struggling readers despite a year of intervention. These results could help school personnel to consider how much intervention to provide before deciding on more intensive services, such as Tier 3 intervention or special education. It is important to realize that not all students who exited Tier 2 were able to maintain strong reading performance when the additional support was removed, suggesting that the inoculation effect found in Coyne and colleagues (2004) may need "booster shots" along the way.

DECISIONS IN THE DESIGN OF SECONDARY INTERVENTIONS

Researchers and school personnel who pursue three-tier models of reading intervention have many decisions to make. As yet, there are too few studies to form firm recommendations regarding how best to proceed. The most progress has been made toward defining the content of the code-based instruction that forms primary intervention, which is usually shared with teachers through ongoing professional development. As schools move toward combinations of primary and secondary intervention, it is important to establish criteria to determine which students should receive secondary intervention, the frequency and duration of this instruction, the content and format for the interventions, grouping and scheduling arrangements, and when to transition toward instruction that is even more explicit and targeted or altogether different (Tier 3 intervention).

Criteria for Selecting Tier 2 Participants

One of the first critical decisions in the implementation of three-tier models is determining how to select students for additional interventions. Using the criteria for reading disability (i.e., a discrepancy between ability and achievement of one or more standard deviations or "outside the normal range" cut-off scores on standardized tests) would enable too many students to fall into the crack of underselection (Stuebing et al., 2002; Torgesen, 2000). This problem is exacerbated by commonly available normed measurement tools, which tend to inflate standard scores at the kindergarten and first-grade levels, making struggling learners even more difficult to identify because "typical readers" are not expected to read very well in these grades. Recent longitudinal prediction studies that use precursors of reading—for example, performance-based measures of segmenting and letter knowledge—to identify students at risk show convergence for levels of skill that place students more or less at risk (Good, Simmons, & Kame'enui, 2001; O'Connor & Jenkins, 1999) in kindergarten and early in first grade. The research of Simmons and colleagues (2003), Vaughn (2003), and O'Connor, Fulmer and colleagues (2005) used measures of phoneme segmentation and letter knowledge to establish two groups of students: one that would continue with only Tier 1 instruction and one that would receive a "minimal dose" of Tier 2 instruction. Although the absolute levels indicating risk on these measures varied by study and research team, individual differences were found in each study as early as in November of kindergarten. In our work, we decided to err on the side of overselection and use monitoring of reading progress (see Chapter 3) to guide our grouping and regrouping decisions.

Once students are receiving secondary intervention, for how long should they receive it? Secondary intervention can be managed by duration (e.g., 10 or 15 weeks of intervention), or by the progress students make in the intervention. If the latter course is chosen in conjunction with progress monitoring, then how good is good enough to be considered on track for adequate progress? If intervention is inoculation, as Coyne and colleagues (2004) suggest, then, over time, studies might converge on absolute levels of performance at particular time points that achieve this protection against future reading failure. Unfortunately, data to strongly recommend either option is lacking because most studies of three-tier interventions published to date are only 1 or 2 years in duration, and the collection of skills that constitutes reading becomes more sophisticated over time. Even within the 2-year studies (O'Connor, 2000; Simmons et al., 2003; Vaughn, 2003), most have found that some students who seem to be "good enough" on target skills such as word attack or word identification may have difficulty once again with the more complex acts of reading text fluently and comprehending it (Coyne et al., 2004; O'Connor, Fulmer et al., 2005). It would be useful for future studies to identify levels of skill that exert long-lasting protection against future reading difficulties.

Content of Secondary Intervention

Should Tier 2 intervention provide a complete reading lesson (e.g., include phoneme awareness, phonics, vocabulary, fluency practice, and comprehension) or focus on reading skills most in need of improvement (e.g., phoneme segmenting or word identification or fluent reading)? Little evidence as of 2006 exists on the comparative effects of this decision. If general education instruction provides a complete package, teachers may be able to help students make more rapid gains by focusing on the student's skill or collection of skills most different from the student's classmates. Alternatively, differentiating the content of Tier 2 for individuals or groups of students could place undue stress on the measurement system to determine specific areas of weakness for each child. Moreover, students gain skills at different rates and, therefore, would need to be frequently regrouped, which is difficult for maintaining routines and also for the schedules of the intervention providers. In the studies introduced in this collection, Blachman and colleagues (1999), Simmons and colleagues (2003), and Vaughn (2003) took the complete package approach, and O'Connor, Fulmer and colleagues (2005) attempted to match instruction to areas of need.

EXAMPLES OF LAYER 2 INSTRUCTION ACROSS GRADES

We have concluded an intervention study in two schools (O'Connor, Harty, & Fulmer, 2005) in which Tier 1 and Tier 2 interventions were implemented across the first 4 years of schooling. For each student selected for Tier 2 intervention, we tried to determine 1) which skills diverged most from those of his or her peers across the skills relevant to reading in that grade and 2) what the student currently could do in that skill domain (e.g., which letter sounds are known, which phoneme positions can be identified, how fast the child currently reads). We used this information to form groups ranging from two to four students in size and used ongoing measurement of progress to determine how long a student would stay in a particular instructional group and when he or she should either return to Tier 1 instruction only or move to a different Tier 2 (or Tier 3) group. We do not claim that this type of Tier 2 intervention is superior to (or even as good as) Tier 2 interventions in other studies, but we use this work to illustrate how the content and logistics can be operationalized over time in schools.

Kindergarten

Several researchers have concluded that for students to make reading progress in the primary grades, the most important understanding is the notion of the alphabetic principle (National Reading Panel, 2000; Share & Stanovich, 1995; Vellutino et al., 1996). To grasp this understanding, students need to be able to hear the speech sounds in words and to associate some of these speech sounds with alphabet letters, which enables students to grasp how reading and writing works. We can decompose this notion into measurable components, including students' ability to segment a spoken word into speech sounds, to provide sounds for alphabet letters, and to match the sounds they hear in words to an appropriate letter, such as children do when generating a spelling for a word. Studies have generated developmental sequences (Vandervelden & Siegel, 1997) and average performance for these skills at various time points in kindergarten (e.g., see Good et al., 2001; O'Connor & Jenkins, 1999), and these recommendations are helpful for determining whether students are making the kind of progress likely to yield adequate reading in first or second grade.

For this study, we selected two schools representing differing demographics and degrees of need in a large city in the northeastern United States. One school was located in an industrial area where fewer than 10% of parents reported any college education. The other was a university-affiliated laboratory school for which most parents paid tuition, although 12% of students received tuition aid. Across the two schools, 15% of third graders—most of whom had a diagnosis of learning disability—were eligible for special education. English was the predominant language of 92% of the participants. We screened students in October; however, we used October scores as a baseline from which to measure gains rather than as a basis for placing students in secondary intervention. To determine which students were eligible for Tier 2 intervention, we assessed students again in January and chose for intervention those students who named fewer than 15 letters or 10 phonemes in a list of 10 words. We released students from Tier 2 intervention when they could name more than 40 letters and identify more than 20 segments in 10 spoken words, which nears the performance of average achievers near the end of kindergarten.

Because of the half-day schedule of most kindergarten classes and the students' short attention spans, instructional sessions were kept brief (10–12 minutes) and were supplemental to the teacher's literacy instruction. The first focus of instruction was on stretched segmenting and cumulative introduction of letters and sounds. We taught and practiced the sounds for *a, m, s,* and *t,* first by practicing with letter cards and then by using games to say and match letter sounds. In these brief sessions, we also spent about 2 minutes segmenting words that contained these sounds and others by saying the words in a stretched fashion (e.g., "Let's see how slowly we can say *sat.*" [The teacher models: "SSSaaat."] "Say it with me. SSSaaat. Now you say it slowly." [The students say *sat* slowly, pausing for a second on each sound.]). When students were able to say words slowly without a teacher model, the teacher introduced Elkonin boxes (Elkonin, 1973), on which students touched each of three joined boxes in sequence as the phonemes in words were stretched.

Within a few weeks, teachers in these small groups asked students to pause on a box they were touching and identify a sound in isolation. As these sounds were identified, students selected a known letter to represent the sound they heard. Because previous work also suggested that some students who reached these benchmarks might still have difficulty applying aspects of the alphabetic principle to reading words (O'Connor & Jenkins, 1995), our instruction included letter manipulation activities to provide students with opportunities to represent most or all sounds in words with letter tiles for the letter sounds they learned in class and in Tier 2 intervention. During this activity, intervention teachers were careful to keep the word choices within the collection of letters and sounds the students already had learned.

By the end of the year, the kindergarten secondary interventions consisted primarily of review of letter sounds, Segment-to-Spell (O'Connor, Notari-Syverson et al., 2005), and sounding out words (decoding aloud the word they had spelled). Of the one hundred students in the initial sample, all but three were able to segment one-syllable words of 3 phonemes and name sounds for 30 or more letters by the end of kindergarten. This outcome was considerably better than what we had achieved when we intervened without the backdrop of Tier 1 intervention. Although these levels of prereading skill placed most of our sample above the threshold for reading disability identified in recent prediction studies (Good et al., 2001; O'Connor & Jenkins, 1999) and would have made most students eligible for the inoculated group described in Coyne and colleagues (2004), not all students who appeared to be helped by this intervention remained in the average range in first grade. Also troubling were the three students who failed to acquire typical levels of segmenting and letter knowledge during Tier 2 intervention, which suggested that a longer duration or greater intensity would be needed for these students than the small-group instruction this secondary intervention provided.

First Grade

With a focus on segmenting and letters, 10 minutes of supplemental instruction allowed most kindergarten students to keep up with their peers; however, much more instruction was needed to help struggling readers catch up to or keep pace with their peers in first grade. The content of secondary intervention in first grade can take various forms depending on whether students 1) responded well in kindergarten, but needed additional practice opportunities to keep up with the demands of instruction in first grade; 2) failed to reach grade-level expectations in kindergarten and needed to continue to work on segmenting, sounds for letters, and blending, in addition to skills being learned by their classmates; or 3) moved to the school from classes elsewhere that had offered limited opportunity for learning the alphabetic principle. This latter group may need secondary interventions at any time point when entering a new school and may respond well when the instruction is appropriate or may need prolonged intervention at the secondary or tertiary levels. Although newcomers present important instructional problems that must be addressed in schoolwide intervention systems, the focus here is on secondary interventions for students who have been continuously enrolled in a school that uses a three-tier model of instruction, measurement, and intervention.

Tier 1 instruction in first-grade classrooms involves more components of reading than in kindergarten and more coordination among the components, which suggests a need to monitor progress monthly or more frequently as the content of reading instruction becomes more varied. Word study that began in September with vowel-consonant (v-c) and consonant-vowel-consonant (c-v-c) forms broadened by November into words with consonant and vowel patterns such as *ch, -ing, –igh,* and *ai,* and quick recognition of frequently occurring sight words became important as students began to read connected text such as sentences and short passages.

Tier 2 intervention was conducted for 30 minutes 3 or 4 days per week in groups of two to four learners, depending on students' needs and teachers' schedules. First grade offered myriad instructional targets for Tier 2 intervention, including continued work on letter sounds, letter patterns, and decoding words; reading and rereading sentences and longer passages; rereading material from prior sessions; spelling or writing and reading back what was written; and vocabulary instruction, story grammars, and retells for comprehension.

We used a gated procedure for determining which skills had been sufficiently mastered and which skills were appropriate targets for measurement and instruction for each child. As examples, we monitored students' progress in auditory segmenting until they could articulate each phoneme in a list of 10 one-syllable words to 90% accuracy. Previous research (O'Connor, 2000) in which we measured students' skills over time showed how students moved from articulating single phonemes to chunking sounds as their reading skills improved, and so continuing to measure one skill long after students move to more complex skills is unproductive. We monitored letter-naming until students could name more than 50 mixed upper- and lowercase letters in a minute; thereafter, we monitored their knowledge of letter sounds and, later still, of letter combinations. As lower-level processes were thoroughly learned, we constructed probes of high-frequency words based on the 25, 50, 75, and 100 most common words in *The Reading Teacher's Book of Lists* (Fry, Kress, & Fountoukidis, 2000). As students began to routinely read connected text, we shifted from word lists to oral reading fluency probes to monitor their progress. We used scores on these measures to form our Tier 2 intervention groups and continued to use them to regroup students periodically. By December, we had regrouped the first graders so that we could focus on particular needs and spent more or less time on specific instructional features depending on the needs of students in the group.

In some groups, we worked hard to break students' habit of guessing at words. For these students, we reinforced letter sounds with a magnetic board and included a few minutes of word formation with students reading back the words they had spelled. We moved students into reading connected text with the *Bob Books* (Maslen & Maslen, 1987), which begin with tightly controlled vocabulary and sight words. Each day, students practiced reading word cards from previous and current lessons. By November, a first-grade teacher stopped us in the hall to tell us that a child's mother had called to announce that her child was sounding out words at home.

By January, only a handful of students lagged due to trouble with particular word or letter pattern confusions, though several students showed difficulties with spelling. The largest single hurdle for Tier 2 participants was reading fluently, which arguably represents the most complex attainment in first grade. Because comprehension of text is tightly linked to the speed of reading words in first and second grades (e.g., correlations above .9 in Deno, 1985 and O'Connor & Jenkins, 1999), midway through first grade we began devoting more of Tier 2 intervention to reading and rereading text.

To ease the scheduling difficulties that began to surface in first grade, we took advantage of students in secondary interventions who arrived at school early, ate breakfast quickly, or attended after school programs in these schools. These opportunities allowed us to deliver interventions without disrupting the school day. Despite the concern of the adults (e.g., classroom teachers, specialists, interventionists), the students rarely minded leaving class for secondary intervention; in fact, in some cases they left their classes amid disappointed looks from the students left behind ("Why don't you pick me?").

Some students made steady progress across all of the early reading skill areas; others had particular difficulties with impulsive guessing (particularly in running text), retaining new letter-sound patterns, retrieval of sounds during decoding, or reading fluently. The three kindergartners who had failed to master segmenting and letter sounds continued to have reading difficulties through the end of third grade; four other students receiving Tier 2 intervention in kindergarten and first grade caught up and remained strong through third grade; and several other students had difficulty with one or several aspects of reading and required Tier 2 intervention for 1 or more years before catching up.

Second Grade

From first to second grade, more changes occurred in our Tier 2 interventions. Students who had responded poorly in kindergarten and first grade received intensive, daily intervention in tertiary, or Tier 3, intervention, which is explained and described in other chapters of this book.

We continued to provide Tier 2 intervention to second graders whose reading achievement fell below average and who needed additional support and practice to improve and/or to maintain reading levels close to those of their peers. Although each group differed from others, especially in the reading levels of materials, two types of Tier 2 sessions predominated. About two thirds of students received intervention that included word study (e.g., recognition of affixes, common letter and syllable patterns, and using these features to decode words) along with reading connected text at their reading level (.5 to 1 year below grade level). These sessions lasted 30 minutes, 3 or 4 days per week, with 8–12 minutes on word and syllable level activities, 10–15 minutes reading and rereading text, and a few minutes on vocabulary and comprehension.

Because the words and ideas in our reading materials were somewhat below the students' grade level, most students needed vocabulary help only with occasional unusual words, phrases, or concepts. One group of students in Tier 2, however, spent about 8 minutes daily on vocabulary and oral language as a result of low scores on receptive and expressive language tests and somewhat lower cognitive ability. One of these students had mild mental retardation, and although the other two had cognitive scores in the average range, comprehension of spoken and written language was more difficult for them than for other students in the intervention groups, which was readily apparent in the fall. None of these students spoke English as a second language. We selected words and concepts from their reading materials and followed guidelines in Carnine, Silbert, and Kame'enui (1997) and Beck, McKeown, and Kucan (2002) for developing definitions, multiple examples of usage, and frequent review of the week's and previous weeks' words and phrases.

The remaining one third of the students had achieved grade-appropriate word recognition skills (e.g., scores of 95 or higher on the (Woodcock Reading Mastery Tests–Revised [WRMT–R] subtests of Word Identification and Word Attack) but were slow readers. Teachers told us that these students just could not get through the material that others could complete during the instructional time. It is important to recall that teachers continued to receive professional development around the essential components of reading and that they were already including fluency practice through partner reading and word study several times a week throughout second grade. Tier 2 sessions for students who only needed fluency practice were 15 minutes, 3 days per week, and included choral reading of paragraphs, closely monitored partner practice, and weekly graphed progress on first readings of text, which many of the students found motivating and reinforcing.

Some students appeared to grow into the average range at particular testing points and then fall behind again later. For example, eight students who had received secondary intervention in first and second grade scored in the average range during the January testing cycle of second grade. We dropped these students from the Tier 2 intervention; however, by the end of second grade, we picked three of them up again because they were unable to maintain average progress without the additional practice secondary intervention provided. Of the second graders whose Tier 2 intervention was directed only toward fluency, none continued to need assistance in third grade.

Third Grade

By third grade, 71% of the students who had received secondary intervention in kindergarten, first grade, and/or second grade read in the average range for skills and fluency (within one standard deviation of mean performance). Of the remaining students, all continued to need additional instruction and practice with words. We introduced a variation of the DISSECT (*D:* discover the context; *I:* isolate the word's prefix; *S:* separate the word's suffix; *S:* say the word's stem; *E:* examine the word's stem; *C:* check with another person to see if you are correct; and *T:* try to find the word in a dictionary) model of Lenz and Hughes (1990), which we called BEST (O'Connor & Bell, 2004), to provide a strategy for reading multisyllable words. In this model, we taught students to *B:* break apart the word into pieces you recognize; *E:* examine the root; *S:* say the parts in order; and *T:* try the whole thing. Students learned the strategy over four consecutive teaching sessions, and we continued to rehearse and refer to the strategy for the rest of the year. During partner reading, we observed students challenging each other to "BEST" a word that was difficult. Most of the students who continued to receive Tier 2 intervention were reading about a year below grade level; and although they continued to make progress, it was slower progress than average.

Scheduling secondary intervention in second and third grade became increasingly difficult because of the competing demands of "specials" such as music, library visits, physical education, and extended projects in social studies and science. Along with scheduling, finding appropriate materials became another serious issue. Instruction in general education classrooms and the practice opportunities that constituted Tier 1 were no longer appropriate for some students. As students entered third grade, the Tier 2 intervention no longer mirrored the instruction offered in general education classrooms, which rarely included word-level instruction or opportunities to read aloud for fluency development. By third grade, some students in need of Tier 3 interventions (4.8% of the original sample) were reading so far below grade level that classroom materials were inappropriate for improving their reading skills (O'Connor et al., 2002) even though the content of grade-level materials was engaging or important. The mismatch between what students can understand and what they can read grows over time. Ideally, in a three-tier system, students will not lag as far behind as they would have in systems without Tier 1; and, indeed, our students in Tier 2 were not as delayed as students selected for intervention in our earlier studies that were conducted outside a three-tier model of reading intervention (O'Connor et al., 2002). Nevertheless, even with the best interventions, some students grow more slowly than others, and seven of the nine students who continued to need specialized reading instruction had moved from secondary to tertiary interventions by December. Of these seven students, one was diagnosed with mental retardation in first grade, one with a behavior disorder in second grade, and the other five with learning disabilities in second, third, or fourth grade.

OUTCOMES OF SECONDARY INTERVENTIONS

One way to view outcomes of layered intervention is by considering diminishing proportions of struggling readers over time and the level of competence the students achieved. By May of first grade, 17% of students (down from 21% earlier that year) continued in Tiers 2 or 3, and their segmenting scores ranged from 24–46 phonemes per minute. Word recognition also showed dramatic gains, with standard score gains of 5–25 points (average 14 points, or nearly a standard deviation) from the beginning to the end of first grade. One third of the Tier 2 students ended first grade with standard scores above 100 on Word Identification and Word Attack subtests; however, average reading rate at the end of first grade was only 32 words per minute, and only 27% of students read more than 40 words per minute on connected text, leaving the others clearly in the danger range. Because most studies of three-tier models of reading intervention have not reported end-of-first-grade fluency, it is difficult to know whether these outcomes are representative. Moreover, although students who continued in Tier 2 or 3 scored lower than those who were "released" in first grade, we did not find distinct differences that identified which students in additional layers would later become eligible for special education.

Studies of students who are typical readers have found no advantage for additional instruction in segmenting and the alphabetic principle when their reading program already included systematic phonics instruction (Foorman, Francis, Novy, & Liberman, 1991; Perfetti, Beck, Bell, & Hughes, 1987). The improvement found across studies of three-tier models of intervention has suggested that even when general class instruction includes explicit phonics instruction and decoding practice, low-skilled students benefit from the specificity, attention to mastery, and practice opportunity that secondary intervention provides.

LESSONS LEARNED

It is important to note that the interventions described in this chapter began with explicit instruction in the alphabetic code: how to hear the sounds in words, represent those sounds with alphabet letters and letter combinations, examine a string of letters and generate blended sounds to produce words, and manipulate sounds in words to form new words. In earlier studies, when instruction in the alphabetic code was compared with instruction in which half or more of the allotted time was spent on comprehension for young students at risk for reading difficulties, the instruction that concentrated on the code showed significant advantages (Juel & Minden-Cupp, 2000; Simmons et al., 2003). Although we added instructional time on fluency, vocabulary, and comprehension for some students in first grade and beyond, only 3 students who continued in Tier 2 past first grade needed no more instruction at the level of individual words. Table 7.1 shows the activities we used at each grade level and the number of students who received each collection.

In keeping with other chapters in this book, providing short term, focused intervention helped to discriminate students who had difficulty getting started or who entered school with less-developed preparatory skills for literacy learning than their peers from students whose reading difficulties were persistent and severe. In keeping with studies of special education over the last several decades, no one "packaged" set of activities addressed the needs of all of the students whose difficulties were most severe. In our most recent work (O'Connor, Harty et al., 2005) first-grade interventions that appeared successful did not inoculate all second graders from struggling once again as reading demands increased. As many studies have indicated, fluency can continue to make reading laborious after other skills have been remediated.

Our data showed that increasing the intensity of instruction while keeping the instruction rooted in the code produced improvements for all students, but

Table 7.1.   Instructional activities in Tier 2 interventions in kindergarten through third grade

Grades	Number of students who participated in each activity	Activities
Kindergarten	31	Cumulative letter-sound instruction
31 students in	31	Stretched blending
Tier 2	31	Stretched segmenting
	31	Manipulating letters while segmenting
First grade	14	Cumulative letter-sound instruction
21 students in	14	Blending and segmenting speech sounds
Tier 2*	14	Decoding
	14	Letter patterns
	14	Spelling with a magnetic board
	14	Practice reading high-frequency words quickly
	14	Reading and rereading text aloud
	7	All other first grade activities, plus vocabulary, story structure, and retells
Second grade	6	Reading and rereading text aloud only
18 students in	9	Word study (decoding)
Tier 2*	9	Reading and rereading text aloud
	3	All of above, plus vocabulary and comprehension
Third grade	2	Reading and rereading text aloud only
9 students in	7	BEST analysis for multisyllable words
Tier 2*	7	Reading and rereading text aloud

Key: BEST = *B*reak apart the word into pieces you recognize, *E*xamine the root, *S*ay the parts in order, and *T*ry the whole thing.

*Some of these students received Tier 2 for only part of the school year.

not cures. Some of the students who received continuous tiers of intervention for all 4 years continued to struggle with reading; however, none of the students were reading fewer than 25 words per minute on grade-level text at the end of third grade. Perhaps these students would have made more progress in an intervention that was quite different from what we offered. Evidence from other studies of second and third graders (outside a three-tier model of reading intervention) suggest that severely delayed readers still make more gains with code-based instruction than with whole-word approaches (Foorman et al., 1998; Shankweiler & Liberman, 1989); however, there may be additional elements to add to instruction for the slowest growers that could improve their trajectory of growth. As layered designs are now in their nascency, there is much to learn about the type and intensity of instruction that can minimize reading disability.

REFERENCES

Ball, E., & Blachman, B. (1991). Does phoneme awareness training in kindergarten make a difference in early word recognition and developmental spelling? *Reading Research Quarterly, 26,* 49–66.

Beck, I., McKeown, M., & Kucan, L. (2002). *Bringing words to life: Robust vocabulary instruction.* New York: The Guilford Press.

Blachman, B., Ball, E., Black, S., & Tangel, D. (1994). Kindergarten teachers develop phoneme awareness in low-income, inner-city classrooms: Does it make a difference? *Reading and Writing: An Interdisciplinary Journal, 6,* 1–17.

Blachman, B.A., Ball, E.W., Black, R., & Tangel, D.M. (2000). *Road to the code: A phonological awareness program for young children.* Baltimore: Paul H. Brookes Publishing Co.

Blachman, B.A., Tangel, D.M., Ball, E.W., Black, R.S., & McGraw, C.K. (1999). Developing phonological awareness and word recognition skills: A two-year intervention with low-income, inner-city children. *Reading and Writing: An Interdisciplinary Journal, 11,* 239–273.

Carnine, D., Silbert, J., & Kame'enui, E. (1997). *Direct instruction reading* (3rd ed.). New York: Merrill.

Coyne, M., Kame'enui, E., Simmons, D., & Harn, B. (2004). Beginning reading intervention as inoculation or insulin: First-grade reading performance of strong responders to kindergarten intervention. *Journal of Learning Disabilities, 37,* 90–106.

Cunningham, A. (1990). Explicit vs. implicit instruction in phonemic awareness. *Journal of Experimental Child Psychology, 50,* 429–444.

Darling-Hammond, L. (2000). Teacher quality and student achievement: A review of state policy evidence [Electronic version]. *Education and Policy Analysis Archives 8*(1).

Deno, S. (1985). Curriculum-based measurement: The emerging alternative. *Exceptional Children, 52,* 219–232.

Elkonin, D.B. (1973). U.S.S.R. In J. Downing (Ed.), *Comparative reading.* (pp. 551–579). New York: Macmillan.

Engelmann, S., & Bruner, E. (1995). *Reading mastery I* (Rainbow ed.). New York: McGraw-Hill.

Foorman, B.R., Francis, D.J., Fletcher, J.M., Schatschneider, C., & Mehta, P. (1998). The role of instruction in learning to read: Preventing reading failure in at-risk children. *Journal of Educational Psychology, 90,* 37–55.

Foorman, B.R., Francis, D.J., Novy, D., & Liberman, D. (1991). How letter-sound instruction mediates progress in first-grade reading and spelling. *Journal of Educational Psychology, 83,* 456–469.

Fry, E.B., Kress, J.E., & Fountoukidis, D.L. (2000). *The reading teacher's book of lists.* Upper Saddle River, NJ: Prentice Hall.

Garet, M.S., Porter, A.C., Desimone, L., Birman, B.F., & Yoon, K.S. (2001). What makes professional development effective? Results from a national sample of teachers. *American Educational Research Journal, 38*(4), 915–945.

Good, R.H., Simmons, D.C., & Kame'enui, E.J. (2001). The importance and decision-making utility of a continuum of fluency-based indicators of foundational reading skills for third-grade high-stakes outcomes. *Scientific Studies of Reading, 5,* 257–288.

Greenwood, C.R., Tapia, Y., Abbott, M., & Walton, C. (2003). A building-based case study of evidence-based literacy practices: Implementation, reading behavior, and growth in reading fluency, K–4. *Journal of Special Education, 37,* 95–110.

Jenkins, J., Fuchs, L., van den Broek, P., Espin, C., & Deno, S. (2003). Accuracy and fluency in list and context reading of skilled and RD groups: Absolute and relative performance levels. *Learning Disabilities Research and Practice, 18,* 237–245.

Juel, C. (1988). Learning to read and write: A longitudinal study of 54 children from first through fourth grades. *Journal of Educational Psychology, 80,* 437–447.

Juel, C., & Minden-Cupp, C. (2000). Learning to read words: Linguistic units and instructional strategies. *Reading Research Quarterly, 35,* 458–492.

Lenz, B.K., & Hughes, C.A. (1990). A word identification strategy for adolescents with learning disabilities. *Journal of Learning Disabilities, 23,* 149–163.

Maslen, B.L., & Maslen, J.R. (1987). *The Bob books.* West Linn, OR: Bob Books Publications.

McCutchen, D., Abbott, R.D., Green, L.B., Beretvas, S.N., Cox, S., Potter, N.S., et al. (2002). Beginning literacy: Links among teacher knowledge, teacher practice, and student learning. *Journal of Learning Disabilities, 35,* 69–86.

National Reading Panel. (2000). *Teaching children to read.* Rockville, MD: NICHD Information Resource Center.

O'Connor, R.E. (1999). Teachers learning Ladders to Literacy. *Learning Disabilities Research and Practice, 14,* 203–214.

O'Connor, R.E. (2000). Increasing the intensity of intervention in kindergarten and first grade. *Learning Disabilities Research and Practice, 15,* 43–54.

O'Connor, R.E., & Bell, K.M. (2004). Teaching students with reading disability to read words. In A. Stone, E. Silliman, B. Ehren, & K. Apel (Eds.), *Handbook of language and literacy: Development and disorders* (pp. 479–496). New York: The Guilford Press.

O'Connor, R.E., Bell, K.M., Harty, K.R., Larkin, L.K., Sackor, S., & Zigmond, N. (2002). Teaching reading to poor readers in the intermediate grades: A comparison of text difficulty. *Journal of Educational Psychology, 94,* 474–485.

O'Connor, R.E., Fulmer, D., Harty, K.R., & Bell, K.M. (2005). Layers of reading intervention in kindergarten through third grade: Changes in teaching and child outcomes. *Journal of Learning Disabilities, 38,* 440–455.

O'Connor, R.E., Harty, K.R., & Fulmer, D. (2005). Tiers of intervention through third grade. *Journal of Learning Disabilities, 38,* 532–538.

O'Connor, R.E., & Jenkins, J.R. (1995). Improving the generalization of sound/symbol knowledge: Teaching spelling to kindergarten children with disabilities. *Journal of Special Education, 29,* 255–275.

O'Connor, R.E., & Jenkins, J.R. (1999). The prediction of reading disabilities in kindergarten and first grade. *Scientific Studies of Reading, 3,* 159–197.

O'Connor, R.E., Jenkins, J.R., & Slocum, T.A. (1995). Transfer among phonological tasks in kindergarten: Essential instructional content. *Journal of Educational Psychology, 2,* 202–217.

O'Connor, R.E., Notari-Syverson, A., & Vadasy, P.F. (1996). Ladders to literacy: The effects of teacher-led phonological activities for kindergarten children with and without disabilities. *Exceptional Children, 63,* 117–130.

O'Connor, R.E., Notari-Syverson, A., & Vadasy, P.F. (2005). *Ladders to literacy: A kindergarten activity book.* (2nd ed.). Baltimore: Paul H. Brookes Publishing Co.

Perfetti, C., Beck, I., Bell, L., & Hughes, C. (1987). Phonemic knowledge and learning to read are reciprocal: A longitudinal study of first-grade children. *Merrill-Palmer Quarterly, 33,* 283–319.

Shankweiler, D., & Liberman, I. (1989). *Phonology and reading disability: Solving the reading puzzle* (pp. 1–33). IARLD Monograph Series. Ann Arbor: University of Michigan Press.

Share, D., Jorm, A., MacLean, R., & Matthews, R. (1984). Sources of individual differences in reading acquisition. *Journal of Educational Psychology, 76,* 1309–1324.

Share, D., & Stanovich, K. (1995). Cognitive processes in early reading development: Accommodating individual differences into a model of acquisition. *Issues in Education: Contributions from Educational Psychology, 1,* 1–57.

Simmons, D.C., Kame'enui, E.J., Stoolmiller, M., Coyne, M.D., & Harn, B. (2003). Accelerating growth and maintaining proficiency: A two-year intervention study of kindergarten and first-grade children at risk for reading difficulties. In B.R. Foorman (Ed.), *Preventing and remediating reading difficulties: Bringing science to scale.* Timonium, MD: York Press.

Stuebing, K., Fletcher, J., LeDoux, J., Lyon, G.R., Shaywitz, S., & Shaywitz, B. (2002). Validity of IQ-discrepancy classifications of reading disabilities: A meta-analysis. *American Educational Research Journal, 39,* 469–518.

Torgesen, J.K. (2000). Individual differences in response to early interventions in reading: The lingering problem of treatment resisters. *Learning Disabilities Research and Practice, 15,* 55–64.

Torgesen, J., Wagner, R., & Rashotte, C. (1997). Prevention and remediation of severe reading disabilities: Keeping the end in mind. *Scientific Studies of Reading, 1,* 217–234.

Vandervelden, M., & Siegel, L. (1997). Teaching phonological processing skills in early literacy: A developmental approach. *Learning Disabilities Quarterly, 20,* 63–81.

Vaughn, S. (2003, December). *How many tiers are needed for response to intervention to achieve acceptable prevention outcomes?* Paper presented at the National Research Center on Learning Disabilities Responsiveness to Intervention Symposium, Kansas City, MO.

Vellutino, F.R., Scanlon, D.M., Sipay, E., Small, S., Pratt, A., Chen, R., et al. (1996). Cognitive profiles of difficult-to-remediate and readily remediated poor readers: Early intervention as a vehicle for distinguishing between cognitive and experiential deficits as basic causes of specific reading disability. *Journal of Educational Psychology, 88,* 601–638.

Tertiary Intervention

8

The Nature and Role of the Third Tier in a Prevention Model for Kindergarten Students

Beth A. Harn, Edward J. Kame'enui, and Deborah C. Simmons

E arly identification and intervention for students with reading difficulties is axiomatic and at the heart of the general recommendation of most recent meta-analyses and national panels (Foorman & Torgesen, 2001; Francis, Shaywitz, Stuebing, Shaywitz, & Fletcher, 1996; National Reading Panel [NRP], 2000; National Research Council [NRC], 1998; Vaughn & Fuchs, 2003). These studies document the long-term consequences of reading failure and the daunting, often futile task of providing intervention services after a child spends years struggling with the complex task of early reading skill development. More empowering, though, is the firm conclusion that we know more now about the intricacies of early reading instruction and the power of prevention. Prevention efforts and targeted intervention provided in kindergarten and first grade have proven successful at decreasing the need for later remediation (Kame'enui, Good, & Harn, 2004). The success of prevention research is the impetus for the current Reading First Initiative (No Child Left Behind Act of 2001; PL 107-110) and influences the development of comprehensive reading programs, both of which impact daily practices in classrooms.

Although a full review of prevention research for children with reading difficulties is beyond the scope of this chapter (see Cavanaugh, Kim, Wanzek, & Vaughn, 2004; Foorman & Torgesen, 2001; Torgesen, 2002), two general conclusions are offered. First, the most common cause of reading difficulty is a child's lack of proficiency in phonological processing, hence the need for prevention and

Preparation of this chapter manuscript was supported in part by Project CIRCUITS, Grant No. H324X010014, and Project ACCEL–S, Grant No. H324M980127, of the Office of Special Education Programs, U.S. Department of Education. This material does not necessarily represent the policy of the U.S. Department of Education nor is the material necessarily endorsed by the federal government.

intervention in kindergarten and first grade (Torgesen, 2002). Second, intervention efforts for students in kindergarten and first grade who display early reading difficulties are successful. In his meta-analysis of early reading intervention studies, Torgesen determined that when students are identified early and provided explicit, systematic instruction in small instructional groups, only 2%–6% of the general population would not develop skills predictive of later reading proficiency.

Additional support for the power of early reading intervention is gained from recent studies documenting how instruction can change the neural functioning in the brain (Papanicolaou et al., 2003; Sandak, Mencl, Frost, & Pugh, 2004; Shaywitz, 2003). Through the use of noninvasive technology involving functional magnetic resonance imaging and magnetic source imaging, researchers are able to capture children's neural activity as they are reading. General conclusions of this research are 1) as early as kindergarten, students displaying overt reading difficulties on traditional measures of early literacy show different neural activity than typically developing readers; and 2) if struggling readers are provided scientifically based intervention, the neural activity of the brain changes to more closely resemble typically developing readers (Papanicolaou et al., 2003; Sandak et al., 2004; Shaywitz, 2003). Papanicolaou and colleagues (2003) concluded that instruction plays a vital role in establishing brain mechanisms and emphasized the importance of early intervention because of the developmental plasticity of neural processes in early reading development. This current line of research broadens the lens and captures the complex processes and variables involved in reading and aids the field in refocusing attention on variables that can be changed to improve reading outcomes: early identification and scientifically based reading interventions.

In this chapter, we provide a framework for employing a Three-Tier Model of reading intervention in schools that focus on preventing children from developing reading difficulties by increasing instructional support in a systematic, responsive manner. Examples of this system of instructional support are provided for each tier, but emphasis will be on the essential features of a Tier 3 intervention, including data from a research study completed with kindergartners identified as at risk for reading difficulties. The essential features of effective Tier 3 interventions are 1) prioritized content, 2) purposeful instructional design and delivery, 3) protected time and grouping, and 4) performance monitoring.

A THREE-TIER MODEL OF INSTRUCTIONAL SUPPORT TO PREVENT READING DIFFICULTIES

The theoretical and conceptual framework we employ for the prevention of reading difficulties is drawn from the public health literature (Caplan & Grunebaum, 1967, cited in Simeonsson, 1994). This framework comprises three individual tiers, or levels, of prevention: primary prevention, secondary prevention, and tertiary prevention (Kame'enui, Simmons, Good, & Chard, 2002). In this framework, the concept of "prevention" is defined in one of two ways: 1) an action that stops an event from happening; or 2) an action designed to reduce a problem or condition that already has been identified.

In the following definitions of primary, secondary, and tertiary prevention, these two meanings are evident. At a systems level, *primary prevention* is concerned with reducing the number of new cases (incidence) of a potential problem (e.g., reading difficulties, learning disabilities, reading disabilities) in the population. Thus, primary prevention directs the sources of information and resources (e.g., instructional and curricular programs, strategies, procedures, approaches in beginning reading) at the school, classroom, and child level to ensure that the needs of all learners are addressed before reading difficulty crystallizes, takes hold, and stabilizes. The primary focus of this strategy is to minimize the number of students requiring more intensive resources or interventions. Primary prevention begins in kindergarten and Grade 1 by implementing scientifically based practices to decrease the likelihood of students developing reading difficulties.

In contrast to primary prevention, *secondary prevention* is concerned with reducing the number of existing cases (prevalence) of an already identified condition or problem in the population. According to the Committee on the Prevention of Reading Difficulties of the National Academy of Science, secondary prevention "involves the promotion of compensatory skills and behaviors. . . . The extra effort is focused on children at higher risk of developing reading difficulties but before any serious, long-term deficit has emerged" (NRC, 1998, p. 16). The focus in secondary efforts is to increase instructional supports to children identified as at-risk to teach them the essential skills they need to benefit from instruction in the primary instructional program as quickly as possible.

Finally, *tertiary prevention* is concerned with reducing the complications associated with an existing and identified problem or condition. According to the NRC (1998), "Programs, strategies, and interventions at this level have an explicit remedial or rehabilitative focus. If children demonstrate inadequate progress under secondary prevention conditions, they may need instruction that is specially designed and supplemental—special education, tutoring from a reading specialist—to their current instruction" (p. 16). The instruction necessary for these students is significantly more intensive, "relentless," and "precise" to accelerate learning rates (Kavale, 1988, p. 335).

The three levels, or tiers, of prevention are depicted in Figure 8.1. As indicated, the level of information, resources, and specialization of support services increases for students demonstrating reading difficulty. The focus of a three-tier prevention model is to intensify instruction systematically in kindergarten through Grade 3 in response to student performance, which should prevent or decrease the number of students needing additional support after Grade 3.

This model of instructional support is based on our collective research and professional development efforts over the past several years to implement, document, and scale up schoolwide systemic strategies and processes for effectively reforming a school's efforts to prevent reading difficulties for all readers (Good,

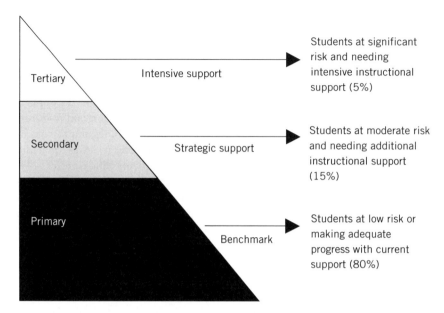

Figure 8.1.   Tiers of instructional support in a prevention model. (Adapted from Walker, H.M., Horner, R.H., Sugai, G., Bullis, M., Sprague, J.R., Bricker, D. et al. [1996]. Integrated approaches to preventing antisocial behavior patterns among school-age children and youth. *Journal of Emotional and Behavioral Disorders, 4,* 202; adapted by permission.)

Simmons, & Kame'enui, 2001; Kame'enui & Simmons, 2002; Simmons et al., 2002; see also http://idea.uoregon.edu:16080/~ibr/ for more information on this research). Although the educational community realizes the need for systems-level prevention research, there is no agreed-on approach or agreed-on metric for evaluating what constitutes an effective prevention model. No large-scale experimental studies of such a prevention model (i.e., random assignment to treatment and control groups) have been conducted, and the nonexperimental studies that have been conducted often do not have student academic outcomes as a dependent variable (Zins, Heron, & Goddard, 1999). Thus, the best method to evaluate prevention efforts has yet to be determined. We propose that one effective method for evaluating efforts on the reading performance of students is to use a formative evaluation system—the Dynamic Indicators of Basic Early Literacy Skills (DIBELS)—on a school or systemswide level within a three-tier prevention model. With this assessment approach, if a student is not progressing as expected, he or she can be identified readily and increased instructional support can be implemented to prevent the reading difficulty from taking hold. In the next section, we discuss implementation of this approach at a systemwide level with particular emphasis on the instructional features, content, and procedures needed to intensify instruction and accelerate learning for struggling readers.

THE THREE-TIER PREVENTION MODEL: SYSTEMATICALLY INCREASING INSTRUCTIONAL INTENSITY BASED ON STUDENT PERFORMANCE

In a prevention model, it is important to determine which students are at risk for later reading difficulties and who requires additional instructional support. The DIBELS was designed to efficiently screen all students on critical literacy skills (e.g., phonological awareness, alphabetic principle, fluency with connected text) on a quarterly basis in relation to established goals (Good & Kaminski, 2003; Good, Simmons, & Kame'enui, 2001). Therefore, in this prevention model, a student's performance on these measures is compared with established DIBELS benchmarks. A student's score is then categorized according to level of risk (low risk, some risk, or at risk) and his or her need for one of three types of instructional recommendations—benchmark, strategic, or intensive. In each category, students are said to be at increased relative risk if their current levels of performance are predictive of later reading failure. To prevent reading difficulties from becoming entrenched, we use the instructional recommendations within the three-tier model to determine which students need increased instructional support.

Benchmark Instruction

Students given a *benchmark* instructional recommendation are considered on track and at low relative risk, which means the odds are in their favor (i.e., 80% or greater) of achieving the next early literacy goal if they continue to receive their current effective, comprehensive instructional support. For these students, the primary, or Tier 1, level of instructional support is considered sufficient for meeting the students' instructional needs.

Strategic Instruction

Students given a recommendation of *strategic* instructional support are at increased relative risk for later reading difficulties because one or more early literacy skills are not at levels predictive of long-term reading success. For these students, secondary, or Tier 2, instructional support is recommended to increase instructional support to accelerate learning.

Intensive Instruction

The odds of reaching the next literacy goal for students given an instructional recommendation of *intensive* are poor (i.e., less than 40%) unless significant additional instructional support is provided immediately, relentlessly, explicitly, and continuously. For these students, the tertiary, or Tier 3, level of instructional support is recommended to significantly increase instructional support to accelerate learning.

INSTRUCTIONAL COMPONENTS
OF A THREE-TIER PREVENTION MODEL

The following section discusses the features related to instruction across each tier of this systemwide approach. The features relate to nature of the instruction (e.g., explicitness, time, grouping), program, setting, and frequency of evaluating student performance.

Primary (Tier 1) Prevention: Benchmark Instructional Support

The purpose of Tier 1 instructional support is to implement a schoolwide comprehensive reading program that emphasizes the essential components of scientifically based reading research to support the needs of all students in acquiring essential early reading skills. In addition to the implementation of a core reading program, the following alterable variables must be considered: allocated and engaged instructional time, group size, instructional focus, and progress monitoring. In Table 8.1, we provide a list of variables that can be manipulated to increase the intensity of instructional support. For example, the instructional intensity of students receiving Tier 1 support, or students with a benchmark instructional recommendation, is not high. Students at benchmark on the DIBELS measures are benefiting from the core curriculum and instructional procedures delivered by the general education teacher. Because these students are on track, assessment with the DIBELS is completed only three times per year (i.e., beginning, middle, and end of the year) to ensure that learning rates predictive of later reading proficiency are maintained. In contrast, students at Tier 2 (strategic) or Tier 3 (intensive) levels require more intensive instructional support—including frequent progress monitoring—across the alterable variables listed in Table 8.1.

In our conceptualization of a prevention model, Tier 1 instructional support represents the core curricular and instructional reading programs with strategies implemented in the general education classroom. Primary prevention in Tier 1 is designed to accommodate the majority of students in a school, or approximately 70%–80% of enrolled K–3 students. More importantly, it is designed to prevent children from becoming at risk for reading problems. Therefore, the core reading program, instructional support (e.g., grouping and teacher direction), time allocated (i.e., 90 minutes), and frequency of progress monitoring represent the primary prevention investments of the K–3 teachers, paraprofessionals, parents, and administrators. Primary prevention also involves a formative assessment system (e.g., DIBELS) that provides practitioners with timely and important information on the reading performance of all students as well as on the effectiveness of the core instructional investments.

Table 8.1. Alterable variables to increase instructional support: Preventing reading difficulties

Alterable variable	Level of recommended instructional support		
	Primary—Tier 1 benchmark	Secondary—Tier 2 strategic	Tertiary—Tier 3 intensive
Curricular program	Research-based core reading program that emphasizes the five essential elements of beginning reading instruction	Research-based core reading program Strategic enhancements of the five essential elements of beginning reading or specific targeted supplemental programs	Research-based reading program with supplemental or accelerated/intervention programs on selected essential elements of beginning reading Carefully selected objectives from grade-level core materials
Nature of teacher-guided instruction	Provided throughout the school day	Increased explicitness of instruction and focus Additional opportunities to practice embedded throughout the day Increased opportunities to review skills	Increased explicitness of instruction and focus Additional opportunities to practice embedded throughout the day Increased opportunities to review skills
Highly qualified instructor	General education teacher	General education teacher Additional general and supplemental support	General education teacher Additional general education or specialized support
Opportunities to learn	Mainly large group with small-group arrangements	A mixture of large- and small-group instruction Deliberate selection of skills targeted for small-group instruction	Mainly small-group instruction Deliberate selection of skills targeted for large group instruction
Allocated instructional time	A minimum of 90 minutes allocated to the essential elements of literacy skills	A minimum of 90 minutes allocated to the essential elements of literacy skills Time specifically set aside to supplement or enhance essential skill development in small groups	A minimum of 90 minutes allocated to the essential elements of literacy skills Time specifically set aside to essential skill development in small groups Additional 20–30 minutes per day provided in a small group settings
Instructional setting	General education classroom	General education classroom	General education classroom with push-in or pull-out instructional support
Evaluating student learning	Assess at the beginning, middle, and end of year	Assess 1–2 times a month	Assess 2–4 times a month

Secondary (Tier 2) Prevention: Strategic Instructional Support

The purpose of Tier 2 instructional support is to identify groups of students with increased risk of not becoming proficient readers and systematically increase instructional support. As specified in Table 8.1, students requiring Tier 2 instructional support are provided instruction in small groups with increased specificity and explicitness and with additional opportunities to practice and review essential early reading skills. Because these students are at risk and additional instructional resources are required, their learning is monitored more frequently (i.e., once or twice a month) using DIBELS. Their instructional plan (i.e., materials, time, grouping) can then be modified as the data warrant.

Because of individual child variation in learning to read in an alphabetic writing system and the reality that one core reading program is not likely to meet the needs of all children, schools must develop and implement a range of reading programs, strategies, and supports. "One size does not fit all" is a pedagogical and instructional reality in schools. Therefore, Tier 2 support involves programs, strategies, and procedures designed and employed to supplement, enhance, and support the core reading program for children identified with marked reading difficulties. The goal of Tier 2 is to increase instructional support to accelerate learning. It is assumed that in a school with effective Tier 1 support, approximately 15%–20% of students will need Tier 2 support to meet high stakes outcomes.

Tertiary (Tier 3) Prevention: Intensive Instructional Support

Students needing Tier 3, or intensive, instructional support demonstrate both low skills and little progress when provided with additional instructional support. Students needing intensive instructional support require significantly more instructional resources delivered with greater intensity and specificity than students receiving Tier 2 instructional support. Tier 3 instructional variables that may differ from Tier 2 may include 1) selecting program materials that are more explicit; 2) focusing on essential skills; and 3) providing more opportunities to practice and review newly introduced skills (see Table 8.1). Because students needing Tier 3 support have the most to learn, additional time for reading instruction provided in small-group settings is critical. To ensure that the intensive instructional program is meeting the students' needs, data are collected at least every other week to evaluate learning rates in a more timely manner. Tier 3 represents reading instruction that is specifically designed and customized for students with marked difficulties in reading or who have not responded to other intervention efforts (e.g., Tier 1 or Tier 2). Often the instruction is delivered by personnel with specialized training (e.g., Title I teachers, special education teachers, reading specialists) employing specially designed instructional materials (i.e., intervention or acceleration programs). It is expected, even in schools implementing the first two tiers of this prevention model, that approximately 5%–10% of students may need this most intensive level of instructional support to achieve critical reading goals.

In summary, the general features of the three-tier prevention model include systematically increasing instructional support in response to student performance by implementing the following:

1. Effective, scientifically based core curriculum and instructional practices

2. Adequate time allocated and judiciously protected for reading instruction

3. A system or continuum of additional interventions and supports

4. Brief, repeatable, valid formative assessment of reading progress used in a timely manner to identify students at risk for later reading difficulty

5. Dynamically evaluated interventions to maximize student learning and problem-solving teams to inform instructional decisions

The next section provides an example of how this prevention model, with each tier representing increased instructional support, is implemented within a particular school district, the Bethel School District in Eugene, Oregon. In this section, we also discuss the results of a study conducted with kindergarteners identified as at risk for reading difficulties. These results illustrate the essential features of effective three-tier interventions: 1) prioritized content, 2) purposeful instructional design and delivery, 3) protected time and grouping, and, 4) performance monitoring.

SCHOOL DISTRICT APPLICATION
OF THE THREE-TIER PREVENTION MODEL

Our relationship with the Bethel School District began 6 years ago with the implementation of a 4-year model demonstration project titled Project ACCEL–S (Accelerating Children's Competence in Early Reading and Literacy–Schoolwide). A full description of this project is provided in Simmons and colleagues (2002), but the primary features included 1) professional development and support in the selection of research-based instructional materials, 2) implementation of a formative assessment system (DIBELS), and 3) research-based instructional strategies and procedures designed to improve reading outcomes. Because Project ACCEL–S was implemented prior to the Reading First initiative, getting schools to agree to use a common core program and to deliver reading instruction for at least 90 minutes a day was a notable accomplishment.

The next section describes the general features of each level of instructional support—mapped onto the alterable variables presented in Table 8.1—for kindergarten through Grade 3. In addition, to aid in understanding exactly what these schools did on a daily basis, we identify the specific commercial reading and intervention programs the schools implemented. These materials were selected by school personnel due to their documented empirical efficacy and are not named here as an endorsement of any specific program, simply as an example of what this school district implemented. We suspect that other programs with similar features and implemented with fidelity may be equally effective.

Primary Prevention: Tier 1

To maximize the reading outcomes for all students, schools adopted and received professional development in using research-based instructional programs delivered by the general education teacher. In Project ACCEL–S, all schools selected *Open Court* (Adams et al., 2000) except for one school that selected *Reading Mastery* (Englemann & Bruner, 1995). Reading instruction was provided for a minimum of 90 minutes each day with a mixture of whole- and small-group arrangements. All students were screened at the beginning, middle, and end of the school year to ensure that they were progressing as expected and to identify students who would need additional instructional support beyond Tier 1. Students identified as "benchmark" on DIBELS were seen as benefiting from the Tier 1 instructional support and not at risk for developing later reading difficulties.

Secondary Prevention: Tier 2

Instructional support was intensified systematically for students identified on the DIBELS assessment as being at moderate risk (i.e., requiring strategic supports). As specified in Table 8.1, the core program was still the primary source of reading instruction. However, during small-group instruction, teachers purposefully focused on the essential reading skill areas (i.e., phonological awareness, phonics, vocabulary) as indicated by DIBELS and other instructional assessments. In some schools, students experienced difficulty in reading connected text fluently. Teachers felt that their core reading programs did not place sufficient emphasis on fluency and adopted a targeted fluency intervention program, *Read Naturally* (Ihnot, 1991), to support and enhance the core program. Other schools developed general fluency strategies incorporating more controlled text reading and rereading in a more systematic manner (Greenwood, Maheady, & Delquadri, 2002; Howell & Nolet, 2001). During both large- and small-group instruction, teachers worked on increasing the number of opportunities students had to actively practice these essential skills. Teachers also increased the explicitness and consistency of teacher instructional language. In many schools, Title I personnel worked in the general classroom providing daily homogeneous small-group (Tier 2) instruction as part of a "push-in" model of service delivery. Because students receiving Tier 2 supports had increased relative risk for reading difficulties, their progress was monitored at least monthly to evaluate the effectiveness of the instructional supports. If progress monitoring data displayed a positive trend predictive of later reading proficiency, intervention services were continued. If progress monitoring data displayed less-than-adequate growth, Tier 2 teachers met to problem-solve and determine if additional instructional or procedural modifications might be necessary. If performance was not adequate, additional instructional support was recommended and typically provided as part of Tier 3 intervention.

Tertiary Prevention: Tier 3

Instructional support was further intensified for students identified as being at high risk (i.e., requiring intensive supports) on the DIBELS assessment or displaying limited growth in response to additional instructional supports in Tier 2. For many of these students, the gap between the instructional objectives of the core reading program in some beginning reading areas (e.g., advanced phonic elements) and the student's skill level (e.g., inconsistent letter-sound knowledge) was so large that the school-level reading team and parents decided that instructional materials other than those being used in the general classroom would be more appropriate. Careful decisions were made on what skills (e.g., vocabulary, comprehension strategies, early phonological awareness, skills review) to teach during whole-group instruction that would benefit all students. Critical skills that needed to be taught with urgency (e.g., alphabetic understanding, word reading, reading connected text) were thought to be best addressed by intervention and acceleration programs specifically designed with careful sequencing of skill introduction and development, ample opportunities to practice and review, and explicit instructional strategies to maximize instructional time and learning. A continuum of instructional supports was developed as schools selected a range of different programs based on student instructional needs, current core program, and instructor familiarity, for example, *Horizons* (Englemann, 1999), *Read Well* (Sprick, Howard, & Fidanque, 2000), *Reading Mastery,* (Englemann & Bruner, 1995), *Read Naturally* (Ihnot, 1991). To accelerate learning, students receiving Tier 3 supports were provided with more than 90 minutes of reading instruction each day, the majority of it provided in small groups by Title I and/or special education personnel. As the alterable variables chart in Table 8.1 indicates, progress monitoring was conducted every other week so that instruction was maximally responsive to student learning. Instructional problem-solving teams met every 2 weeks, and student progress was dynamically evaluated and modifications were made to the instructional program when data indicated a need for acceleration.

ESSENTIAL FEATURES OF TIER 3 INTERVENTIONS

A research study was conducted within the implementation of Project ACCEL–S to better understand the kindergarten intervention attributes (e.g., content, procedures, instructional delivery) required to close the gap between the most at-risk students and their typically developing peers. For a more thorough discussion and a detailed description of this project, see Simmons, Kame'enui, Stoolmiller,

Coyne, and Harn (2003). The next section highlights the general characteristics of the study to illustrate the essential features of effective Tier 3 interventions.

Context and Population of Participants

Participants in this study initially included 111 kindergarten students from seven elementary schools across two school districts in the Pacific Northwest. All of the schools were qualified to receive Title I reading services, were rural in nature, and had similar ethnicity breakdowns (primarily white). The percentage of free and reduced-rate lunch participation ranged from 32%–63% of the school population. The students identified to participate in the intervention were selected as at risk based primarily on their early literacy skills of letter knowledge and beginning phonological awareness, as measured by the DIBELS Letter Naming Fluency and Onset Recognition Fluency (now called Initial Sounds Fluency) measures (Good & Kaminski, 2003). All of the students were screened at the beginning of the school year, and students performing below the 20th percentile—similar to what the DIBELS categorizes as "intensive instructional recommendation"—were invited to participate. Final participants were primarily white (84%) and male (58%) with a small percentage of students from Latino/Hispanic ethnic groups (13%).

Intensive Intervention Characteristics: Essential Features of Tier 3 Interventions

To demonstrate the features of effective Tier 3 interventions, the results of this study are presented to best illustrate the critical components discussed earlier in this chapter: 1) protected time and grouping; 2) performance monitoring; 3) prioritized content; and, 4) purposeful instructional design and delivery. The features consistent across the three interventions are presented first.

Protected Time and Grouping

All students received a half day of kindergarten for 2.5 hours, during which a minimum of 60 minutes was devoted to early literacy activities. Because all of the students in the study were at significant risk for reading difficulties, they were provided with an additional 30 minutes of small-group instruction 5 days a week beyond the general school day. To maximize student learning, all instruction was provided in groups of no more than five students. Intervention began in early November and ended mid-May.

Performance Monitoring

In addition to the assessments completed before and after the intervention, all students were assessed using DIBELS at least monthly. In addition, schools assessed the students monthly as well, so students' growth in phonological awareness and alphabetic principle were monitored twice a month.

Prioritized Content and Purposeful Instructional Design and Delivery

The features of purposeful instructional delivery and prioritized content can best be illustrated within a more general description of the interventions. The following descriptions are condensed to focus on the essential intervention and instructional elements of the interventions to demonstrate how these attributes can accelerate learning rates.

INTERVENTION DESCRIPTIONS

Code Emphasis

Code emphasis (CE)—an experimenter-developed intervention—focused on providing strategic, explicit, and systematic instruction on phonemic awareness and alphabetic understanding in two consecutive 15-minute components. This intervention was not designed to be comprehensive nor to replace the core reading instruction provided in the general classroom. Instead, it was carefully designed to accelerate learning of the most essential skills students need to be able to read.

Prioritized Content

The content for the CE intervention was carefully chosen based on research documenting the importance of these reading skills in later reading (NRP, 2000; Simmons & Kame'enui, 1998). In the first 15 minutes, instruction established and reinforced the essential phonologic skills of 1) first and last sound isolation, 2) sound blending, and 3) sound segmentation. The following fundamental alphabetic skills and strategies also were taught: 1) letter sound and name identification, 2) letter-sound blending to read consonant-vowel-consonant (c-v-c) words, 3) selected irregular word reading, and 4) sentence reading of controlled text. The second 15 minutes extended and deepened phonological and alphabetic skills through instruction in handwriting (e.g., letter dictation and formation) and integrated phonologic and alphabetic skills and spelling.

Purposeful Instructional Design and Delivery

In addition to carefully chosen and prioritized content, the CE intervention contained the following instructional elements: 1) explicit and consistent teacher language, 2) multiple and careful modeling of tasks, 3) careful sequencing of skill introduction and development, 4) ample opportunities to practice and receive corrective feedback on skill performance, 5) systematic and cumulative review of previously learned skills, and 6) purposeful integration of previously learned skills to support more advanced skill learning (i.e., words used in blending activities were also used in sentence reading).

Code and Comprehension Emphasis

The code- and comprehension-emphasis (CCE) intervention also was experimenter-developed but was broader in scope of instruction than the CE intervention. The lessons were provided using strategic, explicit, and systematic instruction on phonemic awareness, alphabetic understanding, story grammar, and vocabulary in two consecutive 15-minute components.

Prioritized Content

The CCE intervention distributed content emphasis across two areas of reading—code (i.e., phonologic and alphabetic) and comprehension (i.e., vocabulary, narrative text structure, story retell)—delivered as two 15-minute consecutive segments that were taught each day. One half of the CCE intervention was allocated to code-based features and the other half to vocabulary and comprehension. The first 15 minutes were the same as the CE intervention and focused on high-priority phonologic and alphabetic skills. The second 15 minutes had two primary foci: 1) receptive and expressive knowledge of vocabulary that appeared in storybooks, and 2) expanded knowledge and development of story structure and story retell through a repeated reading of popular children's literature.

Purposeful Instructional Design and Delivery

The same explicit and systematic instructional elements used in the CE intervention were also applied to the CCE intervention.

Commercial Program

The commercial program (CP) intervention served as a comparison group and included the implementation of a commercial reading program characterized as explicit and systematic with a strong emphasis on phonologic and alphabetic development.

Prioritized Content

The CP intervention comprised the "Sounds and Letters" module of the *Open Court Reading* (Adams et al., 2000) comprehensive reading program. The entire 30 minutes of small-group instructional time was allocated to code-emphasis activities. However, the range of skills taught was much broader. For example, the range of phonological awareness skills covered a full complement of skills from rhyming to sound substitution. In a typical day, children 1) listened to rhymes, poems, and songs, 2) played language and word games to apply knowledge of sounds, letters, and language, 3) engaged in phonemic awareness activities, 4) recited poems for a designated letter, 5) learned a new letter name and sound, 6) used new sounds in sentences, and 7) wrote new letters in the writing workbook.

Purposeful Instructional Design And Delivery

The instructional elements of materials and delivery were less intensive and purposeful than in the CE and CCE interventions. For example, instead of providing specific instructional language for reviewing or correcting skills as in the CE and CCE interventions, this intervention offered 1) directions that designated when and how to introduce and practice a skill, and 2) reminders of what key skills to review when children had difficulty. In contrast to the experimental interventions, the number of teacher models and practice examples were less prescribed, and corrective feedback was less specific. Specific correction procedures were not provided, although directions did direct teachers to point out the task children were to perform (e.g., "If the children have trouble, remind them that the words you are looking for begin with the /s/ sound," Adams et al., 2000, Unit 2, Lesson 11, p. 180).

RESULTS

Changes in children's performance were assessed in the following domains with the corresponding measures: 1) phonological awareness (DIBELS: Phonemic Segmentation Fluency [PSF]; Good & Kaminski, 2003); 2) nonsense or pseudoword reading (DIBELS: Nonsense Word Fluency [NWF]; Good & Kaminski, 2003; Woodcock Reading Mastery Test–Revised (WRMT–R): Word Attack subtest; Woodcock, 1987) and word reading (WRMT–R: Word Identification subtest; Woodcock, 1987); 3) general receptive vocabulary (Peabody Picture Vocabulary Test–Revised; Dunn & Dunn, 1981); 4) targeted expressive vocabulary; and 5) listening comprehension (an experimenter-developed measure designed to tap story retell and story comprehension). The results reported here focus solely on phonologic and alphabetic skills and are organized around progress monitoring measures (using the DIBELS measures) and pre- and postassessments (using the WRMT–R). To determine the efficacy of these interventions, a group of 37 average achieving (AA) students were identified at the beginning of the school year (based on performing at the 50th percentile on the same identification measures in September) and monitored throughout the school year.

Progress Monitoring Measures

Students were monitored monthly using the PSF and NWF measures. Scores on PSF and NWF measures indicated that the typical performer in each of the three intervention groups and the AA group met established end-of-year kindergarten benchmarks of 35 phonemes per minute and 20 letter sounds per minute (Good, Simmons, & Kame'enui, 2001). One-way analyses of variance indicated a significant main effect for group on the May PSF measure, $F(3,135) = 5.245$, $p = .002$, and the May NWF measure, $F(3,134) = 4.548$, $p = .005$ (see Table 8.2 for descriptive statistics). Planned comparisons among the three intervention groups

Table 8.2. Descriptive statistics of phoneme segmentation fluency and nonsense word fluency end-of-kindergarten performance by group

	Students assigned to interventions			Average-achieving students
	CE (n = 32)	CCE (n = 34)	CP (n = 30)	AA (n = 37)
	May phonemic segmentation fluency[a]			
M	47.84	41.44	36.43	49.62
SD	14.42	17.61	17.54	9.88
	May nonsense word fluency[b]			
M	39.38	29.38	25.03	39.68
SD	17.48	17.81	13.60	25.74

Key: CE = code emphasis; CCE = code and comrehension emphasis; CP = commercial program; AA = above average; N = number of students; M = mean; SD = standard deviation. (From Simmons, D.C., Kame'enui, E.K., Stoolmiller, M., Coyne, M.D., & Harn, B. [2003]. Accelerating growth and maintaining proficiency: A two-year intervention study of kindergarten and first-grade children at risk for reading difficulties. In B.R. Foorman [Ed.], *Preventing and remediating reading difficulties: Bringing science to scale.* [p. 206]. Timonium, MD: York Press.)

[a]Phoneme Segmentation Fluency (Good & Kaminski, 2003)

[b]Nonsense Word Fluency (Good & Kaminski, 2003)

using the Tukey-Kramer method (critical point = 2.37 for the studentized range statistic, q for alpha = .05 and 3 simultaneous contrasts) indicated that the CE group was significantly higher than the CP group on both NWF (q = 3.11) and PSF (q = 2.41) and significantly higher than the CCE group on the NWF measure (q = 2.94). Planned comparisons using the Tukey-Kramer method (critical point = 2.37 for q for alpha = .05 and 3 simultaneous contrasts) indicated that the CP group was significantly lower than the AA group on both PSF (q = –2.56) and NWF (q = –3.53).

A noteworthy difference emerged between the AA comparison and intervention groups meeting the NWF criterion by the end of intervention. In May, 88% of students in the CE group identified 20 or more letter sounds in one minute compared with 65% and 63% of students in the CCE and CP groups, respectively. This finding is particularly impressive given that 86% of students in the AA comparison group achieved the benchmark. Chi-square analyses indicated a significant relation among groups and attainment of benchmark, $\chi2(3\ df)$ = 9.55, p = .023. Figure 8.2 illustrates the observed mean growth trajectories on NWF from January through May. Particularly noteworthy is the rate of growth (i.e., slope) of the different groups across the intervention, especially the rate of alphabetic principle development of the CE group when compared with the CP group. Students in the CE intervention not only were more likely to reach benchmark than students in the CP group, they were more likely to reach that benchmark approximately 2 months earlier.

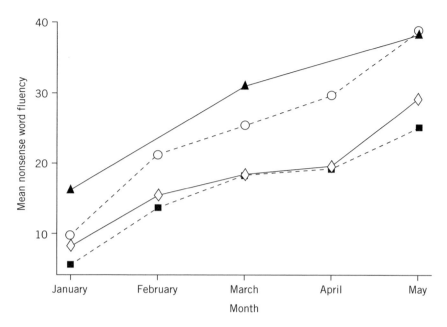

Figure 8.2.   Mean nonsense word fluency performance by intervention group across the intervention. (*Key:* ▲ = above average; ■ = commercial program; ○ = code emphasis; ◇ = code and comprehension emphasis.) (From Simmons, D.C., Kame'enui, E.K., Stoolmiller, M., Coyne, M.D., & Harn, B. [2003]. Accelerating growth and maintaining proficiency: A two-year intervention study of kindergarten and first-grade children at risk for reading difficulties. In B.R. Foorman [Ed.], *Preventing and remediating reading difficulties: Bringing science to scale.* [p. 207]. Timonium, MD: York Press.)

Pre and Postmeasures

Performance on the WRMT–R revealed a strong response to intervention across groups, with mean scores falling well within average ranges. On the Basic Skills Cluster of the WRMT–R (Word Attack and Word Identification subtests composite), respective means for the groups were as follows: CE: M = 109.31; CCE: M = 104.47; CP: M = 100.13; and AA: M = 111.97. One-way analysis of variance indicated a significant main effect for group, $F(3,129)$ = 9.175, $p < .001$. Planned comparisons among the 3 intervention groups using the Tukey-Kramer procedure (critical point q = 2.37 for alpha = .05 and 3 simultaneous contrasts) indicated that the CE group was significantly higher than the CP group (q = 3.28). Planned comparisons using the Tukey-Kramer procedure (critical point q = 2.37 for alpha = .05 and 3 simultaneous contrasts) indicated that the CP (q = –4.91) and CCE (q = –3.43) groups were significantly lower than the AA group (see Table 8.3 for descriptive statistics).

Table 8.3. Descriptive statistics of WRMT-R Basic Skills Cluster end-of-kindergarten performance by group

	Interventions			Average-achieving students
Interventions	CE	CCE	CP	AA
M	109.31	104.47	100.13	111.94
SD	9.79	9.51	14.47	15.27

Key: WRMT-R = Woodcock Reading Mastery Test–Revised; CE = code emphasis; CCE = code and comprehension emphasis; CP = commercial program; AA = above average; M = mean; SD = standard deviation. (From Simmons, D.C., Kame'enui, E.K., Stoolmiller, M., Coyne, M.D., & Harn, B. [2003]. Accelerating growth and maintaining proficiency: A two-year intervention study of kindergarten and first-grade children at risk for reading difficulties. In B.R. Foorman [Ed.], *Preventing and remediating reading difficulties: Bringing science to scale.* [pp. 206–207]. Timonium, MD: York Press.)

Summary of Results

These results provide further evidence for the importance of early intervention. However, when examining these results in relation to the essential features of prioritized content and purposeful instructional delivery, the importance of these alterable elements is clear. The role of purposeful instructional design and delivery is exemplified through the contrast of the CE intervention with the CP intervention. The group size, time, and general content (i.e., phonological awareness and alphabetic principle) were the same. However, students receiving the CE intervention significantly outperformed students in the CP intervention on the PSF, NWF and WRMT–R measures. The role of prioritized content is exemplified through the contrast of the CE intervention with the CCE intervention. These interventions only varied in terms of the breadth of content (i.e., phonological awareness and alphabetic principle vs. phonological awareness, alphabetic principle, vocabulary, and story grammar). Students in the CE intervention significantly outperformed students in the CCE intervention on the NWF measure. It should also be mentioned that students in the CE intervention were not significantly different than students in the AA group across all early reading measures.

CONCLUSIONS AND RECOMMENDATIONS OF ESSENTIAL FEATURES OF EFFECTIVE THREE-TIER INTERVENTIONS

Although the results of this study need to be replicated, the findings provide support for the essential features to improve the efficacy and need for three-tier models of reading intervention. We recommend four actions schools should take when designing instructional supports for their students needing third tier instructional support: 1) purposeful instructional design and delivery, 2) prioritized content, 3) protected time and grouping, and 4) performance monitoring.

Purposeful Instructional Design and Delivery

The results demonstrate the power of carefully designed and delivered instruction in accelerating student learning with the most at-risk students. As Lyon and Chhabra (2004) stated, "Children do not acquire reading ability naturally, easily, or incidentally" (p. 6), it must be taught. The mode or vehicle for teaching is the nature of the instruction employed. In this study, the nature of the instruction across the interventions varied in terms of the explicitness of the instructional *language* and specificity and care of how the instructional skills within the program were *designed*. The primary difference between the experimenter-developed interventions (CE and CCE) and the CP intervention was the level or intensity of instructional support provided. Providing explicit instructional language of how to introduce, model, complete, and correct specific reading tasks gives children the intensive level of instructional support necessary for them to successfully learn the skill (Carnine, Silbert, Kame'enui, & Tarver, 2003; Engelmann & Carnine, 1991; Rosenshine & Stevens, 1984). Although we are not advocating for schools to *design* curricular programs, the architecture of a program must be carefully examined. When schools select programs for students with the most intensive instructional needs, the nature of the instructional language should be carefully considered, especially if the program is going to be delivered by educational assistants who do not have the same level of professional development or training as certified teachers. Related to the instructional language used in delivering the program is the care taken in designing how the instructional objective is taught.

In the experimenter-developed interventions (CE and CCE), careful attention was given to determining when, how long, and how often a skill was taught. A scope and sequence of skill introduction, practice, and review was carefully designed to minimize learner confusion and increase successful learning. Skills that are easily confused (e.g., letter sounds of *b, d, p, q*) were deliberately separated in time. Skills that are more challenging (e.g., segmenting two- to three-phoneme words) were given more time to teach then easier skills (e.g., identifying first sounds). Consistent instructional language and materials were used in teaching the same skill across time so that students' attention was focused on learning the skill rather than being distracted by novel instructional tasks (Kame'enui & Simmons, 1990). Specific time and care also was taken in designing a deliberate and distributed review cycle of skills to maintain mastery of skills across the intervention. For example, a schedule was developed to quickly review previously taught letter sounds in a systematic and distributed way across the intervention. To accelerate learning of essential skills, care must be taken in deciding which skills will be taught during small-group instruction.

Prioritized Content

One of the greatest challenges when working with students needing intensive support is curriculum coverage. Teaching the essential skills that individual children are missing in addition to the many other skills specified within the core reading program in one instructional day is formidable. But if the goal is to get each child to be a reader by the end of Grade 3, schools need to prioritize essential skills and determine which parts of the core reading program must be taught. Fortunately, research has identified skills most predictive of reading success to assist educators in prioritizing (Kame'enui, Carnine, Dixon, Simmons, & Coyne, 2002; NRC, 1998; NRP, 2000; Simmons & Kame'enui, 1998). For example, in teaching phonological awareness to students who are the most behind, the CE intervention prioritized three skills that have the most research support: first and last sound isolation, sound blending, and sound segmentation. In contrast, the CP intervention taught the full range of phonologic skills. As Kame'enui, Carnine, Dixon, Simmons, and Coyne (2002) note, the effect of having too many instructional objectives for at-risk readers is that instruction can be reduced to exposure, which decreases the likelihood that skills are learned at a high criterion. When examining programs for use with students needing third-tier instructional support, time should be taken to examine which skills are taught, in what order, under what timeline, and to what criterion level of performance. As demonstrated by the results of the present study, careful sequencing of prioritized skills can accelerate learning rates in meaningful ways (e.g., students in the CE intervention reached criterion approximately 2 months earlier than students in the CP intervention).

Protected Time and Grouping

Students needing third-tier interventions require more reading instructional time than their peers to catch-up. The school districts participating in our study prioritized a minimum of 60 minutes of reading instruction each day for all kindergarten students. In addition, for their most at-risk kindergarteners, the schools provided an additional 30 minutes of instruction beyond the typical day. Careful planning of instructional time within a given classroom is a significant challenge; however, it is crucial if we are to maximize limited instructional minutes (Kame'enui & Simmons, 1990). Some schools have taken care to map out their reading instructional time within and across grade levels to enable a broader perspective of how to maximize their full range of instructional resources (i.e., Title 1, special education, English language learner, paraprofessionals). By making all instructional support services fully available to support reading instruction, schools have every opportunity to determine how small-group instruction can be most efficiently and effectively accomplished.

Students with the most intensive instructional needs will need more of their instruction delivered in small groups (Vaughn & Bos, 2002). Small-group instruction that is focused on the prioritized skills increases the instructional support in crucial ways by allowing instruction to be targeted specifically at the student's skill level and by increasing students' opportunities to practice skills with corrective feedback from teachers to enhance learning (Howell & Nolet, 2001). Research has clearly indicated that, on average, instructional groups of three students to one teacher are just as effective as one-to-one instruction (Elbaum, Vaughn, Tejero, & Watson Moody, 2000).

Performance Monitoring

Regularly collected progress monitoring data provides the objective information teachers need to document student skill development and evaluate intervention efficacy. Teachers who collect or are given student performance data make more strategic instructional changes (Fuchs, Deno, & Mirkin, 1984). However, in most discussions on intensifying instruction for at-risk readers, this area is not always addressed (Foorman & Torgesen, 2001). Most research studies involving struggling readers use measures that are not designed to assess rate of student performance (slope) on a repeated basis (Lyon & Moats, 1997; Shaywitz & Shaywitz, 1994). Measures of early literacy skills with parallel forms, such as the DIBELS, were designed specifically to assess rate of growth over time and to be sensitive to instruction (Good & Kaminski, 2003; Kaminski & Good, 1996). Collecting and examining a trend line of student performance (learning rate) enables teachers to be more responsive to student learning. For example, if the trend line indicates a learning rate not predictive of attaining empirically validated reading goals, a change in instruction is indicated. As Ysseldyke (2001) notes, examining student performance data regularly assists educators in taking instructional responsibility for student learning and empowers educators to problem solve on variables (e.g., fidelity of program implementation, grouping, time allocation, attendance, accuracy of student performance) that can be altered to improve student outcomes. Evaluating students' rate of progress regularly allows the efficacy of an intervention and the potential need for modification to be assessed in a timely manner.

CONCLUSION

As Foorman and Torgesen (2001) discussed, even with a core reading program delivered consistently and with fidelity, there will still be a need for additional instructional support. Schools should carefully develop each tier of instructional support by identifying students at risk for reading difficulties and systematically increasing instructional support in response to students' instructional needs. The essential features of purposeful instructional design and delivery, prioritized content, protected time and grouping, and performance monitoring can help schools focus on critical factors within their control to maximize the instructional time for students who do not have a minute to lose.

The power of the prevention efforts discussed in this chapter is made even more salient when considering the neurological research discussed in Chapter 6. The neural plasticity of the beginning reader compels us to intensify instruction early. Fortunately, the nuances of what "intensive instruction" looks like are clearer to us now then ever before. This intensive instruction should be empirically based, carefully designed and implemented, prioritized and protected, and responsive to student learning. As Papanicolaou and colleagues (2003) stated, "good instruction is always brain-based" (p. 16).

REFERENCES

Adams, M.J., Bereiter, C., Brown, A., Campione, J., Carruthers, I., Case, R., et al. (2000). *Open Court Reading.* New York: McGraw-Hill.

Caplan, G., & Gunebaum, H. (1967). Perspective on pprimary prevention: A review. *Archives of General Psychiatry, 17*(3), 258–381.

Carnine, D.W., Silbert, J., Kame'enui, E.J., & Tarver, S. (2003). *Direct instruction reading* (4th ed.). Upper Saddle River, NJ: Prentice Hall.

Cavanaugh, C., Kim, A., Wanzek, J., & Vaughn, S. (2004). Kindergarten reading interventions for at-risk students: Twenty years of research. *Learning Disabilities: A Contemporary Journal, 21,* 9–21.

Dunn, L., & Dunn, L. (1981). *Peabody Picture Vocabulary Test* (Rev. ed.). Circle Pines, MN: AGS Publishing.

Elbaum, B., Vaughn, S., Tejero, H., & Watson Moody, S. (2000). How effective are one-to-one tutoring programs in reading for elementary students at risk for reading failure? A meta-analysis of the intervention research. *Journal of Educational Psychology, 92,* 605–619.

Engelmann, S. (1999). *Horizons reading series.* New York: McGraw-Hill.

Englemann, S., & Bruner, E.C. (1995). *Reading mastery: Rainbow edition.* New York: McGraw-Hill.

Engelmann, S., & Carnine, D. (1991). *Theory of instruction: Principles and applications.* Eugene, OR: ADI Press.

Foorman, B.R., & Torgesen, J. (2001). Critical elements of classroom and small-group instruction promote reading success in all children. *Learning Disabilities Research & Practice, 16*(4), 203–212.

Francis, D.J., Shaywitz, S.E., Stuebing, K.K., Shaywitz, B.A., & Fletcher, J.M. (1996). Developmental lag versus deficit models of reading disability: A longitudinal individual growth curves analysis. *Journal of Educational Psychology, 88,* 3–17.

Fuchs, L.S., Deno, S.L., & Mirkin, P.K. (1984). Effects of frequent curriculum-based measurement on pedagogy, student achievement, and student awareness of learning. *American Educational Research Journal, 21,* 449–460.

Good, R.H., & Kaminski, R.A. (2003). *DIBELS: Dynamic Indicators of Basic Early Literacy Skills* (6th ed.). Longmont, CO: Sopris West Educational Services.

Good, R.H., Simmons, D.C., & Kame'enui, E.J. (2001). The importance and decision-making utility of a continuum of fluency-based indicators of foundational reading skills for third-grade high-stakes outcomes. *Scientific Studies of Reading, 5*(3), 257–288.

Greenwood, C., Maheady, L., & Delquadri, J. (2002). Classwide peer tutoring programs. In M. Shinn, H. Walker, & G. Stoner (Eds.), *Interventions for academic and behavior problems II: Preventive and remedial approaches* (pp. 611–650). Washington, DC: National Association of School Psychologists.

Howell, K., & Nolet, V. (2001). *Curriculum-based evaluation: Teacher and decision making* (3rd ed.). Belmont, CA: Wadsworth Publishing.

Ihnot, C. (1991). *Read Naturally reading program.* St. Paul, MN: Read Naturally.

Kame'enui, E., & Simmons, D. (1990). *Designing instructional strategies: The prevention of academic learning problems.* Columbus, OH: Charles E. Merrill.

Kame'enui, E.J., Carnine, D.W., Dixon, R., Simmons, D.C., & Coyne, M.D. (2002). *Effective teaching strategies that accommodate diverse learners* (2nd ed.). Upper Saddle River, NJ: Prentice Hall.

Kame'enui, E.J., Good, R., & Harn, B. (2004). Beginning reading failure and the quantification of risk: Reading behavior as the supreme index. In W. Heward, T. Heron, N. Neef, S. Peterson, D. Sainato, G. Cartledge, et al. (Eds.), *Focus on behavior analysis in education: Achievements, challenges, & opportunities.* Upper Saddle River, NJ: Prentice Hall.

Kame'enui, E.J., & Simmons, D.C. (2002). From an "exploded view" of beginning reading toward a schoolwide beginning reading model: Getting to scale in complex host environments. In R. Bradley, L. Danielson, & D.P. Hallahan (Eds.), *Identification of learning disabilities: Research to practice* (pp. 163–172). Mahwah, NJ: Lawrence Erlbaum Associates.

Kame'enui, E.J., Simmons, D.C., Good, R., III, & Chard, D. (2002). *Focus and nature of primary, secondary, and tertiary prevention: CIRCUITS model.* Unpublished manuscript.

Kaminski, R.A., & Good, R.H., III. (1996). Toward a technology for assessing basic early literacy skills. *School Psychology Review, 25*(2), 215–227.

Kavale, K.A. (1988). The long-term consequences of learning disabilities. In M. Wang & M.C. Reynolds (Eds.), *Handbook of special education: Research and practice: Vol. 2: Mildly handicapped conditions. Advances in education* (pp. 303–344). Elmsford, NY: Pergamon.

Lyon, G.R., & Chhabra, V. (2004). The science of reading research. *Educational Leadership, 61*(6), 12–17.

Lyon, G.R., & Moats, L.C. (1997). Critical conceptual and methodological considerations in reading intervention research. *Journal of Learning Disabilities, 30,* 578–588.

National Reading Panel. (2000). *Teaching children to read: An evidence-based assessment of the scientific research literature on reading and its implications for reading instruction: Reports of the subgroups.* Bethesda, MD: National Institute of Child Health and Human Development.

National Research Council. (1998). *Preventing reading difficulties in young children.* Washington, DC: National Academies Press.

No Child Left Behind Act of 2001, PL 107-110, 115 Stat. 1425, 20 U.S.C. §§ 6301 *et seq.*

Papanicolaou, A.C., Simos, P.G., Fletcher, J., Francis, D., Foorman, B., Castillo, E., et al. (2003). Early development and placitiy of neurophysiological processes involved in reading. In B. Foorman (Ed.), *Preventing and remediating reading difficulties: Bringing science to scale.* Timonium, MD: York Press.

Rosenshine, B., & Stevens, R. (1984). Classroom instruction in reading. In D. Pearson (Ed.), *Handbook of research on reading.* (pp. 745–798). New York: Longman Publishers.

Sandak, R., Mencl, W.E., Frost, S.J., & Pugh, K.R. (2004). The neurobiological basis of skilled and impaired reading: Recent findings and new directions. *Scientific Studies of Reading, 8,* 273–292.

Shaywitz, B.A., & Shaywitz, S.E. (1994). Measuring and analyzing change. In G.R. Lyon (Ed.), *Frames of reference for the assessment of learning disabilities: New views on measurement issues* (pp. 59–68). Baltimore: Paul H. Brookes Publishing Co.

Shaywitz, S. (2003). *Overcoming dyslexia: A new and complete science-based program for reading problems at any level.* New York: Alfred A. Knopf.

Simeonsson, R.J. (1994). Promoting children's health, education, and well-being. In R.J. Simeonsson (Ed.), *Risk, resilience, & prevention: Promoting the well-being of children* (pp. 3–11). Baltimore: Paul H. Brookes Publishing Co.

Simmons, D., & Kame'enui, E. (1998). *What reading research tells us about children with diverse learning needs: Bases and basics.* Mahwah, NJ: Lawrence Erlbaum Associates.

Simmons, D.C., Kame'enui, E.J., Good, R.H., III, Harn, B.A., Cole, C., & Braun, D. (2002). Building, implementing, and sustaining a beginning reading improvement model school by school and lessons learned. In M. Shinn, G. Stoner, & H.M. Walker (Eds.), *Interventions for academic and behavior problems II: Preventive and remedial approaches* (pp. 537–569). Bethesda, MD: National Association of School Psychologists.

Simmons, D.C., Kame'enui, E.J., Stoolmiller, M., Coyne, M.D., & Harn, B. (2003). Accelerating growth and maintaining proficiency: A two-year intervention study of kindergarten and first-grade children at risk for reading difficulties. In B. Foorman (Ed.), *Preventing and remediating reading difficulties: Bringing science to scale* (pp. 197–228). Timonium, MD: York Press.

Sprick, M., Howard, L., & Fidanque, A. (2000). *Read well.* Longmont, CO: Sopris West Educational Services.

Torgesen, J.K. (2002). The prevention of reading difficulties. *Journal of School Psychology, 40,* 7–29.

Vaughn, S., & Bos, C. (2002). *Strategies for teaching students with learning and behavior problems* (5th ed.). Boston: Allyn & Bacon.

Vaughn, S., & Fuchs, L.S. (2003). Redefining learning disabilities as inadequate response to instruction: The promise and potential problems. *Learning Disabilities Research & Practice, 18,* 137–146.

Woodcock, R. (1987). *Woodcock Reading Mastery Test–Revised.* Circle Pines, MN: AGS Publishing.

Ysseldyke, J. (2001). Reflections on a research career: Generalizations from 25 years of research on assessment and instructional decision making. *Exceptional Children, 67,* 295–309.

Zins, J.E., Heron, T.E., & Goddard, Y.L. (1999). Secondary prevention: Applications through intervention assistance teams and inclusive education. In C.R. Reynolds & T.B. Gutkin (Eds.), *The handbook of school psychology* (3rd ed., pp. 800–821). Hoboken, NJ: John Wiley & Sons.

9

Preventing Early Reading Difficulties through Intervention in Kindergarten and First Grade

A Variant of the Three-Tier Model

Frank R. Vellutino, Donna M. Scanlon,
Sheila G. Small, Diane P. Fanuele, and Joan M. Sweeney

Since the mid-1990s, there has been considerable research evaluating responsiveness to intervention as a means of distinguishing between children who may require intensive and protracted remediation to correct their reading problems and children who may only require less intensive and short-term remediation to achieve the same end (Foorman, 2003; Vaughn, Linan-Thompson, & Hickman, 2003). Much of this research has been conducted within the context of questions and issues surrounding the use of responsiveness to intervention in lieu of the IQ-achievement discrepancy to define learning disabilities (Gresham, 2002; Vellutino et al., 1996, Vellutino, Scanlon, & Lyon, 2000). The ultimate and most important objective of virtually all of the research, however, has been the development of assessment and instruction formats and procedures to facilitate functional literacy in all children. The responsiveness to intervention approach to serving the needs of children with reading difficulties has been conceptualized within the framework of what has come to be called the "three-tier model of intervention," which is characterized by three different modes of sequentially ordered remedial treatment (Denton & Mathes, 2003; Fuchs & Fuchs, 1997).

Virtually all of the work discussed in this paper was supported by grants from the National Institute of Child Health and Human Development (NICHD). The data for the intervention study that is the primary focus of the current paper were collected under the auspices of grant R01 HD34598. The data for the intervention study reported in Vellutino and colleagues (1996) were collected as part of a project conducted under the auspices of a special center grant (P50HD25806) awarded to the Kennedy Krieger Institute by NICHD. The authors express their sincere gratitude to the teachers, students, and secretarial and administrative staff in participating schools. We are also grateful to the intervention teachers and data collectors who worked with us on both intervention studies.

Tier 1 entails analysis of the instructional program in the child's classroom to ensure that all children in that classroom are being provided with balanced, explicit, and systematic reading instruction that fosters both code-based and text-based strategies for word identification and comprehension. If the instructional program does not meet these criteria, then steps are taken to modify the program in ways that will significantly improve the rate and level of reading growth for all children in the classroom, including the struggling readers who provided the occasion for modifications in the program. Intervention at this level is based on the assumption that many, if not most, students who struggle with reading will be able to profit from relevant modifications in classroom literacy instruction, despite the fact that they appear to be less well-equipped than their typically achieving classmates to compensate for inadequacies in reading instruction.

Tier 2 of the three-tier model entails supplemental secondary intervention for those children whose reading difficulties are not resolved by enhanced, high-quality classroom instruction. Such intervention generally entails more explicit and more extended instruction in the general education setting, typically in small groups of children with similar needs. Again, many struggling readers respond well to secondary intervention, especially if it is combined with high-quality classroom instruction and incorporates sufficient emphasis on both code-based and meaning-based reading strategies (Denton & Mathes, 2003).

In Tier 3 of the three-tier model, children who continue to have significant reading difficulties, despite provision of primary and secondary intervention, become eligible for special education services and may be classified as having reading disabilities. Such tertiary intervention typically entails more intensive and more highly individualized remedial services (e.g. daily one-to-one tutoring) of greater duration, in most instances as a supplement to classroom instruction in the general education setting. Note, however, that in the three-tier model, consideration of a reading disability classification would be based on inadequate response to primary and secondary remedial intervention and not on the more traditional IQ-achievement discrepancy criterion (Denton & Mathes, 2003; Gresham, 2002).

Denton and Mathes (2003) reviewed existing evidence for the three-tier model and concluded that it holds promise for significantly reducing the number of children who would be diagnosed as having reading disabilities and who require intense and protracted remediation: "If high-quality primary and secondary instruction were regularly provided in our public schools, less than 2% of our children would require tertiary intervention" (p. 239). With regard to tertiary intervention, they further concluded, "From this important research, we can deduce that highly intense tertiary intervention has the potential to 'normalize' the decoding and comprehension skills of many students with severe reading difficulties, and that these effects may be maintained over time" (p. 240). Our own intervention research leads us to agree with these conclusions, with some caveats, as will be shown following.

In this chapter, we summarize selected findings from a kindergarten and first-grade intervention study we have recently completed that incorporated some, but not all, of the components of the three-tier model (Vellutino, Scanlon, Small, & Fanuele, 2006). The study was designed to evaluate a preventive model of intervention that deviated somewhat from the three-tier model in that remedial services were provided for kindergarten children identified as at risk for early reading difficulties before they had any extensive exposure to the classroom language arts program. In addition, the intervention supplemented classroom literacy instruction without any attempt to modify the instruction. Before describing this study, however, it would seem useful to briefly summarize the central features and main findings of a first-grade intervention study we conducted (Vellutino et al., 1996) that led to the design of the present study.

THE FIRST-GRADE INTERVENTION STUDY

Our first-grade intervention study was motivated by serious concerns we had over current psychometric/exclusionary approaches to diagnosing reading disability using the IQ-achievement discrepancy as the central defining criterion (Gresham, 2002). Because we believed that such approaches greatly inflate the number of children classified as having reading disabilities and do not take adequate account of the child's previous educational history (Clay, 1987), we designed a program of intervention research that we hoped would begin to develop criteria for distinguishing cognitive deficits from experiential and instructional deficits as primary causes of early and long-term reading difficulties and for identifying children at risk for early reading difficulties before they are exposed to first-grade reading instruction. To this end, we tracked literacy development in middle- to upper middle-class children, who were identified in mid–first grade as either struggling readers or typically achieving readers, from the time they entered kindergarten (before their reader group status was determined) through the end of fourth grade. These two groups were selected from a larger population of children ($n = 1,407$) we tested at the time they entered kindergarten. Because we were interested in examining the influence of home and preschool literacy experiences on early reading achievement, all of these children were given a large battery of tests evaluating emergent literacy skills (e.g., knowledge of letter names, knowledge of print concepts, phonological awareness) shortly before or at the time they entered kindergarten. Reading-related cognitive abilities also were assessed in kindergarten and again in first and third grade. The cognitive batteries included measures of language and language-based abilities such as listening comprehension, vocabulary knowledge, syntactic knowledge, and verbal memory; visual abilities such as visual-spatial analysis and visual memory; and verbal and nonverbal intelligence. To assess the possible influence of kindergarten literacy instruction on first-grade reading achievement, we periodically observed the kindergarten language arts programs in all schools participating in the study (Scanlon & Vellutino,

1996, 1997). Most importantly, we provided daily one-to-one tutoring (30 minutes per day) for most of the students with reading impairments for a minimum of 15 weeks (a total of 70–80 sessions) and, in some cases—depending on the child's progress—approximately twice this amount. A primary objective of the tutoring program was to facilitate assessment of possible differences between the cognitive profiles of struggling readers who were found to be difficult to remediate and struggling readers who were found to be readily remediated.

The nature of the tutoring program is described in detail elsewhere (Vellutino & Scanlon, 2002). In brief, it was implemented by certified teachers trained by project staff and was highly individualized; in addition, every session involved activities designed to foster both functional use of the alphabetic code and reading for meaning. Approximately 15 minutes of each session was devoted to reading connected text. Along with facilitating reading for meaning, fluency, and enjoyment, a major objective of time spent in text reading was to foster deliberate use of alternative, complementary, and what we have come to call "interactive strategies" for word identification and comprehension: use of contextual cues (e.g., sentence and passage context, pictures) as clues to a word's identity and use of these sources of information to facilitate prediction and comprehension monitoring. Particular emphasis was placed on the conjoint use of contextual and phonological (letter-sound) decoding strategies for word identification. The other 15 minutes of each session was distributed among activities designed to help the child acquire word-level skills such as phonological awareness, phonological decoding, and sight-word identification and to engage the children in some meaningful writing. The child's individual needs determined the amount of time devoted to one or another of the word-level activities. An outline of the types of remedial activities that typically were implemented in a given lesson is presented in Table 9.1.

Because of results obtained in previous intervention studies (e.g., Clay, 1985; Iversen & Tunmer, 1993; Pinell, 1989; Wasik & Slavin, 1993), we expected that daily one-to-one tutoring would facilitate the acquisition of at least average-level reading skills in most of the struggling readers. And, because of extensive research we have conducted in the study of the etiology of reading disability (Vellutino 1979, 1987), we also expected that the cognitive profiles of readily remediated readers would be more like those of the normally achieving readers than like those of difficult-to-remediate readers. These expectations generally were confirmed.

First, approximately 9% of the first-grade population from which our sample was drawn ($n = 1,284$ after attrition) would have qualified for a reading disability classification prior to implementation of our intervention program. Using scores below the 30th percentile as the principal defining criterion, however, only 3% of this population would have qualified for this classification after one semester of remediation. This figure was reduced to 1.5% when the 15th percentile was used as the cutoff. In addition, although the percentage of tutored children who scored at least within the average range was substantially reduced after tutoring was discontinued, such "wash-out effects" occurred primarily among children

Table 9.1. Outline of the activities incorporated in each daily lesson in the first-grade intervention program

Component	Description
Rereading	One or more texts read in a previous session were reread to promote fluency and comprehension. Prior to having the child read the text, the teacher presented words missed in the previous reading for review. The teacher also frequently reminded the child of or had the child recall one or more word identification strategies that the child was learning to use.
Phonological skills	The specific skills focused upon in this component of the lesson depended upon the child's current skills and upon the text the teacher was planning to have the child read later in the session. This was the portion of the lesson during which the teacher would help the child 1) learn the names of the letters and their relationships to sounds, 2) become sensitive to the phonemes in spoken words and how those phonemes were related to the letters in printed words, and 3) learn to decode and spell larger orthographic units such as word families and prefixes and suffixes.
Reading new texts	One or more new texts was read orally each session. Prior to having the child read the text, the teacher introduced the text (title, author, discussion of the probable storyline) and introduced and provided practice in the identification of a few new sight words that the child would encounter in the text. While the child read the text, the teacher provided guidance and feedback on the use of a variety of strategies for word identification. Throughout the reading of the text, the teacher engaged the child in casual conversation about the story to ensure that the child understood the purpose of reading and to promote enjoyment of the story.
High-frequency words	During each session, some time was devoted to helping the child master the most frequently occurring sight words. Practice activities included sight word drills using flash cards, repeated writing of target words, and various game-like activities (such as "Go Fish").
Writing	The child was engaged in writing each day. In early sessions, writing activities often involved the child in dictating a message that was written by the teacher. As the teacher wrote, she engaged the child in analyzing the spoken words into their component phonemes and in deciding which letters to use to represent those sounds. As the child's skills progressed, he or she did more of the writing with guidance from the teacher. To the extent possible, when the child wrote, he or she was encouraged to apply the skills and abilities that had been the focus of earlier aspects of the lesson and of earlier lessons.

Reprinted from *Contemporary Educational Psychology, 27.* Vellutino, F.R., & Scanlon, D.M. The interactive strategies approach to reading intervention. (p. 591). © 2002; with permission from Elsevier.

who showed the least amount of initial growth in response to remediation (Vellutino & Scanlon, 2002; Vellutino, Scanlon, & Jaccard, 2003).

Second, children who were found to be the most difficult to remediate tended to perform below the level of both normally achieving readers and children who were found to be readily remediated on measures of phonologically based skills such as phonological awareness, phonological (letter-sound) decoding, and verbal memory. In addition, the cognitive profiles of the children who were found to be readily remediated were more like those of the normally achieving readers than like those of the children who were found to be difficult to remediate. Third, all children identified as struggling readers in mid–first grade were found to be lacking in foundational literacy skills such as letter identification and phonological awareness at the beginning of kindergarten, thus affording some support for the possibility that early reading difficulties may be due, in many cases, to deficiencies in the quality and/or quantity of early literacy experiences. Fourth, children who had been exposed to balanced and comprehensive language arts instruction in kindergarten that included substantial emphasis on both word-level and text-processing skills were less likely to be identified as poor readers in first grade than were children who had not been exposed to such instructional programs, in accord with the possibility that early reading difficulties may be due, in part, to inadequacies in early literacy instruction (Scanlon & Vellutino, 1996, 1997).

Finally, no significant differences were found between the struggling readers who were difficult to remediate and the struggling readers who were readily remediated on tests of verbal and nonverbal intelligence. Neither were there significant differences on these measures between any of the struggling reader groups and the group consisting of typical readers of average intelligence. At the same time, there were no significant differences between the typical readers of average intelligence and the typical readers of above-average intelligence on measures of basic word-level skills such as word identification and phonological decoding. In addition, IQ-achievement discrepance scores were not significantly correlated with initial growth in reading (Vellutino, Scanlon, & Lyon, 2000).

The major findings from this study make it clear that early reading difficulties in most, though not all, struggling readers can be successfully ameliorated and that experiential and instructional inadequacies are more likely to be the primary cause of such difficulties than are basic cognitive impairments of biological origin. Moreover, they add to the growing body of evidence questioning the validity of the IQ-achievement discrepance to define reading disability (Aaron, 1997; Fletcher et al., 1994; Francis, Shaywitz, Stuebing, & Shaywitz, 1996; Siegel, 1988, 1989; Stanovich & Siegel, 1994). In view of these findings, we suggested that response to remedial intervention supplant the IQ-achievement discrepance and other psychometric/exclusionary criteria as the principal means of identifying children who have a basic reading disability of biological origin. We also suggested that a classification of "reading disability" be deferred in given cases until such diagnostic intervention has been implemented.

Results from the kindergarten assessment and classroom observation components of the Vellutino and colleagues (1996) study, however, strongly suggested that children's prekindergarten literacy experiences and the literacy and language arts instruction they receive in kindergarten may significantly influence their ability to profit from first-grade reading instruction. Given this possibility, we were motivated to further evaluate and extend the major findings from this study by exploring the utility of identifying children at risk for early reading difficulties on entry into kindergarten and initiating intervention in kindergarten in the interest of preventing early reading difficulties in first grade and beyond. We also were interested in further evaluating the utility of using initial response to intervention as the principal means of distinguishing between cognitive factors and experiential and instructional factors as primary sources of individual differences in early reading achievement. To accomplish these objectives, we conducted a second longitudinal study that incorporated small-group kindergarten (Tier 2) intervention for children judged to be at risk for early reading difficulties at the beginning of kindergarten and one-to-one (Tier 3) intervention for children who continued to need supplemental remedial assistance at the beginning of first grade. We discuss selected findings from this study in the remainder of this chapter.

THE KINDERGARTEN AND FIRST-GRADE INTERVENTION PROJECT

Kindergarten Screening

The study was initiated in late spring of 1997 and terminated in late spring of 2002. Participants were lower middle- to upper middle-class children from rural and suburban schools in upstate New York. The initial sample consisted of two cohorts of children (n = 1,373) assessed at the beginning of their kindergarten year. There were approximately equal percentages of males and females in each cohort (54% males in Cohort 1 and 50% males in Cohort 2). In addition, approximately 98% of the total sample consisted of white children, .67% consisted of African American children, .59% consisted of Hispanic children, and .39% consisted of Asian children. Finally, .33% of the children in the total sample were English language learners, and 8.4% of the children in the total sample were eligible for free lunches.

To identify children who were at-risk for early reading difficulties, each child was given a test evaluating knowledge of letter names when he or she entered kindergarten (fall of 1998 and 1999). We used a letter-name test for initial screening of at risk children because all of the impaired readers in our first-grade intervention study (Vellutino et al., 1996) entered kindergarten deficient in letter-name knowledge and because such knowledge has been found to be the single best predictor of early reading achievement, both in our laboratory and elsewhere (Adams, 1990; Scanlon &

Table 9.2.   Performance levels for the at-risk and not-at-risk groups on the kindergarten screening battery (both cohorts)

Selection measures	At-risk[a]	Not-at-risk[b]
WRMT-R Letter Identification raw score (51)[c]		
M	5.75	25.26
SD	4.21	5.82
(n)	(475)	(898)
WRMT-R letter identification standard score		
M	84.05	105.75
SD	6.05	8.74
(n)	(475)	(898)
Rhyme detection raw score (12)[c]		
M	6.71	8.93
SD	2.76	2.86
(n)	(474)	(676)
Alliteration detection raw score (12)[c]		
M	4.16	6.02
SD	1.46	2.70
(n)	(475)	(677)
Rapid automatized naming time (in seconds)		
M	83.36	73.00
SD	21.29	17.48
(n)	(470)	(668)
Counting by 1s (highest number) (40)[c]		
M	23.49	32.94
SD	9.58	8.48
(n)	(475)	(895)
Number identification raw score (12)[c]		
M	4.97	8.67
SD	2.80	1.69
(n)	(475)	(895)

Source: Vellutino et al. (2006).

Key: WRMT-R = Woodcock Reading Mastery Test–Revised; *M* = mean; *SD* = standard deviation; *n* = number of children in each group.

[a]At-risk *n* = 475

[b]Not at-risk *n* = 898

[c]Number in parenthesis indicates maximum possible score on the measure.

Vellutino, 1997). To cross-validate initial screening results based on letter-name knowledge, however, all children also were given tests evaluating phonological awareness (sensitivity to rhyme and alliteration), rapid naming of objects, counting by 1's, and number identification. Approximately 30% of our kindergarten sample tentatively was identified as being "at risk" for early reading difficulties.

Table 9.2 presents results on the letter-name test for the kindergarten children from combined cohorts. Results from the cross-validating measures also are presented. It can be seen that children who qualified for the at-risk group performed well below children who did not qualify for the at-risk group, not only on the letter-name test used to determine risk status but also on all of the cross-validating measures. These findings replicate earlier results (Scanlon & Vellutino, 1997; Vellutino et al., 1996). Taken together, they suggest that performance on a letter-name test administered to entry-level kindergartners is a reasonably good barometer of performance on other measures of emergent literacy skills. Thus, it appears that assessing a child's knowledge of letter names could prove to be a useful (and relatively economical) way of identifying children who may need extra instructional support in the early phases of learning to read.

Kindergarten Intervention

Shortly after initial screening, roughly half of the children in the at-risk group were randomly assigned to a project intervention group (Project Treatment). Children in this group received remedial instruction provided by project teachers. The other half was assigned to a school-based comparison group (School-Based Comparison). The children in this group were not expected to receive any type of supplemental instruction at the outset of the project. Table 9.3 presents results for

Table 9.3.   Performance levels for the project treatment and school-based comparison groups on the kindergarten screening battery (both cohorts)

Selection measures	Project treatment[a]	School-based comparison[b]
WRMT-R letter identification raw score (51)[c]		
M	5.33	6.29
SD	4.01	4.40
WRMT-R letter identification standard score		
M	83.53	84.71
SD	5.98	6.13
Rhyme detection raw score (12)[c]		
M	6.65	6.72
SD	2.87	2.67
Alliteration detection raw score (12)[c]		
M	4.09	4.23
SD	1.45	1.43
Rapid automatized naming time (in seconds)		
M	83.62	82.24
SD	21.81	20.15
Counting by 1s (highest number) (40)[c]		
M	22.81	24.09
SD	10.10	9.02
Number Identification raw score (12)[c]		
M	4.70	5.31
SD	2.86	2.71

Source: Vellutino et al. (1996).

Key: WRMT-R = Woodcock Reading Mastery Test–Revised; *M* = mean; *SD* = standard deviation; *n* = number of children in each group.

[a]Project treatment *n* = 232

[b]School-based treatment *n* = 230

[c]Number in parenthesis indicates maximum possible score on the measure.

these two groups on the tests included in our initial screening battery. It can be seen that the groups were not appreciably different on any of these measures at the outset of the study.

The children who were assigned to the Project Treatment group received supplemental instruction in small groups consisting of no more than two or three children. The instruction was provided by certified teachers trained by project staff. Children in each group met with their teacher twice each week for 30-minute sessions in a room outside of their classrooms. Remedial activities were designed to facilitate development of emergent literacy skills: phonological aware-ness, letter recognition and identification, letter–sound association, functional use of the alphabetic principle, knowledge of print concepts, print awareness, and high-frequency sight words. In each session, the children listened to and/or read stories, spent time working on foundational skills such as phoneme awareness and alphabetic mapping, and participated in shared writing or other writing activities. The goals of the kindergarten intervention program are depicted in Table 9.4. The general approach we used in the intervention program was an adaptation of the "Interactive Strategies" approach we used in our first-grade intervention study

Table 9.4.   Goals for the kindergarten intervention program

1.	Motivation to read and write: The child will develop the belief that reading and writing are enjoyable and informative activities that are not beyond his or her capabilities.
2.	Phoneme awareness: The child will have a conceptual grasp of the fact that words are made up of somewhat separable sound segments. Further, the child will be able to say individual sounds in simple words spoken by the teacher and to blend separate sounds to form whole words.
3.	Letter identification: The child will be able to name, rapidly and accurately, all 26 letters of the alphabet, both upper- and lowercase versions.
4.	Letter–sound association: The child will be able to associate the sounds of the majority of consonants with their printed representations.
5.	Alphabetic principle: The child will understand that the letters in printed words represent the sounds in spoken words. Further, the child will be able to change single consonants at the beginning or end of one-syllable words in accord with requests made by the teacher (e.g., change mat to bat).
6.	Print awareness: The child will understand that the purpose of print is to communicate.
7.	Print conventions: The child will understand some of the most basic print conventions, such as the left to right and top to bottom sequencing of print, where to begin reading a book, the concepts of letter and word, and so forth.
8.	Whole-word identification: The child will learn to recognize, at sight, a small set of high frequency words.

Adapted from Scanlon, D.M., Vellutino, F.R., Small, S.G., Fanuele, D.P., & Sweeney, J.M. (2005). Severe reading difficulties—Can they be prevented? A comparison for prevention and intervention ap-proaches. *Exceptionality, 13*(4), 212; adapted by permission.

(Vellutino et al., 1996; Vellutino & Scanlon, 2002), which is designed to provide the child with alternative and complementary strategies for word identification and comprehension during text reading.

To assess the initial and short-term effects of our kindergarten intervention program, we compared the progress made by the Project Treatment and School-Based Comparison groups through periodic assessment (in December, March, and June) of these groups on measures evaluating letter identification, phonological awareness (detection of rhyme and alliteration, phoneme segmentation, and phoneme blending), print concepts, knowledge of letter sounds, letter-sound (primary) decoding, spelling, and primary word identification. (The primary word identification and primary decoding tests are experimental tests that were constructed and normed in our laboratory to avoid the "floor effects" typically observed with kindergarten and first-grade children on most commercially available standardized tests.) For present purposes, we report results only for the end of the children's kindergarten year (June assessment). These results are presented in Table 9.5. It can be seen that the Project Treatment group performed somewhat better than the School-Based Comparison group on most of the measures. Effect sizes of better than .50 (a widely accepted standard), however, were obtained only on experimental measures of primary word identification, letter-sound (primary) decoding, and phoneme segmentation.

As indicated earlier, the children assigned to the School-Based Comparison group were not expected to receive any type of remedial instruction when the project was initiated. Several of the participating schools, however, decided to implement their own kindergarten intervention program shortly after the start of the project, thereby weakening treatment effects based on comparisons of this group with the Project Treatment group. A more informative assessment of the effects of our kindergarten intervention program is provided by comparisons involving children in the participating schools that offered no intervention program in kindergarten and children from those same schools who received the intervention program provided by project teachers. These results are presented in Table 9.6. As is evident, effect sizes of .50 or higher emerged on tests evaluating knowledge of letter names, knowledge of letter sounds, primary word identification, letter-sound (primary) decoding, spelling, and phoneme segmentation. In contrast, effect sizes were below statistically acceptable standards on tests evaluating print concepts, detection of rhyme, detection of alliteration, and phoneme blending. In both the larger and smaller samples, however, all effect sizes favor the Project Treatment Group. Thus, it seems reasonable to suggest, from these results alone, that early intervention to institute foundational literacy skills in children identified as at risk for early reading difficulties at the beginning of kindergarten can significantly improve such skills and, thereby, help to prepare them for first-grade reading instruction.

Table 9.5.　Performance levels for the project treatment and school-based comparison groups on the kindergarten June follow-up battery (both cohorts)

Kindergarten follow-up measures	Project treatment[a]	School-based comparison[b]	Effect size
WRMT-R letter identification raw score (51)[c]			
M	28.91	27.07	.29
SD	5.13	6.33	
Letter sounds raw score (35)[c]			
M	24.49	20.80	.41
SD	7.80	9.05	
Primary word identification raw score (25)[c]			
M	6.68	4.32	.57
SD	5.18	4.14	
WRMT-R word identification raw score (106)[c]			
M	3.24	2.11	.35
SD	3.84	3.19	
WRMT-R word attack raw score (45)[c]			
M	.91	.28	.47
SD	2.33	1.32	
Primary decoding (30)[c]			
M	6.51	4.15	.52
SD	6.50	4.56	
Print concepts raw score (12)[c]			
M	10.88	10.43	.27
SD	1.31	1.68	
Rhyme detection raw score (12)[c]			
M	8.43	8.03	.14
SD	2.99	2.90	
Alliteration detection raw score (12)[c]			
M	8.38	7.53	.28
SD	3.12	3.03	
Phoneme blending raw score (20)[c]			
M	14.80	12.97	.47
SD	3.59	3.89	
Phoneme segmentation raw score (22)[c]			
M	6.22	2.76	.65
SD	7.45	5.27	
Spelling (30)[c]			
M	13.00	10.62	.40
SD	6.36	6.00	

Key: WRMT-R = Woodcock Reading Mastery Test–Revised; *M* = mean; *SD* = standard deviation; *n* = number of children in each group.

[a]Project treatment *n* = 214

[b]School-based treatment *n* = 214

[c]Number in parenthesis indicates maximum possible score on the measure.

Table 9.6.   Performance levels for project treatment and school-based comparison groups in schools that did not offer school-based intervention on the kindergarten June follow-up battery (both cohorts)

Kindergarten follow-up measures	Project treatment[a]	School-based comparison[b]	Effect size
WRMT-R letter identification raw score (51)[c]			
M	28.52	24.37	.51
SD	3.86	8.14	
Letter sounds raw score (35)[c]			
M	24.69	15.23	.99
SD	7.17	9.54	
Primary word identification raw score (25)[c]			
M	4.38	2.06	1.07
SD	3.30	2.16	
WRMT-R word identification raw score (106)[c]			
M	2.29	1.02	.44
SD	3.07	2.86	
WRMT-R word attack raw score (45)[c]			
M	.92	.01	[d]
SD	2.37	.12	
Primary decoding (30)			
M	6.81	2.36	1.30
SD	7.51	3.42	
Print concepts raw score (12)			
M	10.96	10.48	.25
SD	1.13	1.92	
Rhyme detection raw score (12)			
M	8.13	7.88	.09
SD	2.78	2.93	
Alliteration detection raw score (12)			
M	7.75	6.65	.36
SD	3.36	3.04	
Phoneme blending raw score (20)			
M	14.29	12.44	.47
SD	3.49	3.91	
Phoneme segmentation raw score (22)			
M	6.25	1.05	1.66
SD	7.50	3.13	
Spelling (30)			
M	11.35	7.60	.69
SD	5.99	5.41	

Key: WRMT-R = Woodcock Reading Mastery Test–Revised; *M* = mean; *SD* = standard deviation; *n* = number of children in each group. (From "Response to intervention as a vehicle for distinguishing between children with and without reading disabilities: Evidence for the role of kindergarten and first grade intervention" by F.R. Vellutino, D.M. Scanlon, S.G. Small, & D.P. Fanuele. [2006]. *Journal of Learning Disabilities, 39,* 161. © 2006 by PRO-ED, Inc. Reprinted with permission.)

[a]Project treatment *n* = 48

[b]Comparison *n* = 65

[c]Number in parenthesis indicates maximum possible score on the measure.

[d]Effect size not reported because of floor effects.

First-Grade Screening

Because a primary objective of the preventive model evaluated in this study was to distinguish between children who profited from the supplemental remedial assistance they received in kindergarten and, consequently, were no longer at risk and children who continued to need remedial assistance in first grade despite having received such assistance in kindergarten, all children from our at-risk kindergarten cohorts were reevaluated at the beginning of first grade using the experimental measures evaluating knowledge of letter sounds, letter-sound (primary) decoding, and primary word identification administered in kindergarten, as well as the Letter Identification, Word Identification, and Word Attack subtests from the Woodcock Reading Mastery Test–Revised (WRMT–R; Woodcock, 1987). We then computed, for each child, a composite score based on summed z-scores from each of the tests, and this composite was used to operationally define "poor reader" (PR) and "no longer at-risk" (NLAR) groups. Here we should point out that, in addition to our interest in evaluating the utility of kindergarten intervention as a means of reducing the incidence of early reading difficulty, a major objective of the intervention project was to compare two different approaches to remedial instruction in first grade, one emphasizing phonological skills and the other emphasizing text-processing skills. Thus, to ensure that there would be an adequate number of poor readers in each of these treatment conditions, we adopted a relatively lenient criterion for identifying the NLAR and poor reader groups. Accordingly, we defined a PR as a child whose summed z-score was at or below the mid-point of the z-score distribution for the at-risk children who had been assigned to our Project Treatment group in kindergarten and an NLAR reader as a child whose summed z-score was above this index. Thus by definition, 50% of the kindergarten intervention group qualified as poor readers. Using the same cutoff score, 60% of the kindergarten School-Based Comparison group qualified as poor readers when the entire sample was included in the count, and 80% qualified when the percentage was based only on children from those schools in the kindergarten School-Based Comparison group that did not offer their own kindergarten intervention program. These results suggest that the project-based kindergarten intervention program was reasonably successful in reducing the number of children who qualified as poor readers in first grade. The results also provide support for the type of preventive approach to early reading difficulties evaluated in the present study.

To further assess the utility of this approach for preventing early and long-term reading difficulties, however, we tracked the progress of the NLAR children until the end of third grade (when the project ended). Of special importance here was the question of whether these children would be able to maintain their NLAR status without further remedial assistance. In order to provide a normative standard, we also identified two groups of typically achieving readers at the beginning of first grade and assessed their reading growth as well. Both groups consisted of children whose summed z-scores on the tests included in the screening battery administered at the beginning of first grade were at or above zero. Whereas one group, however, included only children having average intelligence (AvIQNorm), the other group included only children having above-average intelligence (AbAvIQNorm). The typical reader group was dichotomized on the basis of the mean score of the typical reader distribution on the Wechsler Intelligence Scale for Children (3rd ed.; WISC III) Full Scale IQ score (Wechsler, 1991). This test was administered to all target children in third grade. In addition, we followed the progress of the children identified as poor readers at the beginning of first grade. Some of these children received daily one-to-one tutoring provided by project teachers (either code-emphasis or meaning-emphasis intervention), and the remainder received whatever remedial services were available at their home schools.

Finally, the poor readers who received project-based intervention in first grade were dichotomized into two groups, one consisting of children who were found to be difficult to remediate (DR) and a second consisting of children who were found to be less difficult to remediate (LDR). We refer to these children as less difficult to remediate in comparing them to the children we characterize as difficult to remediate because, although they responded more positively to first-grade intervention than did the difficult to remediate children, they did not respond as positively to the kindergarten intervention as the children in the NLAR groups and were therefore more difficult to remediate than the children in the latter group. Children in the DR group all received standard scores below 90 on the Basic Skills Cluster (BSC) of the WRMT–R, a composite of the WRMT–R Word Identification and Word Attack subtests administered at the end of third grade. Children in the LDR group all received standard scores at or above 90 on the BSC. We were especially interested in comparing the cognitive profiles of children in these two groups with the cognitive profiles of children in the NLAR and typical reader groups. Note, however, that because the two first-grade treatment conditions evaluated in this project (see descriptions below) produced statistically equivalent results on measures of basic word level skills, the DR and LDR groups were dichotomized on the basis of scores on the BSC collapsed across the two conditions. It is also important to note that the lack of differences between the two first-grade intervention conditions on word-level skills at the end of third grade should not be taken as evidence that the two conditions were equivalent. In fact, there were notable differences in the distributions of scores for the two conditions, and there was some evidence that the conditions differentially affected comprehension performance. These differences are addressed in another article (Scanlon, Vellutino, Small, Fanuele, & Sweeney, 2005) and are outside the focus of this chapter.

Table 9.7 presents results for the various reader groups on the screening measures administered at the beginning of first grade. It can be seen that the children in the DR and LDR groups do not differ appreciably on most of the measures. It

Table 9.7.   Performance levels for the poor, no-longer-at-risk, and control (normal) reading groups on the first-grade screening battery

First-grade screening measures	Poor reader— difficult to remediate (n = 19)	Poor reader— less difficult to remediate (n = 26)	No longer at-risk (n = 81)	Average IQ control (n = 27)	Above average IQ control (n = 27)
WRMT-R letter identification (51)*					
M	23.16	23.73	32.20	33.12	34.74
SD	6.80	4.83	2.76	2.28	3.08
Letter sounds (35)*					
M	13.05	17.54	28.51	28.08	29.63
SD	5.62	6.59	3.02	4.17	4.46
Primary word identification (25)*					
M	4.00	2.81	9.22	13.70	16.56
SD	3.73	2.67	5.49	7.46	6.43
WRMT-R word identification (106)*					
M	2.00	1.12	5.70	13.68	19.78
SD	2.45	1.80	4.98	9.87	13.43
WRMT-R word attack (45)*					
M	.00	.23	2.72	4.19	6.96
SD	.00	.59	3.37	4.80	5.29
Primary decoding (30)*					
M	1.79	2.58	9.80	10.24	14.89
SD	1.84	1.90	6.01	5.38	8.26
Rhyme detection (12)*					
M	5.32	7.27	9.31	9.96	10.37
SD	2.52	3.21	2.30	2.46	1.52
Alliteration detection (12)*					
M	6.11	7.54	10.43	10.26	10.89
SD	2.56	2.67	1.91	1.89	1.74
Phoneme blending (20)*					
M	11.89	12.69	16.74	16.26	16.89
SD	2.40	2.11	2.56	3.29	3.26
Phoneme segmentation (22)*					
M	2.84	1.96	11.65	9.00	11.33
SD	5.51	4.31	6.74	7.29	7.45

Key: WRMT-R = Woodcock Reading Mastery Test–Revised; M = mean; SD = standard deviation; n = number of children in each group. (From "Response to intervention as a vehicle for distinguishing between children with and without reading disabilities: Evidence for the role of kindergarten and first grade intervention" by F.R. Vellutino, D.M. Scanlon, S.G. Small, & D.P. Fanuele. [2006]. *Journal of Learning Disabilities, 39,* 162. © 2006 by PRO-ED, Inc. Reprinted with permission.)

*Number in parenthesis indicates maximum possible score on the measure.

also can be seen that they performed substantially below both children in the NLAR and typical reader groups on all measures. Note, in addition, that performance levels across groups approximates a linear trend with the two poor reader groups generally performing at the lowest levels, the two typical reader groups performing at the highest levels, and the NLAR group performing at levels intermediate to the former and latter groups. But, of special importance, vis-à-vis the preventive model evaluated in this study, is that the children in the NLAR group were much closer to the typical readers on these measures than were the children in the DR and LDR groups. These results speak for the utility of identifying at-risk children at the beginning of kindergarten and providing them with small-group supplemental instruction in kindergarten as a "first cut" approach in distinguishing between those who may need only a modest degree of support in kindergarten to prepare them for first-grade literacy instruction and children with more severe impairments who may require more intense and more individualized remedial assistance in first grade (and possibly beyond first grade) to ameliorate their reading difficulties. The data also suggest that providing supplemental literacy instruction in kindergarten may be all that is needed to prevent early and long-term reading difficulties in many at-risk children. Results on reading achievement measures administered at the end of first, second, and third grade provide additional support for this suggestion (see discussion below).

First-Grade Intervention

Children from both the kindergarten Project Treatment and School-Based Comparison groups who qualified as poor readers in first grade were randomly assigned to one of three conditions. In two of the conditions, children received one-to-one remedial intervention (30 minutes per session) provided by project teachers. In the third condition, children received the remedial intervention that was offered by their home school. Such intervention varied from school to school and included everything from daily one-to-one tutoring (e.g., Reading Recovery) to small-group remedial reading provided a few times each week. Both of the first-grade intervention programs provided by project teachers involved the same instructional components in each daily lesson: rereading familiar texts and reading new texts, along with activities to improve phonological skills, sight-word identification, and writing. The intervention programs, however, differed with regard to the emphasis placed either on activities designed to facilitate development of phonological skills or on activities designed to facilitate development of text-processing skills. Thus, in the phonological skills emphasis condition, 15 minutes was devoted to the phonological skills component of the lesson and 5 minutes was devoted to each of the other main activities: supported reading of continuous text, sight word development, and writing. The phonological skills component involved direct instruction to facilitate phonemic awareness, knowledge of letter names and letter sounds, letter-sound decoding, and detection and functional use of phonetically and orthographically redundant phonograms (e.g., "at" in "cat," "fat," "rat").

In the text-emphasis condition, 15 minutes was devoted to supported reading of continuous text, and approximately 5 minutes was devoted to each of the other components of the lesson: phonological skills, sight-word development, and writing. Special emphasis was placed on activities designed to foster the use of complementary and interactive strategies for promoting accuracy and fluency in word identification and reading for comprehension, as described earlier. Such activities included conjoint use of picture, context, and letter-sound cues for word identification; use of predictive strategies to aid word identification and comprehension; and comprehension monitoring. More detailed descriptions of these two treatment conditions are presented elsewhere (Scanlon, Vellutino, Small, & Fanuele, 2000; Scanlon, Vellutino, Small, Fanuele, & Sweeney, 2003, Scanlon, Vellutino, Small et al., 2005).

Because we were unable to control for or obtain detailed information about the intervention programs to which children in the kindergarten and first-grade School-Based Comparison groups were exposed, we report results only for the poor reader groups (DR and LDR) that received kindergarten and first-grade intervention provided by project teachers and for the NLAR group that only received kindergarten intervention provided by project teachers, relative to the two typical reader groups.

Table 9.8 presents results from reading achievement measures, in standard score units, for follow-up assessments undertaken at the end of first, second, and third grades for the children in each reader group who were available at the end of third grade. For purposes of comparison, we also graph the raw scores on these measures (see Figure 9.1). It can be seen that a linear trend similar to that observed on the first-grade screening measures is observed on each of the reading measures. On each assessment and on all measures, the DR children performed at the lowest levels, the AvIQNorm and AbAvIQNorm children performed at the highest levels, and the LDR and NLAR children performed at levels intermediate to children in the DR and typical reader groups. Moreover, the children in the LDR and NLAR groups performed at solidly average levels of achievement on all literacy measures across grade levels, with the NLAR group having only a slight advantage over the LDR group on most of the measures. Further, the performance levels in both groups approach those of the typical readers on the word-level measures. Thus, of the total sample of available at-risk children who received only kindergarten intervention or both kindergarten and first-grade intervention provided by project teachers ($n = 117$), 84% achieved at least average levels of reading skill on all literacy measures by the end of third grade (NLAR and LDR groups), and 73% (72/98) of these children (i.e., children in the NLAR group) received only kindergarten intervention, representing 62% of the total sample of at-risk children (72/117).

These findings are encouraging. They also are important. We say this for several reasons. First, they provide strong support for the type of preventive intervention model evaluated in the present study, insofar as they suggest that early and long-term reading difficulties can be prevented in most children found to be at risk for such difficulties if these children are identified at the beginning of kindergarten (if not sooner) and if appropriate intervention to institute foundational

Table 9.8.   Performance levels for the poor, no-longer-at-risk, and control (normal) reading groups on the first, second, and third grade achievement measures

Grade level		Poor reader— difficult to remediate ($n = 19$)	Poor reader— less difficult to remediate ($n = 26$)	No longer at-risk ($n = 72$)	Average IQ control ($n = 27$)	Above average IQ control ($n = 27$)
		Word identification[a]				
First grade	M	94.63	105.73	109.24	118.89	127.33
	SD	8.50	5.72	11.71	13.05	14.69
Second grade	M	83.94	102.73	107.47	117.67	125.78
	SD	11.46	8.37	12.19	14.68	12.21
Third grade	M	79.16	99.50	103.44	109.74	114.81
	SD	11.58	6.63	9.70	11.37	8.13
		Word attack[a]				
First grade	M	93.32	102.23	102.15	109.19	114.52
	SD	7.87	8.80	9.70	10.66	13.08
Second grade	M	84.68	101.54	102.26	110.11	114.96
	SD	10.49	7.61	12.81	11.98	13.34
Third grade	M	79.95	101.62	101.38	107.74	109.56
	SD	6.69	9.61	11.37	10.54	11.39
		Reading comprehension[b]				
First grade	M	86.63	96.27	100.61	107.85	117.15
	SD	5.92	7.16	8.95	11.64	12.68
Second grade	M	86.37	99.65	102.85	108.44	114.81
	SD	9.36	7.81	10.14	10.74	11.64
Third grade	M	88.47	98.23	105.99	109.30	120.11
	SD	7.24	7.00	9.86	9.75	12.73

Key: WRMT-R = Woodcock Reading Mastery Test–Revised; *M* = mean; *SD* = standard deviation; *n* = number of children in each group. (From "Response to intervention as a vehicle for distinguishing between children with and without reading disabilities: Evidence for the role of kindergarten and first grade intervention" by F.R. Vellutino, D.M. Scanlon, S.G. Small, & D.P. Fanuele. [2006]. *Journal of Learning Disabilities, 39,* 163. © 2006 by PRO-ED, Inc. Reprinted with permission.)

[a]Woodcock Reading Mastery Test–R (Woodcock, 1987) standard scores.

[b]Wechsler Individual Achievement Test (Wechsler, 1992) standard scores.

literacy skills is provided throughout kindergarten. Second, the data provide additional support for our suggestion that small-group supplemental remedial instruction in kindergarten may be a sufficient means of ensuring that most at-risk children are prepared for and will be able to profit from classroom literacy instruction in first grade and become functionally independent readers without additional remedial assistance. Third, they suggest that the majority of children who continue to need remedial assistance at the beginning of first grade, despite having received such assistance in kindergarten, can be brought to at least average levels of literacy achievement by the end of first grade. In fact, of the 45 children who qualified for first-grade intervention, only 4 (9%) obtained standard scores below 90 on the BSC at the end of first grade. Moreover, 58% of these children

WRMT-R word identification

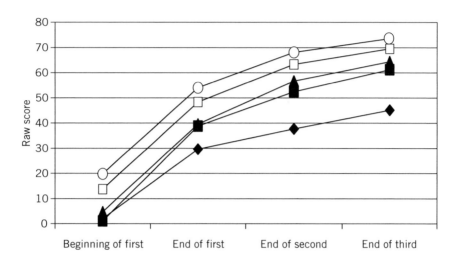

WRMT-R word attack

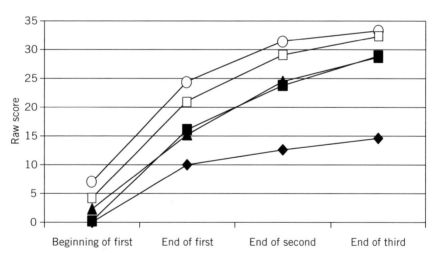

Figure 9.1.   Performance levels across grades for poor, no longer at-risk, and typical reader groups on the reading measures. (*Key:* WRMT-R = Woodcock Reading Mastery Test–Revised; ◆ = poor reader–difficult to remediate; ■ = poor reader–less difficult to remediate; ▲ = no longer at risk; □ = average IQ normal readers; ○ = above average IQ normal readers. WIAT = Wechsler Individual Achievement Test.) (From "Response to intervention as a vehicle for distinguishing between children with and without reading disabilities: Evidence for the role of kindergarten and first grade intervention" by F.R. Vellutino, D.M. Scanlon, S.G. Small, & D.P. Fanuele. [2006]. *Journal of Learning Disabilities, 39,* 164. © 2006 by PRO-ED, Inc. Reprinted with permission.)

WIAT reading comprehension

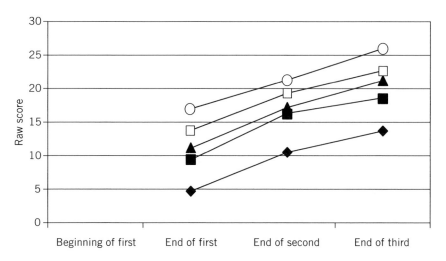

Figure 9.1. *(continued)*

(the 26 children in the LDR group) continued to perform solidly in the average range in second and third grade.

Finally, in accord with results obtained in both our first intervention study (Vellutino et al., 1996) and intervention studies conducted elsewhere (e.g., Torgesen, 2000, Torgesen, Rose, Lindamood, Conway, & Garvan, 1999), the present findings make it clear that a significant percentage of children who receive the amount and types of instruction provided in the kindergarten and first-grade interventions evaluated in this study will, nevertheless, require additional remedial assistance beyond first grade to become functionally independent readers. Thus, of the 45 children who qualified for first-grade intervention (n = 19 in DR group), 42% performed well below the average range on the word-level measures at the end of third grade and only in the low average range on a measure of reading comprehension. Yet, these children generally performed solidly within the average range on the word level measures at the end of first grade. This finding suggests that, although the DR children profited from the additional assistance they received in first grade, they had not yet consolidated their gains when the remedial program was discontinued and needed instruction of a type and/or amount different from that provided by their home schools to maintain these gains. Note, however, that it was not possible to compute percentages of the total sample represented by the number of children in the DR and LDR groups because we were unable to track the entire kindergarten sample through the end of third grade and, therefore, had no reliable way of estimating the attrition rate in this sample.

Cognitive Profiles of Reader Groups

In the first-grade intervention study discussed earlier (Vellutino et al., 1996; Vellutino et al., 2003), we found that poor readers generally performed below typical readers on tests of reading-related cognitive abilities that were administered in kindergarten and first and third grade. These two groups were especially divergent on tests of phonological abilities such as phonological awareness, letter-sound decoding, and verbal memory. We also found that the children in the DR group often performed below the children in the LDR group on many of the same measures. Moreover, the cognitive profiles of the LDR children were more like the cognitive profiles of the AvIQNorm readers than like the cognitive profiles of the DR children. Essentially the same pattern of results emerged in the present study.

Table 9.9 presents results for each of the five reader groups (DR, LDR, NLAR, AvIQNorm, AbAvIQNorm) on selected cognitive measures administered in first and/or third grade. These include tests evaluating rapid automatized naming, phonological memory, memory for digits, receptive vocabulary, listening comprehension, and verbal and nonverbal intelligence. In accord with similar results observed on both the first-grade screening measures and the reading achievement measures, we see a linear trend across groups, whereby the DR and LDR groups performed at the lowest levels, the AvIQNorm and AbAvIQNorm groups performed at the highest levels, and the NLAR group performed at levels that were between these groups. Moreover, the trend is rather stable on the measures that were administered in both first and third grade, notwithstanding substantial gains in performance levels on these measures from first to third grade in all groups. But, whereas the LDR children performed at levels that approximated those of the NLAR children on the reading achievement measures, they more often performed at levels that approximated those of the DR children on all of the cognitive measures save for the rapid-naming measures, on which their performance levels were more like the NLAR children. At the same time, performance levels of children in the NLAR group approximated those of children in the AvIQNorm group on several of the cognitive measures. The only exception to this pattern of results occurred on the test of nonverbal intelligence, on which the DR group mean was not appreciably different from that of either the LDR or the AvIQNorm group means, and all three means were lower than the NLAR group mean. Finally, with the exception of tests evaluating rapid automatized naming skills, the AbAvIQNorm group performed above the AvIQNorm group on all of the language-based measures.

These results are quite in keeping with results obtained in both our first intervention study (Vellutino et al., 1996) and similar intervention studies (e.g., Foorman, 2003; Torgesen, 2000; Torgesen et al., 1999) insofar as they show that language-based abilities, especially phonological abilities, discriminate more strongly and more reliably between children who have difficulty learning to read and children who have little difficulty learning to read than do nonverbal abilities. They, however, provide additional support for these earlier findings in demon-

Table 9.9. Performance levels for the poor, no-longer-at-risk, and control (normal) reading groups on the first- and third-grade cognitive measures

Cognitive measures	Poor reader— difficult to remediate (*n* = 19)	Poor reader— less difficult to remediate (*n* = 26)	No longer at-risk (*n* = 72)	Average IQ control (*n* = 27)	Above average IQ control (*n* = 27)
First-grade rapid naming letters[a]					
M	45.74	40.58	38.71	33.26	32.74
SD	8.28	9.55	9.45	10.47	8.12
Third-grade rapid naming letters[a]					
M	33.89	30.35	28.42	25.67	26.65
SD	6.86	8.39	5.82	5.31	5.25
First-grade rapid naming objects[a]					
M	63.84	57.69	57.88	51.89	49.89
SD	13.41	12.73	11.90	14.62	12.58
Third-grade rapid naming objects[a]					
M	52.42	51.15[b]	47.65	42.81	42.27
SD	12.61	17.31	9.43	8.14	8.04
Third-grade Boston naming spontaneously correct (60)[c]					
M	32.68	34.50	37.22	38.89	42.81
SD	5.51	4.54	4.43	3.41	4.80
First-grade phonological memory raw score (48)[c]					
M	15.79	14.96	17.42	18.04	20.67
SD	4.52	4.56	5.62	3.97	6.82
Third-grade phonological memory raw score (48)[c]					
M	18.89	20.62	24.19	25.07	28.04
SD	3.89	4.77	5.34	4.87	5.83
Third-grade WISC-III digit span scaled score					
M	8.58	8.15	10.46	11.19	13.15
SD	2.17	2.43	3.05	3.03	2.57
Third-grade Peabody Picture Vocabulary Test standard score					
M	97.95	99.73	103.53	102.70	115.33
SD	9.49	9.22	11.19	9.71	10.37
Third-grade WIAT listening comprehension					
M	98.00	98.85	105.75	106.00	115.59
SD	10.97	9.33	10.33	10.02	12.11

(continued)

Table 9.9.   *(continued)*

Cognitive measures	Poor reader— difficult to remediate (*n* = 19)	Poor reader— less difficult to remediate (*n* = 26)	No longer at-risk (*n* = 72)	Average IQ control (*n* = 27)	Above average IQ control (*n* = 27)
Third-grade WISC-III Verbal IQ					
M	93.89	97.15	105.51	107.19	120.56
SD	8.84	11.84	9.02	8.17	7.75
Third-grade WISC-III Performance IQ					
M	98.68	96.04	105.89	99.93	120.67
SD	10.66	11.49	11.78	8.46	7.42
Third-grade WISC-III Full-Scale IQ					
M	95.63	95.92	106.03	103.81	122.59
SD	6.06	10.31	9.41	7.62	5.10

Key: M = mean; *SD* = standard deviation, *n* = number of children in each group; WISC-III = Wechsler Intelligence Scale for Children III; WIAT = Wechsler Individual Achievement Test; LDR = less difficult to remediate. (From "Response to intervention as a vehicle for distinguishing between children with and without reading disabilities: Evidence for the role of kindergarten and first grade intervention" by F.R. Vellutino, D.M. Scanlon, S.G. Small, & D.P. Fanuele. [2006]. *Journal of Learning Disabilities, 39,* 165. © 2006 by PRO-ED, Inc. Reprinted with permission.)

[a]Time in seconds.

[b]Note that one LDR child's naming speed on the Object Naming task was atypical (107 seconds). When this child's score was removed from the distribution the mean LDR score for object naming was 48.92, and the standard deviation was 13.30.

[c]Number in parenthesis indicates maximum possible score on the measure.

strating, once again, that children who have the most difficulty learning to read are less well-equipped in terms of language-based abilities underlying reading ability than are children who have less difficulty learning to read, and both of these groups are not as well-equipped as children who have no difficulty learning to read.

In discussing similar trends in the performance levels of difficult-to-remediate, readily remediated, and typically developing readers, Vellutino and colleagues (1996) suggested that children are differentially endowed with the various cognitive abilities underlying the ability to learn to read and that such endowments might be placed on a continuum that determines the ease with which a child acquires functionally independent literacy skills, relative to the degree and type of literacy experience and instruction to which that child is exposed. Thus, whereas the child who is endowed with an optimum or near optimum mix of reading-related cognitive abilities may acquire strong and perhaps even superior literacy skills with little or no difficulty, despite even less than optimum experiential and instructional circumstances, the child who is endowed with a less-than-optimum mix of reading-related cognitive abilities may find literacy acquisition a more challenging enterprise; such a child may even require supplemental instruction to avoid early reading difficulties. By logical extension, the child who has significant deficiencies in cognitive abilities that underlie reading ability, especially language-based abilities (e.g., phonological coding, phonological awareness, and verbal memory impairments), may have extraordinary difficulty learning to read, even when provided with optimal or near optimal literacy experience and instruction. A child of this description will, quite likely, require more intensive, more individualized, and more extended literacy instruction to become functionally literate. Accordingly, some scholars have suggested that there is what might be called a "gradation of risk" for becoming "reading disabled" that is uniquely determined by the child's natural endowment interacting with the amount and quality of his or her environmental and instructional experiences (Snowling, Gallagher, & Frith, 2003; Vellutino et al., 2003).

IMPLICATIONS OF THE PRESENT FINDINGS

The Three-Tier Model

The preventive approach described in the study we have just summarized departs significantly from the three-tier model we discussed earlier in three important ways. First, unlike the three-tier model, it entails identification of children at risk for early reading difficulties on entry into kindergarten, before they have been exposed to extensive classroom literacy instruction. Second, it uses an emergent literacy measure rather than response to classroom literacy instruction to identify at-risk children. Finally, it implements supplemental literacy instruction on the basis of results on these measures and makes no attempt to evaluate and/or modify inadequacies in the classroom literacy program. Under the three-tier model, Tier 2 supplemental intervention would be initiated only if modifications in classroom literacy instruction did not ameliorate the child's reading difficulties.

Several related questions might be profitably raised about the efficacy of the preventive approach described herein, relative to the demonstrated utility of the three-tier model (Denton & Mathes, 2003). First, one can legitimately question the efficacy of identifying children as being at risk for early reading difficulties at the beginning of kindergarten, using a measure of letter identification to do so, and implementing small-group literacy instruction on the basis of performance on this measure before these children have had extensive exposure to classroom literacy instruction. Indeed, one might worry that this approach incurs the risk of producing an intolerably high number of "false positives" by placing children in the at-risk category prematurely and providing them with supplemental instruction they may not have needed. Second, one also can question the efficacy of using response to supplemental kindergarten intervention as the primary basis for implementing more individualized and intensive (three-tier) instruction in first grade, in the absence of any attempt to evaluate and modify the classroom literacy program in kindergarten. Indeed, considering the fact that classroom literacy instruction is provided for children on a daily basis, unlike the Tier 2 supplemental instruction of the type provided in the present study (which was provided only two times a week), it could be argued that Tier 3-type instruction in first grade may not have been necessary for many of the at-risk children who received supplemental instruction in kindergarten (and who continued to be at risk at the beginning of first grade) if they also had been exposed to classroom literacy instruction in kindergarten that was better balanced and more comprehensive. Finally, one can question the efficacy of implementing Tier 3-type intervention for children who continue to be at risk at the beginning of first grade without evaluating and perhaps modifying the classroom literacy program in first grade. In general, one can question the efficacy of any intervention model that does not also incorporate strategies that address instructional problems at the classroom level (Fuchs, 2002).

With regard to the first of these questions, we justified identification of at-risk children at the beginning of kindergarten on the basis of the finding, in our previous intervention study (Vellutino et al., 1996), that virtually all of the children identified as poor readers in first grade entered kindergarten lacking foundational literacy skills such as knowledge of the alphabet and phonological awareness. We used letter identification to determine at-risk status in the present study because we and others have found this measure to be the single best predictor of early and long-term reading achievement (e.g. Adams, 1990; Scanlon & Vellutino, 1997; Vellutino et al., 2003). In addition, kindergarten children who were found to be deficient on a test of letter identification at the beginning of kindergarten in our previous intervention study (Vellutino et al., 1996) also were found to be deficient on a wide range of tests evaluating cognitive abilities underlying reading ability, and essentially the same pattern of results was observed in the present study. Because the majority of kindergartners in this study received some form of remedial assistance in kindergarten, however, the false positive rate could not be assessed on the full sample of at-risk children identified at the beginning of kindergarten. Nevertheless, it is worth noting that there were 55 at-risk children who did not receive supplemental intervention in kindergarten and who were yet available for testing at the time we administered our first-grade screening battery, and of these children, 78% received standard scores below 90 on WRMT–R Word Identification; 96% received standard scores below 90 on WRMT–R Word Attack; and 98%, 93%, and 89% received scores below the means of the NLAR and AVIQNorm groups on the experimental tests evaluating primary word identification, primary (letter-sound) decoding, and phoneme segmentation (respectively). Thus, the average true positive rate for this group is 91%, and the average false positive rate is 9%. Given that the children in this group had scores on the kindergarten screening battery that were not appreciably different from the total sample of at-risk children (data not shown), it would appear that the false positive rate associated with the use of letter identification to identify at-risk children at the beginning of kindergarten is more tolerable than a false negative rate of similar or greater proportion.

With regard to the question raised about initiating supplemental intervention for at-risk children at the beginning of kindergarten before making any attempt to evaluate and modify their instructional programs, it will suffice to point out that this procedure was motivated by our finding, in the previous intervention study, that children who had not been exposed to a comprehensive and balanced language arts program in kindergarten were much more likely to be identified as poor readers in first grade than children who had been exposed to such a program, even if they had not been lacking in foundational literacy skills when they entered kindergarten (Vellutino et al., 1996). And, given the likelihood that many children will be exposed to kindergarten language arts instruction that may be less than adequate, it seemed to us that supplemental instruction to institute foundational literacy skills at the outset would be a critically important ingredient in any preventive approach to early and long-term reading difficulties. Thus, we were concerned to evaluate the efficacy of an approach that incorporated this strategy independent of variability in the classroom instructional program, and we believe that our results are salutary.

We fully acknowledge, however, the importance of evaluating the classroom literacy program and taking steps to modify and monitor the program when necessary, as prescribed by Tier 1 logic. Indeed, in our first intervention study (Vellutino et al., 1996), we found that inadequate classroom literacy instruction in kindergarten was associated with inadequate literacy development in at-risk children in both kindergarten and first grade, as we have already indicated. Moreover, it is entirely possible that the at-risk children in the present study who profited from Tier 3 intervention in first grade but were unable to consolidate their gains after the intervention was terminated (DR children) were subsequently exposed to classroom instruction that made it difficult to for them to do so (see discussion below). We raised the same question in discussing similar findings obtained in our previous intervention study (Vellutino et al., 2003). Thus, in our view, addressing instructional problems at the classroom level is critically important and would be a vital component of any preventive model designed to reduce the number of children who experience early and long-term reading difficulties. We intuit that the most effective preventive model would incorporate both enhanced classroom instruction and appropriate supplemental instruction for children identified as at risk for early literacy difficulties at the beginning of their school year (i.e., after they are identified as at risk) and would implement both of these strategies simultaneously rather than in tandem as dictated by the three-tier model. We also intuit that the most effective preventive model would incorporate enhanced classroom instruction as an intervention strategy, regardless of whether the supplemental instruction was less intense, less individualized, and short term (Tier 2) or more intense, more individualized, and more protracted (Tier 3). In other words, addressing possible problems in the classroom literacy program would be a critically important component of any preventive intervention model. Moreover, high-quality supplemental instruction should not be a substitute for high-quality classroom instruction, and one should complement the other.

In the interest of assessing the validity of these intuitions, we conducted another intervention study with children from high-poverty schools that compares the preventive type model evaluated in the present study with two other preventive models: one that provides professional development for kindergarten and first-grade teachers before the start of and throughout the school year, with no supplemental intervention for at-risk children in their classrooms; and another that provides kindergarten and first-grade intervention for such children along with professional development for their classroom teachers (Scanlon, Vellutino, Schatschneirder et al., 2005). We expect to replicate the major findings from the current study, but we expect, as well, that professional development will also be effective in reducing the number of children who experience early and long-term reading difficulties, relative to a baseline control group. We fully expect, however, that combining both supplementary intervention for at-risk children and professional development for their classroom teachers will have the most powerful effect. The study is yet ongoing, but results from preliminary analyses are encouraging (Scanlon, Vellutino, Schatschneirder et al., 2005).

Lack of Progress Among Difficult-to-Remediate Children

The finding that children in the DR group were unable to consolidate and build on the substantial gains they achieved by the end of first grade, despite having been exposed to both kindergarten and first-grade intervention, raises questions about their lack of progress. One distinct possibility is that the classroom and/or remedial instruction they received at their home schools after our intervention project was terminated was inadequate. Because we did not collect data on the characteristics of instruction provided by the schools that participated in our project, we were able to evaluate this possibility only in a global way. When school-level outcomes for the nine schools were examined, we found that 80%–100% of the children who received intervention in first grade obtained a standard score of 90 or greater on the BSC at the end of first grade. By contrast, at the end of third grade, the outcomes for four of the schools had fallen to less then 60% of the participating students scoring above 90. The percentages for the remaining five schools were unchanged from the first-grade levels (and four of these schools had 100% of the first-grade intervention students scoring above 90 at both first and third grade). Clearly, this pattern strongly implicates the quality of second and third-grade instruction as an explanatory factor for the low progress (DR) group. Unfortunately, because the number of children who qualified for first-grade intervention in any given school was relatively small (ranging from one to five children in most schools), it was not possible to employ hierarchical linear modeling to examine school effects.

There are, of course, other possible explanations for the outcomes for the DR group. One is that these children simply had yet to achieve sufficient competence as readers when the intervention ended and, thus, without sufficient ongoing support, were unable to maintain the growth they had demonstrated during the intervention period. The fact that the DR children scored substantially below the LDR children at the end of first grade certainly lends credence to this explanation but leaves us to question why the DR group lagged so far behind the LDR group by the end of the intervention period. This suggests yet another possible explanation for the lack of progress in the DR children: Their limited growth in second and third grade and their comparative lack of progress in first grade may have been caused by significant deficiencies in reading-related cognitive abilities. Indeed, although the LDR and DR groups did not differ substantially at the beginning of first grade on many of the language and reading measures, by the end of the intervention period (the end of first grade) the two groups were substantially different on some of the language measures and all of the reading measures. Thus, although both the DR and the LDR groups were at the lower end of the continuum with regard to the cognitive abilities that are important for reading development, it is possible that the LDR children had a somewhat better mix of these abilities and were therefore more responsive to the intensive instruction provided. It is, however, also possible that these LDR children simply received more effective classroom instruction during their first-grade year and that this allowed them to maintain their advantage in subsequent years. Given that the children in the DR group were, predominantly, from a fairly small number of schools, it seems likely that instructional differences may be the strongest explanatory factor.

These explanations notwithstanding, it is clear that the DR children continued to need significant support at the end of first grade. This, of course, raises the question of just what kind of school-based support might have prevented these children from demonstrating such slow growth in early reading skills. At the risk of being unduly speculative, one possible candidate is first-grade classroom instruction at their home school that 1) was more comprehensive and better-balanced, in terms of appropriate emphasis on code-based and text-based skills for word identification and comprehension; 2) provided sufficient opportunity to apply and integrate these skills (Snow, Burns, & Griffin, 1998), and 3) was more compatible with and complementary to the remedial instruction these children were receiving in our first-grade intervention program. It is also possible, and perhaps even likely, that many, if not most, of the DR children had not received the amount of support they needed to maintain and expand on the gains they achieved by the end of first grade. Because of budgetary constraints, few school districts provide the intensive remedial assistance (one-to-one daily tutoring) provided in our first-grade intervention program, and it is possible that many, though perhaps not all, of the DR children may have needed such assistance beyond first grade. Others may have been able to consolidate and expand on their gains with only short-term, small-group instruction beyond first grade and more adequate classroom instruction, and still others may have been able to do so with more adequate classroom instruction and no additional supplemental instruction. In any case, more research is needed to make such distinctions and to develop the means for acquiring the expertise and work force needed to ensure that even the most difficult-to-remediate children become functionally literate.

With regard to the expertise needed to satisfy this objective, there is a pressing need to develop the means for ensuring that classroom and remedial teachers understand and are able to implement research-based instructional practices that have been proven effective in remediating such children (National Reading Panel, 2000; Snow et al., 1998). There is also a pressing need to develop the means for ensuring greater compatibility between classroom and remedial instruction, and more research is needed to satisfy both of these objectives. With regard to the work force needed to ensure that difficult-to-remediate children become functionally literate, our data imply that the financial burden on schools in providing intensive and protracted remediation for such children can be significantly alleviated if they adopt preventive approaches to intervention such as those evaluated in the present study. There is also accumulating evidence that the financial burden on schools also can be alleviated by training paraprofessionals to work with difficult-to-remediate children under the supervision of expert reading teachers (Gelzheiser, Scanlon, & D'Angelo, 2001; Invernizzi, Juel, & Rosemary, 1996; Simmons, Kame'enui, Stoolmiller, Coyne, & Harn, 2003). These latter points underscore yet another implication of our findings; specifically, that the dimensions and extensions of Tier 3-type intervention for difficult-to-remediate children need to be better specified.

Diagnosing Reading Disability Using Response to Intervention

In addition to their implications for developing effective intervention models, the present findings have important implications concerning the role of early identification and early intervention in distinguishing between children with and without reading disabilities. First, they provide additional support for the contention that reading difficulties in most beginning readers are caused primarily by experiential and instructional inadequacies rather than cognitive impairments of biological origin (Clay, 1987; Vellutino et al., 1996). Support for this contention is provided by our finding that deficiencies in foundational literacy skills were ameliorated in most of the at-risk children by the end of kindergarten. Moreover, performance levels in these children on follow-up measures of reading achievement were solidly in the average range from first through third grade and were generally higher than those of poor readers who continued to need remedial assistance in first grade. The data also provide additional support, however, for the contention that reading difficulties in some beginning readers are caused primarily by biologically based cognitive impairments. Support for this contention is provided by our finding that the cognitive profiles of the children who continued to need remedial assistance in first grade were generally weaker than those of both the typical readers and the children in the NLAR group. Taken together, these results imply that an at-risk child's positive response to supplementary intervention in kindergarten can be a reasonably good predictor of the degree to which that child will become a functionally independent reader and writer in first grade and beyond without the need for intensive intervention. In accord with results obtained in our previous intervention study (Vellutino et al., 1996), the results also imply that a positive response to such intervention, at a level that obviates the need for any additional remedial assistance, can act as a "first-cut diagnostic" that aids in determining whether impairments in the at-risk child's ability to acquire foundational literacy skills are caused primarily by experiential and instructional inadequacies or by cognitive impairments of biological origin. By this analysis, the at-risk children in our study who no longer needed remedial assistance after having received only small-group supplemental kindergarten intervention (the NLAR group) would be least defensibly classified as having "reading disabilities," whereas the at-risk children who continued to need remedial assistance, despite having received both kindergarten and first-grade intervention (the DR group) would be most defensibly classified as having "reading disabilities."

Another implication of the present results, vis-à-vis the use of responsiveness to intervention to diagnose reading disability, is inherent in our finding that the intelligence measures did not reliably distinguish between the children who were difficult to remediate (DR) and those who were less difficult to remediate (LDR). Clearly if response to intervention is unrelated to measured intelligence, such measurement serves no useful purpose in a service delivery setting. For research purposes, however, it is interesting to note that, on the test of nonverbal intelligence, the at-risk children in the three intervention groups did not differ from the average IQ of typical readers (AvIQNorm). And, whereas the difficult-to-remediate children (DR and LDR) did perform significantly below the readers in the AvIQNorm group on the test of verbal intelligence, this difference could reasonably be attributed to Matthew Effects (Stanovich, 1986). In our previous intervention study (Vellutino et al., 1996), we evaluated verbal and nonverbal intelligence in both first and third grade and found that the most difficult-to-remediate children were not significantly different from the average IQ typical readers on either measure in first grade but were significantly different on the verbal intelligence measure in third grade, in accord with the present findings. Thus, results on the intelligence measures essentially replicate results on similar measures from the Vellutino and colleagues (1996) study and further undermine the use of the IQ-achievement discrepancy criterion to diagnose reading disability (see also Fletcher et al., 1994; Siegel, 1988, 1989; Stanovich & Siegel, 1994; Vellutino et al., 2000). The obvious implication that emerges from these findings is that responsiveness to intervention approaches to diagnosing reading disability are empirically better grounded and more defensible than are psychometric approaches using the IQ-achievement discrepancy as their central defining criterion.

SUMMARY

The study summarized in this chapter was designed to evaluate the effectiveness of a preventive approach to early reading difficulties that involved: 1) identification of children at risk for such difficulties at the beginning of kindergarten; 2) provision of small-group supplemental kindergarten intervention designed to establish foundational literacy skills in these children, preparatory to first-grade reading instruction; 3) assessment of literacy development in kindergarten to evaluate the effectiveness of kindergarten intervention; 4) assessment of literacy skills at the beginning of first grade to identify both children who were no longer at risk for reading difficulties and children who continued to be at risk for reading difficulties and, thereby, required additional remedial assistance; 5) identification of a comparison group of typical readers; 6) provision of more intensive and more highly individualized supplemental intervention throughout first grade for the children who continued to need remedial assistance; and 7) follow-up assessment of all target children at the end of first, second, and third grade to evaluate the long-term effects of the kindergarten and first-grade interventions.

Results suggest that small-group supplemental intervention in kindergarten can significantly reduce the number of children who may be found to be at risk for reading difficulties in first grade and that more intense and more individualized intervention throughout first grade can remediate reading difficulties in most of these children. The data also suggest, however, that a small percentage of at-risk children will have difficulty consolidating and building on the gains they may achieve through both kindergarten and first-grade supplemental intervention and will require additional assistance to become functionally literate. We provided suggestive evidence that, for the most difficult-to-remediate group, less than optimal classroom instruction may play a significant role in accounting for their slow progress. Taken together, these findings imply that the three-tier model may be usefully modified to include supplemental small-group (Tier 2) intervention for children identified as at risk for early reading difficulties on entry into kindergarten and more intensive, more individualized (Tier 3) intervention for at-risk children who continue to need remedial assistance in first grade, along with any necessary modifications in both the kindergarten and first-grade classroom programs to ensure compatibility between the literacy instruction provided in the various instructional settings. More generally, our data imply that high-quality classroom (Tier 1) and small-group (Tier 2) instruction should be in place in every primary classroom. Supplemental small-group instruction that is responsive to the individual needs of at-risk children can be implemented either in the classroom by the classroom teacher or by an intervention teacher outside the classroom (ideally by an intervention specialist). More intensive and more individualized (Tier 3) instruction should be implemented for at-risk children who continue to need remedial assistance after receiving small-group supplemental instruction, but this more intense form of intervention should not be a substitute for high-quality classroom instruction in any of the grades.

Finally, our data also imply that placement of an at-risk child into the "disabled reader" category should be deferred until that child has been exposed to intensive (Tier 3) instruction tailored to his or her individual needs, which, in turn, implies that a child's response to three tiers of intervention should be assessed before rendering a diagnosis of reading disability.

REFERENCES

Aaron, P.G. (1997). The impending demise of the discrepancy formula. *Review of Educational Research, 67,* 461–502.

Adams, M.J. (1990). *Beginning to read: Thinking and learning about print.* Cambridge, MA: The MIT Press.

Clay, M.M. (1985). *The early detection of reading difficulties* (3rd ed.). Auckland, New Zealand: Heinemann.

Clay, M.M. (1987). Learning to be learning disabled. *New Zealand Journal of Educational Studies, 22,* 155–173.

Denton, C.A., & Mathes, P.G. (2003). Intervention for struggling readers: Possibilities for change. In B.R. Foorman (Ed.), *Preventing and remediating reading difficulties: Bringing science to scale* (pp. 229–251). Timonium, MD: York Press.

Dunn, L.M., & Dunn, L.M. (1997). *Peabody Picture Vocabulary Test–III.* Circle Pines, MN: AGS Publishing.

Fletcher, J.M., Shaywitz, S.E., Shankweiler, D.P., Katz, L., Liberman, I.Y., Stuebing, K.K., et al. (1994). Cognitive profiles of reading disability: Comparisons of discrepancy and low achievement definitions. *Journal of Educational Psychology, 86,* 6–23.

Foorman, B.R. (Ed.). (2003). *Preventing and remediating reading difficulties: Bringing science to scale* (pp. 73–120). Timonium, MD: York Press.

Francis, D.J., Shaywitz, S.E., Stuebing, K.K., & Shaywitz, B.A. (1996). Developmental lag versus deficit models of reading disability: A longitudinal, individual growth curve analysis. *Journal of Educational Psychology, 88*(1), 3–17.

Fuchs, L. (2002). Three conceptualizations of "treatment" in a responsiveness to treatment framework for LD identification. In R. Bradley, L Danielson, & D. Hallahan (Eds.), *Identification of learning disabilities: Research to practice* (pp. 521–529). Mahwah, NJ: Lawrence Erlbaum Associates.

Fuchs, L., & Fuchs, D. (1997). Use of curriculum-based measurement in identifying students with learning disabilities. *Focus on Exceptional Children, 30,* 1–16.

Gelheizer, L.M., Scanlon, D.M., & D'Angelo, C. (2001, April). *The effects of community volunteers and poor readers engaging in interactive reading of thematically-related texts.* Paper presented at the annual conference of the American Educational Research Association, Seattle, WA.

Gresham, F.K. (2002). Responsiveness to intervention: An alterative approach to the identification of learning disabilities. In R. Bradley, L Danielson, & D. Hallahan (Eds.), *Identification of learning disabilities: Research to practice* (pp. 467–419). Mahwah, NJ: Lawrence Erlbaum Associates.

Invernizzi, M., Juel, C., & Rosemary, C.A. (1996). A community volunteer tutorial that works. *The Reading Teacher, 50*(4), 304–311.

Iversen, S., & Tunmer, W. (1993). Phonological processing skills and the reading recovery program. *Journal of Educational Psychology, 85,* 112–126.

National Reading Panel. (2000). *Teaching children to read: An evidence-based assessment of the scientific research literature on reading and its implications for reading instruction.* Washington, DC: National Institute of Child Health and Human Development.

Pinnell, G.S. (1989). Reading recovery: Helping at risk children learn to read. *Elementary School Journal, 90,* 161–184.

Scanlon, D.M., & Vellutino, F.R. (1996). Prerequisite skills, early instruction, and success in first grade reading: Selected results from a longitudinal study. *Mental Retardation and Development Disabilities, 2,* 54–63.

Scanlon, D.M., & Vellutino, F.R. (1997). A comparison of the instructional backgrounds and cognitive profiles of poor, average, and good readers who were initially identified as at risk for reading failure. *Scientific Studies of Reading, 1*(3), 191–215.

Scanlon, D.M., Vellutino, F.R., Schatschnieder, C., Gelzheiser, L.M., & Dunsmore, K. (2005, February). *Instructional and teaching characteristics of kindergarten teachers whose at-risk students make the largest and smallest gains.* Paper presented at the Pacific Coast Research Conference, Coronado, CA.

Scanlon, D.M., Vellutino, F.R., Small, S.G., & Fanuele, D.P. (2000, April). *Severe reading difficulties: Can they be prevented? A comparison of prevention and intervention approaches.* Paper presented at the annual conference of The American Educational Research Association, New Orleans.

Scanlon, D.M., Vellutino, F.R., Small, S.G., Fanuele, D.P., & Sweeney, J.M. (2003, June). *The short- and long-term effects of different types of early literacy intervention on reading comprehension.* Paper presented at the annual conference of the Society for the Scientific Study of Reading, Boulder, CO.

Scanlon, D.M., Vellutino, F.R., Small, S.G., Fauele, D.P., & Sweeney, J.M. (2005). Severe reading difficulties—Can they be prevented?: A Comparison of prevention and intervention approaches. *Exceptionality, 13*(4), 209–227.

Siegel, L.S. (1988). Evidence that IQ scores are irrelevant to the definition and analysis of reading disability. *Canadian Journal of Psychology, 42*(2), 201–215.

Siegel, L.S. (1989). IQ is irrelevant to the definition of learning disabilities. *Journal of Learning Disabilities, 22,* 469–478.

Simmons, D.C., Kame'enui, E.J., Stoolmiller, M., Coyne, M.D., & Harn, B. (2003). Accelerating growth and maintaining proficiency: A two-year intervention study of kindergarten and first-grade children at risk for reading difficulties. In B.R. Foorman (Ed.), *Preventing and remediating reading difficulties: Bringing science to scale* (pp. 197–228). Timonium, MD: York Press.

Snow, C.E., Burns, M.S., & Griffin, P. (Eds.). (1998). *Preventing reading difficulties in young children.* Washington, DC: National Academies Press.

Snowling, M.J., Gallagher, A., & Frith, U. (2003). Family risk of dyslexia is continuous: Individual differences in the precursors of reading skill. *Child Development, 74,* 358–373.

Stanovich, K.E. (1986). Matthew effects in reading: Some consequences of individual differences in the acquisition of literacy. *Reading Research Quarterly, 21,* 360–407.

Stanovich, K.E., & Siegel, L.S. (1994). Phenotypic performance profile of children with reading disabilities: A regression-based test of the phonological-core variable-difference model. *Journal of Educational Psychology, 86*(1), 24–53.

Torgesen, J.K. (2000). Individual differences in response to early interventions in reading: The lingering problem of treatment resisters. *Learning Disabilities Research and Practice, 15*(1), 55–64.

Torgesen, J.K., Rose, E., Lindamood, P., Conway, T., & Garvan, C. (1999). Preventing reading failure in young children with phonological processing disabilities: Group and individual responses to instruction. *Journal of Educational Psychology, 91,* 579–594.

Vaughn, S., Linan-Thompson, S., & Hickman, P. (2003). Response to instruction as a means of identifying students with reading/learning disabilities. *Exceptional Children, 69*(4), 391–409.

Vellutino, F.R. (1979). *Dyslexia: Theory and research.* Cambridge, MA: The MIT Press.

Vellutino, F.R. (1987, March). Dyslexia. *Scientific American, 34*–41.

Vellutino, F.R., & Scanlon, D.M. (2002). The Interactive Strategies approach to reading intervention. *Contemporary Educational Psychology, 27,* 573–635.

Vellutino, F.R., Scanlon, D.M., & Jaccard, J. (2003). Toward distinguishing between cognitive and experiential deficits as primary sources of difficulty in learning to read: A two-year follow-up of difficult to remediate and readily remediated poor readers. In B.R. Foorman (Ed.), *Preventing and remediating reading difficulties: Bringing science to scale* (pp. 73–120). Timonium, MD: York Press.

Vellutino, F.R., Scanlon, D.M., & Lyon, G.R. (2000). Differentiating between difficult-to-remediate and readily remediated poor readers: More evidence against the IQ-achievement discrepancy definition of reading disability. *Journal of Learning Disabilities, 33,* 223–238.

Vellutino, F.R., Scanlon, D.M., Sipay, E.R., Small, S.G., Pratt, A., Chen, R.S., et al. (1996). Cognitive profiles of difficult to remediate and readily remediated poor readers: Early intervention as a vehicle for distinguishing between cognitive and experiential deficits as basic causes of specific reading disability. *Journal of Educational Psychology, 88,* 601–638.

Vellutino, F.R., Scanlon, D.M., Small, S.G., & Fanuele, D.P. (2006). Response to intervention as a vehicle for distinguishing between children with and without reading disabilities: Evidence for the role of kindergarten and first grade interventions. *Journal of Learning Disabilities, 39*(2), 157–169.

Wasik, B.A., & Slavin, R.R. (1993). Preventing early reading failure with one-to-one tutoring: A review of five programs. *Reading Research Quarterly, 28,* 179–200.

Wechsler, D. (1992). *Wechsler Individual Achievement Test.* New York: Psychological Corporation.

Wechsler, D. (1991). *Wechsler Intelligence Scale for Children* (3rd ed.). New York: Psychological Corporation.

Woodcock, R.W. (1987). *Woodcock Reading Mastery Tests–Revised.* Circle Pines, MN: AGS Publishing.

Implementation of
the Three-Tier Model

10

Considerations When Implementing Response to Intervention with Culturally and Linguistically Diverse Students

Janette Klingner, Audrey McCray Sorrells, and Manuel T. Barrera

The Response to Intervention (RTI) model holds promise as a way to improve outcomes for culturally and linguistically diverse students and reduce their disproportionate representation in special education. Certain aspects of the RTI model are particularly encouraging: the emphasis on early intervention; the focus on making sure children receive appropriate instruction at the Tier 1, or classroom, level; and the push to match instruction to a child's needs based on ongoing classroom assessment. The RTI model has the potential to help professionals in the field of learning disabilities shift from focusing on finding disability or within-child deficits to focusing on providing the best instruction for all. Yet, unless researchers and educators capitalize on known and evolving knowledge about appropriate assessments and interventions for culturally and linguistically diverse students, there is also concern that—like with previous eligibility criteria— those implementing the RTI model will presume that if a child does not make adequate progress, he or she must have an internal deficit of some kind or come from a deficit background (making his underachievement something that cannot be helped). In fact, in their description of the RTI model, Vaughn and Fuchs (2003) noted, "When children fail to respond to instruction, the assumption is that some inherent deficit, not the instructional program, explains the lack of response and that some special intervention is required" (p. 142). This assumption is cause for concern, especially as it relates to culturally and linguistically diverse students who historically have been overidentified as having high-incidence disabilities. Disproportionate representation is most apparent among African American and American Indian students when aggregated data are the focus, though there are notable instances of overrepresentation among Hispanics and Asian Americans when data are disaggregated and population subgroups are examined. Hispanic students are overrepresented in some school districts and underrepresented in others (Artiles, Trent, & Palmer, 2004; Donovan & Cross, 2002). It is important to ensure that each child has in fact received culturally responsive, appropriate, quality instruction—instruction that is "evidence-based," with the "evidence" being determined with the target population. As with earlier identification criteria, this model must be based on students having received an adequate opportunity to learn. The concept of "adequate opportunity to learn" is a fundamental aspect of the definition of learning disabilities as part of its exclusionary clause: When a child has not had adequate opportunity to learn, the determination cannot be made that he or she has a learning disability.

Fundamental to the notion of the three-tier model of reading intervention is that instructional practices at each level should be based on scientific evidence about "what works." It is essential, however, to find out specifically what works *with whom, in what contexts,* and *under what circumstances.* What should Tier 1 intervention look like for culturally diverse students? For English language learners? For students living in high-poverty areas? What should Tier 2 intervention look like? Should it be the same for all students? If not, how should it vary, and how should these variations be determined? How can educators ensure that the instruction is, in fact, responsive to children's needs? These are important questions to consider as RTI models are implemented in schools.

The descriptions of the first tier in an RTI model by Vellutino, Scanlon, Small, and Fanuele (2003; see also Chapter 9), Fuchs, Mock, Morgan, and Young (2003), Grimes and Kurns (2003), and Vaughn and Fuchs (2003) are encouraging because they include an analysis of classroom instruction and corresponding modifications to that instruction, if possible, before moving a child to the next tier in the model. Vellutino notes that when establishing a three-tier model, it is important to analyze the instructional program in the child's classroom to ensure that all children in that classroom are being provided with balanced, explicit, and systematic reading instruction. Similarly, Vaughn and Fuchs (2003) also describe the analysis of the general education classroom as part of a problem-solving approach to RTI: "The first criterion was whether the quality of the general education program is such that adequate learning might be expected" (p. 138). Vellutino goes on to say that if it were found that the instructional program is insufficient, then steps must be taken to modify it. Intervention at this level is based on the assumption that many if not most struggling readers will be able to benefit from appropriate modifications in classroom literacy instruction, even though they seemed less able than their normally achieving classmates to compensate for inadequacies in reading instruction. This recognition that many students struggle when their instruction is inadequate is important and has profound implications for culturally and linguistically diverse students who tend to be disproportionately educated in high-poverty, high-need schools in which teachers are often not as qualified as teachers in more affluent schools (Darling-Hammond,

1995; Oakes, Franke, Quartz, & Rogers, 2002). In their investigation of the special education referral process in high-need schools, Harry and Klingner (2006) found that the classroom context was rarely considered when making referral or eligibility decisions; rather, school personnel seemed quick to attribute a child's struggles to internal deficits or the home environment.

Analysis of classrooms should be an essential component of RTI models. When children are struggling, school personnel should first consider the possibility that the students are not receiving adequate instruction before it is assumed that they are not responding because they have deficits of some kind. In addition to considering other factors, observers also should note the extent to which the instruction the child is receiving is culturally responsive.

Some readers may now be saying to themselves, "Culturally responsive? Isn't good instruction just good instruction, no matter who the students are?" We agree that to some extent culturally responsive teaching is "just good teaching," depending on how that is defined. Moje and Hinchman (2004) succinctly noted, "All practice needs to be culturally responsive in order to be best practice" (p. 321). This is a point we elaborate on in this chapter.

Researchers and educators must ask whether they are truly providing an optimal learning environment for all students and doing all they can to improve outcomes for culturally diverse students who seem to be "left behind." If Treatment A is found to be better than Treatment B (or nothing), it should not be assumed that Treatment A is the best treatment. What would happen if Treatment A was adapted to be culturally responsive to a particular group of students and then the Culturally Responsive Treatment A was compared with Traditional Treatment A? When are increased outcomes with a given intervention "good enough"? In other words, how are educators and researchers looking at and thinking about student growth? It is generally considered acceptable for students to make "adequate gains." But what does that mean? Are culturally and linguistically diverse students making modest or adequate gains with the intervention in question while majority students are making outstanding gains? If only slight or modest gains are being seen among culturally and linguistically diverse students in the early grades, this can in part explain why by the third grade an achievement gap already exists. The NRC report (Snow, Burns, & Griffin, 1998) noted that high levels of poverty in a school are a better predictor of children who will have reading problems than a lack of early phonemic awareness:

> For schools in which more than 75 percent of all students received free or reduced-priced lunches (a measure of high poverty), the mean score for students in the fall semester of first grade was at approximately the 44th percentile. By the spring of third grade, the difference had expanded significantly. Children living in high-poverty areas tend to fall further behind, regardless of their initial reading skill level (p. 98).

Gee (1999) interpreted this finding as evidence of the mismatch between schools and students of diverse backgrounds:

A focus on phonological awareness can hide a wider paradox about school success: the more you already know about school itself, and in particular, about school-based language and school practices . . . before you got to school, the better you do in school (p. 367).

Consider the following example: Say that Method A was found to be superior to Method B in an experimental study (randomized control group design) and that 63% of the students in the sample were middle-class white students and the rest were students of other ethnicities and different levels of socioeconomic status (SES). Some were English language learners. Method A was found to be superior at a statistically significant level, and the effect size was impressive—.56. The conclusion would be that Method A is better than Method B. It is important to ask, however, whether it is better for all of the students in the sample. What if the data were then disaggregated by ethnicity, SES, or language proficiency and interactions were examined? What if it turns out that Method B actually was better for some of the students in the sample. After all, not all children learn the same, and some variation is to be expected. What if it turns out that Method A included explicit instruction in phonological awareness and the alphabetic principle and that Method B was precisely the same as Method A but with the addition of "culturally responsive" components? What if the majority of the sample (the middle-class white students) did better with A because, after all, school instruction tends to be compatible culturally with white, middle-class culture? What if many of the culturally and linguistically diverse students did better with B (or perhaps it should be called A+)? What conclusions could be reached?

Should evidence-based interventions be disregarded? Absolutely not. Research substantiates that interventions work with many children, including culturally and linguistically diverse children. There is limited evidence, however, that evidence-based interventions will work with all students. The purpose of using these interventions, as noted by Linan-Thompson, Vaughn, Prater, and Cirino (2006), should be to ameliorate learning difficulties and to increase student engagement in learning. Most approaches to increasing students' motivation, however, are extrinsic in nature and less effective with African American learners, for example, who tend to respond more to intrinsic motives for learning (Chavous et al., 2003; Kaplan & Maehr, 1999; Willis, 2002). Interventions that are disconnected from the affective or a cultural ethos are less responsive to these children. Our position is that it is desirable to include evidence-based instruction at each level of support in an RTI model but that interventions must take place within a context that is culturally and linguistically responsive (Ortiz, 2002). It is important to conduct more research designed to improve instruction for culturally and linguistically diverse students; if Intervention A does not work with some students, educators should then try Intervention B, or A +, and keep trying to find an appropriate intervention instead of assuming that a child has learning disabilities.

In the remainder of this chapter, we detail our perspectives about these issues. We discuss the variability that is to be expected when conducting school-based research as well as the importance of not overgeneralizing research findings. Similarly, we describe issues related to treatment fidelity, the feasibility of transferring an instructional model from one setting or context to another, and implementation challenges. We also convey our concerns about the inadequate descriptions of participant samples and the phenomenon of leaving English language learners out of research studies. We ask what counts as evidence when conducting educational research. Next we discuss the role of culture in learning and then finish with a description of what culturally responsive Tier 1 instruction might look like.

VARIABILITY AND THE
IMPORTANCE OF NOT OVERGENERALIZING

As noted, a foundation of the RTI model is that instruction must be "evidence based." It is important to ask, however, with whom, and under what circumstances? Unfortunately, the results from control-group randomized or quasi-experimental designs tend to be overgeneralized, particularly by educational leaders and policy makers, without a close enough look at variance and possible treatment X attribute interactions or school or teacher effects (Reynolds, 1988; Simmerman & Swanson, 2001; Troia, 1999). In other words, a practice can be determined to be effective and conferred the "evidence-based" label even though a substantial subset of the participants did not in fact achieve superior gains with the model.

Researchers and educators need to pay closer attention to variation. In an RTI model, it is important to look at the "treatment resisters" or "nonresponders" demographically and determine how they differ culturally and linguistically from responders, both from the mainstream and those in a similar cultural group. What aspects of the intervention are they failing to respond to or resist, and how does this connect to what motivates them to respond (intrinsically and extrinsically)?

In addition, at least some variation can be attributed to differences among teachers (Simmerman & Swanson, 2001). It is important to look at who is providing the intervention and whether it is a novice or veteran teacher, a general education or special education teacher, a teacher who has been trained in culturally responsive pedagogy or one who has in fact not received this teacher preparation or who has resisted it. Also, what are teachers being told to do to modify evidence-based practices when they do not work with resisters or nonresponders? Gerber (2003) notes that "Responsiveness to instruction is embedded in but not separable from a complex educational context that includes institutional as well as teacher variables" (p. 2). He cautions that differences in teachers' as well as students' responsiveness to instruction must be considered, emphasizing that "teachers differ as individuals despite the quality of their professional preparation . . . like their students, they cannot be made identical" (p. 6). Likewise, Mastropieri (2003) asks, "Who monitors whether general educators teach this way [using an evidenced-based approach]?" and "What are the teachers doing?" (p. 8). Measures of treatment fidelity have been noticeably lacking in the research. For example, in a critical review of the experimental methodology in 39 studies of phonological awareness, Troia (1999) found that only seven studies met at least two thirds of his evaluative criteria for internal and external validity, and all had at least one fatal flaw (e.g., insufficient or nonexistent assurance of fidelity of treatment).

Similarly, it is important to consider school contexts. Are there culturally diverse children in some schools who respond favorably to a treatment and similar culturally diverse children in another school who do not respond as favorably? This happens frequently (for a classic example, see the First-Grade Studies; Bond & Dykstra, 1967). What is occurring when this happens? Is it the treatment or the school context? That is, when they are numerically a minority, do culturally and linguistically diverse children fail to respond in disproportionate numbers compared with the children who make up the majority of the school population? What is it about the system that facilitates or impedes learning? To simply conclude that the student has failed and thus move him on to the third tier of intervention or decide he belongs in special education is problematic. History shows that a substantial proportion of children do not respond to treatment for various reasons. Research indicates that educators have not done a good enough job teaching culturally and linguistically diverse learners; yet, this research is often overlooked or disregarded as evidence (Hilliard, 1992, 2001; McCray & Garcia, 2002; Pugach, 2001).

It is unreasonable to think that "one size fits all." Consider a few examples from the field of medicine. Much has been made of differential responses to treatment, some of which medical experts are saying seem to be related to race (Bloche, 2004; Committee on Pharmacokinetics and Drug Interaction in the Elderly, Institute of Medicine, 1997; Harder, 2005). Of course, this is controversial and many would say these differences are due to social inequities and disparities in health care provided across ethnic groups (Smedley, Stith, & Nelson, 2003). Regardless of race it is known that individuals vary in their responses to medications. What if a physician insisted on telling everyone to take an aspirin a day to prevent heart disease? If someone with an ulcer takes aspirin, it will not be long before the person's stomach lining begins to bleed. Or consider medications for depression: Although in clinical trials Paxil has been found to be effective for reducing depression in adults, it has been found to increase the incidence of suicide in adolescents and, as such, has been banned in Great Britain (Alliance for Human Research Protection, 2003). Even in adults, Paxil, like other medications for depression, seems to work well for some individuals but not for others. To some extent, the process of identifying the most effective drug for a given individual seems to be one of trial and error. The point is that there is natural variation among humans, and to say definitively that a student has a disability solely on the basis of his lack of response to an "evidence-based intervention" is inappropriate at best and miseducation at worst.

Consider an example closer to home. In Foorman, Francis, Fletcher, Schatschneider, and Mehta's (1998) study of different models of reading instruction, the "direct code" (DC; direct instruction in letter–sound correspondence as practiced in decodable text) group outperformed the "implicit code" (IC) and "embedded code" (EC) groups on a measure of isolated word reading. The authors reported that "only 16% [of the students] in the DC group" exhibited no demonstrable growth in word reading (as compared with 46% of students in IC group, and 44% in EC group" p. 51). This much-cited study is considered evidence in favor of direct code approaches, and certainly this difference among groups is impressive. But what about the 16% of students who did not progress? It would seem important to understand more about them and what happened in their classrooms. This point highlights the problem of looking at all children as a model for effectiveness, especially for learners with disabilities from culturally and linguistically diverse backgrounds.

Other aspects of the study's results also are worthy of scrutiny. The authors noted that although the DC group outperformed the other groups in word reading, they did not do statistically better in reading connected text, and attitudes toward reading were significantly higher in the IC condition. Foorman and colleagues (1998) cautioned that the long- term effects from these programs are not known and that students in the IC and EC conditions could catch-up. Furthermore, they noted that all three conditions, including DC instruction, took place in a "print-rich environment with a significant literature base" (p. 52). Yet this information is rarely mentioned when this study is cited.

Similarly, the National Reading Panel (NRP) report (2000) is touted frequently as supporting direct instruction in phonological awareness and the code. Yet, the limitations of this instruction are rarely reported along with these findings. The report noted the following:

> Taken together, these studies indicate that training in phonological awareness, particularly in association with instruction in letters and letter–sound relationships, makes a contribution to assisting at-risk children in learning to read. The effects of training, although quite consistent, are only moderate in strength, and have so far not been shown to extend to comprehension. Typically, a majority of the trained children narrow the gap between themselves and initially more advanced students in phonological awareness and word reading skills, but few are brought completely up to speed through training, and a few fail to show any gains at all (p. 251).

Critics of the NRP point to other factors, in addition to phonics instruction, that correlate as highly or higher with subsequent reading performance. For example, in their analysis of the same body of work, Camilli, Vargas, and Yurecko (2003) found a smaller effect for systematic phonics instruction than did the NRP ($d = .24$); in addition, they found an effect for systematic language activities of .29 and for tutoring of .40, both higher than the .24 associated with systematic phonics instruction. Furthermore, Camilli and colleagues regression model suggests that the effects of phonics, tutoring, and language activities are additive. Early language abilities also are noted in the NRP as a strong predictor of later reading abilities (e.g., vocabulary, ability to recall and comprehend stories, ability to engage in verbal interactions). The point here is not to diminish the importance of explicit instruction in phonics but to say that this instruction should not be overemphasized at the expense of other aspects of instruction that also are important.

History suggests that the "racehorse mentality of studies that pits one method against another" is ill-advised (Pearson, 2004, p. 8). In summarizing the First-Grade Studies, Bond and Dykstra (1967) noted,

> Children learn to read by a variety of materials and methods. . . . Furthermore, pupils experienced difficulty in each of the programs utilized. No one approach is so distinctively better in all situations and respects than the others that it should be considered the one best method. . . . Reading programs are not equally effective in all situations. . . . Future research might well center on teacher and learning situation characteristics rather than method and materials. The tremendous range among classrooms within any method points out the importance of elements in the learning situation over and above the methods employed (p. 123).

This is not to say that we should scrap experimental studies; on the contrary, it is important to get beyond looking for the method that will be the best in all circumstances and with all students and pay closer attention to context, "noise" (i.e., extraneous variables), moderator variables, and interaction effects so that we can better understand the complexities of real world applications of various instructional approaches.

In 1994, Samuels argued,

> If we wish to make continued progress in our field, we will have to abandon our attempt to find simple, universal laws that can generalize across a variety of populations, conditions, and tasks. Instead, we will have to specify the conditions under which particular processes occur (p. 362).

In summarizing the body of reading research conducted since 1967, Pearson (2004) reiterated this conclusion, "Several large-scale studies of reading methods have shown that no one method is better than any other method in all settings and situations. . . . For every method studied, some children learned to read very well while others had great difficulty." Like these and other reading experts, we believe that the focus of literacy research should not be on finding one best method for all but on better understanding variation and the factors that influence treatment outcomes. Unfortunately, it seems as though the field has come full circle, and we are back to studying similar issues and questions that led to the First-Grade Studies almost 40 years ago.

INSUFFICIENT INFORMATION ABOUT PARTICIPANTS

As discussed earlier in this chapter, variability is to be expected when conducting research. To understand this variability, it is important that researchers provide adequate information about participants as well as contextual features (what some would call the "noise") in research reports. Too often, insufficient demographic data are provided about culturally and linguistically diverse students (Artiles, Trent, & Kuan, 1997; Donovan & Cross, 2002; Gersten & Baker, 2000; Simmerman & Swanson, 2001; Troia, 1999). For this reason, caution should be exercised in interpreting research findings when applied to ethnically diverse students. Research reports should include information about the language proficiency, ethnicity, life experiences (e.g., socioeconomic background, specific family background, community environment and history), and other characteristics of study participants (Bos & Fletcher, 1997; Keogh, Gallimore, & Weisner, 1997) and examine how those variables help explain educational outcomes. Data should be disaggregated to show how intervention(s) may have differentially affected students from diverse backgrounds. It should not be assumed that students from diverse perspectives necessarily respond in the same way as majority students.

A related concern is that culturally and linguistically diverse students, particularly English language learners, are often omitted from participant samples. Language dominance and proficiency are important research variables, yet, too often, these variables are avoided (Ortiz, 1997). For years, special educators have argued for the inclusion of students with disabilities in validation studies of standardized assessments. The same argument can be made regarding the inclusion of English language learners in educational research. Although including English language learners creates some internal validity issues and they are often excluded from studies because of the need to "control" for their lack of English proficiency, this practice limits the external validity and applicability of such studies, especially for teachers who have culturally and linguistically diverse students in their classes. As noted by Pressley, "Experiments should include students who are the intended targets of the instruction being evaluated" (2003, p. 68). Although English language learners do not participate in many studies, research findings generally are touted as applying widely across student populations. For instance, the National Reading Panel report "did not address issues relevant to second language learning" (2000, p. 3), yet the report's conclusions commonly are cited as support for Reading First initiatives applied in schools with English language learners.

Although there is a large body of knowledge on effective research-based strategies for monolingual English speakers and although it may seem appropriate to use these strategies with English language learners, it is important to recognize that instructional strategies for English language learners may need to be adapted or may need to be different in some ways (McCardle, Mele-McCarthy, & Leos, 2005). There is a growing literature base showing promising results for RTI as a way to provide early intervention and assist with the identification of English language learners who need more intensive assistance (Gerber et al., 2004; Haager, 2004; Leafstedt, Richards, & Gerber, 2004; Linan-Thompson et al., 2006; Linan-Thompson, Vaughn, Hickman-Davis, & Kouzekanni, 2003; Vaughn, Linan-Thompson, Hickman, 2003; Vaughn, Mathes, Linan-Thompson, Francis, 2005).

Gerber and his research group implemented progress monitoring and provided intensive small-group supplemental instruction with positive results to English language learners identified as struggling to read. Vaughn and colleagues (2005) described the effectiveness of focused reading interventions coupled with language development activities and English as a second language (ESL) best practices (e.g., use of repetitive language, modeling information, facial expressions, and gestures in teaching vocabulary; explicit instruction in English language usage).

WHAT COUNTS AS EVIDENCE?

Who decides that a practice is evidence based, and what criteria are used? Certainly the What Works Clearinghouse (i.e., the Institute for Educational Science's collection of methods they consider evidence based) would like to have the last word on this. Many would argue, however, that the criteria used are too narrow and too focused on experimental and quasi-experimental designs at the expense of other designs better equipped to answer questions about complex phenomena. Results from carefully designed experimental and quasi-experimental research studies certainly are of value, but it should also be emphasized that much can and should be learned through qualitative means. Whereas quasi-experimental and experimental approaches can help researchers understand which instructional approaches are most effective in a general sense, qualitative methods are ideally suited to answering questions about "how," helping us to understand essential contextual variables that affect the effectiveness of an approach, and facilitating our understanding of implementation challenges and under what circumstances and with whom a practice is most likely to be successful, adding depth not available through other approaches. This emphasis on context when conducting research with diverse populations is essential, especially given the complexity and shifting nature of interactions among political forces, institutions, communities, families, and children. As noted by Shavelson and Towne (2002),

> These features require attention to the physical, social, cultural, economic, and historical environment in the research process because these contextual factors often influence results in significant ways. Because the U.S. education system is so heterogeneous and the nature of teaching and learning so complex, attention to context is especially critical for understanding the extent to which theories and findings may generalize to other times, places, and populations (p. 5).

Gee (2001) discusses the limitations of laboratory and controlled classroom studies when applied to "real world" settings, and calls for "a broader view of both what constitutes empirical research and what sorts of empirical evidence are relevant to complex issues that integrally involve culture, social interaction, institutions, and cognition" (p. 126).

Much can be learned by observing in schools and classrooms where culturally and linguistically diverse students excel as readers. Findings from this type of research are valuable "evidence" that should count as validation of a practice's effectiveness. For example, Taylor, Pearson, Clark, and Walpole (2000) investigated 14 schools across the U.S. that each had a high proportion of students living in poverty. In comparison with less-effective schools, the most-effective schools they identified were noted as having 1) more small-group instruction and more coaching (i.e., scaffolding) by teachers, 2) more teaching of phonics with an emphasis on application during real reading, 3) more higher-order questioning (i.e., questions requiring inferences and integration), 4) greater parental involvement, and 5) more independent reading. There was a balance between skills and holistic instruction (e.g., reading complete texts, composition writing). Also of note was that the more effective schools were characterized by greater student engagement (i.e., students spent more time productively reading and writing). Perhaps these students were more engaged because of these other instructional and climate factors.

In their observational studies of effective programs, Pressley and colleagues (Pressley, Allington, Wharton-McDonald, Block, & Morrow, 2001; Pressley, Wharton-McDonald et al., 2001) noted 1) excellent classroom management; 2) a positive, cooperative classroom environment with much reinforcement of students; 3) explicit instruction in word-level, comprehension, and writing skills; 4) frequent experiences with high-quality literature and students engaged in a great deal of actual reading; 5) teachers making sure students are involved in tasks matched to their competency level, with demands on students accelerating as their competencies improve, 6) teachers carefully monitoring students and providing scaffolded support; 7) teachers encouraging students to self-regulate; and 8) strong connections across the curriculum (e.g., through thematic units). Similarly, Graves, Gersten, and Haager (2004) and Haager (2004) observed first-grade classrooms that included English language learners and suggested that effective teachers enact sophisticated knowledge of reading instruction as well as second language instruction. Their instruction is explicit; draws on the prior knowledge of struggling readers; makes connections with what they know; and places considerable emphasis on explicit and active word identification, phonological awareness, vocabulary instruction, and providing structured opportunities to practice English. Students are highly engaged. Moreover, the classrooms of effective teachers are warm, supportive environments. These important research findings should be taken into account when considering how best to teach reading.

FIDELITY, FEASIBILITY, AND IMPLEMENTATION CHALLENGES

One fundamental underlying assumption of "evidence-based" practices—practices deemed effective through research studies conducted with experimental or quasi-experimental designs—is that the results are generalizable. That is, they are generalizable to the population from which the sample of participants for the research was drawn. But what does that really mean? What aspects of a population make it similar to other populations? Are the students in urban schools in Houston, Texas the "same" as students in urban schools in Miami, Florida? Can results be generalized from a school where 67% of the students receive free or reduced-price lunches to a school where 98% of the students receive free lunches? Can the findings from a school where 12% of the students are English language learners be generalized to a school where 43% of the students are English language learners? What if the percentage of students who are English language learners is the same but at one school the students speak a total of 11 different home languages and at the other school Spanish is the only home language other than English? An intervention tested in one environment with students with a particular set of characteristics may or may not transfer well to or be feasible in another environment.

One critical aspect of generalizability is whether the evidence-based practice is feasible in the new setting and can be implemented with fidelity. The idea of fidelity seems to be related to the belief that "one size fits all"—the assumption that results should be generalizable and transferable from one setting to another and that when results do not transfer, it is because those implementing the model did not do it correctly (Klingner, Cramer, & Harry, 2006). The differences between laboratory or controlled studies and the "real world" are substantial, especially in high-need urban schools. When interpreting the success of a research-based model and considering the extent to which it was implemented with fidelity, it is important to examine the constraints under which those who implemented the model were operating (Herman et al., 2000). For example, the creators of the Success for All (SFA) curriculum offer the caveat that their program is effective only when it is "fully implemented" (Slavin & Madden, 2001, p. 34). This issue of fidelity has been at the center of debates about SFA and other schoolwide instructional models. One of the greatest challenges seems to be students' stagnating and not passing to higher levels of the program, thus recycling through material they already had covered. In their investigation of the various challenges that affected the fidelity with which SFA was implemented across four high-need urban schools with the percentage of students on free lunch in the high 90s. Klingner and colleagues (2006) found numerous grouping and scheduling difficulties, with students of different reading levels and widely varying grade levels placed in the same class. Further complicating implementation was the view of some highly effective teachers that programs such as SFA essentially de-skill and de-professionalize teachers. Klingner and colleagues noted that these schools were confronted with numerous pressures from many levels that complicated both the implementation of the program and its potential for effective outcomes. These pressures included a heightened emphasis on accountability through high-stakes testing, excessive poverty and associated factors that put students at risk for school failure, high mobility rates among teachers and students, and the expectation that schools could implement numerous mandated programs simultaneously. The unique characteristics of the student population and the school context exerted a powerful influence on how these schools implemented SFA. Thus, Klingner and colleagues argued, the issue was not only one of fidelity of implementation but also feasibility in a particular context. They speculated whether

SFA would have been more effective if educators had been empowered to adapt SFA for the local context and their students.

In Foorman and colleagues' (1998) study, the sample was culturally and linguistically diverse (and, it should be added, described in more detail than most samples, although information about language proficiency was not provided). The range of students on free or reduced-price lunches varied from 32.3%– 71.4%. As already noted, however, there are notable differences between schools in this range and schools with free-lunch percentages in the 90s. This is an important point: It cannot be assumed that the results from research conducted in schools where less than 70% of students receive free lunches can transfer to and apply to schools where 99% of students receive free lunches (such as in our SFA example). The students who receive free lunches in each of these schools are not necessarily different from each other in terms of their levels of poverty; it is the tremendous differences in the schools themselves (see, e.g., Kozol's "Savage Inequalities," 1991) that must be taken into account. This is no easy task, in part because schools are so dependent on larger societal influences.

It is interesting to note that the achievement gap decreased from the late 1960s to the early 1980s, but then widened again (Lee, 2002). Gee (1999) makes the point that whatever factors were at work to close the achievement gap were in fact "powerful 'reading interventions' because they significantly increased the scores of at-risk children" (p. 359). Gee suggests that these gains were associated with the social programs of President Johnson's "war on poverty"—programs that were later dismantled. These were not, of course, *reading* interventions. But this line of reasoning does point to the importance of looking at the influence of other factors when considering student achievement, as with Bronfenbrenner's (1977) nested ecological systems model. Instruction does not take place in a vacuum but is influenced by many factors across multiple levels of the home, community, school, and society at large. Thus, debates over instructional methods should be framed within the larger context of how literacy practices interrelate with issues of social practice, culture, and power across these levels (Gee, 1999). Gee's (2002) rejoinder to Snow's critique of his analysis of the NRP report nicely sums up the tension we perceive between our position and that of many mainstream researchers: "She wants to focus on individuals and their internal states (and then move on to the social), whereas I want to focus on social, political, and institutional systems (and then move on to the individual)" (p. 122). That is, insufficient consideration is given to the sociocultural, historical, and political factors that provide the backdrop for individual learning.

As the popularity of the RTI model grows, it seems there is not enough attention on teachers as intervention implementers. With so much variability in knowledge, skills, and dispositions, it is unrealistic to assume with confidence that classroom teachers indelibly will be able to implement interventions in such a way that they are providing students with an adequate opportunity to learn. Indeed, it seems that the difficulties with many such models (e.g., RTI, SFA) may be that they presume too much for implementation, thereby leaving the practitioner to conserve and retrench to their own (sometimes ineffective) "tried and true" methods or to modify research-based interventions in ill-conceived ways because they lack the training (or time) to make the necessary modifications. What if a teacher's underlying belief is that ethnically diverse students can reach mastery on skills-based learning but not succeed with tasks involving higher-order thinking? What type of instruction will this teacher use in a classroom with culturally and linguistically diverse students? It is a mistake to think that evidence-based instruction can be designed without looking at who is going to implement it and without considering how teachers may "resist" teaching all children, even when they are provided with strong professional development.

By not sufficiently acknowledging these challenges, students themselves are held accountable for their reading difficulties, considered to have deficits, and overreferred to and overplaced in special education. Therefore, as the education system starts to move toward RTI models for identifying and remediating students with reading difficulties, it is important to design interventions with culture in mind. But what does it mean to provide culturally responsive literacy instruction? We will turn to a discussion of this shortly, but first let us look more closely at the role of culture in learning.

CULTURE AND LEARNING

To what extent is learning mediated by culture? Rogoff (2003) and Cole (1998) emphasize the cultural processes that are involved in all children's learning. This chapter has discussed the importance of variability and including sufficient demographic information about students' ethnicities in descriptions of participant samples. At the same time, however, it is important to consider that culture is fluid and dynamic and not simply a collection of static or categorical traits. Gutierrez and Rogoff (2003) caution, "Treating cultural differences as traits, in our view, makes it harder to understand the relation of individual learning and the practices of cultural communities, and this in turn sometimes hinders effective assistance to student learning" (p. 19). In any given classroom, there are multiple cultures "as embodied in the cultural toolkit that each person brings to school and the cultures that are created as students, teachers, and school staff interact over time" (Artiles, 2002, p. 696). It is important for teachers to recognize their own assumptions about culture and how these assumptions affect their views of their students' learning.

Students may learn differently because of their cultural backgrounds, but these are precisely that—differences—not deficits. Heath (1982) stresses this point in her descriptions of children growing up in three distinct communities who experienced schooling very differently. It is important for educators to understand the histories and valued practices of cultural groups rather than trying to teach prescriptively according to broad, underexamined generalities and stereotypes about groups. Gutierrez and Rogoff caution that treating cultural differences as individual traits encourages overgeneralization. Disproportionate representation is in part due to the inadequate attention to and oversimplification of culture by researchers and practitioners.

Instructional methods do not work or fail as decontextualized generic practices but only in relationship to the cultural contexts in which they are implemented (Gee, 1999). Thus, there is promise in promoting a culturally responsive pedagogy that is infused throughout general education, multicultural education, and special education. Each of these three areas by itself has its limitations. Though multicultural education's goals of making sure teachers consider students' backgrounds, develop sensitivity and awareness, and connect with their students culturally and affectively are worthy ones, individuals who advocate for multicultural education or culturally responsive education also need to give attention to evidence-based interventions (keeping in mind the caveats about incorporating conditions of cultural and linguistic variability in the conducting of research and the recommendation to reconsider what counts as evidence put forth in this chapter). Conversely, general and special educators tend to focus on instructional interventions without adequately considering the role of sociocultural experiences in learning and without full consideration of affective variables such as motivation and interest. The strongest interventions will come from bringing together multiple voices with diverse perspectives and from examining notions of disability within their full sociocultural and historical contexts.

CULTURALLY RESPONSIVE LITERACY INSTRUCTION (TIER 1)

As mentioned previously, Moje and Hinchman (2004) made the point that "all practice needs to be culturally responsive in order to be best practice" (p. 321). Culturally responsive teaching should not be thought of as an add-on for students from other than mainstream backgrounds but rather as a fundamental condition of effective teaching. This is essential to our conception of what the "first tier" in an RTI model should look like. Culturally responsive teachers build on what *all* learners bring to the classroom. They are able to tap into and connect with students' prior knowledge, interests, motivation, and home language (August & Hakuta, 1997; Au, 2000).

Culturally responsive literacy instruction should be authentic and multifaceted, with frequent opportunities to practice reading with a variety of rich materials in meaningful contexts (Pressley, 2001). In addition, this instruction should include language activities and explicit instruction in phonological awareness, the alphabetic code, vocabulary development, and comprehension strategies (National Reading Panel, 2000; Reyes, 1992; Snow, 2002; Snow, Burns, & Griffin, 1998). A focus on the complete literacy event does not negate the importance of traditional skills. "Rather these skills are situated within a holistic context that is intimately linked with goals and conditions of reading" (Roller, 1996, p. 34).

Literacy instruction should take into account the sociocultural contexts within which students learn (Artiles, 2002; Ruiz, 1998). As stated throughout this chapter, culture matters. When teaching children to read, what does it mean to account for one's culture? First, it entails taking a broad view of what counts as literate in a multiethnic, diverse society. It means being aware that when children start school, they may not have experienced the same interactions with print as their mainstream peers. They still, however, have had valuable experiences on which their teachers can and should build. It requires connecting literacy practices from the home, community, and the school. Culturally responsive literacy instruction involves recognizing that students' discourse and behavioral styles may not match the school's expectations but need to be validated anyway (Brice Heath, 1983; Cazden, 1988). As August and Hakuta (1997) indicate, it means recognizing that bilingualism is an asset and that learning English should be an additive rather than a subtractive process. Teachers do not need to be "insiders" in a particular culture in order to offer culturally responsive instruction. Teachers, however, do need to make an effort to learn about the cultures represented in their classrooms, respect students' values, and view differences in students' literacies as strengths, not deficits (Alvermann, 2003; Ladson-Billings, 1994).

Culturally responsive literacy programs tap into community resources that promote children's literacy, such as by enlisting volunteers to serve as reading tutors (Baker, Gersten, & Keating, 2000; Fitzgerald, 2001; Invernizzi, Juel, & Rosemary, 1997; Wasik, 1998; Wasik & Slavin, 1993). Inviting parents and others in the neighborhood to share their expertise or "funds of knowledge" on a multitude of topics is another way to promote children's literacy (Moll & González, 1994). A concrete example entails including local elders in the schooling of American Indian youth (Aguilera, 2003). Also valuable are programs that focus on developing partnerships with parents and other caregivers to enhance home literacy experiences. Finally, parents can learn to interact with their children in ways that promote literacy achievement (Arnold, Lonigan, Whitehurst, & Epstein, 1994; Dickinson & Smith, 1994; Valdez-Menchaca & Whitehurst, 1992; Whitehurst et al., 1994).

A multipronged approach is recommended to prepare teachers to teach in culturally responsive ways. First, teacher education and professional development programs should include a strong focus on instructional practices and assessment procedures that have been validated with culturally and linguistically diverse students. Second, these programs also should include a strong component designed to help participants develop the attributes of culturally responsive teachers (Gay, 2000; Ladson-Billings, 2001; Villegas & Lucas, 2002).

CONCLUSION

It is crucial for the first tier in RTI models to address the overwhelming difficulties facing culturally and linguistically diverse students as they strive to learn in general education programs. Researchers and educators must ask whether current interventions (for both the first and second tiers) are responsive to the needs of culturally and linguistically diverse students. We have been asked, "But isn't teaching phonological awareness the same regardless of whether the child is white or African American?" Our response is, "Yes, but we must also consider everything else going on in the classroom and school. The context within which discrete skills instruction occurs cannot be ignored or separated from considerations of its effectiveness." In conclusion, a culturally responsive RTI model has tremendous potential to mitigate the effects of cultural and linguistic bias inherent in discrepancy-based identification models and more appropriately differentiate between culturally and linguistically diverse learners who do and do not have true disabilities. Only by doing so can all children achieve their full potential.

REFERENCES

Aguilera, D.E. (2003). *Who defines success: An analysis of competing models of education for American Indian and Alaskan Native students.* Unpublished doctoral dissertation, University of Colorado, Boulder.

Alliance for Human Research Protection. (2003, June 10). *UK health department/British prime minister issue statement warning no Paxil for children!* Retrieved April 16, 2005, from http://www.ahrp.org/infomail/0603/10.php

Alvermann, D. (2003). Exemplary literacy instruction in grades 7–12: What counts and who's counting? In J. Flood and P. Anders (Eds.), *Literary development of students in urban schools: Research and policy.* (pp. 187–201). Newark, DE: International Reading Association.

Arnold, D.H., Lonigan, C.J., Whitehurst, G.J., & Epstein, J.N. (1994). Accelerating language development through picture book reading: Replication and extension to a videotape training format. *Journal of Educational Psychology, 86,* 235–243.

Artiles, A.J. (2002). Culture in learning: The next frontier in reading difficulties research. In R. Bradley, L. Danielson, & D.P. Hallahan (Eds.), *Identification of learning disabilities: Research to policy* (pp. 693–701). Mahwah, NJ: Lawrence Erlbaum Associates.

Artiles, A.J., Trent, S.C., & Kuan, L. (1997). Learning disabilities empirical research on ethnic minority students: An analysis of 22 years of studies published in selected refereed journals. *Learning Disabilities Research & Practice, 12,* 82–91.

Artiles, A.J., Trent, S.C., & Palmer, J. (2004). Culturally diverse students in special education: Legacies and prospects. In J.A. Banks & C.M. Banks (Eds.), *Handbook of research on multicultural education* (2nd ed., pp. 716–735). San Francisco: Jossey-Bass.

Au, K.H. (2000). A multicultural perspective on policies for improving literacy achievement: Equity and excellence. In M.L. Kamil, P.B. Mosenthal, P.D. Pearson, & R. Barr (Eds.), *Handbook of reading research* (Vol. 3, pp. 835–851). Mahwah, NJ: Lawrence Erlbaum Associates.

August, D., & Hakuta, K. (1997). *Improving schooling for language minority children: A research agenda.* Washington, DC: National Academies Press.

Baker, S., Gersten, R., & Keating, T. (2000). When less may be more: A 2-year longitudinal evaluation of a volunteer tutoring program requiring minimal training. *Reading Research Quarterly, 35,* 494–519.

Bloche, M.G. (2004). Race-based therapeutics. *New England Journal of Medicine, 351,* 2035–2037. Extract available at http://content.nejm.org/cgi/content/extract/351/20/2035

Bond, G.L., & Dykstra, R. (1967). The cooperative research program in first-grade reading instruction. *Reading Research Quarterly, 2,* 10–141.

Bos, C.S., & Fletcher, T.V. (1997). Sociocultural considerations in learning disabilities inclusion research: Knowledge gaps and future directions. *Learning Disabilities Research & Practice, 12,* 92–99.

Brice Heath, S. (1983). *Ways with words: Language, life, and work in communities and classrooms.* New York: Cambridge University Press.

Bronfenbrenner, U. (1977, July). Toward an experimental ecology of human development. *American Psychologist,* 513–531.

Camilli, G., Vargas, S., & Yurecko, M. (2003). Teaching children to read: The fragile link between science and federal education policy [Electronic version]. *Education Policy Analysis Archives, 11*(15).

Cazden, C.B. (1988). *Classroom discourse: The language of teaching and learning.* Portsmouth, NH: Heinemann.

Chavous, T.M., Bernat, D.H., Schmeelk-Cone, K., Caldwell, C.H., Kohn-Wood, L., & Zimmerman, M.A. (2003). Racial identity and academic attainment among African American adolescents. *Child Development, 74,* 1076–1090.

Cole, M. (1998). Can cultural psychology help us think about diversity? *Mind, Culture, and Activity, 5*(4), 291–304.

Committee on Pharmacokinetics and Drug Interaction in the Elderly, Institute of Medicine. (1997). *Pharmacokinetics and drug interactions in the elderly and special issues in elderly African-American populations: Workshop summary.* Washington, DC: National Academies Press.

Darling-Hammond, L. (1995). Inequality and access to knowledge. In J.A. Banks & C.A. Banks (Eds.), *The handbook of research on multicultural education* (pp. 465–483). New York: Macmillan.

Dickinson, D.K., & Smith, M.W. (1994). Long-term effects of preschool teachers' book readings on low-income children's vocabulary and story comprehension. *Reading Research Quarterly, 29,* 104–122.

Donovan, S., & Cross, C. (2002). *Minority students in special and gifted education.* Washington, DC: National Academies Press.

Fitzgerald, J. (2001). Can minimally trained college student volunteers help young at-risk children to read better? *Reading Research Quarterly, 36,* 28–47.

Foorman, B.R., Francis, D.J., Fletcher, J.M., Schatschneider, C., & Mehta, P. (1998). The role of instruction in learning to read: Preventing reading failure in at-risk children. *Journal of Educational Psychology, 90*(1), 37–55.

Fuchs, D., Mock, D., Morgan, P.L., & Young, C.L. (2003). Responsiveness to-intervention: Definitions, evidence, and implications for the learning disabilities construct. *Learning Disabilities Research & Practice, 18,* 157–171.

Gay, G. (2000). *Culturally responsive teaching.* New York: Teachers College Press.

Gee, J.P. (1999). Critical issues: Reading and the new literacy studies: Reframing the National Academy of Sciences Report on Reading. *Journal of Literacy Research, 31,* 355–374.

Gee, J.P. (2001). A sociocultural perspective on early literacy development. In S.B. Neuman and D.K. Dickinson (Eds.), *Handbook of early literacy research* (pp. 30–42). New York: The Guilford Press.

Gee, J.P. (2002). The limits of reframing: A response to Professor Snow. *Journal of Literacy Research, 32,* 121–128.

Gerber, M.M. (2003, December). *Teachers are still the test: Limitations of response to instruction strategies for identifying children with learning disabilities.* Paper presented at the National Research Center on Learning Disabilities Responsiveness-to-Intervention Symposium, Kansas City, MO.

Gerber, M.M., Jimenez, T., Leafstedt, J., Villaruz, J., Richards, C., & English, J. (2004). English reading effects of small-group intensive intervention in Spanish for K-1 English learners. *Learning Disabilities Research & Practice, 19,* 239–251.

Gersten, R., & Baker, S. (2000). What we know about effective instructional practices for English-language learners. *Exceptional Children, 66,* 454–470.

Graves, A., Gersten, R., & Haager, D. (2004). Literacy instruction in multiple-language first-grade classrooms: Linking student outcomes to observed instructional practice. *Learning Disabilities Research & Practice, 19,* 262–272.

Grimes J., & Kurns, S. (2003, December). *An intervention-based system for addressing NCLB and IDEA expectations: A multiple tiered model to ensure every child learns.* Paper presented at the National Research Center on Learning Disabilities Responsiveness-to-Intervention Symposium, Kansas City, MO.

Gutierrez, K., & Rogoff, B. (2003). Cultural ways of learning: Individual traits or repertoires of practice. *Educational Researcher, 32*(5), 19–25.

Haager, D. (2004, November). *Promoting literacy development for English language learners learning in English: A case for explicit instruction.* Paper presented at the National Center for Culturally Responsive Educational Systems Conference on English Language Learners, Scottsdale, AZ.

Harder, B. (2005). The race to prescribe: Drug for African Americans may debut among debate. *Science News, 167,* 247–248.

Harry, B., & Klingner, J.K. (2006). *Crossing the border from normalcy to disability: Culturally and linguistically diverse students and the special education placement process.* New York: Teachers College Press.

Heath, S.B. (1982). What no bedtime story means: Narrative skills at home and school. *Language in Society, 11,* 49–76.

Herman, R., Carl, B., Lampron, S., Sussman, A., Berger, A., & Innes, F. (2000). *What we know about comprehensive school reform models.* Washington, DC: American Institutes for Research.

Hilliard, A.G., III. (1992). The pitfalls and promises of special education practice. *Exceptional Children, 52*(2), 168–172.

Hilliard, A.G., III. (2001). Race, identity, hegemony, and education: What do we need to know now? In W.H. Watkins, J.H. Lewis, & V. Chou (Eds.), *Race and education: The roles of history and society in educating African American students* (pp. 1–36). Boston: Allyn & Bacon.

Invernizzi, M., Juel, C., & Rosemary, C.A. (1997). A community tutorial that works. *The Reading Teacher, 50,* 304–311.

Kaplan, A., & Maehr, M.L. (1999). Enhancing the motivation of African American students: An achievement goal theory perspective. *Journal of Negro Education, 68*(1), 23–41.

Keogh, B., Gallimore, R., & Weisner, T. (1997). A sociocultural perspective on learning and learning disabilities. *Learning Disabilities Research & Practice, 12,* 107–113.

Klingner, J.K., Cramer, E., & Harry, B. (2006). Challenges in the implementation of Success for All by four urban schools. *Elementary School Journal, 106,* 333–349.

Kozol, J. (1991). *Savage inequalities: Children in America's schools.* New York: HarperPerennial.

Ladson-Billings, G. (1994). *The dreamkeepers: Successful teachers of African American children.* San Francisco: Jossey-Bass.

Ladson-Billings, G. (2001). *Crossing over to Canaan: The journey of new teachers in diverse classrooms.* San Francisco: Jossey-Bass.

Leafstedt, J.M., Richards, C.R., & Gerber, M.M. (2004). Effectiveness of explicit phonological-awareness instruction for at-risk English learners. *Learning Disabilities Research & Practice, 19,* 252–261.

Lee, J. (2002). Racial and ethnic achievement gap trends: Reversing the progress toward equity? *Educational Researcher, 31,* 3–12.

Linan-Thompson, S., Vaughn, S., Hickman-Davis, P., & Kouzekanni, K. (2003). Effectiveness of supplemental reading instruction for second-grade English language learners with reading difficulties. *Elementary School Journal, 103,* 221–238.

Linan-Thompson, S., Vaughn, S., Prater, K., & Cirino, P.T. (2006). The response to intervention of English language learners at-risk for reading problems. *Journal of Learning Disabilities, 39,* 390–398.

Mastropieri, M.A. (2003, December). *Feasibility and consequences of response to intervention (RTI): Examination of the issues and scientific evidence as a model for the identification of individuals with learning disabilities.* Paper presented at the National Research Center on Learning Disabilities Responsiveness-to-Intervention Symposium, Kansas City, MO.

McCardle, P., Mele-McCarthy, J., & Leos, K. (2005). English language learners and learning disabilities: Research agenda and implications for practice. *Learning Disabilities Research & Practice, 20,* 68–78.

McCray, A.D., & Garcia, S.B. (2002). The stories we must tell: Developing a research agenda for multicultural and bilingual special education. *Qualitative Studies in Education, 15*(6), 599–612.

Moje, E.B., & Hinchman, K. (2004). Culturally responsive practices for youth literacy learning. In T.L. Jetton & J.A. Dole (Eds.), *Adolescent literacy research and practice* (pp. 3211–3350). New York: The Guilford Press.

Moll, L.C., & González, N. (1994). Critical issues: Lessons from research with language-minority children. *JRB: A Journal of Literacy, 26,* 439–456.

National Reading Panel. (2000). *Teaching children to read: An evidence-based assessment of the scientific research literature on reading and its implications for reading instruction: Summary Report.* Washington, DC: National Institute of Child Health and Development. Retrieved January 10, 2005, from http://www.nationalreadingpanel.org/Publications/summary.htm

Oakes, J., Franke, M.L., Quartz, K.H., & Rogers, J. (2002). Research for high-quality urban teaching: Defining it, developing it, assessing it. *Journal of Teacher Education, 53,* 228–234.

Ortiz, A.A. (1997). Learning disabilities occurring concomitantly with linguistic differences. *Journal of Learning Disabilities, 30,* 321–332.

Ortiz, A.A. (2002). Prevention of school failure and early intervention for English language learners. In A.J. Artiles & A.A. Ortiz (Eds.), *English language learners with special education needs: Identification, placement, and instruction* (pp. 31–48). Washington, DC: Center for Applied Linguistics.

Pearson, P.D. (2004). American reading instruction since 1967. In International Reading Association (Ed.), *Preparing reading professionals: A collection from the International Reading Association.* (pp. 6–40.) Newark, DE: Editor.

Pressley, M. (2001). *Effective beginning reading instruction. Executive summary and paper commissioned by the National Reading Conference.* Chicago: National Reading Conference.

Pressley, M. (2003). A few things reading educators should know about instructional experiments. *Reading Teacher, 57*(1), 64–71.

Pressley, M., Allington, R., Wharton-McDonald, R., Block, C.C., & Morrow, L.M. (2001). *Learning to read: Lessons from exemplary first grades.* New York: The Guilford Press.

Pressley, M., Wharton-McDonald, R., Allington, R., Block, C.C., Morrow, L., Tracey, D., et al. (2001). A study of effective grade-1 literacy instruction. *Scientific Studies of Reading, 5,* 35–58.

Pugach, M.C. (2001). The stories we choose to tell: Fulfilling the promise of qualitative research for special education. *Exceptional Children, 67,* 439–453.

Reyes, M. de la Luz. (1992). Challenging venerable assumptions: Literacy instruction for linguistically diverse students. *Harvard Educational Review, 62,* 427–446.

Reynolds, C. (1988). Putting the individual into aptitude-treatment interaction. *Exceptional Children, 54,* 324–331.

Rogoff, B. (2003). *The cultural nature of human development.* New York: Oxford University Press.

Roller, C. (1996). *Variability not disability: Struggling readers in a workshop classroom.* Newark, DE: International Reading Association.

Ruiz, N. (1998). Instructional strategies for children with limited-English proficiency. *Journal of Early Education and Family Review, 5,* 21–22.

Samuels, S.J. (1994). Word recognition. In R.B. Ruddell, M.R. Ruddell, and H. Singer (Eds.), *Theoretical models and processes of reading* (pp. 359–380). Newark, DE: International Reading Association.

Shavelson, R.J., & Towne, L., (Eds.). (2002). *Scientific research in education.* Washington, DC: National Academies Press.

Simmerman, S., & Swanson, H.L. (2001). Treatment outcomes for students with learning disabilities: How important are internal and external validity. *Journal of Learning Disabilities, 34,* 221–235.

Slavin, R.E., & Madden, N.A. (2001). *Success for All and comprehensive school reform: Evidence-based policies for urban education.* Washington, DC: Office of Educational Research and Improvement.

Smedley, B.D., Stith, A.Y, & Nelson, A.R. (Eds.). (2003). *Unequal treatment: Confronting racial and ethnic disparities in health care.* Washington, DC: National Academies Press.

Snow, C.E. (2002). *Reading for understanding: Toward an R&D program in reading comprehension.* Santa Monica, CA: RAND.

Snow, C.E., Burns, M.S., & Griffin, P. (1998). *Preventing reading difficulties in young children.* Washington, DC: National Academies Press.

Taylor, B.M., Pearson, P.D., Clark, K., & Walpole, S. (2000). Effective schools and accomplished teachers: Lessons about primary-grade reading instruction in low-income schools. *Elementary School Journal, 101,* 121–165.

Troia, G.A. (1999). Phonological awareness intervention research: A critical review of the experimental methodology. *Reading Research Quarterly, 34,* 28–52.

Valdez-Menchaca, M.C., & Whitehurst, G.J. (1992). Accelerating language development through picture book reading: A systematic extension to Mexican day care. *Developmental Psychology, 28,* 1106–1114.

Vaughn, S., & Fuchs, L. (2003). Redefining learning disabilities as inadequate response to instruction: The promise and potential problems. *Learning Disabilities Research & Practice, 18,* 137–146.

Vaughn, S., Linan-Thompson, S., & Hickman, P. (2003). Response to instruction as a means of identifying students with reading/learning disabilities. *Exceptional Children, 69,* 391–409.

Vaughn, S., Mathes, P., Linan-Thompson, S., & Francis, D.J. (2005). Teaching English language learners at risk for reading disabilities to read: Putting research into practice. *Learning Disabilities Research & Practice, 20,* 58–67.

Vellutino, F.R., Scanlon, D.M., Small, S., & Fanuele, D. (2003, December). *Response to intervention as a vehicle for distinguishing between reading disabled and non-reading disabled children: Evidence for the role of kindergarten and first-grade intervention.* Paper presented at the National Research Center on Learning Disabilities Responsiveness-to-Intervention Symposium, Kansas City, MO.

Villegas, A.M., & Lucas, T. (2002). Preparing culturally responsive teachers: Rethinking the curriculum. *Journal of Teacher Education; 53 (1),* 20–32.

Wasik, B.A. (1998). Using volunteers as reading tutors: Guidelines for successful practices. *The Reading Teacher, 51*(7), 562–570.

Wasik, B.A., & Slavin, R.E. (1993). Preventing early reading failure with one-to-one tutoring: A review of five programs. *Reading Research Quarterly, 28,* 178–200.

Whitehurst, G.J., Epstein, J.N., Angell, A.L., Payne, A.C., Crone, D.A., & Fischel, J.E. (1994). Outcomes of an emergent literacy intervention in Head Start. *Journal of Educational Psychology, 86,* 542–555.

Willis, A.I. (2002). Dissin' and disremembering: Motivation and culturally and linguistically diverse students' literacy learning. *Reading and Writing Quarterly, 18,* 293–319.

Teacher Roles in
Implementing Intervention

Diane Haager and Jennifer Mahdavi

The notion of Response to Intervention (RTI) as a means of identifying and treating children with learning difficulties is widely recognized as an important and welcome shift from practices that rely on arbitrary and inconsistent discrepancy criteria and focus on student impairments. The reauthorization of special education law with the Individuals with Disabilities Education Improvement Act (IDEA) of 2004 (PL 108-446) indicates that schools may use an RTI approach to identifying students with learning disabilities. As researchers and educators move forward in delineating and validating interventions that support and enhance students' academic learning in an RTI model, practical issues related to implementation must also be examined. Of particular interest is how this shift in practice affects those who are responsible for instruction—general and special education teachers.

Other chapters in this book describe models and instructional practices for reading intervention; therefore, this chapter does so only briefly. Though there are variations in the conceptualization of multitiered models across researchers, the basic framework is similar. The first tier represents core reading instruction that is provided for all students. Instruction in Tier 1 consists of a research-based reading program that is comprehensive in covering the essential early reading skills, is fully implemented, and is delivered by skilled teachers who have received adequate professional development. Tier 2 involves supplemental instruction beyond the core program for students whose performance is significantly below grade level expectations as determined by reliable and valid assessment of essential reading skills. Tier 3 consists of more intensive and specialized instruction for students who have significant learning problems that have not been addressed in a specified amount of time in Tier 2. Some researchers and educators would consider Tier 3 to be special education; others would include a fourth tier that would be reserved for students with recognized disabilities.

Clearly, no one would doubt the merit of adopting a process for early identification and treatment of significant learning problems that would lead to positive reading outcomes for many children. The idea of developing a system of
assessment and intervention that is responsive to student needs is intuitively ap-
pealing. In an RTI approach, educators follow the progress of students showing
early signs of reading difficulty and make educational decisions, such as adaptations to instruction or curriculum, based on students' responses to intervention.
Some students may respond well to intervention and in a short time be able to
discontinue intervention. Continued or more intensive intervention may be war-
ranted for other students based on their inadequate response to intervention.
Such students may require intensive, specialized reading instruction such as is offered in special education programs (Torgesen, 2000).

The RTI approach brings compelling questions to the forefront regarding
teachers' roles. The delineation of roles for general and special education teachers
becomes less clear as students with and without disability labels require specialized instruction. In this chapter, we consider the roles of both general and special
education teachers in a three-tier model of reading intervention. How does this
model change teachers' roles and daily activities? What evidence is there that it is
feasible for general and special educators to adopt the necessary practices and routines? What barriers exist that might prevent full implementation?

To answer these questions, we draw from current research focusing on three-
tier reading intervention models as well as previous studies of prereferral intervention. Based on a review of research, policy, and practices, we suggest a framework
for defining the roles of general and special education teachers in implementing
a three-tiered model. We then describe the processes and roles of general and special education teachers in a specific project implemented over the past 6 years.
Last, we examine lessons learned from implementation, draw conclusions about
potential barriers to implementation, and suggest guiding principles for assisting
teachers in accepting their challenging roles in a three-tier system.

PREREFERRAL INTERVENTION RESEARCH:
WHERE IT ALL BEGAN

Prereferral intervention long has been viewed as an essential component of the educational system (Graden, Casey, & Christenson, 1985; Rock & Zigmond, 2001;
Safran & Safran, 1996). Researchers have noted the importance of using the resources of general education to remediate learning problems prior to considering
issuing a disability label to students experiencing difficulty. By law, before school
personnel may consider a special education placement for an individual student,
they must document attempts to provide appropriate instruction in the general
education program. Some researchers and educators have called for using the
term "intervention assistance" instead of "prereferral intervention" to avoid the
sometimes unwarranted assumption that such assistance would automatically

lead to a referral for special education (Graden, 1989; Whitten & Dieker, 1995). Rather, systematic intervention assistance keeps the intervention focus in the general education system and more clearly differentiates a learning problem from a learning disability.

Studies have documented the importance of systematic prereferral intervention processes and strategies. Studies have shown that effective prereferral intervention practices can decrease spurious requests for special education assessment (Safran & Safran, 1996; Whitten & Dieker, 1995) as well as increase the number of assessed students who qualify for services (McNamara & Hollinger, 2003). Teachers involved in the process tend to appreciate the opportunity to work with colleagues to solve problems as well as the increased communication among staff members that occurs as a result of the prereferral process (Chalfant & Pysh, 1989). When the members of the prereferral team have been trained and supported by the state or a university program, the process is carried out with greater integrity and efficacy (Bahr, Whitten, Dieker, Kocarek, & Manson, 1999; Fuchs, Fuchs, Dulan, Roberts, & Fernstrom 1992; McDougal, Clonan, & Martens, 2000). One unfortunate problem with prereferral intervention approaches has been that general education teachers tend to view the process as a special education function (Gersten & Dimino, 2006).

Prereferral intervention processes that use a strong consultative or collaborative approach generally support the use of interventions. When school psychologists or other consultants provide feedback or coaching to general educators, the teachers' implementation of suggested interventions increases, although student performance may remain variable (Mortenson & Witt, 1998). Giving students responsibility for monitoring their own progress, in conjunction with the use of a contingency-based contract between teachers and students, is another effective prereferral intervention strategy (Bahr, Fuchs, Fuchs, Fernstrom, & Stecker, 1993). Generally, it is the additional support provided by a specialist or colleague that makes prereferral intervention efficacious and desirable to classroom teachers (Lane, Mahdavi, & Borthwick-Duffy, 2003). This support increases treatment integrity by keeping the intervention fresh in the general educator's mind. It also helps make the teacher feel more comfortable with providing the types of specialized intervention suggested by the prereferral team. No matter how professional and knowledgeable the members of the prereferral team or how appropriate and valid the interventions suggested, prereferral intervention only can be effective when teachers and other service providers implement the interventions with integrity (Kovaleski, 1999). Teachers as implementers, then, is an important topic to consider as schools move to widespread use of a three-tier reading intervention model.

It is important to note that almost all of the studies of prereferral intervention practices are published in special education journals despite the fact that prereferral intervention is viewed as a general education function. The problem is not that researchers and educators in general education view prereferral intervention as unimportant. Researchers, practitioners, and policy makers would agree that providing explicit, supplemental reading instruction to prevent reading failure in large numbers of students is a powerful and much-needed change in our educational system. Such intervention could greatly reduce the number of students needing costly, intensive special education (Lyon et al., 2001). Recent research indicates that 25% or more of students in the primary grades may need intervention, at least temporarily, to reach grade-level reading by the end of third grade (Torgesen, 2002; Vaughn, Linan-Thompson, & Hickman, 2003). Despite the intuitive appeal and documented need for early reading intervention, widespread and rapid adoption of any educational innovation raises concerns about implementation. Often following well-meaning policy or legislative decisions, districts scramble to implement new policies while the field is still attempting to distill what constitutes effective practice (Crockett, 2004; Landrum & Tankersley, 2004; Odom et al., 2005).

Despite the enthusiasm of researchers and practitioners to adopt reading intervention models to circumvent later, potentially devastating reading problems, it is important to ask questions about what it takes to accomplish widespread implementation. Oft-cited factors necessary for effective implementation of school reform initiatives include administrative support, fiscal resources, time to refine and adjust procedures, and attitudinal factors (Desimone, 2002; Evans, Baugh & Sheffer, 2005). These factors are likely to be important in implementing an RTI model as well. Intervention delivered by highly skilled and knowledgeable teachers is, of course, a central ingredient to successful implementation of a three-tier model of reading intervention, and this suggests extensive professional development and teacher support. Yet, studies indicate that teachers are overburdened, have little time to devote to individualized instruction, and lack the knowledge and skills to address significant reading problems (Bahr & Kovaleski, 2006; Moats, 2004; Vaughn, Hughes, Schumm, & Klingner, 1998). What, then, can reasonably be expected of teachers in implementing a three-tier intervention system? What will it take to prepare the teaching force?

GENERAL AND SPECIAL EDUCATION TEACHERS' ROLES IN A THREE-TIER MODEL OF READING INTERVENTION

Both general education and special education teachers have assumed critical roles in providing appropriate reading instruction for students with reading difficulties. Historically, the difference in their roles has been the students they serve, with general education teachers responsible for general reading instruction and special education teachers responsible for instructing students with disabilities. Since 2000, the role of special education teachers has changed somewhat with the movement to a more inclusive model of education in which students with disabilities spend all or most of their time in a general education classroom. Students with disabilities, however, still often receive at least some of their reading instruction from a special education teacher. In some classrooms, this may be the time that the special education students leave the classroom to see the special education teacher for specialized reading instruction. In others, the special education students may stay in the classroom and do the same assignments with modifications, or, the special education teacher may come into the general education classroom and pull students to a separate table to deliver an alternate reading lesson. Although both the general and special education teachers may work with students with and without disabilities, the general education teacher is primarily responsible for delivering the core reading program, and the role of the special educator is to provide support for students with disabilities either in the general education curriculum or an alternative reading program.

Though Tier 1 of reading intervention does not appear to change the instructional roles of general and special education teachers significantly, there may be additional responsibilities with regard to assessment. Fuchs and Fuchs (2006) suggest that teachers could use the previous year's high-stakes assessment; however, it would be preferable to assess all students early in the year using a performance-based assessment tool that has designated grade-level benchmarks. Who, then, takes on the role of conducting and interpreting such assessments? This type of assessment is likely new to the role of the general education teacher and might seem burdensome. Such assessments, usually administered individually in the early grades, take away from instructional time and pull the teacher's attention away from the class. Yet, screening assessment does not fall within the typical role of the special education teacher either. Special education typically has been defined as occurring after a student has been identified as having a disability. To implement a multitiered reading intervention model, then, schools must identify who will conduct screening assessments and provide the necessary supports for teachers to take on the extra responsibility.

Tier 2 of a three-tier model of reading intervention requires that someone provide supplemental instruction beyond the core program. Common sense dictates that this would be a well-trained teacher. Who, then, should deliver Tier 2 instruction? General educators are adept at designing and implementing core curricula and instruction geared to help most students meet state academic standards. These teachers may find the work of teaching to the disparate needs of their students daunting, but they are aware of the importance of this role. They, however, may feel less comfortable with their responsibility to take on more intensive intervention by providing Tier 2 services to students with greater learning needs. They may report willingness to take on the responsibility of providing early intervention but express trepidation about their ability to identify a child who needs that instruction and then about how to provide it (Bursuck, Munk, Nelson, & Curran, 2002). Yet, students in Tier 2 instruction do not have identified disabilities and, therefore, instruction does not fall within the scope of the special educator's duties. In some research models, Tier 2 has been delivered by paid interventionists (e.g., Vaughn et al., 2003). Hiring additional personnel to provide intervention is not likely feasible in most schools. Thus, it is important to explore the feasibility of general education teachers providing Tier 2 instruction.

The first step a general educator must take to initiate Tier 2 interventions is assessment. Though teachers could use the typical measures that accompany their reading programs, such as decoding, fluency, and comprehension checks, these do not always have the established reliability and validity in providing cut-off scores or benchmarks to screen students who may need additional assistance. An alternative would be to use a norm-referenced or criterion-referenced assessment designed for this purpose (Fuchs & Fuchs, 2006). General educators might also use informal reading inventories or other informal measures to move from screening and into diagnosing the challenges faced by their pupils. Multiple measures that already have been selected for use in general education classrooms are very useful to identify the strengths and needs of students and to devise instruction that will help students meet their potential (Taylor, Pearson, Clark, & Walpole, 2000). Analyzing the assessment data, perhaps in collaboration with grade-level colleagues, administrators, and the special educator is a vital part of this step.

Once general educators have identified whether students are meeting grade-level expectations, they will be able to form small intervention groups of students with similar learning needs. Not all students below benchmarks will have the same needs. Students identified for Tier 2 intervention should be provided instruction that is intense, targeted to their learning needs, and implemented consistently and with fidelity (Marston, 2005). For example, a first-grade teacher may have three or four students who are struggling with phonemic awareness. This would be a likely group for a short-term intervention group focused specifically on phonemic skills. The teacher may work with these students for 10 minutes per day for a few weeks, then retest to see if they have met the benchmark in this area. Other groups may be formed to focus on other important skills such as decoding or sight word practice. Some students will require intensive Tier 2 intervention in multiple skill areas; however, most students will make adequate progress with the usual lessons the teacher delivers (Vaughn et al., 2003). For this reason, Tier 2 should never supplant Tier 1 intervention. In addition, progress monitoring assessments will help teachers to ensure that the intervention is having desired results.

General educators are also responsible for initiating the prereferral intervention process for students who need it. These referrals, based on assessment results including ongoing progress monitoring of students receiving Tier 2 intervention, may lead to additional strategies for the general educator to try or to a referral for special education assessment (Lane et al., 2003). Indeed, the documentation collected by teachers during Tier 2 intervention may be an important part of the prereferral intervention process as the prereferral team works with the teacher to discuss instructional strategies and evaluate their effectiveness for a student who has been referred for prereferral assistance. Tier 2 intervention documentation also may help inform decisions about the necessity of further assessment to determine special education eligibility (Menzies, Mahdavi, & Lewis, 2006).

Finally, the second tier of intervention requires general educators to increase their collaboration with other professionals and with the parents of their students. Teachers can obtain a wealth of knowledge, information, and resources from their colleagues at their school sites. General educators frequently work with their colleagues to design whole-class lessons; it should not be difficult to extend this support into finding new ideas to address the needs of small groups and individual children. Examining student work and making decisions about grouping and instruction, however, might be more effective if collaboration with other teachers is structured and conducted in an environment in which teachers feel comfortable revealing their weaknesses and confusion about why students are not succeeding (Fuchs, Fuchs, & Bahr, 1990; Fuchs, Fuchs, Bahr, Fernstrom, & Stecker, 1990; Littie, Gearhart, Curry, & Kafka, 2003).

In addition to working with other teachers, classroom teachers should work as closely as possible with the parents of their students who are struggling (Kampwirth, 2003). Parents can provide the teacher with information about a child's background and experiences and may be willing to do a great deal at home to support interventions implemented at school. Parents also are definite stakeholders in the child's future and should work with the teacher and school to maximize the child's potential. A parent can be a true ally in working to help the child reach grade-level expectations.

Special educators also may need to stretch beyond their comfort zone to work at the second tier of intervention. Rather than work strictly in self-contained classrooms or pull-out programs, special educators must make time to support general education students both through indirect and direct consultation. Their more important role in the second tier might be to provide assistance to the general educator in analyzing assessment results and understanding how to use that information to effectively differentiate instruction for small groups of students with greater learning challenges. It may even be feasible for special education teachers to conduct progress monitoring assessments because general education teachers are typically teaching and monitoring a whole classroom. Special educators can further their Tier 2 intervention support by modeling the delivery of specialized instruction and then coaching teachers who are making their first attempts to provide differentiated lessons (Haager & Windmueller, 2001).

The third tier of intervention—a role that special education teachers typically have assumed—requires more intensive work with students and a greater variety of instructional strategies. Tier 3 may be considered special education; however, this in no way bypasses the referral and identification process guaranteed by law. A multidisciplinary team still must conduct the individualized education program (IEP) process to consider special education placement options and make individual decisions based on multiple assessments. Whereas general educators hold the primary responsibility for making certain the students are progressing at the first level of intervention, special educators may take over that function in the third tier for students identified as having disabilities. It is possible that some schools may develop a Tier 3 that serves students without disabilities who have not succeeded in Tier 2 and that this service would be separate from special education.

When a student is identified for special education following a lack of success in Tier 2, the general educator does not relinquish responsibility for the student's learning. At this level, the general educator will implement intervention as directed by the student's IEP or 504 plan, in consultation with the special educator. Very likely, the special educator will take the lead in Tier 3 for providing instruction in basic skills, and the general educator will work to provide the student access to the core curriculum in language arts and the content areas by adapting the core text, assignments, and lesson presentation. The special educator will provide direct services to these students, focusing on important basic skills and helping them strengthen their achievement. In addition, in the third tier, the special educator offers greater assistance to the general educator to prepare to accommodate and modify the core curriculum to meet the needs of the target student. At this tier of intervention, it is imperative that general and special educators maintain open lines of communication to maintain seamless supports to the student with significant learning challenges.

A TIER 2 MODEL OF INTERVENTION FOR URBAN SCHOOLS

For more than six years, we have implemented a project focusing on delivering the second tier of intervention in general education classrooms. Through the PLUS—Promoting Literacy in Urban Schools—project, we have worked with several urban schools where the majority of students are English language learners (ELLs) and virtually all have minority status and come from low socioeconomic status backgrounds. All PLUS schools historically have had high rates of referral to special education and, though all had prereferral teams that operated at varying degrees of effectiveness, none had any systematic intervention practices in place. Our purpose was to develop a model of prereferral reading intervention that would be practical and sustainable in urban schools where there are significant challenges in promoting reading achievement. Rather than use grant money to provide interventionists, a model that would not be sustainable in the long run, our goal was to provide sufficient professional development and support to general and special education teachers working in primary grades for implementing assessment and Tier 2 intervention with existing personnel.

The PLUS model was developed collaboratively with teachers and administrators at one school (Haager & Windmueller, 2001) and then disseminated to additional schools to evaluate its efficacy. The grass-roots development of the model resulted in extensive teacher input into and field testing of the procedures and practices, whereas the research team involvement ensured that practices reflected current research. Although the founding school had nearly full-time support from an on-site reading coach, subsequent sites met with a project consultant only twice a month in grade-level collaborative team meetings, an activity we envisioned could be continued beyond the grant period using existing school personnel as facilitators. Following are components of the PLUS model:

1. School willingness: To participate in the PLUS project, the school administrator and all teachers to be involved (Grades K–2 in the initial project; Grades 1 and 2 in the current project) had to agree to participate in all aspects of the project. Because the intervention program was designed to affect the prereferral intervention process and students identified for intervention would be followed longitudinally, it was important to have the full school staff on board.

2. Professional development: Approximately 25 hours of initial professional development was provided to general and special education teachers working in the primary grade levels. Professional development included training on how to administer, score, and interpret the Dynamic Indicators of Basic Early Literacy Skills (DIBELS) assessment (Good & Kaminski, 2003), a tool that provided the basis for identifying and grouping students for intervention and served as a gauge of long-term intervention effects. Teachers also learned a collection of intervention activities that could be implemented in the context of their core reading program.

3. Assessment: Teachers learned to administer, score, and interpret data obtained using the DIBELS assessment tools for the appropriate grade level. This assessment battery includes assessment of rapid letter naming, phonemic awareness, decoding nonsense words, reading fluency, and oral language production (see Good & Kaminski, 2003; http://dibels.uoregon.edu for additional information about DIBELS subtests and their psychometric properties). Each subtest consists of a timed task to check for automaticity or fluency with specific foundational reading skills. Using established benchmarks and cut scores for at-risk status, teachers learned to identify students in need of intervention and determine appropriate small groups of students with similar needs.

4. Intervention: The PLUS intervention training provided teachers with a menu of short activities focused on the key early reading skills of phonemic awareness, decoding, and fluency. Teachers also learned to integrate English language development and vocabulary instruction into the intervention activities for ELL students who were at the beginning stages of learning the English language. All activities were developed and field-tested at the pilot school and were designed to reflect research-based principles of effective instruction (Haager, Dimino, & Windmueller, 2007). Activities followed a format of introducing and modeling a skill, using manipulatives (such as letter tiles or slinky toys) to make the concept concrete, offering guided practice in which the teacher scaffolded instruction for a small group of students and gave appropriate corrective feedback, and providing opportunities for students to practice and perform the task individually to ensure their active participation and clear understanding of the concept. Unlike commercial intervention programs, the activities were meant to be a menu from which teachers could select specific targeted skills based on students' demonstrated needs assessments and teacher observation. The activities were ordered in

Table 11.1.   Format for collaborative grade-level meetings

Format	Description
Debrief from last meeting (10 minutes)	Teachers report successes and challenges in implementing intervention since the last meeting.
Introduction of the new topic (20 minutes)	The facilitator introduces the topical focus for the discussion and leads an interactive discussion in which teachers share ideas or bring up questions.
Collaborative planning of topic (20 minutes)	Teachers discuss how the topic of the day will be implemented in their specific context. Teachers decide how they will address this issue in their intervention groups and, if relevant, conduct any preparation to do so.
Additional questions or issues that teachers bring up (10 minutes)	The facilitator saves 10 minutes at the end of the meeting for teachers to bring up any questions or problems encountered regarding intervention. The facilitator or teachers may be able to assist teachers with specific problems.

a notebook from easier tasks to more difficult, but our main objective was to help the teachers become skilled at identifying specific student needs and selecting appropriate activities to address them.

5. Collaborative grade-level meetings: Project consultants with extensive experience in working with struggling readers and knowledge of research-based reading practices met twice monthly with teachers in grade-level teams. Consultants facilitated collaborative discussions, guiding teachers through the process of using their data reports effectively, grouping students, and planning intervention. Teachers were encouraged to share their challenges and success with the group and work together to refine and adjust their implementation. Tables 11.1 and 11.2 show the structure used for collaborative grade-level meetings and a list of topics that emerged from participant schools as critical for implementation.

6. Progress monitoring assessment: Teachers learned to use the DIBELS progress monitoring tools as well as their curriculum-based assessments from the school-adopted reading program to monitor individual student progress. Though teachers had agreed to implement all aspects of the PLUS model, we recognized that they had a heavy burden of program-based assessments and did not require the use of the DIBELS progress monitoring tools. Therefore, teachers could bring either DIBELS or the program-based assessments to collaborative team meetings for the purpose of discussing student progress.

CHALLENGES ENCOUNTERED AND LESSONS LEARNED

To date, we can report both successes and challenges from the PLUS implementation. Our initial 5-year PLUS project was designed to be a model development,

Table 11.2.   Topics for collaborative grade-level meetings

Topics	Description
How should intervention be organized?	Teachers need to organize and prepare the schedule and materials. It is important for teachers to contextualize this for their own classroom and routine.
How should intervention be managed?	Teachers need to learn what steps to take with other students so they have uninterrupted time to provide intensive intervention. Paired activities and center activities are useful for this purpose. Teachers also need to learn how to maximize instructional time by making quick transitions from whole-class to small-group instruction.
How should intervention be aligned with the core reading program?	Teachers need to discuss how to adapt intervention activities and materials so they know how to reinforce concepts learned in the core reading program and use the same instructional language during intervention.
What does high-quality intervention look like?	Teachers discuss how to identify specific student skill needs and plan activities accordingly. They decide how to make the instruction focused and intensive and develop strategies for maximizing students' active engagement.
When should new skills be introduced?	Teachers learn to conduct and analyze progress monitoring assessment. Charting student progress enables teachers to see when students are ready to move on to new skills and when they are not.
What should be done when students need additional guidance?	When the progress monitoring data show that an individual student is "stuck" at a certain skill level, it is important for teachers to consider increasing the intensity or duration of intervention. It may also be necessary to try a new approach.
How should intervention adjustments be made for English language learners?	Teachers discuss how to integrate vocabulary and comprehension support into the intervention activities. For example, in a decoding activity that includes eight to ten words, teachers might select two or three to define, then give examples of their use. Selecting words that also occur in the whole-group lesson gives students multiple exposures to new words. Reviewing words on subsequent days gives repeated practice.
How should intervention be taught when students are on different skill levels?	Teachers often find that their at-risk students do not fit neatly into groups based on specific skills. It is helpful for them to discuss this and brainstorm strategies for managing this, such as forming more groups for shorter duration or organizing a swap with the teacher next door.
What should be done when new strategies or ideas are needed?	Teachers need time to reflect on what they learned in professional development and to further their knowledge and skills. They may also need support in extending their learning through professional resources or further training.

and we collected evaluation data from teachers as well as DIBELS scores for students. Though all schools reported gains in achievement as measured by state-mandated high-stakes testing, there were no state scores for the lower grades. We had no comparison schools against which to measure achievement using the DIBELS scores. All participant schools reported notable gains for the students receiving intervention, but it is difficult to discern the extent to which the intervention as opposed to the district's adoption of a solid core reading program produced the results. Three schools for which we could obtain referral data experienced a reduction in referral rate and identified students with learning disabilities earlier than usual (first or second grade instead of third or fourth). Since 2004, we have been replicating the PLUS model in new schools using an experimental design to better test the effects of the program on those students identified as at risk for reading difficulty.

Over the course of implementing this project in urban schools chronically challenged by depressed achievement scores, we have learned valuable lessons in the use of a multitiered reading intervention model. In the next sections, we discuss roadblocks that we encountered along the way and outline what we view as critical features to support teachers' implementation of intervention. A list and explanation of the supports and barriers that emerged from our work are included in Tables 11.3 and 11.4.

There are many reasons general education teachers may resist involvement in delivering Tier 2 assessment and intervention that include the complex maze of challenges they face. Teachers are under increasing pressure to make sure that state standards for the grade are met, test scores are high, and no children are left behind. Yet, concurrently, teachers face the challenges of a changing social demographic, with a more diverse student population, many students learning English as a second language, higher rates of poverty, and increases in single-parent households (Smith, Polloway, Patton, & Dowdy, 2006). Although classrooms are less homogenous than in the past, many teachers find themselves teaching a mandated curriculum that delivers one lesson to all of the children in a class, leaving little time for differentiating instruction based on individual needs. The PLUS teachers certainly expressed these sentiments. Frequent comments highlighted the tremendous pressure teachers faced. Simultaneously with the PLUS project, this particular urban school district adopted a structured, scripted reading program and provided extensive professional development to teachers. Although the PLUS intervention model was not inconsistent with the adopted program, the teachers found it difficult to focus on multiple, competing initiatives.

Though little is known from the literature about how general education teachers view taking on Tier 2 intervention, past studies have indicated resistance to providing adaptations and differentiating instruction. General education teachers typically do not feel equipped to meet the needs of struggling students (Schumm & Vaughn, 1991, 1995). In one study, students with hidden disabilities (mild disabilities that were difficult to identify) were likely to be the ones their

Table 11.3. Supports for a multitiered reading intervention model

Supports	Description
Professional development	Professional development must focus specifically on components of the intervention model, be of sufficient depth to build knowledge and skills, and provide practice opportunities for teachers to apply principles learned. When administrators attend professional development with teachers, they are able to provide specific, focused, site-based support.
Ongoing teacher support	Collaborative grade-level specific meetings should occur at least twice monthly to provide opportunities for teachers to analyze and interpret assessment data together, discuss individual students and their needs, plan intervention activities, and prepare lessons.
Shared focus	When an entire school or grade level commits to implementing a multitiered reading intervention model, it is more likely to succeed because there is a common goal.
Administrator support	A supportive site administrator would be involved in adopting an intervention model, participate in professional development with teachers, provide necessary materials and structure, and have frequent communication with teachers about at-risk students.
Logistical support	An intervention model requires organization and planning to ensure that schedules and materials are in place. The schedule must include in-class and out-of-class time for implementation and planning. The school must refrain from allowing interruptions such as announcements over the loudspeaker or messengers coming in and out. Materials must be purchased, organized, and readied.
Classroom management	Teachers must have a management system that allows them to work uninterrupted with small groups or individuals. Using activities such as paired reading or centers will allow teachers to pull aside small groups of students with similar intervention needs for 20–30 minutes.
Coaching or teacher support	It is helpful for teachers to have peer support in implementing intervention. A peer coach provides valuable feedback, assistance, and modeling.
Assessment	Initial screening and ongoing progress monitoring assessment provide critical data for making informed intervention choices.

general education teachers wished to have removed from the classroom, possibly because they were difficult to work with and it was difficult to keep their disabilities in mind (Cook, 2001). Is it any wonder, then, that general education teachers may resist modifying their instruction to better work with students who have

Table 11.4.   Barriers for a multitiered reading intervention model

Barriers	Description
Competing initiatives or mandates	Teachers become involved in multiple schoolwide or districtwide initiatives or special projects that compete for their in-class and out-of-class time and attention.
Negative attitudes or perceptions	General education teachers often feel reluctant to teach students experiencing reading difficulty or may not view it as their responsibility.
Lack of time	Teachers report that they do not have adequate in-class time to teach small intervention groups or out-of-class time for adequate planning.
Inadequate training	General education teachers may not have the knowledge and skills to work with struggling readers because it was not included in their preservice or in-service preparation.
Lack of support	Without administrative support and a structure for ongoing peer support, implementation may not occur.

different needs and may consider it unfair that these students are in their general education classrooms at all? Our PLUS teachers expressed genuine desire to meet the needs of their struggling students and were eager to learn intervention strategies. A positive outcome of the PLUS project was that teachers felt empowered to work with students who in the past would have caused them great frustration. As one teacher said in an anonymous exit interview, "I now know how to work with my at-risk students. I don't avoid working with small groups anymore."

Many PLUS teachers initially were resistant to the idea of working with struggling students. It is no surprise that general education teachers, who may have no aspirations to work with children who have special needs, would bristle when told that they must provide Tier 2 intervention. "It is not my job to provide this level of intervention," general educators might say, "the reading or resource specialist should be doing this." Certainly, providing intervention is time consuming both at the point of planning the instruction and at the point of implementation. The key factor that changed the PLUS teachers' perceptions was data. Though the teachers clearly did not want the added responsibility of administering "one more assessment," soon after the second benchmark period, when they saw students' scores rising, they began to look forward with anticipation to the next data point. Seeing concrete results in improved reading gave them the encouraging boost needed to see that their efforts paid off.

Teachers offer many other reasons for not wishing to provide Tier 2 intervention. They will often say that changing an assignment or giving extra instruction for one child is unfair to the rest of the class. "They all deserve special attention," teachers sometimes say. Interestingly, students appear to like teachers who make accommodations for students who need them, perhaps because doing so demonstrates to the children that the teacher cares about each individual in the class

(Mercer & Mercer, 2001; Vaughn, Schumm, & Kouzekanani, 1993; Vaughn, Schumm, Niarhos, & Daugherty, 1993).

A lack of time to plan, organize, prepare, or deliver specialized instruction is another reason teachers say that they do not implement interventions (Safran & Safran, 1996). Teachers are faced with many professional demands each day, which may include meetings, paperwork, grading, and parent contacts as well as class sizes of thirty or more students. If teachers feel overwhelmed by the daily requirements of the job, it might be difficult for them to see how or when they can add another responsibility to their list. Undoubtedly, this was the biggest challenge we encountered with PLUS implementation. Implementation validity checks demonstrated that teachers were quite inconsistent in the frequency, duration, and integrity of implementation despite the fact that each teacher had turned in an intervention schedule with daily time blocked out. Teachers continually reported lack of time to plan and found it difficult to squeeze in 20–30 minutes per day to run intervention groups, even when they could see results when they did implement them.

Collaborative grade-level specific meetings helped the PLUS teachers build planning time into their schedule. We found that holding meetings twice a month provided enough opportunity for teachers to discuss their assessment data, individual student needs and progress, and plan intervention activities. It is important to have a facilitator of the meetings to keep the focus on intervention rather than other topics that may emerge, such as the general reading program and other initiatives or challenges. Though it is important for teachers to have time to debrief their intervention experiences and share about specific students or events, it is equally important to keep the meetings focused on practical issues that will facilitate implementation. Again, Tables 11.1 and 11.2 describe a format for conducting meetings and topics that have continually emerged from the PLUS project as critical for sustaining implementation.

Inadequate training and support might be the biggest hurdle to implementing Tier 2 intervention. Teachers who have not learned in their preservice training about the learning needs of students of differing abilities may not understand the necessity of designing instruction that will benefit students at many levels of ability and will not know how to do so. If one enters the teaching profession prepared to use what he or she has learned in the teacher preparation program, then changing what is taught there to better prepare these future teachers is necessary (Denton, Vaughn, & Fletcher, 2003). In-service training is critically important in implementing an intervention program. As one-shot, stand-and-deliver workshops have limited effect on classroom practice, however, it is critical to provide ongoing support that is practical and relevant to teachers' daily planning and management of the initiative. In our pilot school, we provided nearly full-time coaching and support that included modeling lessons, observations and feedback, and collaborative planning sessions. Realizing that this was not feasible for or replicable in most schools, we limited support to two times per month in collaborative grade-level meetings, with additional assistance available for specific needs. Given our spotty implementation, we doubt that this level of support is sufficient to ensure and maintain implementation. We would recommend ongoing support that is closer to the classroom. Though the grade-level meetings were productive and important in the views of teachers, the teachers may have had higher implementation if an administrator or on-site coach had provided in-class assistance.

If teachers have not been taught diverse instructional models and their appropriate uses, they will continue to teach in the only way they know how. Professional development for teachers frequently seems to come in the form of an inservice, in which a topic is introduced and discussed during a short period of time and after which no follow-up support or discussion is offered (Dettmer, Thurston & Dyck, 2002). Left to implement a new strategy without support, or without a true understanding of what the strategy is or why it might be useful, teachers give up easily if the lesson does not go smoothly on the first attempt (Brownell, Adams, Sindelar, Waldron, & Vanhover, 2006). They need the opportunity to see an expert employing differentiated instruction in situ and to see how it can be effective. Then they need the chance to be observed by an expert and to receive feedback about how to improve their instruction (Blachowicz, Obrochta, & Fogelberg, 2005). Good classroom instruction includes ample modeling as well as coaching and feedback for building new skills, yet professional development for teachers often omits these two vital pieces of the educational process.

Last, we cannot emphasize enough how important it is to have the ongoing support of the site-based administrator. In the nine schools with which we have worked, we have seen the spectrum of administrator support and varying administrative styles. When the administrator is actively involved in adopting the model and sends the message through ongoing meetings and discussions that it is a school priority, there is a greater chance of success. When an administrator pays it little heed, teachers will do the same. Or, when an administrator forces it on teachers and mandates it without seeking teacher buy-in or promoting collegial endorsement of it, the chances of success are slim. We offer some examples of the types of administrator support that seemed to make a difference. In one school, after they had made a schoolwide decision to participate, the principal announced that for teachers to be assigned to the primary grades, they would have to agree to fully implement the assessment and intervention. This same principal made sure the grade-level team meetings were scheduled and did not assign competing topics for the meetings. Another principal kept a notebook with the DIBELS results along with notes about individual children. The principal made sure she walked through classrooms during intervention time and then met with teachers individually to discuss the intervention. One principal was quick to order materials that teachers needed, arranged a rotating intervention schedule, and scheduled paraprofessionals into rooms during intervention time. To summarize, these principals demonstrated that the intervention program was a priority and were involved in the daily operation.

SUMMARY

General education teachers typically view Tier 2 intervention as neither their role nor their realm of expertise. For intervention to be part of general education instruction, a schoolwide focus and extensive professional development are needed. Professional development is a necessary but not sufficient component of a successful intervention program. Teachers need assessment data that are directly relevant to the skills taught and ongoing support for implementing intervention. Working in collaborative teams facilitates teachers' implementation and fosters a collective sense of efficacy. Last, administrative support is critical.

REFERENCES

Bahr, M.W., Fuchs, D., Fuchs, L.S., Fernstrom, P., & Stecker, P.M. (1993). Effectiveness of student verses teacher monitoring during prereferral intervention. *Exceptionality, 4*(1), 17–31.

Bahr, M.W., & Kovaleski, J.F. (2006). The need for problem-solving teams: Introduction to the special issue. *Remedial and Special Education, 27*(1), 2–5.

Bahr, M.W., Whitten, E., Dieker, L., Kocarek, C.E., & Manson, D. (1999). A comparison of school-based intervention teams: Implication for educational and legal reform. *Exceptional Children, 66,* 67–83.

Blachowicz, C., Obrochta, C., & Fogelberg, E. (2005). Literacy coaching for change. *Educational Leadership, 62,* 55–58.

Brownell, M.T., Adams, A., Sindelar, P., Waldron, N., & Vanhover, S. (2006). Learning from collaboration: The role of teacher qualities. *Exceptional Children, 72,* 169–185.

Bursuck, W.D., Munk, D.D., Nelson, C., & Curran, M. (2002). Research on the prevention of reading problems: Are kindergarten and first-grade teachers listening? *Preventing School Failure, 47,* 4–9.

Chalfant, J.C. & Pysh, M.V. (1989). Teacher assistance teams: Five descriptive studies on 96 teams. *Remedial and Special Education, 10,* 49–58.

Cook, B.G. (2001). A comparison of teachers' attitudes toward their included students with mild and severe disabilities. *Journal of Special Education, 34,* 203–213.

Crockett, J.B. (2004). Taking stock of science in the schoolhouse: Four ideas to foster effective instruction. *Journal of Learning Disabilities, 37,* 189–199.

Denton, C.A., Vaughn, S., & Fletcher, J.M. (2003). Bringing research-based practice in reading intervention to scale. *Learning Disabilities Research & Practice, 18,* 201–211.

Desimone, L. (2002). How can comprehensive school reform models be successfully implemented? *Review of Educational Research, 11*(3), 433–479.

Dettmer, P., Thurston, L.P., & Dyck, N. (2002). *Consultation, collaboration, and teamwork for students with special needs* (4th ed.). Boston: Allyn & Bacon.

Evans, W., Baugh, C., & Sheffer, J. (2005). A study of the sustained effects of comprehensive school reform programs in Pennsylvania. *School Community Journal, 15,* 15–28.

Fuchs, D., & Fuchs, L.S. (2006). Introduction to response to intervention: What, why and how valid is it? *Reading Research Quarterly, 41,* 93–99.

Fuchs, D., Fuchs, L.S., & Bahr, M.W. (1990). Mainstream assistance teams: A scientific basis for the art of consultation. *Exceptional Children, 57,* 128–139.

Fuchs, D., Fuchs, L.S., Bahr, M.W., Fernstrom, P., & Stecker, P.M. (1990). Prereferral intervention: A prescriptive approach. *Exceptional Children, 56,* 493–513.

Fuchs, D., Fuchs, L.S., Dulan, J., Roberts, H., & Fernstrom, P. (1992). Where is the research on consultation effectiveness? *Journal of Educational and Psychological Consultation, 3*(2), 151–175.

Gersten, R., & Dimino, J.A. (2006). RTI (response to intervention): Rethinking special education for students with reading difficulties (yet again). *Reading Research Quarterly, 41,* 99–108.

Good, R.H., III, & Kaminski, R.A. (2003). *Dynamic Indicators of Basic Early Literacy Skills: Administration and scoring guide.* Longmont, CO: Sopris West Educational Services.

Graden, J.L. (1989). Redefining "prereferral" intervention as intervention assistance: Collaboration between general and special education. *Exceptional Children, 56,* 227–231.

Graden, J.L., Casey, A., & Christenson, L.L. (1985). Implementing a prereferral intervention system: Part I. The model. *Exceptional Children, 51,* 377–384.

Haager, D., Dimino, J.A., & Windmueller, M. (2007). *Interventions for reading success.* Baltimore: Paul H. Brookes Publishing.

Haager, D., & Windmueller, M. (2001). Early literacy intervention for English language learners at-risk for learning disabilities: Student and teacher outcomes in an urban school. *Learning Disability Quarterly, 24,* 235–250.

Individuals with Disabilities Education Improvement Act of 2004, PL 108-446, 20 U.S.C. §§ 1400 *et seq.*

Kampwirth, T.J. (2003). *Collaborative consultation in the schools: Effective practices for students with learning and behavior problems* (2nd ed.). Upper Saddle River, NJ: Prentice Hall.

Kovaleski, J.F. (1999). High versus low implementation of instructional support teams: A case for maintaining program fidelity. *Remedial and Special Education, 20,* 170–183.

Landrum, T.J., & Tankersley, M. (2004). Science in the schoolhouse: An uninvited guest. *Journal of Learning Disabilities, 37,* 207–212.

Lane, K.L., Mahdavi, J.N., & Borthwick-Duffy, S.A. (2003). Teacher perceptions of the prereferral intervention process: A call for assistance with school-based interventions. *Preventing School Failure, 4,* 148–155.

Littie, J.W., Gearhart, M., Curry, M., & Kafka, J. (2003). Looking at student work for teacher learning, teacher community and school reform. *Phi Delta Kappan, 85,* 184–192.

Lyon, G.R., Fletcher, J.M., Shaywitz, S.A., Shaywitz, B.E., Torgesen, J.K., Wood, F.B., et al. (2001). Rethinking learning disabilities. In C.E. Finn, Jr., A.J. Rotherman, & C.R. Hokanson, Jr. (Eds.), *Rethinking special education for a new century* (pp. 259–287). Washington, DC: The Progressive Policy Institute and The Thomas B. Fordham Institute.

Marston, D. (2005). Tiers of intervention in responsiveness to intervention: Prevention outcomes and learning disabilities identification patterns. *Journal of Learning Disabilities, 38,* 539– 544.

McDougal, J.L., Clonan, S.M., & Martens, B.K. (2000). Using organizational change procedures to promote the acceptability of prereferral intervention services: The school-based intervention team project. *School Psychology Quarterly, 15,* 149–171.

McNamara, K., & Hollinger, C. (2003). Intervention-based assessment: Evaluation rates and eligibility findings. *Exceptional Children, 69,* 181–193.

Menzies, H.M., Mahdavi, J.N., & Lewis, J. (2006). *Early reading intervention: From research to practice.* Manuscript submitted for publication.

Mercer, C.D., & Mercer, A.R. (2001). *Teaching students with learning problems.* Upper Saddle River, NJ: Prentice Hall.

Moats, L.C. (2004). Science, language, and imagination in the professional development of reading teachers. In P. McCardle & V. Chhagra (Ed.), *The voice of evidence in reading research* (pp. 269–287). Baltimore: Paul H. Brookes Publishing Co.

Mortenson, B.P., & Witt, J.C. (1998). The use of weekly performance feedback to increase teacher implementation of a prereferral academic intervention. *School Psychology Review, 27,* 613–627.

Odom, S.L., Brantlinger, E., Gersten, R., Horner, R.H., Thompson, B., & Harris, K.R. (2005). Research in special education: Scientific methods and evidence-based practices. *Exceptional Children, 71,* 137–148.

Rock, M.L., & Zigmond., N. (2001). Intervention assistance: Is it substance or symbolism? *Preventing School Failure, 45,* 153–161.

Safran, S.P., & Safran, J.S. (1996). Intervention assistance programs and prereferral teams: Directions for the twenty-first century. *Remedial and Special Education, 17,* 363–369.

Schumm, J.S., & Vaughn, S. (1991). Making adaptations for mainstreamed students: General classroom teachers' perspectives. *Remedial and Special Education, 12,* 18–27.

Schumm, J.S., & Vaughn, S. (1995). Getting ready for inclusion: Is the stage set? *Learning Disabilities Research and Practice, 10,* 169–179.

Smith, T.E.C., Polloway, E.A., Patton, J.R., & Dowdy, C.A. (2006). *Teaching students with special needs in inclusive settings* (4th ed.). Boston: Allyn & Bacon.

Taylor, B.M., Pearson, P.D., Clark, K., & Walpole, S. (2000). Effective schools and accomplished teachers: Lessons about primary-grade reading instruction in low-income schools. *Elementary School Journal, 101*(2), 121–165.

Torgesen, J.K. (2000). Individual differences in response to early interventions in reading: The lingering problem of treatment resisters. *Learning Disabilities Research & Practice, 10*(1), 55–64.

Torgesen, J.K. (2002). The prevention of reading difficulties. *Journal of School Psychology, 40,* 7–26.

Vaughn, S., Hughes, M.T., Schumm, J.S., & Klingner, J. (1998). A collaborative effort to enhance reading and writing. *Learning Disability Quarterly, 21,* 57–74.

Vaughn, S., Linan-Thompson, S., & Hickman, P. (2003). Response to instruction as a means of identifying students with reading/learning disabilities. *Exceptional Children, 69,* 391–409.

Vaughn, S., Schumm, J.S., & Kouzekanani, K. (1993). What do students think when their general education teachers make adaptations? *Journal of Learning Disabilities, 26,* 545–555.

Vaughn, S., Schumm, J.S., Niarhos, F.J., & Daugherty, T. (1993). What do students think when teachers make adaptations? *Teaching and Teacher Education, 9,* 107–118.

Whitten, E., & Dieker, L. (1995). Intervention assistance teams: A broader vision. *Preventing School Failure, 40,* 41–45.

Historical Perspectives and Current Trends in Problem Solving

The Minneapolis Story

Douglas Marston, Amy L. Reschly,
Matthew Y. Lau, Paul Muyskens, and Andrea Canter

In 1992, changes in Minnesota state identification criteria requiring the use of intelligence tests for identification of students with learning disabilities (LD) and cognitive impairments precipitated an institutional, or districtwide, change in identification practices. This chapter discusses the implementation of the Problem-Solving Model (PSM) in the Minneapolis Public Schools. A historical perspective on problem solving in general and in Minneapolis is presented, along with a description of how the model is used in Minneapolis and recent implementation data.

HISTORY OF PROBLEM SOLVING

Problem solving involves applying a logical sequence of steps to address an issue or difficulty. General models of problem solving have been delineated in the literature; however, the application to learning and behavior problems in human services settings began in the 1970s with Bergan's behavioral consultation work (Bergan, 1977; Bergan, Curry, Currin, Haberman, & Nicholson, 1973) and with the Data-Based Program Modification Model and Curriculum-Based Measurement (CBM) work conducted by Deno, Mirkin, and others at the University of Minnesota (Deno, 1985; Deno, Mirkin, & Shinn, 1979; Deno & Mirkin, 1977). Numerous similarities exist in the behavioral consultation and Data-Based Program Modification models. Both of the models 1) are rooted in a broad behavioral approach, 2) focus on learning and behavior problems, 3) use multistep problem solving involving behavioral definitions, collection of data, intervention design and implementation, and evaluation of outcomes, 4) occur in natural contexts such as classrooms, 5) use direct rather than indirect measures of hypothetical constructs such as general intellectual functioning, and 6) focus on changing situations and instruction rather than on internal child-based impairments. The differences are subtle but important. Behavioral consultation (Bergan, 1977, Bergan & Kratochwill, 1990) is an indirect service delivered through a process involving a consultant (e.g., psychologist, counselor), consultee (e.g., teacher, parent), and child. Different levels of consultation were described by Bergan, but by far the most common application has been individual and case-centered. One of the signature advances in the Bergan model is the development of intentional verbal interactions as a means to achieve consultation outcomes. Although applicable to both learning and behavior problems, behavioral consultation is used more frequently with behavior problems (Tombari & Bergan, 1978).

In contrast, Deno's data-based problem solving is used directly by teachers and others as a means to improve child performance. The principal applications have been to academic achievement, especially in reading—the most frequent reason for referrals to special education. Deno's signature achievement was the development of CBM as a means to facilitate problem solving with academic skills problems (Deno, 1985). Academic achievement problems are defined using curriculum-based measures and peer-referenced expectations for performance. Large discrepancies are used to define problems (i.e., a problem is defined as a discrepancy between what is expected and what actually occurs; Deno, 1989). CBM norms for growth per week (e.g., number of words increase in oral reading fluency by typical peers) are used to set individual goals that are formulated to reduce discrepancies between individual and peer performance. Deno (1989) was among the first to apply a problem-solving model to special education. And, as mentioned previously, although problem-solving models did exist in the literature, this model was an important advance. As noted by Deno (1989),

> Although the basic steps are common to most problem-solving models, what makes the approach presented here different from the others is the reliance on a data base created through use of a specific set of measurement procedures to collect time series data as an aid to evaluating problem solving efforts (p. 12).

Arguably, the most important features of data-based problem solving with children experiencing achievement problems are progress monitoring and formative evaluation. Child progress is monitored frequently, and changes are made based on these results. If progress exceeds goals, goals are made more challenging. If progress fails to meet goals, instructional elements are enhanced. Data-based problem solving is applied continuously to produce an ongoing connection between instruction and results.

When conceived, the PSM was not intended as a means of identifying students who have disabilities; however, with the authorization of the Individuals with Disabilities Education Improvement Act of 2004 (PL 108-446), this particular application of problem solving has gained momentum. The first large-scale, or institutional, applications of problem solving (e.g., the state of Iowa, Minneapolis Public Schools) have used this model to identify students with disabilities, to design interventions and modifications for students in general and special education, and as an organizational approach for special education services. The use of similar approaches has increased across the United States (Barbour, 2002).

MINNEAPOLIS PUBLIC SCHOOLS

Minneapolis Public Schools were in a unique position as a district to undertake a significant change in special education identification practices. This was due, in part, to the long-standing collaboration between the district and the University of Minnesota and the many staff members who completed graduate work at the university. Individuals at the Minneapolis Public Schools and the University of Minnesota have collaborated for more than 25 years in the development of data-based problem solving and CBM. In some respects, the evolution of problem solving and CBM is mirrored in work conducted in the Minneapolis public schools. In the early to mid-1980s, Minneapolis Public Schools implemented CBM districtwide in special education for prereferral interventions, writing an individual education plans, and measuring student progress (Marston & Magnusson, 1985). In the late 1980s, Hiawatha Elementary, an Minneapolis Public Schools site, used CBM in general and special education in a cooperative teaching project that promoted a problem-solving approach (Self, Benning, Marston, & Magnusson, 1991). In the 1990s, Minneapolis Public Schools utilized CBM for the PSM and measuring student growth in general and special education (Marston, Muysken, Lau, & Canter, 2003).

Another reason that the Minneapolis School District was in a good position to undertake this change was that it was less oriented to the traditional refer–test–place model of special education services. Prior to 1992, state special education rules did not require intelligence testing for determining eligibility for mild mental impairment or LD. In 1992, the state of Minnesota special education rules were changed, requiring an IQ test for cognitive impairments and LD. This change in special education rules also brought changes to school psychology practice within the district. Canter's (1991) analysis of psychologists' time from 1979 to 1991 revealed that Minneapolis Public Schools psychologists evenly divided their time between assessment, consultation, and direct services. For example, before the required use of IQ tests by the state of Minnesota, these school psychologists spent about 30% of their time assessing students, 35% of their time consulting with school staff, and 35% of their time in direct interaction with students and/or parents. Following the state rule change, time spent on testing increased substantially. For example, in 1993, Minneapolis Public School psychologists spent about 58% of their time in assessment (Canter, 1995), bringing the system more in line with traditional school psychology assessment patterns (Reschly & Wilson, 1995; Hosp & Reschly, 2002).

At the time the Minneapolis school district applied for a waiver from state criteria and proposed the use of a problem-solving model, school psychologists were well-prepared to use skills other than administering and scoring intelligence tests. In addition, staff in the schools had many philosophical concerns over the use of intelligence tests for the identification of students with disabilities and were interested in improving the assessment practices for students with disabilities. Staff interest could be traced to educational research that was generating national attention in the 1980s. The first line of research raised issues regarding the appropriate use of intelligence tests for decision making in special education (Ysseldyke et al., 1983). Although the demographics of Minneapolis have changed, there are, and have been for many years, a significant number of minority students, students who do not speak English as a first language, students from low socioeconomic status backgrounds, and students whose families are highly mobile enrolled in the district. Concerns over overrepresentation of certain minority groups in special education programs, questions of fairness, and a history of litigation (e.g., Larry P. vs. Riles, Marshall vs. Georgia) have surrounded the use of intelligence tests for identifying students for special education. Moreover, in a district where a large number of students do not perform well on these measures, many staff believed that IQ tests may not be the best measure of a student's potential (Siegal, 1989). In addition, the National Academy of Sciences raised questions regarding the utility of intelligence tests for the identification of students with mental retardation (Heller, Holtzman, & Messick, 1982). Questions also were being raised about the technical adequacy and usefulness of IQ-achievement discrepancy formulas for LD, the lack of treatment validity of many commonly used assessment devices, and a misplaced focus on eligibility rather than intervention (Reschly, 1988a, 1988b).

In the fall of 1993, the Minneapolis school district pursued a waiver from the state of Minnesota for the required use of intelligence tests. This waiver was granted on a renewable basis. We proposed using the PSM as an alternative assessment approach, in which the student's response to an academic intervention would be used to evaluate the need for more intensive services including special education. Prior to the large-scale implementation of problem solving for the identification of students with disabilities in places such as Iowa and Minneapolis, the PSM had been used for individual students in remedial or special education programs. The utility of this model for identifying students in need of more intensive programs was readily apparent, but its use was not limited to special education eligibility. In Minneapolis, the PSM is used to identify students with academic and behavior difficulties in general education, evaluate effectiveness of interventions, and implement interventions of increasing intensity before special education eligibility is even considered.

THE MINNEAPOLIS PROBLEM-SOLVING MODEL

The PSM is a comprehensive approach to identifying student academic and behavioral needs, selecting empirically based instructional interventions that address specific concerns, monitoring student progress through frequent and repeated measurement, evaluating instructional effectiveness, and making modifications or referral for other services, as needed. The foundation of the Minneapolis model is a sequential approach to problem solving that starts with the classroom teacher in general education and moves through increasingly intensive stages of intervention and evaluation involving increasing levels of team collaboration.

The PSM enhances the school's effectiveness in meeting student academic and behavioral needs in three major areas:

1. It provides a data-based approach within the school to deliver and evaluate the continuum of interventions and services used for accelerating achievement for students.

2. The focus on student response to intervention may reduce the effect of possible test bias.

3. It contributes to the school improvement planning process.

Problem-Solving Components

The major components of problem solving are as follows

1. *Describe the student's behavior and/or academic performance.* Detailed descriptions of student strengths and weaknesses allow staff to develop more appropriate hypotheses about the student's needs and likely effective intervention strategies. Formal assessment procedures used to evaluate students' skills must be technically adequate.

2. *Develop hypotheses regarding the student's needs and select relevant, empirically based intervention strategies.* After the collection of student data instructional strategies that match the academic and behavioral needs of the student are identified. Interventions are selected on the basis of potential for success, given the realities of staff and program resources and organizational considerations, as well as empirical evidence.

3. *Implement interventions with fidelity.* Selected interventions must be implemented as intended by the researchers, authors, and/or publishers of these methods. Staff develop an implementation plan to ensure follow-through.

4. *Monitor progress and evaluate intervention effectiveness.* Student academic and behavior data are collected frequently to evaluate progress toward goals and intervention effectiveness. CBM (Fuchs, Deno, & Mirkin, 1984; Deno, 1985) procedures play an important role in this step because of their sensitivity to short-term growth and their ability to measure responsiveness to intervention. Schools are trained to collect data on a frequent basis, review graphed student CBM data through a district website, and document interventions on a classroom intervention worksheet.

5. *Repeat the cycle in response to student data.* The PSM can be characterized as a "teach-test-teach-test" model in which the student's response to intervention

guides instructional modifications. Follow-up meetings of the team are essential to monitor intervention effectiveness, determine the need for changes or new strategies, or determine the need for a special education evaluation when well-designed and faithfully implemented strategies do not yield expected progress.

This problem-solving sequence is followed at three successive stages (see Figure 12.1). The process is started in general education—Stage 1—when the teacher selects an additional intervention to implement in the classroom for a student performing poorly. If the student does not respond to interventions at this level, the efforts of building a multidisciplinary team are initiated at Stage 2. This collaborative problem-solving team develops hypotheses about student difficulties and designs the next phase of intervention strategies. Stage 3 is implemented for those students who show inadequate response to the team's problem-solving interventions. At this stage, the students begin special education evaluation.

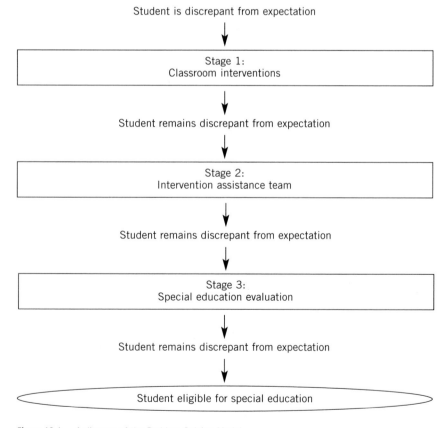

Figure 12.1.   A diagram of the Problem-Solving Model.

Problem-Solving Stages

The student's response to general education interventions is the primary determinant of need for more intensive instruction. Changes and modifications of instructional interventions are documented on a worksheet specific to each stage of the model. Descriptions of the three stages of the Minneapolis PSM are provided below, with a graphic representation shown in Figure 12.1.

Stage 1: Classroom Interventions

In Stage 1 the classroom teacher uses district academic and behavior screening data to identify those students who are in most need of extra support. Teachers modify their instructions for theses students and collect data to help evaluate whether the changes are succeeding. To help teachers follow this process, they use a classroom intervention worksheet to complete the problem-solving process within this stage. The elements of this worksheet include: specific concerns about the student; current levels of student performance; student strengths; relevant health and cultural information; past interventions implemented and their results; and information from the student, the student's school files, the parents or guardians, and other members of the school staff.

Stage 2: Intervention Assistance Team

A student who does not respond to the interventions at Stage 1 enters Stage 2, where the intervention assistance team, also referred to as the problem-solving team, begins to implement the problem-solving process. This team, which is typically composed of the school social worker, a general and a special education teacher, and the school psychologist, repeats the steps of describing the problem, implementing a general education intervention, and evaluating the response to the intervention. Areas to be addressed and defined on a team interventions worksheet include: specific behaviors; the student's current level of performance; specific goals for interventions; and possible intervention strategies, intervention plans, and ways to follow up on the intervention. The team then reviews the student data after the intervention is implemented.

Stage 3: Special Education Evaluation

If the problem-solving team determines that a student did not respond to the regular education interventions at Stage 2, a special education evaluation is initiated at Stage 3. At this point, the assessment team plans the evaluation for the student, which includes a review of interventions conducted at Stages 1 and 2. In addition, the evaluation addresses health history, cognitive functioning, achievement, adaptive behavior, direct observation of the student, and parent concerns. The evaluation, as in any comprehensive special education assessment, will consider other areas of concern, including behavior, speech, and motor skills. The team also addresses the influence of cultural, linguistic, and economic factors before determining special education eligibility. Based on state-approved alternative criteria, the student may be identified as eligible with PSM if he or she shows a severe discrepancy between expected achievement level and academic skills, and the student may need a more intensive intervention not found in the general education environment. These students are called "students needing alternative programming," and the team will write an Individual Education Plan (IEP) for each individual.

Implementation

Use of PSM in Minneapolis began in 1994 with a phased-in implementation of the model. Initially, six elementary schools utilized the three-stage approach to implementing interventions in general education and reviewing student progress through indicators such as curriculum-based measurement. In 1998, the district's implementation of PSM was integrated in a voluntary compliance agreement with Minneapolis's Office for Civil Rights (OCR). The goal of the OCR agreement was to reduce bias in special education evaluation and placement by creating a system across the district in which students were screened for academics and behavior, provided extra general education interventions for lower performing students, monitoring of student progress, and set up multidisciplinary school teams to review student progress. The activities delineated by the OCR agreement were supportive of PSM implementation.

Several factors contribute to successful implementation of PSM and sustaining the effort at the building level. Most critical is the commitment of the staff to using a data-based decision-making model. Those schools that build a system of screening, progress monitoring, and reviewing data into the school schedule increase the probability of PSM success. Central administration can support this effort by providing training, consultation, technical assistance, and the technology when needed. Strong administrative leadership at the school also enhances implementation. As the school's instructional leader, a principal can create the conditions where staff welcome student data review, promote a staff development model that provides a range of evidenced-based interventions for diverse learners, and view PSM as an integrated system of delivering services to all students—not just a path to special education services. Finally, the success of PSM is related to creating a multidisciplinary team that works collaboratively to problem solve for all students. Shared ownership of student problems increases the likelihood of accelerated academic achievement.

INTERVENTIONS IN THE PROBLEM-SOLVING MODEL

As part of an external evaluation of the PSM, Reschly and Starkweather (1997) compared the use of prereferral strategies for students who were identified as needing special education with the PSM compared with the traditional eligibility criteria. There were significantly more students in the PSM (88%) who had at least one documented prereferral intervention than in the traditional model (36%). A review of these prereferral interventions showed a wide variety of types of interventions used in both models. Those types of interventions that appeared significantly more often in the PSM were modified instruction, peer involvement, small-group instruction, individual instruction from the teacher, individual instruction from an aide, Title I service, and home study time. In addition, Reschley and Starkweather (1997) determined the average number of interventions that were implemented for students in each condition. The number of classroom, school, and family interventions were significantly greater for students in PSM compared with traditional eligibility systems. These researchers concluded, "Based on these analyses, it appears that the waiver program is clearly superior to the traditional system in the number and variety of prereferral interventions attempted prior to the consideration of special education eligibility" (p. 39).

As described previously, the selection of evidence-based interventions in the PSM is critical for student improvement. To meet this need, our district has had several initiatives promoting the use of researched best practices. In one major effort, staff from the district's major departments, including Title I, ELL, special education, and Research and Evaluation came together to identify the best practices for reading instruction. Drawing on the published work of Adams (1990), Ysseldyke and Christenson (1993), the National Center to Improve the Tools of Education (NCITE; Smith, Simmons, & Kame'enui, 1995; Chard, Simmons, & Kame'enui, 1995: NCITE, 1996), the National Institute for Children and Human Development (Grossen, 1997), and the National Academy of Sciences (Snow, Burns, & Griffin, 1998), our staff developed a checklist to help elementary school teachers evaluate the extent to which they used research-based strategies in their reading instruction (Minneapolis Public Schools, 1998). Our checklist delineates the essential elements of successful reading within the following main categories: instructional components, appropriate level of instruction, engaged time, assessment and progress monitoring, classroom management, and home involvement. A four-point rating scale is used to assess the degree of implementation of each of the 33 items. For those items for which an implementation rating of "1" or "2" is found, the teacher is encouraged to consult district curriculum consultants or use the district's professional development process to increase awareness in these areas.

Initially, the PSM was utilized in our district to help classroom teachers and building assistance teams find effective interventions for students who may need to be referred for special education evaluation. As part of a Voluntary Compliance Agreement with the Office for Civil Rights, however, the PSM became the framework for the districtwide screening of students with academic and behavior difficulties, the documentation of general education interventions, and the monitoring of student progress and response to the interventions. In the districtwide screening, all students below the 25th percentile on the district-adopted achievement test, the Northwest Achievement Levels Reading Test (NALT; Northwest Evaluation Association, 2002) enter Stage 1 of the PSM process. The teachers of these students are asked to provide an extra intervention in general education, which vary in their scope and intensity. Students who do not make sufficient progress advance to Stage 2, in which the intervention assistance team develops an intervention program. This PSM team, as noted earlier, varies in composition but is typically comprised of the student's general education teacher; social worker; Title I staff; ELL staff, if necessary; special education staff; and, at times, the school psychologist or other specialists. In Stage 2, more intensive interventions are identified by the problem-solving team and implemented over approximately an 8-week period. Data—typically CBM measures for reading—are collected by the team for determining the student's response to intervention. Students who do not respond to Stage 2 interventions and remain discrepant from expectations move to Stage 3 intervention. Stage 3 of the PSM is the beginning of formal special education evaluation.

Documentation of student baseline data, initial interventions implemented with the student, and results of the interventions are entered into the district's web-based student information management system. Classroom teachers record a description of the Stage 1 interventions and Problem-Solving Team members share the responsibility of recording the Stage 2 interventions. We asked the question, "What are the interventions used in Stage 2 and documented on the district information management system?" To answer this question, we reviewed the descriptions of the reading interventions of a sample of 250 students who had entered Stage 2 of the PSM. These students were in Grades 1–8, with 12.8% in Grade 1, 21.5% in Grade 2, 28.5% in Grade 3, 16.9% in Grade 4, 5.8% in Grade 5, 4.1% in Grade 6, 5.8% in Grade 7, and 4.5% in Grade 8. Sixty percent of the students were male and 41.6% received ELL services. A breakdown of ethnic status showed that 3.6% were American Indian, 47.6% were African American, 16.0% were Asian American, 20.8% were Hispanic American, and 12% were white.

For the 250 students, a total of 726 interventions for reading difficulties were implemented. The average number of interventions for each student in Stage 2 was 2.86 (standard deviation [SD] = 1.4). Approximately 83% of the sample had two or more interventions at this level of the PSM. See Figure 12.2 for more detailed information.

In our analysis of the 726 reading interventions, we identified 20 types of descriptions of the interventions. These types of intervention included the following:

- Curriculum that had been published or was commercially available
- Alphabetic understanding and phonemic awareness
- Decoding, sight words, and/or fluency
- Vocabulary
- Comprehension
- Title I service
- ELL service

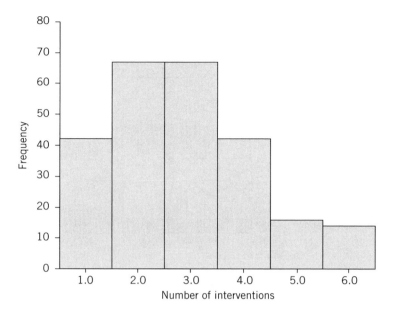

Figure 12.2. Frequency distribution of the number of reading interventions for each student in Stage 2 of the Problem-Solving Model.

- Small reading group
- One-to-one ratio of educational assistant, tutor, or mentor to student
- Peer tutoring or pairing
- Specialist consultation (speech-language, sensory)
- After-school program
- Home program or parent consultation
- Behavior, social skills, or friendship program
- Instructional environment (curriculum or assignment modification, seating change, allocated time)
- Assessment
- Physical/multisensory development
- Language activities
- Spelling
- Other

The number of interventions implemented for each of these categories is provided in Figure 12.3.

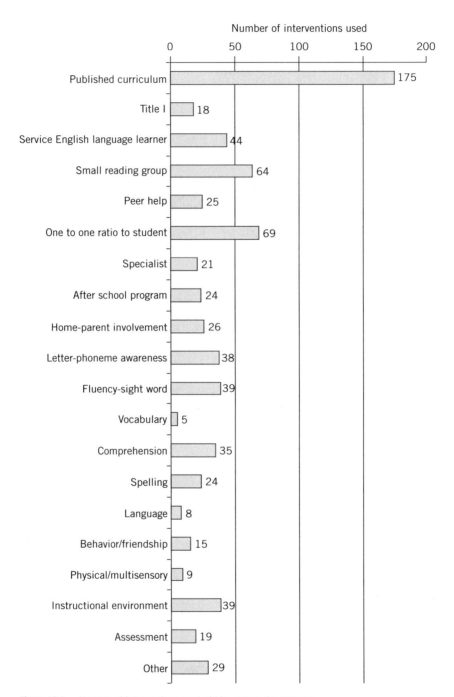

Figure 12.3.   Number of interventions used within each major category.

We then divided the 20 types of intervention into 3 major categories. The first descriptive category, which was by far the largest type of intervention with 175 entries, is "curriculum that had been published or was commercially available." The remaining documented interventions did not specify a curriculum but could be categorized by "the format of the academic support" or by "the content of the reading intervention." The format of the academic support included intervention programs or personnel that implemented the instruction. Examples of this category include Title I, small reading groups, ELL (English language learner) classrooms, peer tutoring, and after-school mentoring. The "content of the reading intervention" included descriptions that specified the area addressed in the intervention. Examples of this category include the five major elements of National Reading Panel (a summary of research on reading instruction), spelling, language activities, and assessments. In all, 24.1% of the documented interventions were commercially available reading curriculum or instructional materials, 40% of the interventions were described as academic support, and 31.8% of the interventions were described by their content.

Our review of the "curriculum that had been published or was commercially available" category showed the most frequently used published curricula were Direct Instruction (including Engelmann and Bruner's [1995] Reading Mastery and Engelmann and colleagues' [1999] Corrective Reading) at 28% and Computer Curriculum Corporation (CCC) computer labs at 18.9%. Within the "format of the academic support" category, the most popular interventions described by the respondents were "one-to-one ratio of educational assistant, tutor, or mentor to student" at 29.8% and "small reading group" at 21.9%. Within the "content of the reading intervention" category, the concepts endorsed most often were alphabetic knowledge and phonemic awareness at 16.4%, fluency and sight word knowledge at 16.9%, comprehension at 15.1%, and management of instructional environment at 16.9%.

READING INTERVENTIONS IN THE PROBLEM-SOLVING MODEL: SPECIAL EDUCATION

At the time of our initial implementation of the PSM, we conducted a formal investigation of the efficacy of several promising interventions in the area of reading. We found the most effective reading instruction approaches for students with mild disabilities were a computer-assisted reading program, reciprocal teaching, and a direct-instruction group (Marston, Deno, Kim, Diment, & Rogers, 1995). As a follow-up to this study, we instituted a reporting process for special education resource teachers in the district. In addition to measuring all special education students with high-incidence disabilities in the fall, winter, and spring with CBM procedures, teachers are asked to report the "major intervention" used for teaching reading to the student. Teachers review a drop-down menu on the district's web site and select the intervention that most closely corresponds to their

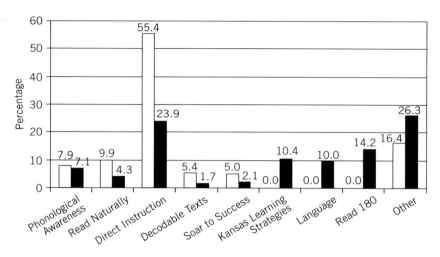

Figure 12.4. Reading interventions used for students in the special education portion of the Problem-Solving Model. (*Key:* Kindergarten through Grade 5 = ☐; Grade 6 through Grade 12 = ■.)

instructional approach. The data in Figure 12.4 show the most popular reading interventions used for elementary (Grades K–5) students and intermediate and secondary (Grades 6–12) students for our population of students with high-incidence disabilities. As can be seen in the figure, the most popular intervention at the elementary level is Direct Instruction, at 55.4%. At the intermediate and secondary level, Direct Instruction remains the most popular intervention, at 23.9%, although it is used less than in elementary grades.

MONITORING STUDENT PROGRESS IN RESPONSE TO INTERVENTION

Evaluating the student's response to an intervention is dependent on using a measurement system that is valid and reliable and can be administered on a frequent basis. As noted earlier in this chapter, Deno's (1985; 1986) Fuchs, Fuchs, and Maxwell's (1988) work on CBM fulfills this formative evaluation role. Minneapolis Public Schools began using CBM in the early 1980s (Marston & Magnusson, 1985, 1988) and continues to use it at present (Tindal & Marston, 1996; Marston, Muyskens, Lau, & Canter, 2003). Our district used the frequent administration of reading probes for progress monitoring. Our district also had probes available in the areas of readiness, written expression, spelling, and math, which can be used for the following decisions in special education: screening, supplementing assessments used in placement, IEP development, progress monitoring of goals and objectives, and program evaluation. Although initially used in special education, the utility of CBM has spread to more than 50 elementary

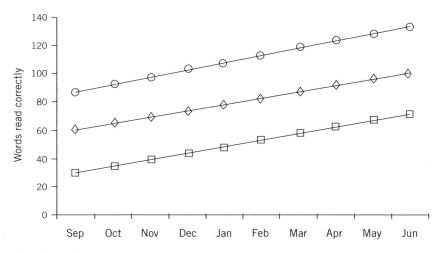

Figure 12.5. Words read correctly performance for third-grade students at the 20th, 50th, and 80th percentiles. (*Key:* 25th percentile = □; 50th percentile = ◇; 75th percentile = ○.)

schools in the Minneapolis district, with particular emphasis on fulfilling the progress monitoring aspects of the PSM in the area of reading. In 1997, district staff found CBM reading measures were highly correlated with high stakes test such as the Minnesota Basic Standards Test of Reading (Fuchs, Deno, & Marston, 1997). Further work showed correlations between CBM and performance on 3rd and 5th grade Minnesota Comprehensive Assessments of Reading that ranged from .60 to .75 (Marston, Muyskens, Betts, & Heistad, 2005). As a result, district staff have developed benchmarks for "passing" state accountability reading tests. In addition, normative charts showing student monthly growth on words read correctly are provided to staff. The chart, shown in Figure 12.5, which comes from Performance Assessment of Academic Skills in the Problem-Solving Model (MPS, 2003), can be used in the PSM to help teachers evaluate whether the student is making adequate progress. This figure shows the CBM performance levels of Third Grade students at the 25th, 50th, and 75th percentile from September to June.

In connection with the PSM, our district also has developed early literacy measures that can be used to evaluate student growth. Marston, Pickart, Reschly, Heistad, Muyskens, and Tindal (in press) reviewed the technical adequacy of letter sounds, onset phoneme identification, and phoneme segmentation with Minneapolis students. All three of these measures were valid, had good reliability, and showed evidence of sensitivity to short-term growth. The correlations of these three measures administered at the end of kindergarten with words read correctly at the end of first grade were .50 for onset phonemes, .57 for phoneme segments, and .70 for letter sounds. Test–retest reliability for these measures ranged from

.90–.97 and for interrater reliability ranged from .95–.99. The average letter sounds for the kindergarten students in this sample was 3 in the fall and 18 in the spring. For first grade students, the average letter sounds ranged from 17 in the fall to 38 in the winter.

EVALUATING IMPLEMENTATION OF
THE RESPONSE TO INTERVENTION MODEL

In the previous sections, we have discussed the importance of using research-based reading interventions and progress monitoring in the RTI model. Although application of RTI to reading problems is predicated on using evidence-based reading interventions and technically adequate progress monitoring procedures, the overall success of the model in improving student achievement is dependent on the best practice implementation of all problem-solving features. Recognizing the importance of an ideal implementation of all components of problem solving, Reschly, Tilly, and Grimes (1998) developed the Problem-Solving Innovation Configuration Rating Scale. This staff-development tool provides PSM implementers with a method to review the extent to which the PSM is being applied in an ideal fashion at their school. Their checklist identified nine critical areas, including the following (p. 236)

- Parent involvement
- Problem statement
- Systematic data collection
- Problem analysis
- Goal
- Intervention plan development
- Intervention plan implementation
- Progress monitoring
- Decision making

For each of these areas, Tilly, Reschly, and Grimes (1998) developed a range of descriptions of practice that may occur during initial implementation. These variations range from "unacceptable" to "ideal." The purpose of the checklist was for staff to improve their implementation of the PSM by comparing their implementation with the "ideal" descriptors and improving those areas in which the school fell short of acceptable practice. Using the Problem-Solving Innovation Configuration as a model, we modified the Tilly and colleagues (1998) checklist to fit PSM implementation in the Minneapolis Public Schools. The areas addressed in our implementation checklist were expanded to include the component of PSM at Stage 1, 2, and 3. Ratings on this implementation checklist are then used by district staff to determine school sites that need more intensive testing and follow-up.

OUTCOMES OF IMPLEMENTING THE PROBLEM-SOLVING MODEL

Elsewhere we have described some of the important outcomes of using a student-focused PSM. Marston and colleagues (2003) showed the model did not increase the number of students with high-incidence disabilities, reduced the use of labels, and had positive support from parents. In that article, Marston and colleagues also showed typical growth trends on CBM procedures for students in general education and at Stages 1, 2, and 3 of the PSM. Not surprisingly, the initial performance and slope of improvement often varied as a function of the student's stage in PSM. Highest initial levels of reading and slopes were typically found in general education students. Students who passed through Stages 1, 2, and 3 of PSM and who were found eligible for special education were usually lower on both measures of CBM performance. For this chapter, we replicated part of this analysis with an examination of the performance of Stage 2 students as a function of their Stage 2 outcome.

In our analysis, we reviewed the growth of 391 students who transitioned from Stage 1 to Stage 2 interventions and were measured with CBM grade-level passages in the fall and spring of the academic year. The PSM appeared to be effective in identifying students who did not respond to interventions and needed further intensive intervention. Differences were found between students who responded to Stage 2 interventions and students in Stage 2 who were eventually identified as needing more intensive interventions in special education. Intervention responders averaged a 29.9 words correct increase from fall to spring (number of students $n = 321$, SD = 17.1) as compared to students who entered special education and had an average gain of 20.7 words correct ($n = 70$, SD = 12.9).

Of further interest is the educational placement outcome for students served in the PSM. Historically, the referral of a student to special education has meant almost certain identification for these services. The classroom teacher would identify the student as having either academic difficulties or behavior difficulties, and the child would be referred to special education for a more intensive educational intervention. Algozzine, Christenson, and Ysseldyke (1982) described this "referral to placement" process as a virtual guarantee that the student would be found to have disabilities and, therefore, be eligible for service. These findings were later replicated by Ysseldyke, Vanderwood, and Shriner (1997). RTI data, however, does not indicate that the same relationship exists. Vaughn (2003) implemented a three-tier model of reading intervention and reported that most students responded to Tier 1 and 2 interventions, and only about 24% went on to the more intensive interventions provided in Tier 3. A review of PSM implementation in Minneapolis Public Schools shows that in the past 3 years, about 28%, 26%, and 27% of the students referred to Stage 2 interventions were later identified as having disabilities. These reports would seem to indicate that almost three fourths of the students with academic difficulties appear to receive effective interventions in general education settings.

How does RTI or PSM effect overall child count data? In an experimental study of RTI implementation, O'Connor (2003) reported 15% of control students in the traditional eligibility model were placed in special education compared with 8% placed in special education as part of an RTI model. These data are consistent with Marston and colleagues (2003), which showed the percentage of high-incidence disabilities was approximately 7% in the PSM model, which has been stable since the implementation of PSM.

Lau, Sieler, Muyskens, Canter, Van Keuren, and Marston (2006) described the implementation of the PSM in Minneapolis Public Schools and the positive effect on the roles of different school personnel. For the principal and teaching staff, utilizing PSM moves the school toward using more research-based interventions and increases the monitoring of student progress. Improvements for special education staff are evident during the referral-evaluation process, which focuses on documented interventions and student response data that is relevant to eligibility decisions and writing individual education plans. For the school psychologist, "PSM expanded this role from one of gate-keeping psychometrician to data-based problem solver" (p. 122).

SUMMARY

In this chapter, we have traced the historical roots of the PSM model from its inception in educational psychology to implementation in the Minneapolis Public Schools. In general, the outcomes using the model have been favorable. The data and procedures presented here and cited from other researchers (Burns, Appleton, & Stehouwer, 2005) show that the RTI model is associated with using research-based interventions, collects technically adequate progress monitoring data for student decision making, has been successfully integrated into web-based student performance monitoring systems that are easily accessed by staff, and has improved the prospects of students with academic difficulties receiving effective instruction before placement in special education.

Lau and colleagues (2006) provided several ideas for successfully implementing the PSM with respect to support and training, using the process, and evaluation of PSM. Regarding support of the model and inservicing staff, they recommend participation of key stakeholders, strong administrative leadership, and in-depth staff development that extends beyond introductory training to include mentoring, modeling, and coaching. Successful day-to-day use of PSM relies on a diverse PSM team composed of general and special education staff that meets regularly, has parent input, and focuses on both interventions for individual students and creating schoolwide interventions for large numbers of low performing students. Finally, effective use of the model includes a regular review and/or evaluation of the PSM that casts a critical eye on student achievement, child count data, instructional integrity, and staff input (Lau et al, 2006).

Quality implementation of RTI does not, however, happen overnight. Improving the quality of implementation is a product of collaboration between general and special educators, a commitment to using research-based interventions, districtwide adoption of formative evaluation procedures for monitoring response to interventions, maintaining the integrity of these interventions, systematic internal review of implementation, and time for professional development.

REFERENCES

Adams, M.J. (1990). *Beginning to read: Thinking and learning about print.* Cambridge, MA: The MIT Press.

Algozzine, B., Christenson, S., & Ysseldyke, J.E. (1982). Probabilities associated with the referral to placement process. *Teacher Education and Special Education, 5*(3), 19–23.

Barbour, B. (2002). Best practices in promoting educational reform at a school district level. In A. Thomas & J. Grimes (Eds.), *Best practices in school psychology* (4th ed.; pp. 293–300). Bethesda, MD: National Association of School Psychologists.

Bergan, J.R. (1977). *Behavioral consultation.* Columbus, OH: Charles E. Merrill.

Bergan, J.R., Curry, D.R., Currin, S., Haberman, K., & Nicholson, E. (1973). *Tucson early education psychological services.* Tucson: Arizona Center for Educational Research and Development, College of Education, University of Arizona.

Bergan, J.R., & Kratochwill, T.R. (1990). *Behavioral consultation and therapy.* New York: Plenum.

Burns, M.K., Appleton, J.J., & Stehouwer, J.D. (2005). Meta-analytic review of responsiveness-to-intervention research: Examining field-based research-implemented models. *Journal of Psychoeducational Assessment, 23*(4), 362–380.

Canter, A. (1991). Effective psychological services for all students: A data based model of service delivery. In G. Stoner, M. Shinn, & H. Walker (Eds), *Interventions for achievement and behavior problems* (pp. 49–78). Washington, DC: National Association of School Psychologists.

Canter, A. (1995). *School psychology department annual report.* Minneapolis, MN: Minneapolis Public Schools.

Chard, D., Simmons, D.C., Kame'enui, E.J. (1995). *Understanding the primary role of word recognition in the reading process: Synthesis of research on beginning reading.* (Synthesis of Research, Technical Report No. 15). Eugene, OR: National Center to Improve the Tools of Educators.

Deno, S.L. (1985). Curriculum-based measurement: The emerging alternative. *Exceptional Children, 52,* 219–232.

Deno, S.L. (1986). Formative evaluation of individual student programs: A new role for school psychologists. *School Psychology Review, 15,* 358–374.

Deno, S.L. (1989). Curriculum-based measurement and special education services: A fundamental and direct relationship. In M. Shinn (Ed.), *Curriculum-based measurement: Assessing special children.* (pp. 1–17). New York: The Gilford Press.

Deno, S.L., & Mirkin, P.K. (1977). *Data-based program modification: A manual.* Minneapolis, MN: Leadership Training Institute for Special Education, University of Minnesota. (ERIC Document Reproduction Service No. ED144270)

Deno, S.L., Mirkin, P.K., & Shinn, M. (1979). *Behavioral perspectives on the assessment of learning disabled children.* Minneapolis, MN: Institute for Research on Learning Disabilities, University of Minnesota. (ERIC Document Reproduction Service No. ED185769)

Engelmann, S., & Bruner, E.C. (1995). *Reading Mastery.* New York: McGraw-Hill.

Engelman, S., Meyer, L., Carnine, L., Becker, W., Eisole, J., & Johnson, G. (1999). *Corrective Reading.* New York: McGraw-Hill.

Fuchs, L.S., Deno, S.L., & Marston, D. (1997, February) *Alternative measures of student progress and state standards testing.* La Jolla, CA: Pacific Coast Research Conference.

Fuchs, L.S., Deno, S.L., & Mirkin, P.K. (1984). The effects of frequent curriculum-based measurement and evaluation on pedagogy, student achievement, and student awareness of learning. *American Educational Research Journal, 21,* 449–460.

Fuchs, L.S., Fuchs, D., & Maxwell, L. (1988). The validity of informal reading comprehension measures. *Remedial and Special Education, 9*(2), 20–29.

Grossen, B. (1997). *30 years of NICHD research: What we now know about how children learn to read.* Santa Cruz, CA: The Center for the Future of Teaching and Learning.

Heller, K., Holtzman, W., & Messick, S. (1982). *National Research Council Special Task Force report.* Washington, DC: National Academies Press.

Hosp, J.L., & Reschly D.J. (2002). Regional differences in school psychology practice. *School Psychology Review, 31,* 11–29.

Individuals with Disabilities Education Improvement Act of 2004, PL 108-446, 20 U.S.C. §§ 1400 *et seq.*

Larry P. vs. Riles, 793 F. 2ed 969 (9th cir. 1984).

Lau, M.Y., Sieler, J.D., Muyskens, P., Canter, A., Van Kevren, B., & Marston, D. (2006). Perspectives on the use of the problem-solving model from the viewpoint of a school psychologist, administration, and teacher. *Psychology in the Schools, 43*(1), 117–127.

Marston, D., Pickart, M., Reschly, A., Heistad, D., Muyskens, P., & Tindal, G. (in press). Early literacy measures for improving student reading achievement: Translating research into practice. *Exceptionality.*

Marston, D., Deno, S.L., Kim, D., Diment, K., & Rogers, D. (1995). Comparison of reading intervention approaches for students with mild disabilities. *Exceptional Children, 62*(1), 20–37.

Marston, D., & Magnusson, D. (1985). Implementing Curriculum-Based Measurement in special and regular education settings. *Exceptional Children, 52*(3), 266–276.

Marston, D., Muyskens, P., Lau, M., & Canter, A. (2003). Problem-Solving Model for decision-making with high-incidence disabilities: The Minneapolis experience. *Learning Disabilities Research and Practice, 18*(3), 187–200.

Marston, D., & Magnusson, D. (1988). Curriculum-based measurement: District level implementation. In J.L. Graden, J.E. Zins, & M.J. Curtis (Eds.), *Alternative educational delivery systems: enhancing instructional options for all students.* Washington, DC: National Association of School Psychologists.

Marston, D., Muyskens, P., Betts, J., & Heistad, D. (2005). *Tracking the progress of diverse learns toward success on tests of accountability: A three year study.* Minneapolis, MN: Minneapolis Pubic Schools. Manuscript in review.

Minneapolis Public Schools. (1998). *Reading instruction: Best practices for diverse learners.* Minneapolis, MN: Author.

Minneapolis Public Schools. (2003). *Performance assessment of academic skills in the problem-solving model.* Minneapolis, MN: Author.

National Center to Improve the Tools of Education. (1996). *Learning to read, reading to learn: Helping children with learning disabilities to succeed.* Project funded by the Office of Special Education Programs, U.S. Department of Education.

Northwest Evaluation Association. (2002). *Northwest Achievement Levels Test (NALT)*. Portland, OR: Author.

O'Connor, R. (2003, December). *Tiers of intervention in kindergarten through third grade.* Presented at National Research Center on Learning Disabilities RTI Symposium, Kansas City, MO.

Reschly, D.J. (1988a). Special education reform: School psychology revolution. *School Psychology Review, 17,* 459–475.

Reschly, D.J. (1988b). Obstacles, starting points, and doldrums notwithstanding: Reform/revolution from outcomes criteria. *School Psychology Review, 17,* 495–501.

Reschly, D.J., & Starkweather, A. (1997). *Evaluation of an alterative special education assessment and classification program in Minneapolis Public Schools.* Ames: Iowa State University.

Reschly, D.J., Tilly, W.J., & Grimes, J.P. (1998). *Functional and noncategorical identification and intervention in special education.* Des Moines: Iowa Department of Education.

Reschly, D.J., & Wilson, M.S. (1995). School psychology faculty and practitioners: 1986 to 1991 trends in demographic characteristics, roles, satisfaction, and system reform. *School Psychology Review, 24,* 62–80.

Siegal, L.S. (1989). IQ is irrelevant to the definition of learning disabilities. *Journal of Learning Disabilities, 22,* 469–486.

Self, H., Benning, A., Marston, D., & Magnusson, D. (1991). Cooperative teaching project: A model for students at risk. *Exceptional Children, 58,* 26–34.

Smith, S.B., Simmons, D.C., & Kame'enui, E.J. (1995). *Synthesis of research on phonological awareness: Principles and implications for reading acquisition.* (Synthesis of research, Technical Report No. 21). Eugene, OR: National Center to Improve the Tools of Educators.

Snow, C.E., Burns, S., & Griffin, P. (1998). *Preventing reading difficulties in young children.* Washington, DC: National Academies Press.

Tilly, W.D., Reschly, D.J., & Grimes, J.P. (1998). Disability determination in problem-solving systems: Connectional foundations and critical components. In D.J. Reschly, W.D. Tilly, & J.P Grimes. *Functional and Noncategorical Identification in Intervention in Special Education.* Des Moines, IA: Department of Education.

Tindal, G., & Marston, D. (1996). Alternative reading measures as performance assessments. *Exceptionality,* 6(4), 201–230.

Tombari, M., & Bergan, J. (1978). Consultant cues, teacher problem definitions, judgments, and expectancies for children's adjustment problems. *Journal of School Psychology, 16,* 212–219.

Vaughn, S. (2003, December). *How many tiers are needed for response to intervention to achieve acceptable prevention outcomes?* Presented at National Research Center on Learning Disabilities RTI Symposium, Kansas City, MO.

Ysseldyke, J.E., & Christenson, S. (1993). *The Instructional Environment System-II (TIES-II): A system to identify a student's instructional needs.* Longmont, CO: Sopris West Educational Services.

Ysseldyke, J.E., Thurlow, M., Grade, J., Wesson, C., Algozinne, B., & Deno, S.L. (1983). Generalizations from five years of research on assessment and decision-making: The University of Minnesota Institute. *Exceptional Children Quarterly, 4,* 75–93.

Ysseldyke, J.E., Vanderwood, M.L., & Shriner, J. (1997). Changes over the past decade in special education referral to placement probability: An incredibly reliable practice. *Diagnostique, 23,* 193–201.

What Are the Issues in Response to Intervention Research?

Deborah L. Speece and Caroline Y. Walker

Response to Intervention (RTI) has emerged as an alternative to IQ-score–achievement discrepance in the identification of learning disabilities (LD). The reasons for this shift are well-documented and discussed both in terms of the shortcomings of discrepancy models and the potential of RTI models (e.g., Fletcher et al., 1998; Fuchs, 1995; Fuchs & Fuchs, 1998; Speece, Case, & Molloy, 2003; Vaughn & Fuchs, 2003). The IQ-score–achievement discrepance model of LD identification lacks coverage, requires too much time for children to exhibit discrepancies, and carries no implications for instruction. RTI *potentially* negates each of these problems by capturing all children who are not learning, allowing implementation of the model early in a child's school career, and having a direct, low-inference connection to instruction. The emphasis in this volume is on reading disabilities, but, conceptually, RTI also could be applied to other academic domains such as math, spelling, and writing.

We emphasize "potentially" in the previous summary of RTI benefits because RTI has been subject to less than 10 years of active empirical investigation despite deeper historical roots. The promise of RTI swamps the evidence; therefore, some reflection on important questions seems appropriate. The outward simplicity of the model (i.e., child is not learning, change instruction) belies the complexity of a multicomponent system that has overlapping goals of prevention, identification, and remediation. In this response chapter, we consider four elements of RTI models that we believe require investigation: screening procedures, intensity and content of instruction, definition of responsiveness, and implications for postprimary-grade children. Our perspective is broader than the aims of the volume as we attempt to situate validated instructional practices within the larger context of RTI and LD. We conclude with some thoughts on what RTI might mean to the construct of LD.

UNIVERSAL SCREENING

Identification of LD in the public schools begins with teacher referral to a school-based child-study team. If children are not referred by this screening process, they will not, for all practical purposes, be identified. Several studies of teacher-based referrals suggest this procedure leads to overidentification of males and children with behavioral issues and underidentification of females with reading difficulties (MacMillan & Siperstein, 2002; Shaywitz, Shaywitz, Fletcher, & Escobar, 1990). The problem encompasses both false positive and false negative identification, with the latter typically viewed as more problematic because children who need more intensive instruction are not identified. This is not an indictment of teacher judgment but rather an acknowledgement that it can be inaccurate when it is the sole screening variable. False positive identification is not without problems, most notably the costs associated with delivering interventions to children who do not need them.

RTI frameworks, in which "responsiveness" is used at each stage (tier) of decision making including screening decisions, reduces the likelihood of false negative cases. As proposed by Fuchs and Fuchs (L.S. Fuchs, 1995; L.S. Fuchs & Fuchs, 1998), all children in a classroom are screened on a regular basis (e.g., weekly, biweekly). Children who perform below classmates (or any normative group) on growth over time and level of performance are candidates for instructional modification. This method reflects a universal screen based on responsiveness—all children receive progress-monitoring assessments with regular reviews of responsiveness. An important feature of this perspective on screening is that it considers a core tenet of LD: Does the child fail to respond to adequate instruction? If the mean level and slope of an entire classroom are below other classrooms, then the assumption of adequate instruction is not tenable. Classroom-level intervention in the form of improved instruction is necessary before any child receives secondary intervention (L.S. Fuchs & Fuchs, 1998).

It is difficult to argue with the logic of this type of universal screen, but the continuous progress monitoring approach may not be acceptable to consumers (or researchers for that matter) for practical reasons. This is an empirical matter. Universal screens may not need to be as demanding as weekly progress monitoring. Attempts to identify a set of measures that can be administered at one point in time and that accurately identify children who later exhibit reading problems, however, have not been successful (Jenkins & O'Connor, 2002; Scarborough, 1998). These approaches typically are better at identifying who will not have problems rather than those who will (Speece, 2005). Screening criteria can be set to produce virtually no false-negative cases, but the trade-off is an increase in false-positive cases. In the literature on early identification of reading disabilities, approximately twice as many children are labeled at risk as are diagnosed, though the goal is to capture all the children who later exhibit problems (Ritchey & Speece, 2004).

From these issues emerge research questions regarding screening and how best to identify children for secondary interventions within an RTI framework. Is there some combination of procedures and measures that are efficient yet will improve the accuracy of screening for the second tier of instruction? How can the adequacy of classroom instruction be assessed? For example, although teacher referral alone may lack precision, perhaps teacher ratings, combined with a brief set of measures, could be devised and tested against alternatives such as continuous progress monitoring and teacher referral. We recognize that RTI researchers focus more on the intervention than how children get to the intervention. Lack of attention to other issues, however, such as the development of reasonable screening protocols that include the quality of classroom instruction, may lead us to the same place as did the IQ-score–achievement discrepance: failure to attend to the instructional conditions that preceded academic problems. It could be argued that Tier 2 intervention will solve the problem of the adequacy of general education instruction. Children who respond immediately are probably the ones who received inadequate instruction in general education. Then what? Without a mechanism to strengthen instruction, knowing that it is substandard does not get us very far.

RTI studies vary in how children are identified for secondary interventions. The continuous progress monitoring approach to screening, emphasizing comparisons to average-achieving children, identifies a group of children who require more intensive instruction (McMaster, Fuchs, Fuchs, & Compton, 2005; Speece & Case, 2001). These children appear to have greater impairments than those identified as low achievers or IQ-achievement discrepant. By the same token, researchers using teacher referral and screening measures also identify children who require more intensive instruction (Vaughn & Fuchs, 2003; Vellutino et al., 1996). What remains unknown with the latter method is whether children were missed (i.e., false negatives) and the extent to which they received reasonable instruction prior to instructional modifications. An important item on the RTI research agenda will be to test competing screening models (e.g., see Fuchs & Fuchs, Chapter 3) and determine the percentage of false negative and false positive cases in the context of a classroom environment in which most children are learning.

INTENSITY AND CONTENT OF INSTRUCTION

The authors in the previous chapters discuss a number of variations to a three-tier model of reading intervention. Taken as a whole, these discussions provide a rich framework for understanding and enacting three-tier reading instruction. The variety of approaches discussed in this volume, however, also underscores the unresolved elements of the three-tier model. Chief among these are the differences in defining first-tier "good instruction" approaches and differences in the dividing point between second- and third-tier instruction.

Tier 1 Interventions

There is a consensus among the authors in this volume that Tier 1 instruction should be research based and validated—backed by evidence illustrating its use in successfully teaching reading to the majority of students. In addition, it is hoped that such "good instruction" will reduce the number of students who display learning difficulties in the area of reading. There is a great deal of variability in what counts as effective Tier 1 instruction. Generally, curriculum with a strong decoding component is viewed as effective (Foorman, 1995).

Some researchers have advocated for the Open Court program (see Fuchs & Fuchs, Chapter 3; Harn et al., Chapter 8), whereas others have promoted code-based programs in general (O'Connor, Chapter 7). The difference in reading curricula is only the start. Many researchers have emphasized a need for professional development, but consistent intensity has not been established (O'Connor, Chapter 7; Vaughn et al., Chapter 2). Other classroom-level or Tier 1 interventions have been shown to be more effective than standard classwide instruction. These interventions include classwide peer tutoring (Fuchs, Fuchs, Kazdan, & Allen, 1999; Greenwood, 1996) and instructional intervention teams (Kovaleski, Tucker, & Stevens, 1996). Research is needed to determine which combination of models is the most effective.

Some schools are already using research-based reading instruction as a requirement of receipt of Reading First grants. In 2001, as a part of the No Child Left Behind (PL 107-110) initiative, these schools were required to implement research-validated reading instructional practices, programs akin to those advocated for Tier 1 instruction. Schools who accept these grants must adopt programs whose positive results are published in peer-reviewed journals or approved by "a panel of independent experts through . . . scientific review" (20 U.S.C. § 6368(6)). In addition, these schools no longer can rely on ad hoc programs if there is no scientific validation of their effectiveness.

This raises the question of the extent to which schools must enact research-based programs to maintain the instruction's proven effectiveness. Can teachers adapt a program to their particular classroom situations and achieve the same, or better, results than those documented in the research? Or should teachers, both as a matter of instructional fidelity and strict adherence to the Reading First grant requirements, be required to implement reading programs with minimal alteration? If this is the ideal, is it even possible? There is good evidence of a research-to-practice gap (Carnine, 1997; Kennedy, 1997; Malouf & Schiller, 1995; Vaughn, Klingner & Hughes, 2000). Some of the factors that hinder teachers' ability to maintain instructional techniques include curricular constraints such as the intrusion of high-stakes testing; the need to cover specific curriculum; mismatches between teacher beliefs and the instruction; mismatches between students' competence and instructional material; scheduling problems; and teachers either forgetting, modifying, or dropping components of the instructional intervention (Greenwood, Terry, Arreaga-Mayer, & Finney, 1992; Klingner, Vaughn, Hughes, & Arguelles, 1999).

What in-school procedures would take the place of stringent research proto-cols to ensure that teachers implement programs with maximum fidelity, or, is this even a priority? The research on the success of the three-tier model of read-ing intervention has necessarily taken place within an environment of strict pro-tocols that enhance fidelity of intervention for Tier 1 instruction. Whether com-parable successes can be achieved outside the experimental setting has yet to be seen, although O'Connor (Chapter 7) suggests that professional development for teachers can improve student outcomes. A necessary component of the research on the effectiveness of the three-tier model should be an examination of the ex-tent to which Tier 1 instructional programs can be faithfully executed in schools within a "real world" context and what, if any, diminution in student outcomes results from failures to adhere to the program's protocols.

In addition, there is a need for research that compares the effectiveness of different Tier 1 interventions to determine which components are most vital in producing successful reading instruction for the majority of students and not sim-ply those students who appear to be struggling or are defined as having LD. It is important to know which products and strategies have the greatest positive im-pact on the greatest number of students and what steps are needed to allow effec-tive, large-scale implementation of those programs.

The Differences Between Tier 2 and Tier 3 Instruction

The Three-Tier Model of Reading Instruction attempts to conceptualize reading interventions into three strata. Tier 1 instruction is classroomwide, takes place within the general education context, and is based on research-validated best in-structional practices. This level of instruction should be sufficient for most stu-dents. A sizeable minority of students, however, will not make adequate progress in reading with only Tier 1 instruction. These students will need additional in-struction in small groups, with a more intensive focus. Such additional instruc-tion makes up the second and third tiers of reading instruction in the three-tier model. There is, however, a lack of consistency in the field regarding which qual-ities are essential to the second and third tiers of instruction or regarding which attributes differentiate Tier 2 from Tier 3 instruction. These differences may cause one to wonder how important a stringent, three-tier concept is to the effective-ness of this form of reading instruction.

Group Size and Who Delivers the Instruction

Tier 2 instruction invariably is described as taking place in small groups; however, researchers differ on the number of students that compose such groups. Tier 2 small-group instruction ranges anywhere from a single student per group (Fuchs & Fuchs, Chapter 3) to five students per group (Blachman, Ball, Black, & Tan-gel, 2000). Researchers also differ in their conceptions of who should deliver Tier 2 instruction. Some suggest that Tier 2 instruction should be delivered by paraprofessionals supervised by a lead classroom teacher (Fuchs & Fuchs, Chapter 3), some suggest certified teachers (Vellutino et al., Chapter 9), and others suggest a specialized reading teacher (Haager et al., Chapter 11). Studies that manipulate group size and the credentials of those providing Tier 2 instruction help guide schools in determining how to best allocate existing resources without negatively affecting the successful results of the three-tier model.

Intensity of Instruction

Studies vary in the duration of instruction provided in Tier 2. Duration comprises the length of time devoted to each Tier 2 session and the length of time devoted to overall Tier 2 interventions provided to the students. Tier 2 interventions have been described as lasting between 10 and 45 minutes per session (O'Connor, Chapter 7; Fuchs & Fuchs, Chapter 3), with sessions taking place between 2 and 5 times per weeks (Vellutino et al., Chapter 9; Vaughn et al., Chapter 2), with the intervention lasting between 10 and 30 weeks (Vaughn, Linan-Thompson, & Hickman-Davis, 2003).

Authors' descriptions of Tier 2 instruction also differ on where the instruction takes place. Some researchers have discussed Tier 2 interventions taking place within the general education classroom (Fuchs & Fuchs, Chapter 3); others have indicated that they should be done through a pull-out model (Vellutino et al., Chapter 9), whereas many other authors are silent on the subject.

In addition, authors describe "increased intensity" in a number of ways. Many authors conceptualized intensity as a focus on remedial and foundational concepts of reading such as phonological awareness, letter recognition, letter-sound awareness, the alphabetic principle, and sight word reading (Vellutino et al., Chapter 9; Fuchs & Fuchs, Chapter 3; O'Connor, Chapter 7). Other characteristics of increased intensity mentioned by researchers have included highly explicit instruction (Fuchs & Fuchs, Chapter 3; Harn et al., Chapter 8), increased specificity (Harn et al., Chapter 8), and additional opportunities to practice fundamental skills (Harn et al., Chapter 8).

Research is needed to examine which, if any, of these intensity of instruction variables are vital to the success of Tier 2 instruction. Because the current studies differ on a number of variables related to intensity, more focused research is needed to isolate individual elements such as duration of sessions, number of sessions per week, number of weeks, location of instruction, and form of remedial or explicit instruction. These components need to be tied to improvement and maintenance of students' skills. Such studies could help school administrators and teachers make decisions in adapting three-tier instruction to their school environments.

Entering and Exiting Tiers

Authors differ on the criteria used to move students from Tier 2 to Tier 3 instruction or from Tier 2 back to Tier 1. Authors split on whether the duration of Tier 2 intervention should be simply a prescribed amount of time or should be based on a certain level of mastery or growth in reading achievement. For example, Fuchs and Fuchs (Chapter 3) appeared to reevaluate students on a fixed schedule, every 8 weeks, but moved students between tiers based on achievement of a pre-defined level of growth, represented as a weekly increase in the number of items scored correctly on a curriculum-based measurement. Similarly, interventions in the study by Vaughn and colleagues (2003) lasted either 10, 20, or 30 weeks depending on how long it took students to achieve a passing score on screening and progress monitoring measures of fluency. Other authors such as O'Connor (Chapter 7) seemed to reevaluate students on a periodic basis, by semester, and move them from tier to tier as needed.

Given the three-tier model's emphasis on individualization and monitoring of student progress, it would seem to make sense for instructors to move students in and out of tiers based on the students reaching predetermined levels of mastery rather than to adhere to a strict time schedule. Preset times for evaluation (e.g., 10 weeks, quarterly, every semester), however, would seem to provide useful guideposts for tracking student progress on a larger scale. It might be useful for future research to compare the set time schedule and level of mastery approaches to examine whether one or the other is more effective in identifying the proper point for moving students from Tier 2 instruction, as determined by later student reading success.

Purpose of Research and Its Influence on the Conclusions

In recommending avenues of research, it is important to remember that many of the differences can be accounted for by authors' differing purposes in conducting research on the three-tier model of reading intervention. Authors using the three-tier model to identify students with LD tend to use larger groups of students, with shorter fixed durations of intervention. Researchers who are more concerned with testing the three-tier approach as a form of remediation are more likely to use small-group instruction of a longer duration.

Tier 3 Variations

Greater agreement among researchers appears to exist with regard to some of the characteristics of Tier 3 instruction. Tier 3 instruction generally is described as more individually focused and relying less on a standard curriculum, focusing in-stead on individual student needs. There is general agreement that Tier 3 instruction is one-to-one instruction with the content of the intervention tailored to the specific student's needs, although some researchers indicate that small-group in-struction of up to five students also can be effective (Harn et al., Chapter 8). Who provides the instruction is also less problematic in Tier 3 instruction; many re-searchers seem to agree that special educators should be the prime providers of Tier 3 instruction (Vaughn et al., Chapter 2; Vellutino et al., Chapter 9; Fuchs & Fuchs, Chapter 3). Continuing with Tier 3 intervention's similarity to traditional special education, most authors seemed to provide Tier 3 instruction in a pull-out setting, although few stated this explicitly (Vellutino et al., Chapter 9). Few authors also discussed the length of Tier 3 instructional sessions or the length of the intervention. The kindergarteners in the study conducted by Harn and colleagues (Chapter 8) received an additional 30 minutes of small-group instruction 5 days a week, with intervention beginning in early November and ending in mid-May. As work continues on Tier 3 instruction, it is important not to lose sight of accountability. Special education or Tier 3 instruction also has to be based on research-proven methods in order to improve student outcomes.

DEFINITION OF RESPONSIVENESS

Perhaps one of the more important understandings to come out of the RTI "movement" is the necessity of keeping track of children's progress, especially those at risk for poor academic outcomes. Accountability is a long-acknowledged cornerstone of Curriculum-Based Measurement (CBM; Deno, 1985; Shinn, 1989) and is now foundational to RTI. This is very good news. It is, however, easier to agree on the concept than it is to define it. At this point, the definitions of "response" and "nonresponse" in the literature are quite variable. Researchers sometimes opt for benchmarks to guide decisions but often the standards for establishing the benchmarks are either not articulated or difficult to defend. Another approach relies on norm-referenced tests, but a noted problem is their inability to index growth over a short period of time. Yet another method is using discrepancies from a reference group on level and growth on CBMs, but the amount of discrepancy required is usually arbitrary. This is a dizzying array of possibilities with no clear winner.

Fuchs, Fuchs, and Compton (2004) compared several approaches to defining responsiveness in a sample of first- and second-grade children. Each definition was applied to form groups of "responsive" and "nonresponsive" children who had received a secondary (Tier 2) intervention. The groups then were compared on several reading outcome and growth variables. Large group differences were interpreted as better ways of defining responsiveness. For first graders, nonresponsiveness was best defined by the median split on a CBM word-reading fluency measure. The second best method was a normative standard (< 90 standard score) on a published test. For second graders, nonresponsiveness was best defined by the median split on CBM passage reading fluency and by a normative criterion that used both CBM passage reading fluency performance and growth (dual discrepancy).

In the previous summary, "best" is defined as those methods that produced the most significant differences. The fact that the median split approach yielded large and significant differences is disconcerting because it is totally dependent on the sample.

Interesting aspects of the Fuchs and colleagues (2004) analyses include the varying proportion of children identified as nonresponsive depending on criterion used with the corresponding implication for classification reliability. If RTI is to be used as an ingredient in the definition of LD (i.e., admission to Tier 3), much more work is required on the thorny issue of responsiveness.

THIRD GRADE AND BEYOND

With reading difficulties, early detection and intervention is certainly the goal, and the majority of research in the field focuses on children in kindergarten through third grade. The research described in the preceding chapters is no exception. Vellutino and colleagues (Chapter 9), Vaughn and colleagues (Chapter 2), and O'Connor (Chapter 7) begin their interventions with kindergarteners and follow them through third grade.

Not all students who will develop reading-based LD, however, will be identified by third grade. To our knowledge, there are no studies with a cohort identified in third grade. Studies have placed the prevalence for late-emerging reading disabilities, those that occur after third grade, at between 22% and 42% of the total number of students identified as having reading disabilities (Kavale & Reese, 1992, Shaywitz, Escobar, Shaywitz, Fletcher, & Makuch, 1992). Given these estimates, although it seems likely that most students who will be diagnosed with reading disabilities will show signs early in their academic careers, a sizeable minority will only be identified later on, presumably when the instructional focus shifts from learning to read to reading to learn. It seems important then to examine the utility of the Three-Tier Model of Reading Intervention for students with such late-onset reading disabilities. Specifically, one should question the extent to which a three-tier approach is necessary for identifying older students with reading disabilities and whether implementation of such an approach past third grade is practical.

Identifying Late-Onset Reading Disabilities

Little research has focused on students who develop reading-based LD in third grade and beyond. Although it is recognized that as many as 74% of students identified as having reading disabilities by the third grade maintain this diagnosis into middle and high school, few researchers have examined students who appear to be typically achieving as late as third or fourth grade and then develop reading-based LD (Lyon, 1996 in McCray, Vaughn, & Neal, 2001).

One of the few studies to focus on such students, conducted by Leach, Scarborough, and Rescorla (2003), found that students who were identified with reading-based LD after third grade were a heterogeneous group. Confirming earlier studies indicating a comprehension-based reading slump in fourth grade (Catts & Hogan, 2002), many of the late-identified students in the Leach and colleagues study demonstrated weak comprehension skills with good basic decoding skills (32%). Thirty-five percent, however, displayed word-level processing impairments and adequate comprehension skills, whereas 32% showed both word-level processing and comprehension difficulties. This was in contrast to a comparison group of students whose difficulties had been identified during or prior to third grade. Of the students with LD identified in or before third grade, only 6% showed comprehension-only difficulties, 49% displayed word-level processing problems, and 46% exhibited both word-processing and comprehension problems. These results illustrate that few of the early-identified students showed problems only in comprehension. In addition, a majority (61%) of students with word-level only or combined word-processing and comprehension difficulties were identified by third grade or sooner.

Leach and colleagues (2003) also found that 47% of the fourth and fifth graders in their sample who possessed reading-based LD were identified after third grade. To ascertain whether these students' disabilities had simply been overlooked in the earlier grades or whether these students did not in fact develop difficulties until after third grade, the authors examined the students' third-, fourth-, and fifth-grade reading achievement test scores. From analysis of these data, the authors concluded that the students with late-identified LD possessed reading difficulties that were late emerging and not simply previously overlooked.

The implication of this research for the three-tier model of reading intervention is that screening and progress monitoring need to be extended to third grade and beyond to identify and treat the sizeable number of students who will not develop serious reading difficulties until the fourth grade or later. Although some may argue that such students would be apparent to teachers in these older grades without screening measures, the study by Leach and colleagues (2003) belies such an assumption. Many of the students who met the study's criteria for reading disabilities had not been previously identified by their schools; this speaks to the fact that older students with reading disabilities are not always easy to identify absent a structured screening process. To ensure that students with both early- and late-emerging reading disabilities are identified, both screening and progress monitoring need to incorporate metrics that specifically examine students' comprehension abilities in addition to more basic word-level decoding skills.

Fuchs and Fuchs (Chapter 3) discuss extending screening and monitoring beyond third grade. In addition, it would seem relatively easy to continue the three-tier approach into fourth grade and beyond. Screening and progress monitoring do not need to take significant amounts of time away from classroom instruction and require little additional training for teachers and other school staff. The extension of these techniques at least through the intermediate grades and perhaps into middle school should not represent a significant drain on school resources.

Some, however, might argue that if a three-tier model of reading intervention is implemented with fidelity, almost all students with decoding-based reading disabilities should be identified prior to fourth grade. So long as one is careful in monitoring student achievement and growth, one should be able to identify those students who are struggling with basic word-level reading skills, and if the threshold level for Tier 2 intervention is set at a conservative level, these students would likely receive some intensive small-group instruction prior to fourth grade. Introduction of measures that can predict comprehension-based reading difficulties prior to fourth grade might provide an effective screen for students with this type of learning disability at an earlier age. For example, recent research suggests that working memory is closely related to students' abilities to comprehend texts in the third through fifth grades, and so screens of working memory might serve to predict later reading comprehension difficulties (Cain, Oakhill & Bryant, 2004). The limited prior research on students with late-emerging LD occurred in schools that had not implemented the three-tier model of reading intervention. This makes it difficult to know whether the 22%–42% of students with LD not diagnosed until fourth grade or later would hold true within the three-tier context.

It is also important to note that the prior research on students with late-identified and/or late-emerging LD was primarily concerned with identifying such students and categorizing the varieties of reading LDs that they displayed. These studies give us no indication as to whether students with these forms of LD would be more, less, or equally receptive to remediation as students whose LD is identified in the earlier grades. It would, therefore, be interesting to compare the effectiveness of the Three-Tier Model of Reading Intervention with cohorts comprised of students with early-emerging and late-emerging LD.

The Practicality of Three-Tier Instruction in the Higher Grades

Although it should be simple to extend the screening and progress monitoring aspects of the Three-Tier Model of Reading Intervention beyond the third grade, there remains the question of whether the approach itself can be effectively implemented in the later grades. As students transition from learning to read to reading to learn, will the three-tier approach prove a practical means of improving student performance for those who are not benefiting from general education instruction?

It can be hoped that exposure to good three-tier instruction in the lower grades would ameliorate many reading difficulties before students reach the higher grades; however, previous research on the persistence of reading disabilities suggests that many students would still possess significant impairments requiring Tier 2 and Tier 3 instruction. In these later grades, such instruction might more resemble traditional special education, with pull-out instruction for small groups of students to work on both basic decoding and higher-level comprehension skills.

IMPLICATIONS FOR THE CONSTRUCT OF LEARNING DISABILITIES

Developing quality interventions, understanding the optimal conditions for delivering instruction, and using assessment data to guide decisions are necessary to understanding the promise of RTI. Resolving these issues, however, is not sufficient to address the problem of LD identification. RTI, in its many forms and at its heart, is presumably a method for identifying LD. The reauthorization language of IDEA states specifically that RTI may replace IQ-achievement discrepancy methods (see http://www.copaa.org/pdf/IDEA97-04COMP.pdf). That RTI also has other outcomes such as prevention and earlier remediation are notable nontrivial features that serve to strengthen the reasons for continued research.

So, what is known about LD from the RTI research? Few studies have taken this as a focus. It is known that young, at-risk children who are nonresponsive to general education reading instruction over the course of a year have poorer skills than children with IQ-score–achievement discrepancies. Importantly, the nonresponsive group exhibits gender and ethnic characteristics that are proportional to the population from which they were drawn (Speece & Case, 2001). Also, at-risk children who are persistently nonresponsive across the early elementary grades and who would therefore likely qualify for Tier 3 intervention have poorer reading and behavioral outcomes than at-risk children who demonstrate better levels of responsiveness (Case, Speece, & Molloy, 2003; Vaughn et al., 2003).

The LD–RTI connection clearly needs elaboration beyond these initial findings. When one steps back from a focus on tiers and interventions and considers the issues of classification and identification, the children who enter Tier 3 are of the highest interest for those concerned with how the LD construct will evolve in the postdiscrepancy world. Who are these children? Are they homogeneous on a set of characteristics (besides responsiveness) that make them distinct from children who respond adequately to secondary intervention? Or, are there subtypes that may emerge when one examines, for example, dimensions of attention, neurobiology, social background, and academic skills?

In addition to individual differences, are there differential interventions that will be more successful when tailored to a child's profile? It is important to note how difficult it is to address a child's reading problems that persist beyond excellent primary and secondary interventions (Fuchs, Fuchs, McMaster, & Al Otaiba, 2003). Understanding the links between low responders' cognitive, neurobiological, and social profiles and responsiveness to carefully planned intervention will be key in describing the evolution of the LD construct. Blashfield and Draguns (1976) said that a good classification system must communicate with practitioners and build theory. We are hopeful that the RTI research will not stop with defining interventions but will use the strong base evident in this volume to build a better understanding of LD.

REFERENCES

Blachman, B.A., Ball, E.W., Black, R., & Tangel, D.M. (2000). *Road to the code: A phonological awareness program for young children.* Baltimore: Paul H. Brookes Publishing Co.

Blashfield, R.K., & Draguns, J.G. (1976). Evaluative criteria for psychiatric classification. *Journal of Abnormal Psychology, 85,* 140–150.

Cain, K., Oakhill, J., & Bryant, P. (2004). Children's reading comprehension ability: Concurrent prediction by working memory, verbal ability, and component skills. *Journal of Educational Psychology, 96,* 31–42.

Carnine, D. (1997). Bridging the research-to-practice gap. *Exceptional Children, 63,* 513–522.

Case, L.P., Speece, D.L., & Molloy, D.E. (2003). The validity of a response-to-instruction paradigm to identify reading disabilities: A longitudinal analysis of individual differences and contextual factors. *School Psychology Review, 32,* 557–582.

Catts, H.W., & Hogan, T.P. (2002, June). *The fourth grade slump: Late emerging poor readers.* Paper presented at the annual meeting of the Society for the Scientific Study of Reading, Chicago.

The Council of Parent Attorneys and Advocates. (2004). *Individuals with Disabilities Education Improvement Act of 2004 Compared to IDEA'97.* Retrieved January 12, 2005, from http://www.copaa.org/pdf/IDEA97-04COMP.pdf

Deno, S.L. (1985). Curriculum-based measurement: The emerging alternative. *Exceptional Children, 52,* 219–232

Fletcher, J.M., Francis, D.J., Shaywitz, S.E., Lyon, G.R., Foorman, B.R., Stuebing, K.K., et al. (1998). Intelligent testing and the discrepancy model for children with LD. *Learning Disabilities Research and Practice, 13,* 186–203.

Foorman, B.R. (1995). Research on "The great debate": Code-oriented versus whole language approaches to reading instruction. *School Psychology Review, 24,* 376–392.

Fuchs, D., Fuchs, L.S., & Compton, D.L. (2004). Identifying reading disabilities by responsiveness-to-instruction: Specifying measures and criteria. *Learning Disability Quarterly, 27,* 216–227.

Fuchs, D., Fuchs, L.S., McMaster, K.N., & Al Otaiba, S. (2003). Identifying children at risk for reading failure: Curriculum-based measurement and the dual-discrepancy approach. In L. Swanson, K.R. Harris, & S. Graham (Eds.), *Handbook of learning disabilities* (pp. 431–449). New York: The Guilford Press.

Fuchs, L.S. (1995, May). *Incorporating curriculum-based measurement into the eligibility decision-making process: A focus on treatment validity and student growth.* Paper presented at the Workshop on IQ Testing and Educational Decision Making, National Research Council, National Academy of Science, Washington, DC.

Fuchs, L.S., & Fuchs, D. (1998). Treatment validity: A unifying concept for reconceptualizing the identification of learning disabilities. *Learning Disabilities Research and Practice, 13,* 204–219.

Fuchs, L.S., Fuchs, D., Kazdan, S., & Allen, S. (1999). Effects of peer-assisted learning strategies in reading with and without training in elaborated help giving. *Elementary School Journal, 99,* 201–220.

Greenwood, C.R. (1996). Research on the practices and behavior of effective teachers at the Juniper gardens children's project: Implications for the education of diverse learners. In D.L. Speece & B.K. Keogh (Eds.), *Research on classroom ecologies* (pp. 39–79). Mahwah, NJ: Lawrence Erlbaum Associates.

Greenwood, C.R., Terry, B., Arreaga-Mayer, C., & Finney, R. (1992). The ClassWide Peer Tutoring Program: Implementation factors moderating students' achievement. *Journal of Applied Behavioral Analysis, 25,* 101–116.

Jenkins, J.R., & O'Connor, R.E. (2002). Early identification and intervention for young children with reading/learning disabilities. In R. Bradley, L. Danielson, & D.P. Hallahan (Eds.), *Identification of learning disabilities: Research to Practice* (pp. 99–149). Mahwah, NJ: Lawrence Erlbaum Associates.

Kavale, K.A., & Reese, J.H. (1992). The character of learning disabilities: An Iowa profile. *Learning Disability Quarterly, 15,* 74–94.

Kennedy, M.M. (1997). The connection between research and practice. *Educational Researcher, 26*(7), 4–12.

Klingner, J.K., Vaughn, S., Hughes, M.T., & Arguelles, M.E. (1999). Sustaining research-based practices in reading: A 3-year follow-up. *Remedial and Special Education, 20,* 263–274, 287.

Kovaleski, J.F., Tucker, J.A., & Stevens, L. (1996). Bridging special and regular education: The Pennsylvania initiative. *Educational Leadership, 53*(5), 44–47.

Leach, J.M., Scarborough, H.S., & Rescorla, L. (2003). Late-emerging reading disabilities. *Journal of Educational Psychology, 95,* 211–224.

MacMillan, D.L., & Siperstein, G.N. (2002). Learning disabilities as operationally defined by schools. In R. Bradley, L. Danielson, & D.P. Hallahan (Eds.), *Identification of learning disabilities: Research to practice* (pp. 287–333). Mahwah, NJ: Lawrence Erlbaum Associates.

Malouf, D.B., & Schiller, E.P. (1995). Practice and research in special education. *Exceptional Children, 61,* 414–424.

McCray, A.D., Vaughn, S., & Neal, L.I. (2001). Not all students learn to read by third grade: Middle school students speak out about their reading disabilities. *Journal of Special Education, 35,* 17–33.

McMaster, K.L., Fuchs, D., Fuchs, L.S., & Compton, D.L. (2005). Responding to non-responders: An experimental field trial of identification and intervention models. *Exceptional Children, 71,* 445–463.

No Child Left Behind Act of 2001, PL 107-110, 115 Stat. 1425, 20 U.S.C. §§ 6301 *et seq.*

Richley, K.D., & Speece, D.L. (2004). Early identification of reading disabilities: Current status and new directions. *Assessment for Effective Intervention, 29,* 13–24.

Scarborough, H.S. (1998). Early identification of children at risk for reading disabilities: Phonological awareness and some other promising predictors. In B.K. Shapiro, P.J. Accardo, & A.J. Capute (Eds.), *Specific reading disability: A view of the spectrum* (pp. 75–107). Timonium, MD: York Press.

Shaywitz, S.E., Escobar, M.D., Shaywitz, B.A., Fletcher, J.M., & Makuch, R. (1992). Evidence that dyslexia may represent the lower tail of a normal distribution of reading ability. *New England Journal of Medicine, 326,* 145–150.

Shaywitz, S.E., Shaywitz, B.A., Fletcher, J.M., & Escobar, M.D. (1990). Prevalence of reading disability in boys and girls: Results of the Connecticut longitudinal study. *Journal of the American Medical Association, 264,* 998–1002.

Shinn, M.R. (Ed.). (1989). *Curriculum-based measurement: Assessing special children.* New York: The Guilford Press.

Speece, D.L. (2005). Hitting the moving target known as reading development: Some thoughts on screening first-grade children for secondary interventions. *Journal of Learning Disabilities, 38,* 437–493.

Speece, D.L., & Case, L.P. (2001). Classification in context: An alternative approach to identifying early reading disability. *Journal of Educational Psychology, 93,* 735–749.

Speece, D.L., Case, L.P., & Molloy, D.E. (2003). Responsiveness to general education instruction as the first gate to learning disabilities identification. *Learning Disabilities Research & Practice, 18,* 147–156.

Vaughn, S., & Fuchs, L.S. (2003). Redefining learning disabilities as inadequate response to instruction: The promise and potential problems. *Learning Disabilities Research & Practice, 18,* 137–146.

Vaughn, S.R., Klingner, J., & Hughes, M. (2000). Sustainability of research-based practices. *Exceptional Children, 66,* 163–171.

Vaughn, S., Linan-Thompson, S., & Hickman-Davis, P. (2003). Response to treatment as a means of identifying students with reading/learning disabilities. *Exceptional Children, 69,* 391–409.

Vellutino, F.R., Scanlon, D.M., Sipay, E.R., Small, S.G., Pratt, A., Chen, R.S., et al. (1996). Cognitive profiles of difficult to remediate and readily remediated poor readers: Early intervention as a vehicle for distinguishing between cognitive and experiential deficits as basic causes of specific reading disability. *Journal of Educational Psychology, 88,* 607–638.

Appendix of General References

READING

http://www.texasreading.org
A variety of resources and links from the Texas Center for Reading and Language Arts at the University of Texas at Austin for teaching reading

http://cars.uth.tmc.edu
Resources from the Center for Academic and Reading Skills at the University of Texas—Houston, Health Science Center, and the University of Houston on the assessment and teaching of reading

http://www.kidsource.com/kidsource/pages/ed.k12.html
Informative articles on a variety of topics, including teaching children to read

http://www.readingrockets.org/teaching
Web site of a national project that offers research-based and best-practice information on teaching reading, with particular emphasis on teaching struggling readers

http://www.ldresources.com/readwrite/readingtolearn.html
Overview of learning to read, including phonological awareness, word identification, and so forth

ASSESSMENT

http://teacher.scholastic.com/reading/bestpractices/assessment.htm
Information about informal reading assessment; contains useful teacher tools

http://www.sedl.org/reading/rad/
Descriptions of many early reading assessment tools that have been published; includes information about the utility and reliability of various reading assessment tools for children in prekindergarten through third grade

http://idea.uoregon.edu/assessment/
Reading First Assessment Committee's analysis of reading assessment instruments

http://dibels.uoregon.edu
Free, downloadable early reading assessments and an administration manual for
the widely used *Dynamic Indicators of Basic Early Literacy Skills* (DIBELS);
information regarding the reliability and validity of the instrument as well as
useful information about administering and scoring assessments

http://www.balancedreading.com/assessment.html
An array of informal reading assessment tools and information

http://www.fcrr.org/assessment/
Articles, reviews, and helpful charts of various reading assessment tools

http://www.studentprogress.org/
Information from the National Center on Student Progress Monitoring about
conducting and using progress monitoring assessments

http://www.interventioncentral.org/htmdocs/interventions/cbmwarehouse.
  shtml
Free and useful tools for progress monitoring from the Currriculum-Based
Measurement Warehouse of the Website for Intervention Central

PHONOLOGICAL AWARENESS

http://www.NationalReadingPanel.org
A current review of the research on teaching reading, with specific information
on teaching phonological awareness and the alphabetic principle, from the
National Reading Panel

http://www.ciera.org
Resources in teaching early reading from the Center for Improvement of Early
Reading Achievement

http://readbygrade3.com
Information on how to teach students how to learn to read with an emphasis
on phonological awareness and word recognition

http://ericec.org
Information on phonological awareness

http://www.ldresources.com/
Overview of learning to read, including phonological awareness, word
identification, and so forth

http://www.ldonline.org/ld_indepth/
Information on alphabetical principle, phonemic awareness, and phonics as well
as on the identification and assessment of reading difficulties with a focus on
phonemic awareness

http://pbskids.org/lions
Contains information and activities for learning to read, with emphasis on
phonological awareness and phonics; web site is for the Public Broadcasting
Service show *Between the Lions*

PHONICS/WORD STUDY

http://www.NationalReadingPanel.org
A current review of the research on teaching reading from the National Reading
Panel

http://www.reading.org
A wide variety of resources for teaching reading from the International Reading
Association

http://www.ciera.org
Resources for teaching early reading from the Center for Improvement of Early
Reading Achievement

http://www.texasreading.org
A variety of resources and links for teaching reading from the Texas Center for
Reading and Language Arts at the University of Texas at Austin

http://www.starfall.com
Interactive games to provide practice in decoding using the analogizing strategy
of using "word families" or patterns to decode words

http://www.aft.org/pubs-reports/american_educator/spring_sum98/
    moats.pdf
Article written by Louisa Moats about decoding—what it is, why it is
important and how to teach it

http://www.ldonline.org/ld_indepth/reading/ldrp_chard_guidelines.html
Information on phonics and word recognition instruction in early reading programs

http://www.ldonline.org/ld_indepth/reading/teaching_children_to_read.
  html
Information on alphabetic principle, phonemic awareness, and phonics

http://pbskids.org/lions
Contains information and activities for learning to read, with emphasis on
phonological awareness and phonics; web site is for the Public Broadcasting
Service show *Between the Lions*

http://www.readingrockets.org/
An array of information and updates regarding reading instruction.

READING FLUENCY

http://www.rfbd.org/
Information about accessing recorded books and players for students with
reading disabilities and dyslexia

http://teacher.scholastic.com/professional/teachstrat/readingfluency
  strategies.htm
A concise summary of effective teaching strategies for building reading fluency

http://www.ldonline.org/ld_indepth/reading/reading_fluency.html
Information about and teaching tools for building reading fluency

http://www.nifl.gov/partnershipforreading/
Information and research briefs on various reading topics including reading fluency

http://www.prel.org/products/re_/assessing-fluency.htm
Information about assessing and charting reading fluency

http://www.studentprogress.org/
Information and resources for conducting ongoing fluency assessment from the
National Center on Student Progress Monitoring

VOCABULARY AND COMPREHENSION

http://www.readingrockets.org/lp.php?SCID=15
An overview of reading comprehension, research findings on reading
comprehension, and practical tips for teachers

http://www.readingrockets.org/lp.php?CID=59
Descriptions of current research on teaching reading to English language
learners, including instructional strategies for teaching reading comprehension

http://www.literacy.uconn.edu/compre.htm
Information and articles about the complex processes involved in reading
comprehension, including vocabulary instruction, text comprehension
instruction, and comprehension strategies instruction; also contains valuable
links that students can visit to practice their use of comprehension strategies
with fiction and nonfiction texts at a variety of reading levels

http://www.edhelper.com/
Teaching resources and information for teachers on a variety of subjects,
including reading comprehension and vocabulary

LEARNING DISABILITIES

http://www.ldonline.com/
Information and resources on a variety of topics related to learning disabilities

http://www.interdys.org
Resources from the International Dyslexia Association for teaching individuals
with learning disabilities

http://www.ncld.org
Resources from the National Center for Learning Disabilities related to reading
and other learning disabilities

http://www.ldaamerica.org/
Resources from the Learning Disabilities Association of America for families of
children with learning disabilities

DIVERSITY

http://www.cal.org/
Information and many resources for teaching English language learners; topic
areas include English as a second language literacy, bilingual education,
dialects/ebonics, immigrant education, language testing, literacy
(prekindergarten through twelfth grade), refugee concerns, and two-way
immersion, among others

http://www.cal.org/crede/
Numerous useful research reports, educational practice reports, occasional
publications, directories, research briefs, practitioner briefs, and CD-ROM
materials from the Center for Research on Educational Diversity and Excellence
that focus on literacy development for English language learners

http://knowledgeloom.org/index.jsp
Information about culturally responsive teaching and literacy instruction in
kindergarten through third grade; reports include "Meeting the Literacy Needs
of English Language Learners (ELLs)" and "Technology and Teaching Children
to Read

http://www.nabe.org/
Links to National Association for Bilingual Education (NABE) publications—
available for free on-line—including the *NABE News Magazine, Bilingual
Research Journal,* and the *NABE Journal of Research and Practice*

http://www.nameorg.org/
Position papers, press releases, publications, frequently asked questions, and
other resources related to educating culturally and linguistically diverse students;
also provides access to National Association for Multicultural Education
(NAME) journal, *Multicultural Perspectives*

http://www.nccrest.org
Access to an extensive on-line library, practitioner briefs, professional
development materials, self-assessment guides, and position statements from the
National Center for Culturally Responsive Educational Systems; designed to
help educators enhance educational opportunities for culturally and
linguistically diverse students

http://urbanschools.org
Numerous resources, including professional development materials, an on-line
library, position statements, syntheses of research, and other reports

http://www.ncela.gwu.edu/
Information from the National Clearinghouse for English Language Acquisition
(NCELA), formerly the National Clearinghouse for Bilingual Education
(NCBE) about language instruction educational programs for English language
learners as well as related programs

http://www.ed.gov/about/offices/list/oela/index.html
Information about current programs, as well as access to reports and resources,
from the Office of English Language Acquisition, Language Enhancement, and
Academic Achievement of the U.S. Department of Education

http://www.rethinkingschools.org/
Access to in-depth special collections on relevant topics, including bilingual education and minority student education; also includes links to numerous publications on various educational issues

SELECTED READINGS RELATED
TO RESPONSE TO INTERVENTION

Arreaga-Mayer, C. (1998). Increasing active student responding and improving academic performance through classwide peer tutoring. *Intervention in School & Clinic, 34,* 89–94.

Artiles, A.J., & Ortiz A.A. (Eds.). (2002), *English language learners with special education needs: Identification, placement, and instruction.* Washington, DC: Center for Applied Linguistics.

August, D., Carlo, M., Dressler, C., & Snow, C. (2005). The critical role of vocabulary development for English language learners. *Learning Disabilities Research & Practice, 20*(1), 50–57.

August, D., & Hakuta, K. (1997). *Improving schooling for language minority children: A research agenda.* Washington, DC: National Academies Press.

Baca, L.M., & Cervantes, H.T. (Eds.). (1998). *The bilingual special education interface.* Upper Saddle River, NJ: Prentice Hall.

Bear, D.R., Invernizzi, M., Templeton, S., and Johnston, F. (2003). *Words their way: Word study for phonics, vocabulary, and spelling instruction* (3rd ed.). Columbus, OH: Charles E. Merrill.

Blachman, B.A., Ball, E.W., Black, R., & Tangel, D.M. (2000). *Road to the code: A phonological awareness program for young children.* Baltimore: Paul H. Brookes Publishing Co.

Bos, C.S., & Vaughn, S. (2006). *Strategies for teaching students with learning and behavior problems* (6th ed.). Indianapolis, IN: Pearson.

Carnine, D., Silbert, J., Kame'enui, E.J., & Tarver, S.G. (2003). *Direct instruction reading* (4th ed.). Columbus, OH: Charles E. Merrill.

Chall, J.S., and Popp, H.M. (1996). *Teaching and assessing phonics: Why, what, when, how.* Cambridge, MA: Educators Publishing Service.

Chamberlin, S.P. (2005). Recognizing and responding to cultural difference in education of culturally and linguistically diverse learners. *Intervention in School and Clinic, 40,* 195–211.

Chard, D.J., and Dickson, S.V. (1999). Phonological awareness: Instructional and assessment guidelines. *Intervention in Clinic and School, 34*(5), 261–270.

Cunningham, P.M. (2004). *Phonics they use: Words for reading and writing* (4th ed.). Boston: Allyn & Bacon.

De La Colina, M.G., Parker, R.I., Hasbrouck, J.E., & Lara-Alecio, R. (2001). Intensive intervention in reading fluency for at-risk beginning Spanish readers. *Bilingual Research Journal, 25,* 503–538.

Delpit, L. (1995). *Other people's children.* New York: The New Press.

Denton, C.A., Anthony, J.L., Parker, R., & Hasbrouck, J. (2004). Effects of two tutoring programs on the English reading development of Spanish-English bilingual students. *The Elementary School Journal, 104,* 289–305.

Donovan, S., & Cross, C. (2002). *Minority students in special and gifted education*. Washington, DC: National Academies Press.

Escamilla, K., Loera, M., Ruiz, O., & Rodriguez, Y. (1998). An examination of sustaining effects in Descubriendo La Lectura programs. *Literacy Teaching and Learning: An International Journal of Early Reading and Writing, 3*(2), 59–81.

Fernald, G.M., & Idol, L. (1988). *Remedial techniques in basic school subjects*. Austin, TX: PRO-ED.

Fuchs, L.S., Hamlett, C., & Fuchs, D. (1990). *Monitoring basic skills progress: Basic math*. Austin, TX: PRO-ED.

Garcia, G.E. (1991). Factors influencing the English reading test performance of Spanish speaking Hispanic children. *Reading Research Quarterly, 26*, 371–392.

Garcia, S.B., & Malkin, D.H. (1993). Towards defining programs and services for culturally and linguistically diverse learners in special education. *Teaching Exceptional Children, 26*(1), 52–58.

Garcia, S.B., & Ortiz, A.A. (1988, June). Preventing inappropriate referrals of language minority students to special education. *FOCUS/NCBE, 5,* 1–17.

Garcia, S.B., Wilkinson, C.Y., & Ortiz, A. (1995). Enhancing achievement for language minority students: Classroom, school, and family contexts. *Education and Urban Society, 27,* 441–462.

Gaskins, I.W. (with Cress, C., O'Hara, C., & Donnelly, K.). (1998). *Word detectives: Benchmark extended word identification program for beginning readers*. Media, PA: Benchmark Press.

Gay, G. (2000). *Culturally responsive teaching: Theory, research, and practice*. New York: Teachers College Press.

Gersten, R., & Baker, S. (2000). What we know about effective instructional practices for English-language learners. *Exceptional Children, 66,* 454–470.

Gersten, R., Baker, S.K., Haager, D., & Graves, A. (2005). Exploring the role of teacher quality in predicting reading outcomes for first grade English learners: An observational study. *Remedial and Special Education, 26,* 197–206.

Gersten, R., & Jiménez, R. (1998). *Promoting learning for culturally and linguistically diverse students: Classroom applications from contemporary research*. Belmont, CA: Wadsworth Publishing.

Gillingham, A., & Stillman, B.W. (1973). *Remedial training for children with specific disability in reading, spelling, and penmanship*. Cambridge, MA: Educators Publishing Service.

Graves, A., Gersten, R., & Haager, D. (2004). Literacy instruction in multiple language first grade classrooms: Linking student outcomes to observed instructional practice. *Learning Disabilities Research and Practice, 19,* 262–272.

Greenwood, C.R., Arreaga-Mayer, C., Utley, C.A., Gavin, K.M., & Terry, B.J. (2001). ClassWide Peer Tutoring Learning Management System: Applications with elementary-level English language learners. *Remedial & Special Education, 22,* 34–47.

Gunning, T.G. (2001). *Building words: A resource manual for teaching word analysis and spelling patterns*. Boston: Allyn & Bacon.

Gunning, T.G. (2004). *Creating literacy instruction for all children* (3rd ed.). Boston: Allyn & Bacon.

Gunning, T.G. (2006). *Assessing and correcting reading and writing difficulties* (3rd ed.). Boston: Allyn & Bacon.

Gunning, T.G. (2006). *Closing the literacy gap*. Boston: Allyn and Bacon.

Haager, D., Dimino, J.A., & Windmueller, M. (2007). *Interventions for reading success.* Baltimore: Paul H. Brookes Publishing.

Haager, D., & Klingner, J.K. (2005). *Differentiating instruction in inclusive classrooms: The special educator's guide.* Boston: Allyn & Bacon.

Harry, B. (1992). Restructuring the participation of African American parents in special education. *Exceptional Children, 59*(2), 123–131.

Harry, B., & Klingner, J.K. (2005). *Why are so many minority students in special education? Understanding race and disability in schools.* New York: Teachers College Press.

Jiménez, R.T. (2001). "It's a difference that changes us": An alternative view of the language and literacy needs of Latina/o students. *The Reading Teacher, 54,* 736–742.

Jiménez, R., & Gersten, R. (1999). Lessons and dilemmas derived from the literary instruction of two Latina/o teachers. *American Education Research Journal, 36,* 265–301.

Kalyanpur, M., & Harry, B. (1999). *Culture in special education: Building reciprocal family–professional relationships.* Baltimore: Paul H. Brookes Publishing Co.

Kame'enui, E.J., Carnine, D.W., Dixon, R.C., Simmons, D.C., & Coyne, M.D. (2001). *Effective teaching strategies that accommodate diverse learners.* Upper Saddle River, NJ: Prentice Hall.

Keogh, B., Gallimore, R., & Weisner, T. (1997). A sociocultural perspective on learning and learning disabilities. *Learning Disabilities Research and Practice, 12,* 107–113.

Klingner, J., & Artiles, A.J. (2003). Bilingual special education: Contemporary challenges and prospective solutions. *Educational Leadership, 61*(2), 66–71.

Klingner, J.K., Artiles, A.J., Kozleski, E., Harry, B., Zion, S., Tate, W., et al. (2005). Addressing the disproportionate representation of culturally and linguistically diverse students in special education through culturally responsive educational systems. *Education Policy Analysis Archives, 13*(38), 1–39.

Klingner, J.K., & Edwards, P. (2006). Cultural considerations with response to intervention models. *Reading Research Quarterly, 41,* 108–117.

Ladson-Billings, G. (1994). *The dreamkeepers: Successful teachers of African American children.* San Francisco: Jossey-Bass.

Linan-Thompson, S., Vaughn, S., Hickman-Davis, P., & Kouzekanani, K. (2003). Effectiveness of supplemental reading instruction for second-grade English language learners with reading difficulties. *Elementary School Journal, 103,* 221–238.

Linan-Thompson, S., Vaughn, S., Prater, K., and Cirino, P.T. (in press). The response to intervention of English language learners at-risk for reading problems. *Journal of Learning Disabilities.*

Maldonado-Colon, E. (1986). Assessment: Interpreting data of linguistically/culturally different students referred for disabilities or disorders. *Journal of Reading, Writing, and Learning Disabilities International, 2,* 73–83.

McCardle, P., Mele-McCarthy, J., & Leos, K. (2005). English language learners and learning disabilities: Research agenda and implications for practice. *Learning Disabilities Research & Practice, 20,* 68–78.

McKenna, M.C., & Stahl, S.A. (2003). *Assessment for reading instruction.* New York: The Guilford Press.

Moats, L.C. (2000). *Speech to print: Language essentials for teachers.* Baltimore: Paul H. Brookes Publishing Co.

Montgomery, W. (2001). Literature discussion in the elementary school classroom: Developing cultural understanding. *Multicultural Education, 8,* 33–36.

Nag-Arulmani, S., Reddy, V., & Buckley, S. (2003). Targeting phonological representations can help in the early stages of reading in a non-dominant language. *Journal of Research in Reading, 26,* 49–68.

National Alliance of Black School Educators & IDEA Local Implementation by Local Administrators Project. (2002). *Addressing over-representation of African American students in special education: The prereferral intervention process.* Washington, DC: National Alliance of Black School Educators.

National Association for Bilingual Education & IDEA Local Implementation by Local Administrators Project. (2002). *Determining appropriate referrals of English language learners to special education: A self-assessment guide for principals.* Washington, DC: National Association for Bilingual Education.

National Reading Panel. (2000). *Teaching children to read: An evidence-based assessment of the scientific research literature on reading and its implications for reading instruction.* Bethesda, MD: National Institute of Child Health and Human Development, National Institutes of Health.

Neal, J.C., & Kelly, P.R. (1999). The success of Reading Recovery for English language learners and Descubriendo La Lectura for bilingual students in California. *Literacy Teaching and Learning, 2,* 81–108

Nieto, S. (1999). *The light in their eyes.* New York: Teachers College Press.

O'Connor, R.E., Notari-Syverson, A., & Vadasy, P.F. (2005). *Ladders to literacy: A kindergarten activity book* (2nd ed.). Baltimore: Paul H. Brookes Publishing Co.

Ortiz, A.A. (2001). *English language learners with special needs: Effective instructional strategies.* Washington, DC: Educational Resources Information Center Education Reports.

Ortiz, A.A., & Maldonado-Colon, E. (1986). Recognizing learning disabilities in bilingual children: How to lessen inappropriate referrals of language minority students to special education. *Journal of Reading, Writing and Learning Disabilities International, 2,* 43–56.

Padrón, Y.N., & Waxman, H.C. (1999). Classroom observations of the five standards of effective teaching in urban classrooms with English language learners. *Teaching and Change, 7,* 79–100.

Pressley, M. (2006). *Reading instruction that works: The case for balanced teaching.* New York: The Guilford Press.

Pressley, M., Allington, R., Wharton-McDonald, R., Block, C.C., & Morrow, L.M. (2001). *Learning to read: Lessons from exemplary first grades.* New York: The Guilford Press.

Rathvon, N. (2004). *Early reading assessment: A practitioner's handbook.* New York: The Guilford Press.

Rueda, R., MacGillivray, L., & Monzó, L. (2001). *Engaged reading: A multilevel approach to considering sociocultural factors with diverse learners.* Ann Arbor, MI: Center for the Improvement of Early Reading Achievement.

Ruiz, N. (1998). Instructional strategies for children with limited-English proficiency. *Journal of Early Education and Family Review, 5,* 21–22.

Salend, S.J., Garrick Duhaney, L.M., & Montgomery, W. (2002). A comprehensive approach to identifying and addressing issues of disproportionate representation. *Remedial and Special Education, 23,* 289–299.

Snow, C.E., Burns, M.S., & Griffin, P. (Eds.). (1998). *Preventing reading difficulties in young children.* Washington, DC: National Academies Press.

Steele, C., Perry, T., & Hilliard, A., III. (2004). *Young, gifted, and black: Promoting high achievement among African American students.* Boston: Beacon Press.

Swanson, H.L., with Hoskyn, M., & Lee, C. (1999). *Intervention for students with learning disabilities: A meta-analysis of treatment outcomes.* New York: The Guilford Press.

Taylor, B.M., Pearson, P.D., Clark, K., & Walpole, S. (2000). Effective schools and accomplished teachers: Lessons about primary-grade reading instruction in low-income schools. *Elementary School Journal, 101,* 121–165.

Tikunoff, W.J., Ward, B.A., van Broekhuizen, L.D., Romero, M., Castaneda, L.V., Lucas, T., et al. (1991). *Final report: A descriptive study of significant features of exemplary special alternative instructional programs.* Los Alamitos, CA: The Southwest Regional Educational Laboratory.

Vaughn, S., & Linan-Thompson, S. (2004). *Research-based methods of reading instruction.* Alexandria, VA: Association for Supervision and Curriculum Development.

Vaughn, S., Mathes, P.G., Linan-Thompson, S., & Francis, D.J. (2005). Teaching English language learners at risk for reading disabilities to read: Putting research to practice. *Learning Disabilities Research & Practice, 20,* 58–67.

Wagner, R.K., Francis, D.J., & Morris, R.D. (2005). Identifying English language learners with learning disabilities: Key challenges and possible approaches. *Learning Disabilities Research & Practice, 20,* 6–15.

Wiley, T.G. (1996). *Literacy and language diversity in the United States.* Washington, DC: Center for Applied Linguistics and Delta Systems Co.

Zeno, S.M., Ivens, S.H., Millard, R.T., & Duvvuri, R. (1995). *The educator's word frequency guide.* Brewster, NY: Touchstone Applied Science Associates.

Index

Page references followed by *t* or *f* indicate tables or figures, respectively.